FRANK ZAPPA'S AMERICA

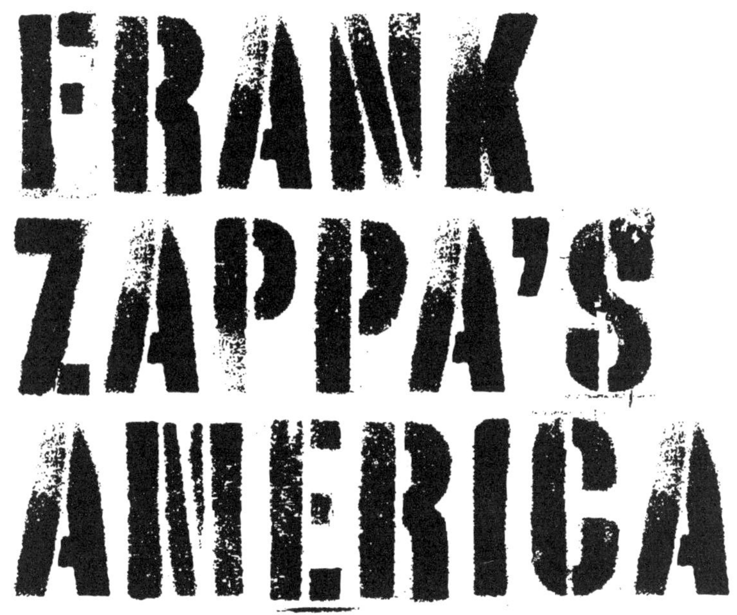

Bradley Morgan

LOUISIANA STATE UNIVERSITY PRESS
BATON ROUGE

Published with the assistance of the V. Ray Cardozier Fund.

Published by Louisiana State University Press
lsupress.org

Manufactured in the United States of America
First printing

DESIGNER: Michelle A. Neustrom
TYPEFACE: Whitman
PRINTER AND BINDER: Sheridan Books, Inc.

JACKET AND FRONTISPIECE PHOTOGRAPH: Frank Zappa, ca. 1985.
Courtesy Ebet Roberts Photography.

LIBRARY OF CONGRESS CATALOGING-IN-PUBLICATION DATA

Names: Morgan, Bradley, author.
Title: Frank Zappa's America / Bradley Morgan.
Description: Baton Rouge : Louisiana State University Press, 2025. | Includes bibliographical references and index.
Identifiers: LCCN 2024048463 (print) | LCCN 2024048464 (ebook) | ISBN 978-0-8071-8392-2 (cloth) | ISBN 978-0-8071-8445-5 (epub) | ISBN 978-0-8071-8446-2 (pdf)
Subjects: LCSH: Zappa, Frank—Criticism and interpretation. | Rock Music—United States—History and criticism. | Rock music—Social aspects—United States—History—20th century. | Rock music—Political aspects—United States—History—20th century.
Classification: LCC ML410.Z285 M67 2025 (print) | LCC ML410.Z285 (ebook) | DDC 782.42166092—dc23/eng/20241015
LC record available at https://lccn.loc.gov/2024048463
LC ebook record available at https://lccn.loc.gov/2024048464

CONTENTS

FOREWORD, BY JEREMY RICHEY / vii

ACKNOWLEDGMENTS / xi

AUTHOR'S NOTE / xv

PROLOGUE: UNDERSTANDING AMERICA / 1

1 IT CAN'T HAPPEN HERE / 8

2 A TOKEN OF MY EXTREME / 39

3 THE MEEK SHALL INHERIT NOTHING / 69

4 THE "TORCHUM" NEVER STOPS / 106

5 PORN WARS / 138

6 JESUS THINKS YOU'RE A JERK / 172

7 AMNERIKA / 204

EPILOGUE: HAVE I OFFENDED SOMEONE? / 227

NOTES / 245

REFERENCES / 259

INDEX / 279

FOREWORD

I'll never forget the first time I heard Frank Zappa. It was a late afternoon in 1990 during my seventeenth year when my buddy Dave's voice punctuated the boredom of the evening by asking if I had ever heard *Joe's Garage*. I admitted I hadn't, and he excitedly made his way over to his growing music collection, where he pulled out a fat-looking CD box-set. Of course, I was familiar with Frank Zappa as a personality, and I flashed on images of the bearded young man I had seen in my back issues of *Rolling Stone* and *Creem* and the older shaven gentleman I had watched speaking so eloquently against the PMRC on MTV—but I had never heard the music.

"Now, this is something really different," Dave assured me, despite my relative disinterest. After all, I had already cut my teeth on albums like Lou Reed's *Metal Machine Music* and Nico's *The Marble Index*, so a record from the 1970s about some dude's garage held little interest for me—until I heard the music. With the widest grin I had ever seen on his face, Dave told me to prepare to have my mind blown as the music began, and as I first heard mention of "The Central Scrutinizer," my mind was indeed very much blown.

My little Indiana town looked much different to me driving home that evening with sounds from *Joe's Garage* pouring out from my car's cassette player. Matter of fact, life growing up in America in the late 1980s felt profoundly altered after being introduced to Mr. Frank Vincent Zappa that evening. Always a decade or two ahead of everyone else, Zappa's music from the 1960s and 1970s felt tailor-made for the 1980s paranoia and peril that continue to affect so many of us all these decades later. As Bradley writes early in these pages:

"With his first album composed and released during a tumultuous period for the country, Zappa introduced himself and his vision of America to the world. With a message that not only captured the moment of its era, Zappa's music proved to be ahead of its time due to the enduring relevance of his cultural commentary."

Despite my adoration for both *Joe's Garage* and then the mind-melting *Hot Rats,* I was more intimidated by Zappa's discography than by any other. Was I smart enough for this massive catalog of music? Informed enough? Zappa's music made me doubt myself, which made me challenge my notion of how art should behave. It was the same thing that Lou Reed, John Cale, and Nico had done for me, but their music challenged me on a more emotional level, whereas Zappa hit me intellectually. There was something profoundly European about the Velvet Underground, no surprise considering Cale and Nico's presence, but Zappa felt distinctly American to me, and his satirical slaps at my country ended up having a much more profound effect on me than any of the many American history books I read throughout my college years.

Zappa, along with being one of America's most prolific composers, was also one of its most perceptive critics. With his massive body of recorded and visual material, Zappa chronicled our ridiculous modern life like no other. Starting with the early Mothers of Invention albums that, save for the Doors, made all the other West Coast bands of the later 1960s seem conservative and traditional, Zappa savaged American culture and its many hypocrisies, picking up where Lenny Bruce had left off. Detailing a key early track, Bradley writes, "With tracks like 'Who Are the Brain Police?' we see the earliest instances in Zappa's music in which he earned his reputation as a cynic, primarily for expressing his belief that many people will sacrifice their own individuality for social and cultural conformity. Using plastic for the lyrical imagery, Zappa comments that much of society is just as synthetic as the material that has come to symbolize the aesthetics of the era, with the concept of plasticity meant to represent a society that can be molded and pressed into anything at the will of those in power."

Like his great and sometimes nemesis and peer Lou Reed, Zappa never became predictable. In fact, like Reed, the artistic moves of his later life turned out to be among his most surprising and even moving. He could do anything.

Take, for example, the overwhelming version of "Stairway to Heaven" that Zappa and his crackerjack band performed in 1988. Who else could take classic rock's most overplayed song and transform it into something so fresh and unique? I admit, the first time I heard Zappa's take on the Page and Plant monolith, I broke down in tears. Zappa's "Stairway to Heaven" is a monumental elegy for both rock and roll and America as we watch both slip further and further away.

The timing couldn't be more ideal for this incredibly insightful book you are holding in your hands. Unlike all those years ago when *Joe's Garage, Hot Rats,* and a handful of other titles were all my buddy and I could track down, streaming has made the once daunting task of listening to all of Zappa's work possible. I often wonder what Zappa would have made of streaming and the way it has changed the way listeners acquire and consume music.

Bradley captures and details both the emotion and intelligence found throughout Zappa's work in this remarkable book. While reading it, I felt as though I was being given the opportunity to hear Zappa's music again for the very first time, but now with more experienced ears. Much more than a traditional tell-all biography, this book gets at the heart of what made Zappa "Zappa," with all the complexities and contradictions in their necessary places. By locating the focus on the music, where it belongs, Bradley has gotten closer to Zappa the man than any traditional biography could accomplish.

This isn't just a book about Frank Zappa, but America in all of its contradictory terms, and Bradley dives deep into Zappa's discography on musical, political, and societal levels. Writing on *Bongo Fury,* one of the astonishing projects Zappa and Captain Beefheart collaborated on, Bradley writes that the project chronicles "the blatant commercialism surrounding the nation's anniversary as a critique of the corporatization of America" and that Zappa's catalog "features songs that critique popular culture and people's egocentricities concerning it."

Bradley's book arrives at the most dangerous and frightening time in our country's history. We so badly need figures like Lou Reed and Frank Zappa to help us understand not only what America was, but what it's becoming. As Bradley writes in one of his most perceptively terrifying passages, Zappa, "through his music, attempt[s] to dispel one of the biggest myths plaguing America: it can't happen here." It can. It is.

While there have been many books written about Zappa throughout the years, none have ever connected his work to the American cultural and political landscape like this one. We lost Frank Zappa over thirty years ago, but his music and ideas have never felt more relevant and, with this book, Bradley presents us with the most compelling portrait of this great American artist we've ever had.

—Jeremy Richey

ACKNOWLEDGMENTS

I did not know what to expect after my first book was published, but it changed my life. I appreciate the opportunities and personal relationships that came from the experience, and I am profoundly grateful to those who have continued to support me over the years. When I was unsure if I had a second book in me, and even after I began to write it, I was fortunate enough to always be around people who encouraged me to do my best work. While I learned a lot going through this process the first time, I knew my second book would be harder to get out into the world because of the subject, and so friends' advice and guidance kept me motivated to keep pushing ahead. I am so thankful for their friendship and for being an important part in this book coming together. Thank you Steven Anderson, Lily Bacon, Adam Balling, Michael Bennett, Paul Birza, Keith Bjorklund, Paul Blanding, Andy Bugay, Rene Calvo, Shawn Campbell, Cécile Carrié, Craig Cobane, Aaron Cohen, Mimi Cole, Mary Conway, Bethany Doerfler, Tim Donovan, Craig Duff, Juliann Esqueda, Josh Friedberg, Al Gabor, Joe Held, Taylor Hodgkins, Chris Holda, Karen Johnson, Melissa Karalis, Carolyn Kassnoff, Debra LaRocco, Jennifer Lizak, Jean Mahony, Dan Menna, Julie Mueller, Kyle Sanders, Eric Sinclair, Amelia Vargas, and Anne Zender.

Jeremy Richey is one of the cleverest and most passionate film critics and historians out there, so I was thrilled when he agreed to write the foreword. When I read his book on Sylvia Kristel, I was amazed by the grace and dignity he afforded to a celluloid icon most known for her provocative work. As my book was meant to fill in a missing piece of another provocateur's legacy, I felt a connection between what I was trying to do with Frank with what Jeremy did so majestically with Sylvia. When I read his comments, it was the first time I felt confident that I accomplished what I had set out to do, and I thank him for that.

I also appreciate the support and guidance that Michael Farmer gave me. Way before I actually started writing this book, when I was still unsure of what a book on Frank Zappa would look like, Michael became one of my earliest champions and helped me navigate the complex world of the mustachioed one's catalog. Michael has a brilliant musical mind and is incredibly savvy when it comes to music commentary and criticism, so I was grateful to have him involved so early. As I was going through the process of writing this book, Michael's feedback on the material was critical to its success, providing not just expert commentary on the music and life of Zappa, but also another perspective in which to view his legacy.

My deepest gratitude goes to Louisiana State University Press for being such a great home for this book, and to their staff who work tirelessly to make it one of the most revered university presses around. Thank you so much to James Long for being such a huge champion for this book, and for his support in guiding me through the world of university publishing. I also want to thank my copyeditor, Stan Ivester, for his editing prowess and for helping to make this the best book it could be.

Thank you so much to Andrew Greenaway, Julie Klausner, and Ray White for providing endorsement blurbs for the book. I truly appreciate the generosity of their time, and for their faith in taking a chance on me. I look forward to the opportunity to pay their kindness forward.

Thank you to Ebet Roberts for permission to use her stellar portrait of Frank as the book's cover and frontispiece. Ebet's photo was very inspirational to me while writing this book, and I strived to capture in words what her portrait conveyed to me. There is no other photo of Frank I would have wanted in this book, and I am thrilled that Ebet's portrait will be the first thing people see when they open it.

I owe a huge debt of gratitude to Avo Raup of afka.net and all the dedicated fans who digitized and compiled an amazing archive of Zappa articles and interviews. This book would have taken much longer to finish if it were not for them. They are doing great work.

There are not enough words to express my gratitude for the Chicago Public

Library and all of its wonderful staff, who are truly the lifeblood of the city's greatest institution. The only reason I was able to write either of my books was because of the amazing resources CPL provided that helped turn my dreams into reality. Libraries are an essential part of every community, a safe public space where people can pursue educational opportunities, explore preserved cultural heritage and history, find empowerment through job assistance, provide safety and security for the homeless, and grow resource access for marginalized communities. Library workers are truly the backbone of a thriving society, and their work is more crucial now than ever. There are an alarming number of communities that have turned their backs on libraries, and it is the people who need libraries the most that will feel the greatest impact of their absence. The people whose goals are to censor and intimidate library workers only do so because they allow their insecurity to become an excuse for lashing out against groups who, by exploring information in a library, are just trying to find their voice. Being able to find that voice should be an absolute and irrevocable right. By being able to get the research material I needed from CPL, I had the privilege that comes from having unobstructed and equitable access to educational resources. The tireless efforts of the CPL staff allowed me to find my voice and finish this book. I am so grateful to them for that, and I stand by all the library workers throughout the country fighting hard to make sure every voice within their community matters and is heard because they truly understand the danger that comes when access to information is threatened.

And, finally, I am eternally grateful for the love and support of my family. None of this would have been possible without them, and I hope I have made them proud. Thank you, and I love you.

/ / /

Thank you to the following publications that granted me permission to quote from their works:

High Times. Quotes from Frank Zappa from the December 1989 interview "Frank Zappa: Somebody Up There Doesn't Like Me" with Elin Wilder. Reprinted with permission.

Mother Jones. Excerpts from "American Myths Are Made of White Grievance—and the Jan. 6 Big Lie Is Just the Latest," by Anthony Conwright, from *Mother Jones* magazine, January and February 2023. www.motherjones.com/politics/2023/01/trump-jan-january-6-insurrection-big-lie-white-supremacy-confederate/. Reprinted with permission.

Politico. Excerpts from "There Is a Real Sense That the Apocalypse Is Coming," by Ian Ward, from *Politico*, January 27, 2023. www.politico.com/news/magazine/2023/01/27/apocalypse-coming-christian-nationalism-00079317. Reprinted with permission.

PopMatters. Excerpts from "It's Time We Hung Out at Joe's Garage Again with Frank Zappa," by Bradley Morgan, from *PopMatters*, September 13, 2022. www.popmatters.com/frank-zappa-joes-garage-atr. Reprinted with permission.

Pulse! Quotes from Frank Zappa from the August 1993 interview "Frank Zappa" with Dan Ouellette. Reprinted with permission.

T'Mershi Duween. Quotes from Ike Willis from the October 1996 interview "Thing-Fish Rap: Ike Willis Chats." Reprinted with permission.

AUTHOR'S NOTE

Frank Zappa was one of the most prolific musicians of the twentieth century. In both the number of albums he released as well as the compositions on each, Zappa's discography is one of the most expansive and dense catalogs in popular music. With so many different opportunities to approach Zappa's music, there are seemingly countless ways in which listeners can experience it.

One consequence of having such a vast musical output over a storied career is that some of Zappa's albums and creative periods get overlooked in favor of his more renowned releases. As this book covers some of Zappa's least critically acclaimed and commercially successful albums, I thought it would be helpful to include a brief note detailing which albums are explored in each chapter, should you wish to listen to them before reading their respective chapters.

The titles of the book's prologue and epilogue are references to two different compilations. *Understanding America* is a compilation that was mastered in 1993 just before Zappa's passing but not released until 2012 and features a collection of songs showcasing Zappa's varying social, political, and cultural commentary. Released posthumously in 1997, *Have I Offended Someone?* gathers some of Zappa's most sardonically satirical songs, several of which have been considered his most offensive. The prologue and epilogue do not specifically address these albums, but rather their themes help set the narrative and context for the book. These compilations are good starting points for those less familiar with Zappa's work in general.

Each of the book's main chapters covers one or more of the following albums:

CHAPTER 1

Freak Out! (1966) (as the Mothers of Invention)
Absolutely Free (1967) (as the Mothers of Invention)
We're Only in It for the Money (1968) (as the Mothers of Invention)

CHAPTER 2

Joe's Garage Acts I, II, & III (1979)

CHAPTER 3

You Are What You Is (1981)

CHAPTER 4

Thing-Fish (1984)

CHAPTER 5

Frank Zappa Meets the Mothers of Prevention (1985)
Congress Shall Make No Law . . . (2010)

CHAPTER 6

Broadway the Hard Way (1988)

CHAPTER 7

The Yellow Shark (1993)
Civilization Phaze III (1994)

Thank you so much for picking up my book. Whether you are new to Frank Zappa's music or are a longtime fan, I hope you will find something meaningful while reading it.

FRANK ZAPPA'S AMERICA

PROLOGUE

Understanding America

Have you ever thought about what Albert Einstein, Jack Kevorkian, Muhammad Ali, Socrates, and Anita Hill have in common? Likely not. However, if you have ever taken Chicago's "L" train north of the city's Loop, through its River North neighborhood, you will see why such a question could pop into your head. Featuring a list of sixty-nine names printed in white lettering against a black banner seventy-two feet tall, the *Freedom Wall* is an art installation created in August 1994 by Columbia College professor Adam Brooks to capture both conservative and liberal voices whose ideas and opinions represent some aspect of the concept of freedom. As one-half of a collaborative conceptual duo in Chicago called Industry of the Ordinary, Brooks sought to understand what freedom meant and people's relationship with it, because "there are as many interpretations of that as there are people."[1] Brooks compiled the list of names by polling users on America Online forums and through direct email requests, asking them to provide up to three names of people they felt embodied freedom in whatever way they chose to interpret it. He ranked the names based on how frequently they were nominated, with Martin Luther King Jr. at the top for getting the most votes.[2]

There are some truly inspiring names on the *Freedom Wall* that represent varying aspects of the purest notions behind the concept of freedom. There are icons who universally symbolize the concept through their tireless efforts to advance racial justice and fight systemic inequality such as Nelson Mandela, Harriet Tubman, Wilma Mankiller, Rosa Parks, and Frederick Douglass. Some of the country's founders, George Washington and Thomas Jefferson, are also included but fall a few places behind a couple of their presidential successors, Abraham Lincoln and John F. Kennedy, each of whom represent similar but different ideas about freedom with the former pair having owned slaves. Several artists, musicians, and writers are also featured, notable for their individual contributions to the betterment of our culture through creative expression that speaks to our collective humanity, including bell hooks, John Lennon, Robert Mapplethorpe, William Blake, Lenny Bruce, Anne Frank, Wolfgang Amadeus Mozart, and Elie Wiesel. Even some religious figures are featured, including Moses coming ahead of both Mother Teresa and the fourteenth Dalai Lama, with Jesus Christ not even breaking the top ten and Buddha sitting comfortably toward the bottom of the list.

However, there are names included that, especially when viewed in a modern context, are rather perplexing. Rush Limbaugh, who was already a controversial figure when the *Freedom Wall* was originally installed, would spend the next couple of decades fostering a culture of grievance and mistrust that would fuel modern conservative movements driven by conspiracy theories. There is also Aung San Suu Kyi, who had won the Nobel Peace Prize in 1991 for her nonviolent movement to promote democracy and human rights in Myanmar, but who would three decades later be ousted out of power by a military coup and be accused of systemizing genocide against the country's Muslim population.[3] Curiously above Noam Chomsky, Ayn Rand earns a spot on the list for her philosophy of objectivism, the "concept of man as a heroic being, with his own happiness as the moral purpose of his life, with productive achievement as his noblest activity, and reason as his only absolute,"[4] and whose enduring legacy can be felt with the many political leaders and entrepreneurs who leverage industries and systems of power to advance their individual interests over those of a collective society. With so many names representing a diverse array of identities and opinions, Brooks's intention with the *Freedom Wall* was not to take on "one particular stance" but rather to open the scope of the project "to multiple participants with multiple viewpoints."

On his intention with the *Freedom Wall*, Brooks said, "I felt that it was critically important for the project to be viewed as not just another piece of liberal activism, to include as many voices from across the political spectrum as possible. It may not be fair and balanced, but it certainly was broad enough and eclectic enough ultimately, in order to ask some important questions about what freedom is, what it means to be free, who decides how we define that."[5]

Like many other commuters who passed by it, I had wondered about this list as well. Until I had learned what it was and what it represented, I would try to read the names on the list as I rolled along the track and speculate why those particular names and in that particular order. With the "L" steadily moving, you only have a few seconds to read, and then try to remember, all the names you can, thus necessitating several trips to appreciate it in its entirety unless you visit the *Freedom Wall* directly on the street. It is a remarkable work of art that elicits profound conversation and debate, inviting people who view it to invest time and emotion in understanding the zeitgeist it captured when Brooks conceptualized it as a response to the 1992 presidential election, with him saying he wanted "passersby and viewers to do a bit of work to make connections between all of the names on that list."[6] Taking in the *Freedom Wall*'s mystifying vagueness and size, those same qualities reflect a symbolic allegory as to what makes America both contradictorily inclusive yet divisive, a country representing a wide swath of people existing in one place at one time trying to make sense of the dichotomous rift between the American Dream and the American Reality built into the foundation of its national identity and which fuels the myths that stem from it.

The *Freedom Wall* provokes a reaction in everyone who sees it. People who look at the list, attempting to decipher what it means, react to the names on it and what they represent to them. Every single person who looks at it has different ideas about the social, cultural, and political figures who grace the towering black landscape. Capitalized in sans-serif Helvetica font,[7] the names convey nothing yet everything, subject to the beliefs and biases of those who read them. No two people who look at the *Freedom Wall* have the same thoughts about it. Some names prompt different reactions than others, resulting in thinking about who else we would include or who we would replace. Everyone who sees it has a name they gravitate toward, for whatever reason. For me, when I passed by the *Freedom Wall* for the first time during my commute in early 2011, that name was Frank Zappa.

Zappa pushed the limits of conventionality in his music, both in taste and in style, blending social and cultural commentary with an eclectic blend of

Freedom Wall, 1994, by Adam Brooks. Photograph by Robert Loerzel.

genres that included rock and roll, jazz, classical, doo-wop, and avant-garde music. From his debut as founder of the Mothers of Invention during the mid-1960s through his success as a solo performer throughout the 1970s, Zappa would earn a reputation that simultaneously both lauded him as a musical virtuoso and criticized him for being a provocateur, resulting in a complex public image where "his unconventional aspect often overshadowed his brilliance" despite being "highly respected as a musical pioneer."[8] Unapologetic and refusing to capitulate to the expectations and demands of his critics, Zappa's notoriety as a controversial artist would continue to be one of the defining characteristics of his career, shaping the public's perception of him as a cultural icon who would have a sizable impact on how we think about the freedom of artistic expression.

However, as the 1980s arrived, and along with it a rising conservative countermovement based on Christian fundamentalism, Zappa's role as an artist would irreversibly change. Though Zappa had demonstrated his penchant for imbuing social and cultural commentary in his music since his album debut in 1966, the prospective consequences of this fundamentalist movement on individual freedoms and civil liberties for all Americans motivated him to reevaluate his art and its impact on effecting social change. Throughout the 1980s, and until his death in 1993, Zappa would increasingly cultivate his art to challenge and push back against the rise of extremist religious influence on American politics and culture despite mounting critical and commercial pressures. By composing music that spoke to how this movement would usher in a fascist theocracy that would have a severely negative impact on the safety and security of non-white, non-male, and non-Christian people, Zappa would become the music industry's biggest advocate of democratic ideals several decades before white Christian nationalism would be legitimized as part of a major political party's platform with the purpose of limiting democratic freedoms in order to elevate and preserve dangerous elements of a white patriarchal society. However, despite this important work Zappa was doing with his music to address how the dangers of this movement hurts all Americans, and especially among its marginalized citizens, it is a period within Zappa's oeuvre that has gone underappreciated, overshadowed by his more commercially successful and notorious work. As a result, there is a disparity between Zappa's reputation and musical output—one that presents an incomplete profile of one of the most prolific and influential musicians and advocates of democracy of the last sixty years.

This book serves as my explanation as to why Frank Zappa is on the *Freedom Wall*, and how he embodies the concept of freedom for me. While this book does offer insights into Zappa's life and work, it is not a traditional biography. Instead, it presents an analytical overview of how Zappa crafted his art to increasingly oppose white nationalism and Christian fundamentalism. With this book, my primary focus is on the parts of Zappa's work that address these themes, centering key albums and compositions from 1979 through his death in 1993, with the opening chapter providing a cursory overview of his work prior to 1979 to illustrate that many of these values had been held since the beginning of his career. There are several reasons for this approach. The main one is that this period aligns with historical events that facilitated the creeping influence of extremist religious principles and values in American politics and culture in ways that still reverberate today. The other reason is that this period is also Zappa's least understood and represented. By analyzing the recurring themes and concepts within this neglected period and connecting them with historical events arising from the influence of this extreme religious movement, I attempt to fill in missing pieces of Zappa's legacy that legitimize his art and cultural value in order to make a case that his work continues to be relevant in ways that many critics, and even some fans, fail to recognize. Many of the points he was making in his commentary, through his music and public statements, are evergreen and speak to the current cultural condition in ways that have, in many instances, proven to be prescient. I demonstrate this by drawing parallels between the issues Zappa was addressing and what is happening now decades later as there is often a direct connection regarding how and why these dangerous elements have grown in stature and impact. I am making the case that the core of Zappa's commentary is both progressive and rooted in liberal democratic principles, noting that most criticisms lobbed against Zappa have less to do with what he is actually saying and more to do with the misinformation surrounding his reputation. However, this book is not fan service either. While I do champion Zappa and his messaging, there are times in which my analysis requires me to challenge him over some of the more problematic aspects of his work and legacy. In these instances, though the book's narrative is largely about how his later career addressed white nationalism and Christian fundamentalism, I do explore his other work that does not directly speak to those themes when addressing particular qualities and aspects of Zappa's life and career. In order to fully appreciate Zappa's music and its impact on society and culture, one needs a more complete understanding of the man behind it.

With the *Freedom Wall*, Adam Brooks sought to explore one of America's most definitive, yet complicated, qualities. To make sense of freedom in America is to accept that the construct is just that, a construct, with its meaning malleable in ways where one's view juxtaposes with another's in ways that can contradict as well as complement. I know what the construct means for me and for the journey I have gone on as an American to understand it. Part of that journey has required me to understand the legacies and lessons of many people who appear on the *Freedom Wall*. Some of them are more well-known than others, having had an impact that can be felt and experienced in obvious ways years, decades, or even centuries later. Others made waves that still ripple throughout our society, but whose impact has faded and is felt in less direct ways, the result of time being the greatest equalizer of all. This journey to understand America is endless, requiring constant evaluation and self-reflection as to what my values are and freedom's relationship to them. In that journey toward understanding America, I sought to understand Frank Zappa and what freedom meant to him.

IT CAN'T HAPPEN HERE

By 1966, the United States had changed considerably since Lyndon Johnson was sworn into office following his predecessor's assassination on November 22, 1963. When John F. Kennedy became president-elect in 1960, his victory symbolized the dawning of a new generation that was coming-of-age, with eyes gazing toward the future and the promises that lay beyond the horizon. Kennedy's ascent to the White House "inspired a generation to accept responsibility for its government, and its world, by taking political and social action."[1] With his attention toward social and cultural progress, Kennedy sought to move America forward despite the turbulent times in which he served as president, which included Black Americans fighting against white segregationists for equal rights as well as the threat of nuclear war being an ever-looming specter in the ideological Cold War against communism. Intelligent, handsome, and charismatic, Kennedy "evoked a sense of security and a spirit of idealism which reassured Americans of their nation's strengths and inspired them to serve their country and the world."[2] As these things not only defined the legacy of his presidency, but also perpetuated national myths brought on by the collective trauma of his tragic demise, the America of the Kennedy years would stand in stark contrast to those of Johnson's presidency. Though the Johnson administration would pass legislation that resulted in sweeping changes and reforms that embodied the spirit of what Kennedy championed, including the Civil Rights Act of 1964 and his extension of the New Deal with the Great Society—Johnson's series of domestic programs designed to promote racial justice while ending poverty and promoting education—the nation became increasingly divided. Between rising domestic racial tensions and an international conflict brewing in Southeast Asia, the idealism of the Kennedy presidency would soon fade away and be replaced by political polarization and the arrival of a conservative counterrevolution, one with a legacy that would endure and grow in strength sixty years on. Amid this cultural chaos, an iconoclastic musical genius would emerge with his eyes, and guitar, set on exposing the insanity of it all.

Frank Zappa, born in Baltimore, Maryland, in 1940, would become one of the most prolific musicians of the twentieth century, with over sixty albums released during his lifetime and dozens more posthumously, working with a diverse array of genres including jazz, rock, classical, fusion, musique concrète, and more. His interest in music would begin as a teenager, performing in bands during high school and developing a deep appreciation not just for the conventional music of his formative years, like rhythm and blues and doo-wop, but also contemporary modernists like Igor Stravinsky and sound experimentalists like Edgard Varèse. As Zappa's career as a musician and composer further developed, so did his reputation as a musical malcontent and subversive satirist. By his death in 1993, Zappa would be remembered for his free-speech advocacy "dedicated to upsetting American suburban complacency and puncturing the hypocrisy and pretensions of both the U.S. political establishment and the counterculture that opposed it."[3] Though this was a profile Zappa worked prodigiously to earn throughout his life, his drive to expose American hypocrisies and pretensions had been front and center for him as an artist since the very beginning. With his first album composed and released during a tumultuous period for the country, Zappa introduced himself and his vision of America to the world. With a message that not only captured the moment of its era, Zappa's music proved to be ahead of its time due to the enduring relevance of his cultural commentary.

Released in 1966, *Freak Out!* is an intrepid and uncompromisingly artistic debut album, with Zappa, as founder of the Mothers of Invention, using the album as a platform to mock American popular culture and the artificially pliable divisions in society that define and shape it. Considered to be one of the first rock "concept" albums, it is a defiant work of art that challenges prevailing notions of taste by presenting highbrow concepts and musicality with a seemingly lowbrow aesthetic. After all, the band does indeed look freaky on the cover. However, that aesthetic and all the biases that can be projected onto it belie the depth and complexity of the album's themes and ideas that challenge the elements of American society firmly rooted in traditional social constructs. As abrasive as this album may sound when juxtaposed with its often uninspired and prosaic chart-topping contemporaries, the purpose of *Freak Out!* is not to drive people away but rather to bring them into the fold so they can be "emancipated from our national social slavery."[4] It is an invitation for all those who hear this music to join in and freak out within a society that discourages such revolutionary, zeitgeist-shifting behavior.

The opening track, "Hungry Freaks, Daddy," is a bold introduction of the band's ethos, with the Mothers of Invention unafraid to tell the truth of what they believe in. Commenting on the United States' worsening education system and its inability to effectively teach, the band calls out Mr. America, their moniker for the older generation as a personification of the state of the country and their grievances with it, for oppressing new ways of thinking to project a sense of emptiness and meaningless existence on its population. The Mothers warn Mr. America that all the tricks he has pulled and lies he has told, meaning the systemic forces used to maintain conventional conservative order in the country, will not be enough to push back against the burgeoning social and cultural forces that would replace traditional and orthodox values in order to make way for more radical ideas. Specifically, the Mothers tell Mr. America that the groups within society still marginalized after Johnson's Great Society programs will not be afraid to use their freedom of expression against conformist elements of society, which the band cheekily refer to as a midwestern hardware-store philosophy as satire of the morals and ethics of small-town America. In the liner notes for *Freak Out!* the band encourages the listener to drop out of school and to instead educate themselves at the library,[5] a radical act of defiance against a system that enforces uniformity and compliance in lieu of knowledge and individualism. As an opening track on a debut album, "Hungry Freaks, Daddy" presents powerful philosophical ideas that not only set the tone for the remainder of the album but for the rest of Zappa's career and life as well: the act of rising up and resisting.

Though the subtext of "Hungry Freaks, Daddy" advocates for a revolutionary resolution to the generational power play at the heart of the countercultural movement and the conservative resistance to it, it is not the only perspective of American life during the mid-1960s captured on the album. "Who Are the Brain Police?" features distorted drones, eerie echoes, and sinister sounds to convey a sense of paranoia that was pervasively creeping throughout the mid-1960s, a narrative at odds with the peace-and-love mythos that has since defined the era. According to Kevin Courrier, author of *Dangerous Kitchen: The Subversive World of Zappa*, Zappa is "satirizing the manner by which listeners identify with the music on the album in their efforts to form an identity."[6] Its presence early on within *Freak Out!* conveys conceptual notions that the preservation of cultural paranoia is deeply rooted within the people oppressed by powerful systems. When asked in 1988 about who the "brain police" were, Zappa said they are any individuals who actively police their own minds to the point that they essentially become citizen soldiers within society by self-policing themselves.[7] This brings to mind the concept of the panopticon. Initially developed by eighteenth-century English philosopher and social theorist Jeremy Bentham, and later expanded upon during the 1970s by French philosopher Michel Foucault, the panopticon is a design for a circular prison in which inmates can be observed at all times by guards in a central watchtower that the inmates cannot see. Meant to convey the feeling that they are being watched at all times, the purpose of this surveillance method within the panopticon is to motivate inmates to be compliant in providing functioning utility within a prison by behaving in ways to avoid punishment. This idea reflects self-imposed policing among citizens as a product of the fear and paranoia over the control emanating from the power of the state. Within the album, "Who Are the Brain Police?" largely blames people complicit in their own oppression, an idea about which the *New Musical Express* declared that while Zappa "raged against the slave-masters . . . he had little sympathy for the slaves."[8]

With tracks like "Who Are the Brain Police?" we see the earliest instances in Zappa's music in which he earned his reputation as a cynic, primarily for expressing his belief that many people will sacrifice their own individuality for social and cultural conformity. Using plastic for the lyrical imagery, Zappa comments that much of society is just as synthetic as the material that has come to symbolize the aesthetics of the era, with the concept of plasticity meant to represent a society that can be molded and pressed into anything at the will of those in power. Satirizing the stereotypical countercultural teenage girl, "You're Probably Wondering Why I'm Here" addresses the excess that comes with a society driven by commercialization and commoditization. As the girl prefers to check out the hippie scene with her friends, the Mothers question the seriousness of her place in society and wonder why they are watching the scene unfold as they challenge the authenticity of the counterculture's leaders and their refusal to "look at themselves with the same critical eye with which they looked at the rest of society."[9] Zappa attacks the superficial elements of youth culture, with the band directly calling out the interactions young Americans engage in that trivialize the culture's legitimacy in shaping society.

This abrasive attitude about the frivolity of American youth culture, with its continuation of the previous generation's conformist middle-class values, is a recurring theme throughout *Freak Out!* Zappa's lampooning of love songs with "I Ain't Got No Heart," the comically delivered doo-wop satire "Go Cry on Somebody Else's Shoulder," the free-love spoof ode to groupies with "Motherly Love," the heartbreak of unreciprocated feelings in "How Could I Be Such a Fool," longing and loneliness of waiting by the phone within "You Didn't Try to Call Me," the freedom of leaving a troubled romance behind as heard in "Any Way the Wind Blows," and the melodramatic teenage suicide note that is "I'm Not Satisfied," which all feature the hallmarks of a potential commercial pop hit, contain inherent themes and ideas ridiculing the type of teenage angst and rebellion that unwittingly perpetuates hackneyed ideas of what it means to be a free youth in American society.

Zappa told *Jazz & Pop* in 1967 that, if one were to "graphically analyze the different types of directions of all the songs" from the album, then you would find something "slanted for every type of social orientation within our consumer group, which happens to be six to eighty," with Zappa noting that record executives had told him their children loved the song "Wowie Zowie,"[10] the subversive bubblegum pop parody on *Freak Out!* Zappa's use of commercial musical stylings, although including avant-garde elements, represents what he outlines in the album's liner notes as "freaking out," which is when individuals shed themselves of outdated societal and cultural standards in order to creatively assess and express their relationship with the "immediate environment and the social structure as a whole."[11] This approach of mimicking more popular musical forms, but infusing them with a bit of freakiness, becomes an effective way in which Zappa's ideas about free expression within society can be heard. With these songs also featured in sequence on the album, which helps craft the loose narrative exploring the range of mid-1960s teenage emotional drama, their combined freaky qualities set the tone for the more offbeat and experimental tracks toward the end of the album that address similar themes. However, there are still obstacles that prevent a complete and total freak out from happening in society. On the noise collage track "It Can't Happen Here," the third movement of the suite "Help, I'm a Rock" which fuses vocal noises with imagery about being a societal reject, Zappa is telling the listener that the act of freaking out cannot happen in the more rural and conservative parts of the country where the plastic people live, with him providing a satirical commentary that recalls the themes of totalitarianism in Sinclair Lewis's classic novel *It Can't Happen Here,* published three decades earlier in 1935, to account for why truly free creative expression will never be welcomed in America. It is Zappa molding the plastic around him to reflect his views on modern cultural decline.

While much of the messaging of *Freak Out!* is wrapped in multiple sardonic layers of satire, both musically and lyrically, the bluesy "Trouble Every Day" stands out as one of the album's signature tracks for being its only clearly direct protest song. Written as a response to the Watts Rebellion, Zappa lambasts those responsible for the media exploitation of the violent confrontations that plagued the neighborhood and its Black residents, presenting a pointed critique not just because of the severity in which the riots played out and were reported on, but also because of the implications regarding the effects such exploitation can have on American society. In August 1965, violence broke out between members of the Los Angeles Police Department and residents of the predominantly Black neighborhood of Watts, as well as its surrounding neighborhoods, after a twenty-one-year-old Black man named Marquette Frye was stopped for driving while intoxicated two blocks from his house. After his brother Ronald went to get their mother, a skirmish erupted that resulted in the police using extra force, and all three were taken into custody. Several hundred people from the neighborhood had gathered at the scene following the arrest, further escalating the situation by throwing rocks at cars and physically assaulting any white people they encountered. As rioting continued through the night, with some local businesses being looted and torched, additional city resources were brought in to stem the rising tide of violence, ultimately resulting in the mobilization of fourteen thousand National Guard troops deployed to secure and patrol the neighborhoods. The violent clashes lasted six days and resulted in thirty-four deaths and over one thousand injuries, as well as accumulating more than $40 million in property damage.[12]

In the opening verse, Zappa sings that the media saturation of the news coverage of the riots is making him feel ill. He clings to some semblance of hope that the violence will subside, so much so that he is willing to pray to some divine power to end the chaos. However, Zappa as an atheist knows that his gesture is in vain as he hears the news project the narrative that more trouble is coming and we are powerless to slow it down, let alone end it entirely. As the song progresses, Zappa recounts the violence he sees on television, notably the police throwing rocks and other debris at crowds, provoking more destructive acts like burning down local businesses. As the violence plays out on the screen, Zappa is well aware of the role the media has been playing in the riots and uses the song to investigate it with a critical lens, challenging them for their sensationalist coverage and running unconfirmed reports so they can break the news before their competitors. It is a dynamic in which Zappa emphasizes the profit-driven model that news departments operate under, one in which they prioritize voyeuristic entertainment over objective journalism, thus turning a tragic event into must-see TV.

Within the first half of "Trouble Every Day," Zappa places a lot of blame on the police and the media for the intensity of the riots. As a cultural commentary on police brutality and the state's willingness to wield it, in addition to examining how media can simplify and agitate complex racial and social issues, "Trouble Every Day" is as powerful a protest song as any to come out of the era and defined Zappa's reputation as a social commentator early in his career. However, what truly makes the messaging of this song important is the way in which Zappa relies on the Watts Rebellion narrative to offer a broader cultural commentary on the ideological underpinnings of American society. Halfway through the song, Zappa makes a personal admission that sounds startling at first, but with each subsequent listen further unveils his complex understanding of systemic racism. Zappa acknowledges that, though he is not Black, there are many instances in which he feels shame and embarrassment for being white. It is a compelling and potent political statement in which Zappa admits the privileges that come with being white in America. Though Zappa's comment implies that he prefers being white to being Black, because of the country's history of systemic inequality that has oppressed and harmed Black lives, it is that very distinction that causes him to have a difficult internal dialogue about what it truly means to be white in America, as in having privilege that can be leveraged for systemic advantages not available to non-white communities and the personal responsibility inherent within that social dynamic. It is a poignant moment in the song that not only exhibits Zappa's understanding of the social issues of the day, but also reveals a lot about his personal character.

In the second half of "Trouble Every Day," Zappa introduces ideas about the inevitable consequences of media sensationalizing racial violence. He addresses the looting and burning of local businesses, specifically criticizing attitudes that rationalize such destruction on the basis that some of the store owners may be white, with Zappa condemning this outlook as discrimination that inflames the already precarious divisions rampant during that time. Zappa is suggesting that the angle in which media portray racial violence on television and in newspapers has a direct effect on how educated the public is about an issue, with him blaming the media for the mass stupidity their reports on race-based violence fosters. Zappa's point is that many people watching these reports do not pay attention to the intricate details of race and systemic power at the root of the riots, with some viewers instead using the footage to reinforce white supremacist attitudes. Zappa is saying that footage of flaming storefronts can make some viewers, especially frightened white people, think they too are at risk of having violence committed against them for political or ideological reasons. Zappa is concerned that, if enough people share this view, it could completely dismantle Johnson's vision for the Great Society, potentially slowing, or even reversing, America's social and racial progress. From there, Zappa closes the song with a recognition of the class-based power imbalance inherent within American society, commenting that the only people who have real advantages in society are those born into wealth while the rest are forced to work menial labor to earn a meager living and left to sing songs about being poor.

"Trouble Every Day" demonstrates how clever and forward-thinking Zappa was as an artist and social commentator, with its critique and themes standing out as particularly timeless and enduring. Looking at Zappa's lyrics concerning how some Americans might react to a bombardment of media images foretelling their societal and cultural doom, the response to the Watts Rebellion is reminiscent of the way many reacted to the protests that erupted in the wake of George Floyd's murder at the hands of police in 2020. Any violence and looting that circumstantially spun off from what were largely peaceful demonstrations fueled skewed narratives in which civil unrest provided "an opportune moment for bad actors to spread disinformation and to divide society," which can "create a volatile information environment,"[13] most notably among conservative politicians who used footage of the protests without context in campaign ads to instill anxiety and resentment in voters. The very idea that such parallels can be drawn between now and a tragic event that happened over half a century earlier speaks volumes about the underlying subtext of Zappa's messaging in "Trouble Every Day." It is a track that challenges accusations of racism and cynicism against Zappa, especially considering its presence on a debut album and that Zappa continued throughout his life to address the larger issues within it. In an August 1993 interview with *Pulse!* Zappa commented on the legacy of "Trouble Every Day" and its themes, saying, "Nothing has changed. We have the same racial hatred, the same unwillingness to face the causes of racial unrest. We've had years to examine the causes of the Watts riots, but no one has done anything about it. There were studies and reports and conclusions then, just like there were studies and reports and conclusions reached after [the Rodney King] riots. There's a certain type of American adolescent behavior that hasn't gotten any better since the 60's."[14]

Absolutely Free, released in 1967 by Verve Records as the Mothers' second album, continued the trend of Zappa composing music in a conceptualized way that addressed the current political, social, and cultural trends of the day through deeply thought-provoking and provocative satire. As opposed to the double album *Freak Out!*, *Absolutely Free* was released as a single album, with each side featuring separate "Underground Oratorios,"[15] together representing a cohesive artistic vision. Zappa told *Song Hits* magazine in September 1967 that *Absolutely Free* was "not exactly rock and roll" with "songs edited together in a continuous piece of music presenting a panorama of life in America today."[16] The first oratorio, named after the album, is "a violently nonsensical outburst of musical hysteria, built around absurd dada imagery," with the second, called "The M.O.I. American Pageant," being "an insane journey through suburban America, a vivid musical collage characterised by rapid shifts through a bewildering variety of musical styles and moods, from beautiful orchestral passages to cabaret-style jazz."[17]

The release of *Absolutely Free* was delayed by four months due to MGM, Verve Records' parent company at the time, finding some of the lyrics on the album to be objectionable. Zappa had wanted the lyrics to be printed onto a separate sheet, as a libretto, with the intention that it be included in the album's packaging. Instead, *Absolutely Free* was packaged and distributed without the libretto.[18] During an interview with *Jazz & Pop* in 1967, Zappa was asked if he had deliberately made some of the lyrics unintelligible on the album in order to avoid being censored by the label. Zappa laid the rumors to rest by saying that he wanted to print the libretto as the album's liner notes but ran into complications because, legally speaking, lyrics on paper are a different matter than lyrics on an album. "You can sing it, and that's part of a work of art," said Zappa, "but the liner notes to an album are not—you can't defend that in court as a work of art."[19] In lieu of the libretto being initially included in the album, *Absolutely Free* contained an advertisement within its gatefold, opposite an image of Zappa with the caption "Kill Ugly Radio," featuring a note saying that a "Clean American Version" of the libretto could be mail-ordered for a minimum of one dollar.[20]

In addition to featuring the lyrics for the album, *Absolutely Free*'s libretto also included a foreword by Zappa explaining the album's premise and underlying concepts. Quoting John Tasker Howard, an early twentieth-century American music historian and composer, Zappa opens the foreword saying, "Music has always shown how people think and feel." For Zappa, the music of the Mothers of Invention represents the sentiments and attitudes of a group of people he refers to as "the vast minority," meaning those who are marginalized into the fringes of American society. This is the audience Zappa wants to reach through his music because he wants to motivate listeners to find "the power within themselves to cause or motivate social change but have never used it for one reason or another,"[21] encouraging them to discover that power within themselves in order for them to better understand who they are as individuals. By forming this kind of connection with listeners, Zappa wanted the meaning behind his lyrics to be understood in order to shift the direction in which he felt America was heading. With the power of music, Zappa believed he could inspire people to rise up and resist the elements of society that were restricting individualization and personal freedoms. Though the libretto would not be Zappa's last brush with censorship, it would foreshadow the obstacles he would have to overcome throughout his life, not necessarily just having his music be understood at all but even to have it be heard in the first place. It exemplifies a lot of Zappa's motivation for being a provocateur, which ultimately was to provoke resistance to institutional power and authority that thrive on systemic oppression.

The first of the oratorios begins with "Plastic People." Starting with a mock introduction of the president of the United States set against a loose arrangement of the Richard Berry–penned classic "Louie Louie," which had previously been a hit for the Kingsmen in 1963, "Plastic People" blends experimental rock with modernistic instrumentation amid confounding spoken-word lines from Zappa about CIA agents creeping around Laurel Canyon, an ill president Johnson, and people marching down Sunset Boulevard. As with *Freak Out!* Zappa continues the theme of critiquing society and its plastic inhabitants. Zappa encourages people to observe what is happening in their town at the hands of the Nazis who run it, delivering a call to action to those who do not want to be plastic members of society. In the libretto for the album, Zappa says the lyrics refer to the youth riots that occurred in Los Angeles the year before outside the restaurant Pandora's Box.

The theme of societal plasticity resurfaces later, during the album's second oratorio, on "Uncle Bernie's Farm," with Zappa describing the song as being about people who make ugly toys for ugly people,[22] including a plastic congress and plastic nations up for sale as well as toys promoting murder and societal devastation. According to Ben Watson in *Frank Zappa: The Negative Dialectics of Poodle Play,* "Uncle Bernie's Farm" is meant to decry "the war-toys that are promoted at Christmas and compares authority and parents to robot simulacra: the paranoid vision of the world as an assemblage of artificial objects."[23] As part of *Absolutely Free,* the track lambasts one of the systems in which plastic people are generated by examining ways in which children can be indoctrinated into plasticity, which Zappa's music and messaging were designed to deter. As Zappa told the *Detroit Free Press* in July 1966, "We play the new free music—music as absolutely free, unencumbered by American cultural suppression. We are systematically trying to do away with the creative roadblocks that our helpful American educational system has installed to make sure nothing creative leaks through to mass audiences."[24]

Toward the end of "Plastic People," Zappa refers to a prune as a vegetable to imply how plastic people, such as government leaders, spread misinformation. It is a joke concept found occasionally throughout Zappa's discography, such as him calling ketchup a vegetable in his takedown of the Republican establishment on 1988's "When the Lie's So Big." However, on *Absolutely Free,* this vegetable concept is explored to make a broader statement about America during the mid-1960s. On "The Duke of Prunes," the first part of a three-part suite, Zappa uses prunes to evoke surrealistic lyrics meant to transpose the sexual imagery within country and blues music, and is followed with "Amnesia Vivace," a free-association composition chronicling the Duke of Prune's failed attempt at picking up a couple of cheerleaders before getting his face smashed with a rock.[25] Stricken with amnesia from the assault, the Duke calls out for his Duchess of Prunes in the suite's final part, "The Duke Regains His Chops," offering his love in the form of prunes and cheesy fat. This amnesia the Duke of Prunes experiences has less to do with the medical diagnosis of memory loss and is more a term to describe a psychological psychosis attributed to a nightmarish Orwellian version of the United States, a theme that would later be revisited on Zappa's posthumous 1994 album *Civilization Phaze III,* thus revealing a continuity in his attitudes about the slow decline of American society from the beginning of his career through the end of it.

More vegetables are then brought into the fold with "Call Any Vegetable," the first part of the second three-piece suite within the album's first oratorio. Using vegetables to symbolize inactive and irresponsible people who ignore their societal responsibilities, "Call Any Vegetable" signifies Zappa's belief that people can use their internal power to foster social change and that they will rise up if you call upon them with the right motivation. Following the suite's second part, the psychedelic garage-rock track "Invocation & Ritual Dance of the Young Pumpkin," in which a young pumpkin dances until it gets amnesia,[26] "Soft-Sell Conclusion" closes the suite with Zappa saying that, while some people may not bother with vegetables, meaning the people who have not been awakened and made aware of their internal power to enact societal change, a lot of good can be done if you just call them and explain your feelings to them. By doing that, it is likely the vegetable will hear you and respond, allowing you to reconnect with your vegetable friends.

Opening the second oratorio is "America Drinks," a drunken lament from a poor schmuck whose heart was broken by a girl with a lot of flashy tricks. It is a scene the listener returns to again later with the album's closing, "America Drinks & Goes Home," with the lyrics repeated amid parody showcasing the horror of cocktail lounges complete with tinkling glasses and cash-register sound effects, demonstrating Zappa's subversive style of humor as it takes aim at the music of the parent generation as well as the disrespect shown by alcoholics to music performers. On the song and its capturing of that atmosphere, Zappa told *Jazz & Pop* in 1967, "The one thing that I think is really good about our music is that the settings for the lyrics are so carefully designed. Supposing you had to listen to 'America Drinks and Goes Home' for a million times—it would drive you crazy. . . . But eventually, if you're the average stupid layman who hates music anyway, you might realize how perfect that setting is. . . . Those things are so carefully constructed that it breaks my heart when people don't dig into them and see all the levels that I put into them."[27]

This thematic and conceptual attention to detail is not just contained within individual tracks or even pairs of them, but is rather woven throughout in a way that speaks to the album's larger themes about being an outsider living on the fringes. "Status Back Baby" chronicles the struggles of an all-American high-school football star who is losing his standing in the school's social hierarchy. Zappa expressed in the album's libretto that he found it unfortunate that so many young people worry about their reputation in high school, suggesting that the only thing that really happens for the pretty and popular people at school is getting drunkenly impregnated in somebody's car, smashing the perception that there is anything to be envious about those high up on the school's social ladder. For Zappa, they are just plastic people.

"Status Back Baby" as a song, and within a larger work, also reflects Zappa's views on the education system and how its flaws affect youth. Zappa believed that the system begins to break down after kindergarten, and that high-school students are essentially just being babysat in order to keep them from getting into trouble or annoying their parents. Instead, he encouraged self-education at public libraries while also recommending that teenagers should have the freedom to do what they want because it would be the only way in which they could truly learn just how awful life can be firsthand,[28] all for the purpose of resisting systems that reinforce cultural ignorance. "I feel a lot of people don't know what high school is," Zappa told *Rolling Stone* in July 1968, "including those who are in it. My material is provided to give them some perspective. People are stupid. They never stop to question things. They just accept. Can you imagine a nation who never questions the validity of cheerleaders and pom-poms?"[29]

The oratorio continues with "Uncle Bernie's Farm" and is followed by "Son of Suzy Creamcheese," the titular character being a fictional groupie who first appeared on *Freak Out!* On the back of that album is a letter attributed to Suzy Creamcheese, though actually penned by Zappa, in which she describes the Mothers of Invention as a group of crazy people who smell bad and dance with other weirdos, then closing the letter saying that none of the other kids at school listen to the Mothers because their teacher explained what their songs meant. The character of Suzy Creamcheese is also heard in the opening of the album's closing track, "The Return of the Son of Monster Magnet," in which her conscience asks Suzy about what has got into her before the track's experimental musique concrète composition kicks in. On *Absolutely Free*, the question posed by her conscience returns for this acid garage-rock track profiling what Zappa referred to in the album's libretto as the "stirring saga of a young groupie" who is preoccupied with psychedelia and staying connected with the scene.[30] On "Son of Suzy Creamcheese," Suzy takes too much acid and steals her boyfriend's car to attend a protest rally in Berkeley. Though Suzy was a character Zappa had imagined, she did embody a cliché that could be found throughout the hippie scene in Los Angeles, with Zappa saying that he started encountering people who identified with the character.[31] Her appearance within the context of *Absolutely Free* represents one of the types of people that inhabit the fringes of society but who can also precariously embody one of the plastic people. Despite her appearing on his first two albums, Zappa was dismissive about the character. "The Suzy Creamcheese line was a carefully planned hype," Zappa told *Hit Parader* in a June 1967 interview. "It has little or no meaning on any level. People can make it as bland or as nasty as they like. Girls come up to us and say 'I'm Suzy Creamcheese' and I say 'I know you are.' But really, it doesn't mean anything." While Zappa may have asserted that the character of Suzy Creamcheese lacked any real meaning, the placement of "Son of Suzy Creamcheese" implies that she does within the context of the album. After the uninhibited groupie madness profiled in "Son of Suzy Creamcheese," the penultimate track on *Absolutely Free*, "Brown Shoes Don't Make It," and its commentary about conservative sexual repression certainly leaves a thematic impression. According to the album's libretto, "Brown Shoes Don't Make It" is about the machinations of government institutions that create laws that impact personal and civil liberties, with Zappa blaming bureaucrats and politicians because of their repressed sexual desires, saying "Dirty old men have no business running your country."[32]

With a length of seven-and-a-half minutes, and blending multiple genres including psychedelic rock, jazz, and experimentalism, "Brown Shoes Don't Make It" is about a lecherous government leader who dreams about having sex with a thirteen-year-old girl, fantasizing about smothering her with chocolate syrup and ravaging her on the White House lawn. After the climax, the politician snaps back into reality, satisfied with himself and his life running City Hall. The track's title was inspired by a *Time* magazine article written by Hugh Sidey in which Sidey observed President Johnson's choice of shoes as a sign that something troubling was happening in the White House, with him saying "When President Lyndon Johnson once showed up for some morning ceremonial duties in a gray suit and brown shoes, the people traveling with him were immediately alert for a change in the day's doings. Johnson was fastidious about the trappings of office, and even the slight dissonance of brown and gray hinted a new mood or schedule."[33] As disturbing as the subject matter of "Brown Shoes Don't Make It" is, its legacy as a countercultural statement has endured, with the song included among the "500 Songs that Shaped Rock and Roll" by the Rock & Roll Hall of Fame[34] for its "indictment of male power" and "savage critique of male hegemony."[35]

The third album from the Mothers of Invention, 1968's *We're Only in It for the Money*, continued the band's streak of producing concept albums that derided the counterculture as well as the conservative reactions to a more liberalized America. Most notably, the album placed a heavy satirical emphasis on the hippie subculture which had grown considerably since the release of *Absolutely Free* the year before. Blending psychedelic rock, musique concrète, and orchestral arrangements, the themes and messaging within *We're Only in It for the Money* pokes holes in the narrow-minded and phony mores that permeated American culture during the late 1960s. The album has been recognized and celebrated as a profound cultural document of its era, inducted into the Library of Congress's National Recording Preservation Board in 2005 for its "unique political stance, both anti-conservative and anti-counterculture" and "scathing satire of hippiedom and America's reactions to it."[36]

Unlike the Mothers' previous two albums, one of the album's celebrated satirical qualities is its cover, which parodies the Beatles' 1967 *Sgt. Pepper's Lonely Hearts Club Band.* While the Mothers were recording *We're Only in It for the Money,* the Beatles had released their landmark album to great commercial and critical success. Considering that among the themes Zappa was exploring in *We're Only in It for the Money* was the exploitation of youth culture, including corporate manipulation for financial gain, the Liverpudlian quartet became prime targets for Zappa to criticize the disingenuous ways in which musicians compromised art for money, believing them to not be serious about music. In essence, he believed the Beatles were only in the music business to make money instead of contributing to the culture in the interest of authentic artistic expression. With the rise of the hippie subculture, which echoed the same hyperbole about love as the Beatles, Zappa saw a direct connection.

On the subject of *We're Only in It for the Money*'s title and cover, Zappa said, "I mean anybody who looked at that album could tell that the reason that it was titled that was because it was a parody of the Beatles only being in it for the money. And anyway, a group that looked like we did and played what we did couldn't have been in it for money because there was no way we could really make money doing it."[37]

When asked by an interviewer for *Down Beat* if the Mothers were only in it for the money, Zappa said:

> No . . . because on the day that that album was released, the thing that escaped everybody was the fact that it was designed to show that *the Beatles* were only in it for the money, not that we were. If we were only in it for the money, we'd be doing something else! . . . But automatically everybody assumed that that was the exact truth, and nobody stopped to question for a minute the relationship between the *Sgt. Pepper* cover style and the title. You know, they never once questioned that the Beatles might be anything other than directly descended from heaven. And I personally felt for a long time that they were extremely plastic, and flat-out commercial.[38]

Much like the Mothers' prior two albums, *We're Only in It for the Money* contains avant-garde and eccentric musical stylings and elements, imbuing social and cultural commentary throughout. "Nasal Retentive Calliope Music" and the album closer, "The Chrome Plated Megaphone of Destiny," contain musique concrète experimentation that continued to showcase Zappa's penchant and admiration for the weird and unconventional ways in which music can be composed. "Let's Make the Water Turn Black," based on a true story, profiles Zappa's neighbors who would light their farts on fire, keep their urine in jars, and smear their bodily mucus on their bedroom window. Drawing inspiration from comedian Lenny Bruce's "To Is a Preposition, Come Is a Verb," the track "Harry, You're a Beast" tests the limits of censorship amid the sexual revolution and promise of female liberation, which reflects Zappa's abrasive interpretation of ideas popularized several years earlier by Betty Friedan in her 1963 book *The Feminine Mystique*. Even the album's interludes, with the opener "Are You Hung Up?" along with "Telephone Conversation" and "Hot Poop," add a bizarre flair that bucks up against the conformist standards of how an album can be arranged, resulting in an exciting and challenging listening experience.

The first actual song on the album, "Who Needs the Peace Corps?" pokes fun at the San Francisco hippie scene using a first-person narrative to hammer out the finer points of its subcultural satire. In the opening lines, the young person who is at the center of the song's narrative is questioning his life and not finding a lot of meaning within it. Instead of doing things that could actually provide some structure and direction in his life, like volunteering with the Peace Corps, he decides to drop out of school and goes to the City by the Bay to be among the others with flowers in their hair, hanging out in phony psychedelic dungeons. As the song progresses, we hear about all the plans this aspiring hippie has for when he hits the scene, including dancing at the Fillmore East stoned, getting uncomfortable venereal diseases from all the free love, and even crashing at the residence of Augustus Owsley Stanley, the sound engineer for the Grateful Dead and the first private manufacturer of large quantities of LSD.[39] The song ends with him rattling off a list of stereotypically hippie activities he would like to perform, including wearing beads and feathers, wandering the streets barefoot while high on marijuana, sleeping on the floor with other hippie bands, and getting beaten up by police as he preaches at them about peace and love. All of these activities reveal not only the naivete and ignorance of the song's narrator, but also exposes the superficiality of the entire subculture, with the narrator leaving for home after a week of playing pretend in a movement that *We're Only in It for the Money* argues is not serious. Similar ideas get expressed in "Flower Punk," a hippie satire modeled after the song "Hey Joe" popularized by the Jimi Hendrix Experience, replacing the gun in Joe's hand with hippie paraphernalia. Much like Joe, the hippie is on a journey, making his way to San Francisco to play in a psychedelic band until he is on the verge of a nervous breakdown.

"Who Needs the Peace Corps?" and "Flower Punk" are quite effective satirical takedowns about the principles and legitimacy of the hippie movement, but Zappa's animosity toward the subculture addresses other elements within it, and in ways that ensure the album's theme stays interwoven. "Absolutely Free," borrowing its title from the Mothers' previous album, parodies the very idea that drugs can be used to expand the scope of one's mind and consciousness. Despite his offbeat appearance, Zappa was strongly opposed to drugs and drug culture. In his 1989 autobiography, *The Real Frank Zappa Book*, Zappa said drugs became excuses for people to behave like assholes and that they had no moral or immoral characteristics on their own because they were merely chemical compounds.[40] Zappa opens the track by defining the word "discorporate," which he explains as the process of mentally detaching from your material body, signifying the attitude that a lot of hippies had about drug use. "Absolutely Free" features absurdist lyrics that mock the hippie rhetoric surrounding taking acid or other mind-altering substances to unlock hidden parts of the brain, with Zappa ridiculing the notion that freedom can come from numbing one's mind and senses through substance abuse.

Though several tracks on *We're Only in It for the Money* are fairly short, with some barely over a minute long, they convey themes that extend beyond the scope of their length. On the doo-wop inspired "What's the Ugliest Part of Your Body?" a question is posed to a young woman named Annie about her most unattractive quality, with the narrator saying it is her mind that is the most unappealing thing about her because of the creeps she hangs out with. Amid the vocal harmonization, Zappa interrupts, sounding as if he is preaching from the pulpit, sharing his truth about how the youth generation has been systemically victimized by a society that perpetuates long-standing myths in order to keep them ignorant. These same lines are repeated with echoed distortion later on in "Lonely Little Girl," a song about a despondent young woman who feels isolated and misunderstood by her parents because they have been disconnected from reality for too long. A reprise of "What's the Ugliest Part of Your Body?" follows, with the same lines repeated before dissolving into cacophony, implying that the reason this young woman feels so lonely is because her mind has been corrupted.

We're Only in It for the Money delves further into the family dynamic across several songs, examining the effects of the counterculture and the generational conflict surrounding it that further divides the household. On "Mom & Dad," two alcoholic parents hear reports that some youths have been gunned down by police, believing they deserved it for looking different. Zappa confronts them for failing to educate and express love to their children, revealing at the end of the track that it was their child who was killed while kneeling by her friends who had just been shot, eerily foreshadowing the massacre at Kent State a couple of years later. As for the parents, the darkly comic Tin Pan Alley–sounding "Bow Tie Daddy" that immediately follows "Mom & Dad" assures the father he has nothing to worry about and that he can continue drowning his feelings with booze before returning home in his Lincoln Town Car, expressed with gallows humor directed at the previous generation for damaging their children. On "The Idiot Bastard Son," a song Zappa dedicated to both Richard Nixon[41] and Ronald Reagan[42] during live performances, the lyrics offer a look into the extent of that damage as well as intimate insights into the family structure itself, providing a glimpse into its tragic elements. The song's titular bastard embodies several strange characteristics, all derived from abstract lyrics about his spending time in church but also him seemingly destined to be kept in a jar after dying in the back of someone's car. His father is a member of Congress who leans so far right that he is effectively a fascist, and the mother is a sex worker in Los Angeles. As he lives his life in this strange and sad situation, he grows up to learn that the world is filled with untrustworthy people. "The Idiot Bastard Son," though a rather confusing song on its own, adds texture to the theme of cultural and societal discord heard throughout *We're Only in It for the Money.*

These tracks, presenting ideas threaded throughout the album, reinforce Zappa's critique of the hippie subculture in a way that erodes the mythology surrounding it that has since endured. On hippies, Zappa said, "I think that what they do is a definite indication of their inability to love, because the whole hippie scene is wishful thinking. They wish they could love but they're full of shit, and they're kidding themselves into saying, 'I love! I love! I love!' And the more times they say it, the more times they think they love. But like it doesn't work, and most of them don't have the guts to admit to themselves that it's a lie."[43]

Zappa's outlook on love and how subcultures wielded the concept for their own purposes is rather cynical, primarily because he challenged the authenticity behind it. It is one of the reasons why he garnered such a reputation as being an anti-idealist, and he was certainly vocal about it during the height of the flower-power movement. "I think it's easier to make somebody mad than to make somebody love," said Zappa, "and seeing how hate is the absolute negative of love, if you can evoke hatred and it[']s really there, you could polarise it and you could really have love."[44] With a lot of Zappa's notoriety centered on his being a cynic, it can make one wonder, especially among fresh listeners or critics of his work, what can be gained from such overbearing misanthropic attitudes. After all, a lot of his musical critiques involved tearing down and exposing phony idealism. However, that is not enough to make a good critique. You cannot point out a problem without having some idea of a solution and still have it be an effective commentary.

Though Zappa has been labeled as an opponent of idealism, there is idealism inherent within his musical commentary, even if it is not readily apparent at times. As seen in the libretto for *Absolutely Free*, Zappa did not want to tear apart people's values or ideas just for the sake of doing so. His purpose was for them to see the bigger picture about their place in society, albeit based on his outlook, so they could realize their own power from within and manifest it in ways to enact positive social change on a systemic level. While the hippie subculture Zappa is criticizing believed that was what they were also doing, Zappa had an understanding about institutional power and authority that conflicted with their ideas based on his observations that things were just not getting better. Zappa, in 1978, referred to hippies as stupid people who were sensitive to criticism, saying, "They always take themselves too seriously. So anybody who impugns the process, whether it's a peace march or love beads or whatever it is—that person is the enemy and must be dealt with severely. So we came under a lot of criticism, because we dared to suggest that perhaps what was going on was really stupid."[45]

Even his mockery of the Summer of Love contained within it deeply idealistic views. Though delivered in a satirical tone of voice, "Take Your Clothes Off When You Dance" contains lyrics that speak to the underlying themes of Zappa's libretto from his previous album. The song presents a utopian vision of a society where people are free to be themselves and feel love without being ashamed of their bodies. It is a vision of a place where a person's worth is not measured by fashion or hairstyle, and where even evil can be overcome when it threatens the serenity of this social paradise. The track expresses what life could be like without prejudices and biases projected onto people, offering a brief glimpse of Zappa without his cynical mask in a song about recognition and acceptance.

These themes are also at the heart of "Mother People," the penultimate track on *We're Only in It for the Money*. It features the Mothers telling you that they have found a way to reach you, confronting the way you think about them and whether you find them creepy because of their clothes and hair, and demanding you know that they are just another person like anyone else. Some lines allude to the rejection of someone else's romantic feelings, but they are an abstraction as an expression of the tension and conflict that can arise when a group is marginalized because of biases, resulting in the otherized group's more direct tone in demanding to be recognized and accepted with dignity. Both "Mother People" and "Take Your Clothes Off When You Dance" stand out not only as idealistic highlights on the album, but also as anthems for the Mothers and what they represent.

With songs that explore social friction and hostility, such as "Mom & Dad" and "The Idiot Bastard Son," as well as those that respond to the consequences of that dynamic, like "Mother People" and "Take Your Clothes Off When You Dance," *We're Only in It for the Money* provides an essential cultural documentation of the era. However, the album goes a bit further than that. Beyond just taking a snapshot of American life in 1968, it also acts as a warning about what may happen if such a societal imbalance threatens the institutional foundation of the country. "Concentration Moon," another track evoking a Tin Pan Alley aesthetic, juxtaposes the jocular tone of its vocals with foreboding notions about what will become of the counterculture if it gains too much momentum in a way that, in Zappa's view, is entirely phony and directionless. Based on unsubstantiated and alarmist rumors over Ronald Reagan, then governor of California, repurposing the state's World War II–era Japanese internment camps in order to imprison hippies, "Concentration Moon" recalls the killing of young people by police to make the point that such antiestablishment sentiments could potentially result in imprisonment as directed by the government. The song features a group of hippies who were forced into the camp after the threat of police violence during a protest demonstration, looking up at the moon and singing how they wish they were free to run around and grow their hair out. For an album that heavily jeers at hippies and the perfunctory philosophy of the counterculture movement, at the heart of *We're Only in It for the Money* is a commentary that elevates individualism and its resistance to institutions that work to quash it.

After *We're Only in It for the Money,* Zappa would continue to release albums with varying degrees of conceptual themes and ideas. Among these were a quartet of releases that were developed as part of a conceptual continuity project called *No Commercial Potential.* This project started with *We're Only in It for the Money* and would also include an album of dual musique concrète pieces that combined hundreds of hours of spoken word tape with orchestral and surf rock samples (*Lumpy Gravy,* 1968), a doo-wop homage album performed as a fictional Chicano band consisting of humanoid dog creatures (*Cruising with Ruben & the Jets,* 1968), and a soundtrack for a proposed science-fiction film based on salaciously sexual stories from the Mothers of Invention's life on the road (*Uncle Meat,* 1969).[46] However, none of these other concept albums would contain as much critique of American society within their narrative as did the Mothers' opening triptych of releases. Arguably, Zappa would not even record another album with such a robustly developed commentary on America until 1979 with the release of *Joe's Garage,* eleven years after *We're Only in It for the Money.* While none of his albums during that time would have such a strong socially conscious focus as to suggest some semblance of a conceptual narrative, Zappa still composed and recorded songs for them that did provide a platform in which he applied a critical lens to American culture while challenging government, religion, media, and other establishment institutions in often intelligent, and sometimes perplexing, ways. Though the themes of these songs would largely not be carried through the entirety of any of his albums released between *We're Only in It for the Money* and *Joe's Garage,* they still contained within them profound and provocative satire and criticism.

"Uncle Remus," from Zappa's 1974 solo album *Apostrophe (')*, is a track that stands out for showcasing how Zappa continued to observe the failures over America's struggle to absolve itself of its original sin. Cowritten with keyboardist George Duke (Duke composed the music while Zappa wrote the lyrics), "Uncle Remus" is a poignant piano piece that asks tough questions about "the relative quiescence of the movement for black emancipation." Ben Watson, author of *Frank Zappa: The Complete Guide to His Music,* calls the song a "gentle reprimand, noting how protest was being abandoned for fashion."[47] Much like "Trouble Every Day" from *Freak Out!* which served as a commentary about the media's exploitation of racial violence, "Uncle Remus" is a song in which Zappa attempts to navigate the complexity of measuring racial progress in the United

States, recalling the fictional freed slave created by Joel Chandler Harris whose stories about plantation life in the Old South have been seen as both idealizing slavery and anti-racist.[48] Zappa opens the track by asking rhetorically whether civil rights are advancing at a much slower pace than they should. As Zappa asks Uncle Remus if he sees what has been happening since the civil rights movement of the previous decade, he notes that, while Black people may now hold more economic buying power than they previously had, which allows them to afford luxuries like fine clothing, it makes no difference when you are on the wet end of a high-powered hose, representing the idea, symbolically as well as literally, that they are still systemically marginalized and are therefore susceptible to state violence.

In the second verse, Zappa points out that society has told Black people that the best way for them to get ahead in America and earn equality is through hard work, specifically by keeping their nose to the grindstone. It is a degrading dynamic, one in which Zappa recommends that the best alternative for Black people, until true racial equity is achieved, is to just go to rich white people's houses and damage the racist caricatured jockeys on their lawn. Composed in a way that had been uncharacteristic for Zappa so far in his catalog, "Uncle Remus" is a complicated and affecting song about racial dynamics from the perspective of whiteness and its understanding of institutional oppression. It captures a lot of feelings about the limits America places on marginalized people, but centers on the experience of someone who cannot possibly understand that dynamic. This was something Zappa had a grasp on, telling an interviewer for *Hot Flash*, "It's not exactly from the point of view of a black person. I don't think that a black person would actually write that song. It's not exactly. . . . there are subtle differences in point of view in there. I think that it's something that should have been said. If you've ever seen these little jockeys on the lawn. They've had it coming for a long time."[49]

Though Zappa railed against media throughout his career, especially when it concerned matters over art and the freedom of expression, no song captured his vehemence and ire over it more than "I'm the Slime." Released as a single in 1973 in support of his album *Over-Nite Sensation*, "I'm the Slime" captures Zappa's attitudes about the role media play in society and their malleability to always reflect and elevate controlling interests. The song opens with Zappa playing a guessing game, dropping clues for the listener to pick up what he is putting down. Delivering the lines with a first-person narrative, Zappa almost sounds as if he is describing himself, as if he is trying to capture his own provocative reputation through words. He says he is gross, perverted, and deranged, and that these qualities about him have been consistent for years. After all, with the release of this song, Zappa had spent nearly a decade in the music business being told he was all these things and more. However, Zappa is not talking about himself but rather a tool that the government and businesses use to manufacture consent through laws and regulations.

With all these hints, Zappa asks the listener if they can guess who he is talking about, with the reveal being that the slime represents what television media broadcasts on behalf of those who control it. With that, those watching their screens are forced to obey and swallow what the television force-feeds them, leaving them helpless and unable to look away because their minds have been brainwashed. Ultimately, at the heart of the song is the message that money controls what is shown on television, with the highest bidder the one who rules the airwaves. Zappa believed that the United States would never crumble as a nation because television, and the profit it generates, has so much control that it would prevent such a collapse. "I don't think the United States will totally break down," Zappa said in 1977. "No way, because there's only one thing that matters in this country, and that's money. And money is a matter of pride to the people who control it. They'll do anything they can to keep the country going just so they can play with their money. That's all it's about."[50] Though Zappa's perception about the robustness of American media seems rather quaint over five decades on, especially considering how the entertainment-media landscape has shifted power away from the United States in favor of ideological competitors like China in recent years,[51] the core messaging of "I'm the Slime" does apply to the same power that social media hold over society as television's successor in being the biggest propaganda tool in the establishment-institution arsenal.

While several songs in Zappa's discography during this period do address larger existential issues in American culture, there are instances peppered throughout where the social commentary borders on being an airing of personal and professional grievances. "Flakes" from 1979's *Sheik Yerbouti* is one of those songs in which Zappa trades deep insight for what can come across as pettiness, referring to unionized plumbers and mechanics in California as inept and lazy. Including a humorous monologue by Adrian Belew delivered in the style of Bob Dylan complaining about a mechanic not fixing his car but billing him anyway, "Flakes" echoes Zappa's beliefs about the breakdown in the quality of American craftsmanship and how Zappa places a lot of the blame on the American public. After the Dylanesque monologue, Zappa portrays an average American guy, described as a moron, whose wife uses a paper knife to frost her cake, a reference to signify the disposable nature of goods in a corporatist-oriented society that promotes plasticity. Everything in their house was cheaply made in the United States and is organized to indicate the absence of any real culture. When something in their home breaks down, they call some flakes who come to make things worse and gouge them for their services. Zappa closes by singing that millions of union-protected flakes will usher in the downfall of American civilization, snidely commenting that such an unceremonious end to society is likely a product of divine will. Even if the potency of Zappa's commentary is lost amid his complaining, "Flakes" does offer an astute critique about personal responsibility and how systems of power thrive on ignorance and complicit behavior. It is a substantive quality that gets lost within the narratives of Zappa's other anti-union songs such as the cartoonish "Rudy Wants to Buy Yez a Drink" from 1970's *Chunga's Revenge* and the faux-reggae rally cry that is "Stick Together" on *The Man from Utopia* from 1983. While those songs have themes that tangentially address the forces behind the crumbling of American industry, such as graft and corruption, they lack the same critique of how institutional power is often derived from the people it dominates.

Zappa earned a reputation as a provocateur very near the beginning of his career, and it has since endured as one of the defining aspects of his legacy. Though a lot of this provocation came in the form of social and cultural satire, especially during the recording of the first three Mothers of Invention albums, Zappa would increasingly become more notorious for using scatological and sexual humor as his career progressed, further complicating his image in the public eye.

As with any other topic or subject he had addressed in his music throughout the years, Zappa tended to heavily rely on tropes to convey certain ideas about his perception of various elements of American society and culture at the time. For example, during the early 1970s, groupies were a regularly occurring trope in his music because of his band's experiences while touring, which resulted in songs like "What Kind of Girl Do You Think We Are?" (*Fillmore East, June 1971*) and "Daddy, Daddy, Daddy" (*200 Motels* soundtrack). Zappa would rely on the groupie trope throughout the rest of the decade, with such notable tracks as "Penguin in Bondage" from 1974's *Roxy & Elsewhere,* "Carolina Hard-Core Ecstasy" from 1975's *Bongo Fury,* "Crew Slut" from 1979's *Joe's Garage,* and even into the 1980s with "Pick Me, I'm Clean" from *Tinsel Town Rebellion,* released in 1981.

Zappa also often explored sexual kinks and fetishes in his music, several of which with a satirically humorous slant. As examples, "Ms. Pinky," from 1976's *Zoot Allures,* is a heavy metal proto-punk ode to a blow-up doll, while "Dirty Love" off 1973's *Over-Nite Sensation* masquerades as a strikingly deviant track because of Tina Turner's sultry groaning backing vocal and the effect that slows Zappa's vocals by a complete step[52] but is just a silly tune at its core, with its various references to poodles. Even "Titties & Beer," from the acclaimed 1978 live album *Zappa in New York,* is just a rollicking good time where Zappa outsmarts Satan, played by drummer Terry Bozzio, in order to get back his case of beer and girlfriend with the voluptuous mammalian protruberances. "Titties & Beer" ends with Zappa being the loser of his own story as his, now, former girlfriend gives him the finger and speeds away on the motorcycle. Songs like these represent an absurd perspective on sex, one distorted by a funhouse-mirror reflection of the lifestyle of a famous rock-and-roll band, which provides the listener with a cathartic and entertaining experience.

Though many of these songs are infused with a lot of humor, others broach the topic of sex in rather difficult and uncomfortable ways. While "Brown Shoes Don't Make It" from *Absolutely Free* is celebrated as one of Zappa's greatest satirical songs, even with the disturbing imagery involving a teenage girl doused in chocolate syrup, "Magdelana" from 1972's *Just Another Band from L.A.* continues that theme but with heightened overt incestual overtones in the lyrics that present one of the most difficult listening experiences one can have with Zappa's music. Fortunately, unlike some of the other tracks mentioned,

Zappa said "Magdalena" was not based on a true story but that it does represent something that could happen somewhere,[53] offering a revealing look into one of the darkest corners of Zappa's commentary about American culture. While some of these songs with this kind of subject matter do have some vague concept in them that critiques some sexual or gendered construct, it is often the case with many of them that the meaning is difficult to discern, or arguably even lost, when Zappa turns the provocative humor dial up, which makes it understandable why someone could be offended by Zappa's music.

Zappa would also express his social and cultural commentary in more abstract ways. Two tracks from 1975's *Bongo Fury,* a collaboration between the Mothers of Invention and Captain Beefheart, feature commentary about America's approaching bicentennial, but veiled in surrealist imagery. In "200 Years Old," a man has an existential crisis while staring into his bowl of cornflakes in a diner, while "Poofter's Froth Wyoming Plans Ahead" is a rocking cowboy song about the blatant commercialism surrounding the nation's anniversary as a critique of the corporatization of America. In a 1975 interview with the *Dallas Times Herald,* when asked about all the festivities being planned for the bicentennial, Zappa said he considered it "perfectly logical in an industrial nation" to become so corrupted after so much time, adding, "We stole from the Indians; we subjugated race after race in the name of God (they've got that spelled wrong, it should read G-N-P) and the immortal dollar-sign. . . . There has never been a better example of a society founded on the concept of greed."[54] These songs provide an alternative vision of America, unveiled as being a cultural wasteland; they act as needles popping the balloons at America's birthday in order to stamp out the national myths that the celebrations are designed to uphold and preserve.

This commitment to expose the hypocrisies that put the country on a trajectory toward a cultural dystopia is consistent throughout Zappa's work and is presented in a variety of ways. As is the case with "Billy the Mountain," the epic folkloric road song that takes up an entire side of *Just Another Band from L.A.*, Zappa's commentary would be buried in layers of theatrical flair. In the song, a mountain named Billy and his wife Ethel, a tree, earn a living as the scenic backdrop for souvenir postcards. When Billy and Ethel receive a royalty check for their work, they decide to go on a vacation to New York

City. Unfortunately, the sheer magnitude of Billy causes him to destroy everything in his path. While passing through Columbus, Ohio, Billy receives a draft notice but chooses not to follow its demands, which in turn gets the couple labeled as communists. In the meantime, as Billy and Ethel continue toward their vacation destination, the government categorizes them as a threat for all the damage they are causing along their journey. After a failed attempt by the government in stopping Billy, which included launching a missile at him, they hire a man named Studebaker Hoch, a mysterious superhero, to stop Billy from destroying more real estate. Studebaker then covers himself with enough Aunt Jemima pancake syrup in order to attract thousands of flies that whisk him away to Billy's peak, where Studebaker threatens the mountain and his wife with violence if he does not go in for his enlistment medical screening. Amused by the audacity of Studebaker's efforts to force him to follow through on the draft, Billy laughs out so loud that Studebaker loses his footing and falls off the side of the mountain. Ending with the sage advice that one should never fuck with a mountain,[55] the song represents Zappa's beliefs about the power of the individual. Zappa would continue this custom of communicating his cultural critique of the country through melodramatic stories throughout his career, including in scales grander than "Billy the Mountain" such as with the 1979 three-LP rock opera *Joe's Garage* and his failed 1984 Broadway production *Thing-Fish*. Though Zappa's success with these releases would vary, he did persist in exploring new satirical ways to share his vision of America.

Zappa's catalog also features songs that critique popular culture and people's egocentricities concerning it. "Disco Boy," Zappa's second single to chart on the *Billboard 200* after 1974's "Don't Eat the Yellow Snow," is a poppy satire about the conceit and self-absorption of disco culture, an art form Zappa explored further with musical caricatures through the end of the 1970s, most notably with "Dancin' Fool" on *Sheik Yerbouti*. Included on 1984's *Them or Us*, "Be in My Video" mocks the music-video culture pioneered by MTV, particularly David Bowie's dominance of the channel's airwaves with his hit singles from his 1983 album *Let's Dance*. Zappa ridicules the medium's clichés, including the depiction of sadomasochistic domination of women, bound in cages and leather collars while being forced to smell the glove a la *This Is Spinal Tap*.

Zappa's humorous takes on popular culture during the 1980s would result in his biggest hit with "Valley Girl," released in 1982 as the first single for *Ship Arriving Too Late to Save a Drowning Witch.* It featured his then fourteen-year-old daughter Moon Unit on lead vocals, perfectly capturing the vapidness of youth culture in Ronald Reagan's America through the vocal affect of a materialistic upper-class San Fernando Valley teenage girl. While the theme of "Valley Girl" explores the era's consumerist greed culture, with the song criticizing the modern corporatist manifestation of the plasticity Zappa documented in the 1960s with the Mothers of Invention, life would imitate art as the farcical figure Moon portrayed would ironically become a nationwide phenomenon,[56] making the truth inherent in Frank's and Moon's satire more palpable. Though "Valley Girl" is feasibly the leading example in Zappa's catalog, it is not the only one in which Zappa's music accurately reflected a view of the culture at the time. "Tinsel Town Rebellion," released the prior year on the album of the same name, chronicles the story of aspiring bands looking to make it big in the music industry, with many sacrificing their integrity and talent in order to appeal to the masses and get a check from a record label. These songs, even if they each on the surface address different scenarios and ideas, condemn the ways in which popular culture can be shaped by the objectively worst aspects of society, especially those that Zappa argued hindered America's intellectual development.

As his career continued, Zappa recognized the ways in which the issues he was addressing in the mid-1960s evolved new methods to limit cultural progress. "We're Turning Again," from 1985's *Frank Zappa Meets the Mothers of Prevention,* illustrates Zappa's views on how the acid-taking hippies of the 1960s grew up into yuppies of the 1980s who live dull and meaningless lives. Zappa drew these parallels in order to address, as Kevin Courrier says in his book *Dangerous Kitchen: The Subversive World of Zappa,* that, "While the Reagan era was committed to wiping out '60s reform, there were movements afoot that sentimentalized aspects of that divisive decade by treating it romantically and nostalgically." Part of Zappa's commentary was to expose the myths surrounding the hippie generation, which Courrier described as "counterfeit" and which "could become repressive and authoritarian."[57] In other words, during a decade in which the nation's leadership was backed by fundamentalist Christianity, nostalgia for the good old days of the 1960s could potentially resurrect the turmoil and instability that harmed Black and other marginalized people—especially, as Zappa would illustrate through the commentary in his music, if religious ideology was guiding it.

Though Zappa had largely withdrawn from making albums with overt political commentary during the 1970s, that would begin to change by the end of the decade. Just as it had during the 1960s when Zappa first began to form his identity as a musician, a conservative counterrevolution was beginning to take shape again, forming in direct opposition to the liberal progressivism that had begun to make headway as the country sought to heal itself following the cultural divisiveness of the Vietnam War. Just like the one following the Kennedy assassination, this conservative uprising was mobilizing in the wake of a national trauma, emboldened to change the ideological direction of the country to reflect its views that restricted the civil liberties and personal freedoms of all Americans, with people of color and other marginalized communities most susceptible to the harm those views would cause through legislation and other tools of systemic power. Though the cultural and media landscape had changed in ways that would make it more difficult for his music to be heard, and despite the critical and commercial pressure that came with it, Zappa would increasingly commit himself toward making music with a message designed to motivate people to fight back against the rising tide of authoritarianism. By 1979, just as he did in 1966 on his first album, Zappa would once again, through his music, attempt to dispel one of the biggest myths plaguing America: It can't happen here.

A TOKEN OF MY EXTREME

Considered inconsequential and unknown at the start of the campaign for the 1976 presidential election, Jimmy Carter would emerge victorious in securing the Democratic Party nomination after early primary victories distanced him from his opponents, with him ultimately winning the presidency with just 50.1 percent of the popular vote. Carter's appeal came from both running on a campaign branding him as a Washington, DC, outsider and voters experiencing fatigue over Republicans due to issues like the Vietnam War and the Watergate scandal. Aspiring to make government competent and compassionate, Carter believed morality "existed as the best foundation for exerting U.S. power and influence," supporting a platform that prioritized peace, the recognition of human rights, and increased cooperation with the international community.[1] However, shortly after entering office, Carter's presidency would come up against rapidly shifting political winds, brought on by issues at home and abroad. Frustrated with what was perceived as a lack of effective leadership on the part of Carter, the voting public's confidence in their president was beginning to be tested, with much opposition coming from the conservative right. Though nearly half of evangelical voters gave Carter their support during his 1976 campaign, white evangelicals, at odds with Carter's progressive brand of liberalism, would begin to coalesce in opposition to what they thought of more and more as a moral crusade, targeting Carter as the enemy of their deeply cherished traditional values.

Carter's tenure as a one-term president is often remembered as being filled with complex domestic and foreign challenges, all of which informed and shaped his popularity with voters. Some of these challenges would be overcome and result in considerable diplomatic success for Carter and his administration. The Camp David Accords, which led to a peace treaty between Egypt and Israel signed in 1978, and the warming relationship between the United States and China, in which the two nations would formally recognize the other after several months of confidential and secret negotiations,[2] have contributed to Carter's legacy as a conscientious humanitarian, which has only grown over the decades since losing his bid for reelection. However, while he was president, several economic crises surfaced that, at the time, gave voters the impression that Carter was an ineffectual leader. Inflation, as high as 14 percent and which triggered a recession during his reelection campaign, was a product of the staggering prices and long lines at the pump during the gas shortage in 1979,[3] with voters carrying that economic struggle with them into the voting booth. Then, there was Iran.

Prior to 1979, Iran was ruled by the Shah, Mohammad Reza Pahlavi, a dictator who "repressed dissent and restricted political freedoms" while also advocating for Iran to "adopt Western-oriented secular modernization, allowing some degree of cultural freedom." The Shah came into monarchical rule in 1953 after the U.S. Central Intelligence Agency and the U.K. Secret Intelligence overthrew Mohammad Mosaddegh, Iran's democratically elected prime minster, following not one, but two attempts at a coup, after Mosaddegh sought to nationalize the country's oil industry.[4] The Shah's rule oversaw the expansion of Iran's economy and education system, the formation of major alliances with the United States and the United Kingdom over its oil industry, and the building of industrial infrastructure across the country. Due to the country's oil reserves, the Shah could position Iran as being a modern nation that adhered to the principles and values of a pro-Western secular government. Iran reflected this modernization through the expansion of personal freedoms such as women being allowed to seek an education, men and women being able to interact together freely in public, and for citizens to wear cosmopolitan and westernized fashions.[5]

However, the prioritization to modernize Iran, as well as the "Shah's increasingly authoritarian measures and his eventual dismissal of multiparty rule," stirred resentment among Iranians who were communists or practiced traditional or fundamentalist religious beliefs. There were few opportunities that fostered engagement and participation with the political process, with some parties, such as the National Front and the pro-Soviet Tūdeh, enduring restrictions with civil protests being met with detention, and even torture, by the Shah's police force and government. Reforms enacted by the Shah, such as centralizing Persian identity in Iranian society, resulted in the rights of local and indigenous tribes to be infringed upon,[6] all of which fueled animosity toward the Shah. The White Revolution, the Shah's program to modernize Iran, which lasted from 1963 through 1979, "upended the wealth and influence of the traditional landowning classes, altered rural economies, and led to rapid urbanization and Westernization. The program was economically successful, but the benefits were unevenly distributed, while changes to social norms and traditional institutions were pervasive."[7] Though this led Iran through a period of significant economic growth, factors including aggressive government spending and rising oil prices would force Iranians to bear the brunt of high inflation through the reduction of their buying power and standard of living.[8]

The clerics felt disenfranchised by these new reforms, especially since the government implemented a decrease in religious education.[9] Many who opposed the government, including conservative clerics and the secular left, who united under the common Shi'i identity, credited the "government extravagance, corruption, brutality, and the suppression of individual rights"[10] for igniting their opposition. It was during this period in which Ruhollah Khomeini, who had received the distinction of ayatollah in the 1950s, became critical of the Shah, often organizing riots protesting his regime. In 1964, after being imprisoned for a year, Khomeini would eventually be exiled from Iran for his anti-government actions. While in exile, Khomeini developed his theoretical concept of *velāyat-e faqīh*, a system of government that proposes a hierarchy where the clergy represent the supreme power and where the Islamic faith grants appointed jurists custodianship over its people. This would "lay the foundations of an Islamic republic in Iran" with Khomeini fomenting the development of a "strong and influential network that positioned him to play a commanding role in the overthrow of the shah." Khomeini relied on a network of supporters to relay tape recordings of his messages and sermons, resulting in increasingly violent large-scale acts of civil disruption and political demonstrations until the Shah fled Iran on January 16, 1979. On February 1, Khomeini had returned from exile in order to assume power as the new religious leader of Iran amid the chaos of the revolution. A new government would be formed four days later and, by February 11, the army became a neutral force. In April, a national referendum would reveal "overwhelming support for the institution of an Islamic republic," with the constitution approved by December. As part of his religious doctrine, Khomeini would eliminate all facets of Westernization implemented by the Shah and disseminate his brand of revolutionary Islam to surrounding Muslim countries.[11]

Empowered by his theocratic government, Khomeini would oversee an adversarial relationship develop between Iran and Western nations, including his referring to the United States as the "Great Satan." Perhaps the most notable crisis to unfold during Carter's presidency occurred when Khomeini advocated that Iranian students seize control of the U.S. embassy in Tehrān, which resulted in fifty-two American hostages being held captive for 444 days.[12] An early response by the United States was to cease all purchasing and imports of Iranian oil. As oil production in Iran slowed, the Organization of the Petroleum Exporting Countries (OPEC) offset the reduction in refinement by raising prices. This ultimately triggered a shortage, resulting in Americans waiting in long lines for gas. Carter would promise to decrease the United States' dependence on foreign oil imports, with added focus to bolstering energy efficiency, but the damage to his reputation as president was already done.[13]

As Carter's influence as a political leader was shrinking, Khomeini's profile was growing. In a controversial decision, Khomeini was declared "Person of the Year" by *Time* magazine in 1980. Detailing the reasons for their decision in giving the fundamentalist leader the honorary distinction, *Time* said, "The lean figure of Khomeini towered malignly over the globe. As the leader of Iran's revolution he gave the 20th-century world a frightening lesson in the shattering power of irrationality, of the ease with which terrorism can be adopted as government policy. . . . Khomeini's importance far transcends the nightmare of the embassy seizure, transcends indeed the overthrow of the Shah of Iran. The revolution that he led to triumph threatens to upset the world balance of power more than any other political event since Hitler's conquest of Europe."[14]

The pressure on Carter and his administration was palpable. In the wake of the Iranian Revolution and its consequential oil shortage and energy crisis, Carter gave a speech that tried to reframe American economic woes on a "moral and civic plane" in order to "unify around a sense of civic sacrifice." On July 15, Carter delivered his televised "Crisis of Confidence" speech, though dubbed his "malaise speech" despite that word not being used.[15] In the speech, Carter acknowledged that "the true problems of our Nation are much deeper" than the effects of the energy crisis or recession. Carter read comments he had heard from citizens, all of which conveyed notions that the American people were suffering economically as a result of the energy crisis and that Carter was not doing enough as president to address that. Recognizing that what was behind those sentiments was something more complex than the energy crisis itself, Carter used the speech to address a much larger issue, referring to "a fundamental threat to American democracy."[16]

Carter addressed the threat as being a "crisis of confidence," an ominous invisible presence that disrupts national unity and purpose, "threatening to destroy the social and the political fabric of America." Carter asserted that this confidence had guided American principles, which included "public institutions and private enterprise, our own families, and the very Constitution of the United States." When Americans lose their confidence in the future, Carter said, we "close the door on our past" and the democratic principles that humanity upholds. Carter laid bare the possible future direction of America and the freedom that could come with energy independence, based on the response to his concerns about its national confidence, saying:

> We are at a turning point in our history. There are two paths to choose. One is a path I've warned about tonight, the path that leads to fragmentation and self-interest. Down that road lies a mistaken idea of freedom, the right to grasp for ourselves some advantage over others. That path would be one of constant conflict between narrow interests ending in chaos and immobility. It is a certain route to failure. All the traditions of our past, all the lessons of our heritage, all the promises of our future point to another path, the path of common purpose and the restoration of American values. That path leads to true freedom for our nation and ourselves. We can take the first steps down that path as we begin to solve our energy problem.[17]

According to Kevin Mattson, an American historian and author of *"What the Heck Are You Up To, Mr. President?": Jimmy Carter, America's "Malaise," and the Speech That Should Have Changed the Country*, Carter "had grown increasingly convinced that Americans had to face up to the energy crisis, but they only could do this if they faced up to the crisis in their own values," noting that Carter conveyed in his speech that "the American way of life . . . our consumerism, our materialism have really gotten in the way of this problem."

"It's from then on," said Mattson, "that Carter had a really difficult time at bouncing back and being seen on the part of the American people as a strong and significant leader—especially a leader that could take America through solving the energy crisis."[18] After narrowly defeating Massachusetts Senator Ted Kennedy for the Democratic nomination in 1980, Carter's position out of the gate as the party's front-runner was already weakened due to the various domestic and foreign issues plaguing his presidency.[19] Ronald Reagan, Carter's opponent in the general election, breezed through the contest for the Republican nomination due to supporters positively responding to his politics that "increasingly reflected the mythic western image of rugged independence and self-reliance."[20]

Reagan offered rhetorical support for the Christian Right as he "endorsed the movement's attempt to bring religion into politics" during the campaign as evangelical supporters "expected his administration to roll back abortion rights, curb the gay rights movement, restore prayer in schools, and lead the nation back to morality" while "abandoning their pretense of nonpartisanship."[21] According to Randall Balmer, a professor of religion at Dartmouth College, the election of Reagan represented the first time American evangelicals actively engaged in politics, marrying the goals of evangelicalism with the political platform of the Republican Party. With Reagan, evangelicals "had a president who shared their distaste for modern whirls of social change." Evangelicals felt encouraged to no longer stay silent when it came to their opposition to Carter and the liberal values in which he was guiding America; they were "hostile to his agenda and to him personally."[22]

While a conservative evangelical coalition was forming in the United States to elect a new leader that would represent them and their values, Khomeini was leveraging his newly acquired power to carry out his fundamentalist vision of Iran. One aspect of that plan involved assuming control over all media and culture within the nation. In July 1979, Khomeini enacted a total ban on music being broadcasted in Iran, referring to it as opium in that it "stupefies persons listening to it and makes their brain inactive and frivolous." Khomeini gave the instructions for this ban while at Radio Darya, an Iranian broadcast station, saying the station's programming had "corrupted Iranian youth" by robbing them of their "strength and virility." "If you want independence for your country," said Khomeini, "you must suppress music and not fear to be called old-fashioned. Music is a betrayal of the nation and of youth."[23] In accordance with this ruling, anyone caught listening to music that was not viewed in alignment with traditional Islam "could be fined, lashed or imprisoned for 'causing corruption on earth' under Iranian law."[24] Though those with a taste for westernized music had to recede into the cultural underground, the people of Iran were subject to fundamentalist religious principles designed to control them.

When Khomeini banned music due to its supposed role in corrupting the religious values of Iranian youth, Zappa certainly took notice. As an artistic response to the building of this theocratic regime in Iran, Zappa would record and release a three-part rock opera by the tail end of 1979 before Khomeini would solidify total control and his doctrine of *velāyat-e faqīh* be cemented in the post-revolution constitution. *Joe's Garage,* with act 1 released as a single LP in September, followed by the second and third acts compiled as a double LP released in November, would reflect "a distinct mixture of Zappa's contempt for the music industry combined with this deep love of music,"[25] drawing inspiration from the state of global and domestic affairs to creatively demonstrate parallels between Iran after the revolution and the cultural and political temperature of the United States ahead of the 1980 election.

The heart of the plot within *Joe's Garage* is a cautionary tale demonizing music for all the ways it can lead to one's self-destruction: by exposing youth to culturally progressive ideas that lead to sexual promiscuity, disease, and insanity. In this story, we follow the journey of a young man named Joe, whose passion for music leads to his eventual downfall as he forms a band during a time when the government is modifying the Constitution to criminalize music. We follow Joe's path of personal destruction, experiencing the myriad ways in which music pollutes minds and society, resulting in a dystopia where the desire for musical expression is banned, and freedom comes through an autonomous commitment to government-sanctioned labor and consumerism.[26]

Narrating *Joe's Garage* is a government employee called the Central Scrutinizer, voiced by Zappa, who is a seemingly omnipresent figure whose official responsibility is to enforce laws that have not yet been passed and ratified. As he also oversees the addition of laws written in tiny print, so as not to be obvious about their constitutional violations, the Central Scrutinizer also warns listeners about mundane activities they might be engaged in that could result in the death penalty or adversely affect their parents' credit rating. The reason for all these bureaucratic and legal changes is because all the criminal institutions are filled with young people who were driven to a life of crime, in the sense that they strayed from traditional conservative values by the damagingly seductive allure of music ("The Central Scrutinizer").

Following the Central Scrutinizer's introduction opening act 1 of the album, we are introduced to Joe, portrayed by Ike Willis, a young all-American guy. He just wants to jam with his friends, eschewing drugs to hang out with his buds and thrill the local girls over some cold brews and hot tunes. Loosely autobiographical based on Zappa's experiences during the 1950s with his earliest groups such as the Blackouts, forming a band with his motivation to play music for his intended audience solely, we see Joe promised a recording contract that never comes to fruition. However, as the years go by and audiences are introduced to newer, more liberal styles of music since his garage-band days, such as disco, heavy metal, and new wave, Joe believes it's time to give the music business another shot. Unfortunately, his return to the garage conflicts with the impending authoritarianism creeping across the country ("Joe's Garage").

Local law enforcement then interferes with Joe's dreams of becoming a musician. To set the young man on the straight and narrow path, Joe is encouraged to instead pursue wholesome church-oriented youth activities. However, at the Catholic Youth Organization (CYO) Joe joins, the activities are anything but innocent, with Father Riley, the homosexual minister, also played by Zappa, turning down the lights while the boys learn about the carnal proclivities of the fairer sex. Things begin to look brighter for Joe when he meets a young Catholic girl named Mary, portrayed by Dale Bozzio, at the social club with whom he spends time holding hands while thinking pure thoughts until music corrupts the serenity of this scene ("Catholic Girls").

Mary eventually quits going to the CYO and instead pursues a groupie lifestyle, following one of the touring rock bands that have come into town, seduced by the allure of excitement that none of the local guys can give the thrill-seeking girls living in the industrial towns on the outskirts of the big city ("Crew Slut," "On the Bus"). Though, after a few weeks with the guys on the bus, Mary is dumped in one of the towns along the tour route. To get the money to buy a bus ticket back home, she excitedly competes in a wet T-shirt contest emceed by Zappa's Father Riley, now defrocked and embracing his new persona as Buddy Jones, proclaiming that Mary represents the type of all-American girl who would do anything for a bit of cash ("Fembot In a Wet T-Shirt").[27]

Unaware that he would find Mary in such a place, Joe becomes disillusioned by his former girlfriend's path toward sexual promiscuity and wanders the streets in a daze before meeting Lucille, a girl who works at Jack-in-the-Box. Joe sleeps with Lucille and gets a sexually transmitted disease, an unpronounceable one according to the Central Scrutinizer, lamenting that it hurts when he urinates ("Why Does It Hurt When I Pee?"). As act 1 comes to a close, Joe is distraught by his erotic affliction and finds comfort singing along to a tune from an old Jeff Simmons album, originally produced by Zappa in 1969 and written under the pseudonym La Marr Bruister, hoping to soothe the pain caused by the lover whose song is her namesake ("Lucille Has Messed My Mind Up").

In act 1, the listener is introduced to a strange, sardonic world that represents Zappa's vision of the initial consequences of the confluence between religion, business, law enforcement, and government. In essence, his belief is that these institutions' overlapping interests work harmoniously to negatively impact the pursuit of artistic expression and individual freedoms. In the liner notes for act 1, Zappa directly addresses this by saying, "Desperate nerds in high offices all over the world" work steadfastly to enact legislation for the sole purpose of getting votes, even going so far as to suggest that the recent passing of environmental laws is purely to get votes (a dig at the oil crisis that year in the wake of the Iranian Revolution). Furthermore, according to Zappa, the principled anti-smut campaigns are less about cleaning society's moral ills and are rather about seeking a desired state-sanctioned saintliness for the officeholder.

Zappa also says that whichever candidate generates the most media coverage gets more votes within this system. The business interests that fund their candidacy benefit financially from the legislation their candidate will soon enact. Ultimately, the point Zappa is making here is that voters can be influenced by a specific presentation sold to them, such as an American flag background or Christian iconography, that convinces them to support dangerous legislation that impacts constitutionally protected freedoms in favor of superfluous culture-war issues like slightly cheaper gas at the pump. The threat of this happening in America is very real for Zappa as he tells the reader, if any of this sounds silly or far-fetched, to just look at Iran to see how state-sanctioned fundamentalist religious zealotry can change a country very quickly.[28]

Though act 1 of *Joe's Garage* introduces the listener to characters and circumstances that eventually reveal the complexity and depth of the album's plot and inherent themes as the story unfolds, the origin of the album was rather simple. Zappa composed *Joe's Garage* much in the same way as his other larger musical works, describing it "as an example of continuity imposed on a series of events that were never meant to be contiguous." Zappa told *Rolling Stone* in a 1979 interview that the band went into the studio to record "Joe's Garage" as a single with "Catholic Girls" as its B-side. However, they stayed in the studio long enough to record sixteen other tracks before Zappa would eventually construct a narrative that threaded them together. "It's all exercise," Zappa said about the process. "It's like doing crossword puzzles. In looking at it, I saw that not only did it make a continuous story, but it made a good continuous story."[29]

Despite the original intent Zappa may have had for the album, the final result of his rock opera reveals a conscientious approach with well-constructed ideas rooted in its narrative foundation that provides the listener with a clear understanding that there is a cohesive story playing out, serving as an allegory to larger cultural and societal issues. Even from the album's opening, with the introduction of the Central Scrutinizer as the narrator, Zappa wastes no time in making the case that the world of *Joe's Garage* is not far off from that of the United States on the cusp of the 1980s, taking real-world influences and reflecting them in the nightmarish funhouse mirror of life outside of Joe's garage. On the role of the album's narrator, which explains his being the first character to be introduced in the story, Zappa told *Record Review* in a February 1980 interview:

> So our story is being told by a character called the Central Scrutinizer. Remember back in high school when they used to send the narks over with this little, "If you take these pills, it leads to the weed which leads to the needle . . ."? The Scrutinizer is sent around in the same way to talk to young people about music. Music will lead you on this terrible downward path. It's kind of like reverse psychology if you just tell them that it's bad so the Scrutinizer has this demonstration, the tragic tale of Joe and *Joe's Garage.*[30]

Even the garage itself, as the first setting of the album's story, carries with it a significance that illustrates a grander artistic vision meant to convey a juxtaposition between the real world and the reality that could be. Within the album's narrative, the garage becomes a symbol of purity. For Joe and his bandmates and friends, it is their own safe haven from the changing world outside, one in which they can relish the seemingly limitless freedom they feel as kids more concerned with having fun playing music than with the inevitability of adulthood that exists on the other side of the garage door. As new forms of musical and artistic expression come along that increasingly worry the cultural and societal forces at odds with increased liberalism, the barrier between Joe's chosen world and that of the real one disappears—thus destroying a sense of innocence Joe associated with the garage and that period of time in which he was young, one in which individualization was valued.

The garage as a setting in *Joe's Garage* is not based on reality and is instead romanticized to enhance the drama and depth of the album's story. When asked by *Rolling Stone* if the story of a musician being humiliated and misunderstood within a future where music is systematically outlawed by a government influenced by business and religion reflected any truth to Zappa's own experiences, Zappa says the depiction of the garage in the album is one based on fantasy. He acknowledged that his experiences playing in garages did not involve teenage girls dancing around, but rather a group of guys performing out of tune. "If I wrote a song about the way it really was in the garages I played in," Zappa told *Rolling Stone*, "it would be totally disgusting." Instead, the only autobiographical part of the song is the reference to a nameless record company man asking Joe and his friends to sign a contract promising good times to be had as musicians.[31] Zappa twists the meaning of the garage in a musical context to provide a larger commentary about America's relationship with nostalgia, one in which he walks an incredibly fine line between the rose-colored-glasses view of yesteryear and determining at which point cultural and societal decline begins. "The garage is sort of a common denominator for America," Zappa told WLIR in 1981.[32]

Beginning act 2, the listener finds Joe seeking grace from the depths of despair. This path toward salvation ultimately leads him to the First Church of Appliantology, founded by spiritual leader L. Ron Hoover, performed by Zappa as a not-so-subtle dig at Scientology and its founder decades before *South Park* or Tom Cruise's couch-jumping popularized satirizing the science-fiction–based religious movement. Hoover convinces the impressionably fragile-minded Joe that he is a latent appliance fetishist and that progressing along his spiritual journey means he must admit to himself that sexual gratification can only be achieved through machines ("A Token of My Extreme").

Not quite convinced by Hoover's proclamation, but having already given him all his money anyway, Joe decides to at least explore the idea by visiting the Closet, a club filled with machines that get sexually excited by German-speaking housewives. There he becomes entranced by the many dancing machines before becoming sexually attracted to one named Sy Borg, portrayed by Warren Cuccurullo and Ed Mann, that resembles a chrome-plated combination of an industrial vacuum cleaner and a piggy bank covered in sex toys, with Joe singing his desire to be penetrated by Sy's curly chrome phallus first in German and then in English ("Stick It Out").[33]

Sy Borg soon takes Joe back to his apartment, where they have a ménage à trois with a "miniature rubberized homo-replica," and engage in sex with bondage and humiliation. The scene comes to a dramatic close when Joe, after "plooking" his playmates too hard, unintentionally destroys Sy Borg with a golden shower. The Central Scrutinizer then shows up with law enforcement to arrest Joe for the destruction of government-issued property ("Sy Borg").

While being admitted to prison, Joe comes across Father Riley after he has ceased being Buddy Jones. He is now the prison chaplain in this institution that houses musicians and record executives. Father Riley escorts Joe through the prison and tells him how much the other prisoners love new inmates, especially a giant of a man called Bald-Headed John, King of the Plookers, portrayed by Terry Bozzio ("Dong Work for Yuda"). Father Riley's advice for Joe is to keep his behind lubed up so the experience of being plooked will be less painful ("Keep It Greasy"). Closing the prison scene and act 2, Joe, having been raped by the music executives, becomes sullen and withdrawn, with him only able to find solace within the depths of his imagination, where he is free to play the music in his mind for an audience of just himself ("Outside Now").[34]

During the second act of the album, not only does the listener continue to follow Joe as he continues his downfall amid this disturbing version of America, but we gain insights into the larger existential issues Zappa raises within the narrative. In an interview with Bob Marshall in 1988, nearly a decade after the release of *Joe's Garage*, Zappa said of the album that its underlying subtext was a commentary on the "criminalization of America" because the legal framework of the country had become so complicated as to result in situations where someone could be in violation of the law without even knowing it.[35]

This observation over the increased criminalization of personal freedoms and liberties in America also speaks to the concern Zappa had regarding the hubris of its own citizens. Zappa told the *Gold Coast Free Press*, a former alternative weekly newspaper distributed in Los Angeles, in a 1979 interview that Americans were becoming increasingly immune to being shocked after years of being exposed to horrific content on the news, which he says has left them with a false confidence that such horrors could never happen in the United States. As a means of pushing back against that apathy, in order to demonstrate the very real danger posed to American citizens and their rights, Zappa said of the ideas conveyed through *Joe's Garage* that "it can't do any harm to just remind people that having their liberties taken away or having things that make life beautiful held back from them by the government is something that they should always be careful to avoid."[36] He elaborated: "I'll tell you how it *could* happen here in America: You can get any law passed, no matter how perverted it is, as long as you tell people that it's gonna lower their taxes. If you told them making music illegal would lower taxes, people would vote for it. If you told 'em that making carrots illegal would do it, they'd vote for that, too."[37]

Though not very subtle due to its graphic nature, even Joe's experience with the record executives signifies a larger commentary. Zappa told *Rolling Stone* he works like a journalist, a reason that the story within *Joe's Garage* does not reflect a personal biography despite there being symbolic connections that some listeners may interpret as being more biographical than Zappa lets on. Instead, Zappa declares that, in centering the album's story on a character named Joe, the character becomes a means for Zappa to speak on behalf of all the Joes who have had negative experiences within the music business. It is a point of view that Zappa acknowledges as being cynical, but he dismisses any criticism over that quality. For him, his cynicism is a positive quality because, by telling a truth he knows within the album that others who are likeminded will recognize and appreciate, he then considers himself more successful in doing his job as an artist.[38] By drawing the connections between the systems of power in America whose strength and influence are emboldened by the complicities of whole swaths within its own population, Zappa closes the second act with a tone that paves the way for the consequences that unfold in the album's final act as a result of such a cultural and social power imbalance.

Act 3 opens with Joe leaving prison and venturing into a new world where music has become illegal. He wanders the streets and observes people lining up to collect welfare checks to pay for obsolete and irreparable appliances, and who instead use the broken junk to build statues dedicated to the "Quality of American Craftsmanship," echoing Zappa's grievances about shoddy workmanship in "Flakes" on *Sheik Yerbouti* released earlier the same year ("He Used to Cut the Grass"). Dismayed by this new world without music, he returns to the inner sanctum of his mind. Joe performs his imaginary guitar music and responds to imaginary negative reviews by imaginary rock critics, a scene that becomes an outlet for Zappa to express his grievances over the role he believes music journalists play as a tool for the government to subvert and delegitimize artistic expression ("Packard Goose").[39]

Having worked himself into hysteria, Joe comes to terms with the reality that freedoms once seemingly guaranteed will likely never return when rescinded by the government. So, in a final effort to live out his dreams of becoming a musician, even if only in his mind, Joe performs one last guitar solo, one so profoundly moving and gorgeous that it is often considered one of Zappa's best ("Watermelon in Easter Hay"). With that final burst of passionate, creative expression, Joe gives up music for good by exorcising it from his very being. Joe symbolically hocks his imaginary guitar before getting a job working the day shift at the Utility Muffin Research Kitchen. Act 3, and the album, end as the Central Scrutinizer turns off his megaphone, leaving Zappa to sing in his regular voice for the final song, a silly and spirited nonsensical affair featuring the album's cast singing about the little green rosetta Joe puts on top of the muffins ("A Little Green Rosetta").

The album's ending represents the extreme extent to which total authoritarian control can be exerted over a population. Joe was exploited by a religious institution, although a seemingly fringe one, before being arrested for unintentionally destroying government property and serving a prison sentence, until being released in a world where artistic expression and individual freedom have become casualties while consumerist and traditional values have been elevated.

In the liner notes for the second and third acts, Zappa cheekily evokes religion to illustrate our innate differences as individuals within a species by saying, "It was discovered that God did not want us to be all the same," which he asserts was unwelcome news for the government. In response to this epiphany about the uniqueness and agency of mankind, the government, with the help of business, media, and religion, sought to bind humanity to more uniform standards. However, there were problems with the enforcement because people are not the same and, thus, demand freedoms that reinforce their individuality. So, these institutions with overlapping interests in maintaining human uniformity advanced the principle of Total Criminalization, which forced the population to easily capitulate so as not to be seen as criminals and have other seemingly inalienable freedoms taken away. And that, as Zappa writes in the liner notes, is how music was eventually made illegal in the story of *Joe's Garage*.[40]

The third act of *Joe's Garage* expands on ideas Zappa expressed earlier throughout the album, but now we get a glimpse into the future, a potentially not-so-alternative history if individuality is criminalized through the confluence of the institutions of business, media, and religion within government. Within that dynamic, we see Zappa at times cross the threshold between storyteller to fortune teller, often imbuing the album's commentary with direct personal grievances that offer insight into what was most troubling about the potential decline depicted in *Joe's Garage.*

For example, the track "Packard Goose" presents the clearest look at Zappa's personal politics in relation to the overall themes of the album. In a November 1978 issue of the *Aquarian Night Owl*, a New Jersey alternative weekly newspaper, "Packard Goose" was noted as being dedicated to the "the rock press establishment" and an outlet for which Zappa vented his hostilities.[41] While Zappa considered himself a journalist when it came to his own music, he did not respect many within journalism for the ways in which they perceived his and other people's musical work. In the song, he refers to journalists as government whores whose sole purpose is to keep Americans ill-informed and uneducated, suggesting that they are paid for symbolically fellating their masters. In this commentary, Zappa declares that such a relationship is financial in nature, evoking shekels as imagery to illustrate coded language that toes the line of being anti-Semitic with its implications that Jews run the media, a dangerous trope with a pervasiveness that has continued to endure. Though, the potentially implicit anti-Semitism in "Packard Goose" is not an isolated incident. "Jewish Princess" from *Sheik Yerbouti* is Zappa's most famous example concerning accusations of anti-Semitism. The song, a satirical take on disco club culture being inhabited by the Jewish Princess, a "stereotypical well-to-do or spoiled American Jewish girl or woman,"[42] earned the condemnation of the Anti-Defamation League of B'nai B'rith in Pasadena when they protested the song's heavy airplay on the radio station KROQ. David Lehrer, the attorney representing the ADL, said, "There's no doubt that the words are anti-semitic and that they promote offensive stereotypes, but the basis for the complaint is obscenity,"[43] a harbinger of the battle Zappa would fight just a few years later before the U.S. Senate.

Zappa would push back against the criticism, saying that he believed the issue at hand was about censorship. "The ADL is perpetuating the primitive concept that words can corrupt you," Zappa said. "Who are they to decide? If you don't like it, you can turn it off."[44] As part of his defense of the song, Zappa said that the stereotype of the "Jewish American Princess" existed elsewhere and that his satire had some kernels of truth within it because he met people who he felt fit within that stereotype. Kelly Fisher Lowe, in his book *The Words and Music of Frank Zappa,* rejects the validity of Zappa's claim, saying that his "music has always been about forcing people to realize the relationship between freedom and responsibility and the relationship between systems and the individual," specifically noting that "Jewish Princess" fails to fall into either category, with Lowe instead suggesting that the only way the song's commentary can make sense is if it is viewed in the same lens as some of Zappa's folkloric road songs. Despite Zappa's assertions about the song, "the worry of the Anti-Defamation League is that it gives people who might have an intent more harmful than Zappa's . . . the right to their own anti-Semitism."[45] All of this is to say that, regardless of his intent, Zappa not being Jewish presents a cultural conundrum when we consider the meaning and impact of his work.

Though I do not consider Zappa to be anti-Semitic, he did rely on tropes that have evolved into or further rationalized hatred toward Jews by those who can be considered unequivocal anti-Semites. However, if there is any doubt regarding Zappa's intention as an artist with "Jewish Princess," even when it is difficult to justify, he did express similar attitudes toward Catholicism, which he directly understood and experienced because his family raised him within it.[46] That attitude exhibited in "Jewish Princess," as well as the reactions to it, would inform Zappa's approach to "Catholic Girls," with him saying, "It will be just as true of Catholic girls as 'Jewish Princess' is of Jewish princesses."[47] An equal opportunity approach to lyrically lampooning different religious beliefs does not let Zappa entirely off the hook, since songs like these do have an impact on his image and how people may perceive it, but the ongoing cultural dialogue over representation of marginalized communities does add some interesting things to consider when we talk about complicated artists. When we take into account the intent of an artist's work, as a singular concept amid an entire portfolio of artistic expression with varying degrees of quality, sometimes the more difficult characteristics of an artist can potentially overshadow their more socially constructive qualities. Songs like "Jewish Princess" and "Catholic Girls" are among the best-known songs of Zappa's oeuvre, but only because of their salaciousness and the strong reactions they elicit. Zappa has so much more music that would not be considered offensive to the average listener than music that some would have objections to, but they are not as well-known because of their aesthetics, lack of availability before streaming, and limited commercial viability. So, yes, while it can be argued that these songs scuff up his reputation, Zappa has still created much more music that positively contributes to his legacy as an artist and cultural commentator. There are reasons why someone like Al Jolson is not so revered today. Despite his difficulties, there is a timelessness and relevancy that threads its way throughout Zappa's catalog.

Even beyond the moments within "Packard Goose" that elicit concerns over anti-Semitism, the narrative of the song does blur the line between what is integral to the plot of *Joe's Garage* and what is merely just Zappa blowing off steam. There is a lot of animosity in the song toward journalists. Even within the hazy realm of his mind as he struggles to adjust to a world of criminalized artistic expression and individuality, Joe's anger in the song is directed at one particular group: journalists. He calls journalism scary and says that people should not believe in it so easily, telling rock writers who write negative reviews of groups to just stick their pencils up their ass and spin on them. Though expressed by Joe within the context of the album, it is a sentiment Zappa has shared throughout his career. In a 1988 interview with *Los Angeles Times Magazine,* Zappa referred to consumer journalism as "a shady business . . . repackaged by an even shadier business."[48]

In 1979, the same year *Joe's Garage* was released, when asked by a journalist for *Oui,* a men's adult magazine, if his sex life was as weird as his music, Zappa responded by saying:

> First of all, you have to get rid of your preconceptions. You're talking to a human being who happens to be pretty intelligent, who works real hard to do what he does—and there's nothing weird about that at all. Remember, I'm rational. I think *you're* weird. What's weird about my music? As an accurate journalist and a person with a conscience, it's your job to bring the truth to the people of the world. There isn't anything weird about my music. . . . The thing that makes my music unusual is that people only hear one kind of music all the time over the radio. It's wallpaper to their

lives. Audile wallpaper. . . . Just because I don't deal in those terms doesn't mean I'm weird.[49]

Still, "Packard Goose" is not just an outlet for Zappa to vent his frustrations over the music press. It does serve an important role within *Joe's Garage* by illustrating the conditions and circumstances that perpetuate American ignorance as Zappa sees it, something Ben Watson in *Frank Zappa: The Negative Dialectics of Poodle Play* describes by saying, "Any attempt at transcendence is immediately rubbished in a welter of trivial Americana."[50] Within the album's liner notes for the third act, the government wanted to enforce a uniformity among its citizens despite it being in violation of God's plan for mankind, a clever appropriation of religion on Zappa's part to advocate personal freedoms and individual expression. In 1980, Zappa told *Rock Australia Magazine* that, when a government wants to operate more effectively and efficiently, they implement systems that result in an "enforceable sameness." "Now obviously, if everybody's the same," said Zappa, "then there are going to be fewer problems in the world. Now, this is going to be difficult to legislate, because people aren't the same, they're all different, see, so some wise guy comes up with the idea of total criminalisation. . . . So, that's where the government comes up with this idea that the easiest thing to do, to get a whole new bunch of crooks, is to make music illegal. And if you like music, then you get to be a crook, and then everyone's the same."[51]

As a musician opposed to the cultural and social institutions that enforce sameness when it comes to the freedom of expression, Zappa composed "Packard Goose" to include one of his more memorable musical moments. In what stands out as an enduringly quotable philosophy, frequently shared in memes across Zappa fan sites and social media circles, a brief monologue appears from a vision of Mary that Joe experiences. In this monologue, Mary breaks down a secret of the universe, or something that is not that much of a secret if you ever have heard Zappa offer his opinion on the matter, which is that music is truly the best thing about our existence. Above everything else Mary mentions, like information, knowledge, wisdom, truth, beauty, and even love, music represents the zenith of human accomplishment and satisfaction. Zappa told Bob Marshall in a 1988 interview that one of the ways to define the monologue is that, within the artistic statement being presented on *Joe's Garage*, music represents whatever concept you may want it to be, and the listeners have to figure out what that means for themselves.[52] Though Zappa's comment suggests that he is speaking broadly when it comes to the concept of music representing freedom in an abstract sense, for himself he literally means music.

Joe's Garage was a warning for America because Zappa foresaw how, through the scapegoating and criminalization of free expression and individual freedoms, the country could follow the same path as Iran. In a November 1979 interview with *Sweet Potato*, an independent music tabloid based in Minneapolis, Zappa was asked how realistic he thought his ideas expressed in *Joe's Garage* were and whether "unwanted behavior" within society could result in music being banned by the government. In his response, Zappa said, "It's not out of the question, I don't think, because you see it's already happening in Iran, and it's totally controlled in the Soviet Communist countries. You know what kind of music they get to hear over there. So when you consider the bad management our country is famous for during the last few years, I don't think it's too far-fetched to imagine somebody could get in and go and do the same thing here."[53]

For Zappa, the path where this eventuality could play out was being paved by the Moral Majority, founded by televangelist preacher Jerry Falwell in 1979. The Moral Majority was a religious and political organization and movement that expanded on Richard Nixon's idea of the "silent majority," a group of conservative constituents who did not voice their opinions publicly, but which were leveraged to "split social traditionalists from the Democratic party, and to harness the energy of the evangelical movement to the GOP."[54] Zappa believed the reason the Moral Majority was so accomplished at suppressing creative expression was because it could make its small coalition sound much bigger than it was if they were loud enough. "The Moral Majority is neither moral nor the majority," said Zappa. "There's not more of them than there is of us. They just make more noise." As a result of this agitation from the Moral Majority, Zappa said congressional members and other political leaders can be engineered into supporting specific legislation because they have been manipulated into thinking a highly vocal and mobilized minority speaks on behalf of the entire country.[55]

While evangelical movements are found throughout the history of the United States, with Christian nationalist movements prior to the Moral Majority having roots in Depression-era Nazi sympathizers and the John Birch Society,[56] Falwell achieved significantly more progress in advancing a conservative evangelical agenda by motivating his followers to support political candidates that upheld his fundamentalist vision on a national level. After its supporters collectively ensured an overwhelming victory for Reagan during the 1980 presidential election, the Moral Majority soon found its way into the White House as it influenced an array of policies within Reagan's administration, including social issues like abortion and gay rights and even foreign policy matters such as defense spending and anti-communism efforts.[57] During a sermon delivered on July 4, 1976, Falwell said, "The idea that religion and politics don't mix was invented by the Devil to keep Christians from running their own country. If [there is] any place in the world we need Christianity, it's in Washington. And that's why preachers long since need to get over that intimidation forced upon us by liberals, that if we mention anything about politics, we are degrading our ministry."[58] Even before Carter was elected president, when he was just running for the office, Falwell's vision for an evangelical conservative government laid bare the foundations of his grander plans for America.

At the core of Zappa's reasoning on how what was happening in Iran could happen in the United States was that the rhetoric espoused by Khomeini and Falwell were similar. Both figures, with their respective religious movements, sought to censor and control people who did not share their ideologies. Any means by which people express their individuality, in the minds of these religious zealots, must be restrained if what is being expressed is antithetical to their dogma. Music, as well as other forms of expression, become easy targets for censorship because of how ideas can permeate a society and its culture. Beyond aesthetics, the underlying purpose of censoring music and art is to police and control words and ideas, as well as our ability to express them.

Throughout his career, Zappa was a vocal advocate for the freedom of expression—not just because he wanted to say whatever he wanted through his music, but also because he saw how the same calls to censor him could legitimize evangelical religious tenets within government and other institutions. In 1980, Zappa rhetorically asked an interviewer for *High Times* what they thought of a society so socially underdeveloped that its citizens actually believed hearing certain words would eternally corrupt them, instantly manifesting pornography out of thin air. Zappa argued that words were just ways to share ideas, but, he implied, culture-war debates over the broadcast suitability of certain types of words ushered in an environment where people with certain beliefs developed an actual fear of specific words.[59] This situation then becomes the basis upon which people prioritize their religion over individual freedom, which for them requires the suppression of words and ideas that they feel are in direct conflict with their faith. Zappa would later become notable for bringing this perspective to the issue of lyric censorship during the 1985 Senate hearing with the Parents Music Resource Center. Speaking on the subject during a lecture in Washington, DC, in 1986, Zappa said, "There is absolutely no science to support the theory that words on a record endanger the listener, and until there is scientific demonstration of deleterious effect, legislation should not be used."[60] Pointing out an inherent hypocrisy within the types of expression being targeted for censorship, and as a statement on the hollowness of dogmatic ideals, Zappa said, "Statistically there are more songs written about love than anything else; if words can affect you, then why don't people love each other?"[61]

Falwell would become one of the leading figures of the book-banning movement during the 1980s. In the same spirit as the religious and political groups coalescing in recent years to ban books by queer and non-white writers, the Moral Majority bombarded libraries and schools with their demands, suggesting that their requests to remove books they believed inappropriate for children were not based on censorship. However, the climate they created strongly indicated otherwise, and for reasons that did not seem readily apparent or even tangible. Judith P. Krug, then director of the Office of Intellectual Freedom of the American Library Association, said in 1982 that "an atmosphere conducive to censorship hovers over the country" and that she believed the censors within the Moral Majority were "searching for something unreal—the good old days. It's 'Alice in Wonderland' thinking."[62] Krug's assessment is not wrong, as Falwell confirmed in his 1981 statement "Listen America," saying, "I believe that Americans want to see this country come back to basics, back to values, back to biblical morality, back to sensibility, and back to patriotism. Americans are looking for leadership and guidance."[63]

Much in the same way that Khomeini decried music as an avenue by which the youth of a nation could be corrupted, as a means of ideologically controlling them, so did Falwell attack anything in which secularism could provide an attractive alternative to his evangelical proselytizing. Chris Finan, director of American Booksellers for Free Expression, said in 2015 that "Reagan didn't run on a campaign of anti-pornography, but he nevertheless ran an election that depowered those who fought for First Amendment freedoms. [His] election encouraged challenges by people who were unhappy with books in schools and libraries that were increasingly realistic in their depiction of life."[64] It is this realistic depiction of life that Falwell, as well as his followers and ideological successors, opposed because it contrasted with their view of what America should be, regardless of popular opinion. In "Listen America," on the conditions where his followers "must share a deep concern and burden for our country," Falwell said:

> We must reverse the trend America finds herself in today. Young people between the ages of twenty-five and forty have been born and reared in a different world than Americans of years past. The television set has been their primary baby-sitter. From the television set they have learned situation ethics and immorality—they have learned a loss of respect for human life. They have learned to disrespect the family as God has established it. They have been educated in a public-school system that is permeated with secular humanism. They have been taught that the Bible is just another book of literature. They have been taught that there are no absolutes in our world today. They have been introduced to the drug culture. They have been reared by the family and the public school in a society that is greatly void of discipline and character-building. These same young people have been reared under the influence of a government that has taught them socialism and welfarism. They have been taught to believe that the world owes them a living whether they work or not.[65]

Falwell's agenda for the Moral Majority meant more than just growing his evangelical base to have a disproportionately powerful influence on the culture of the United States. He wanted to leverage his following in order to facilitate systemic changes to the U.S. Constitution and how government functioned and enforced laws, all for the purpose of prioritizing his beliefs over others'. Believing that God directly contributed to the development of the Constitution and its principles, Falwell said that, while "we are endowed by our Creator with certain inalienable rights," it is only through the strict adherence to "those laws established by our Creator that He will continue to bless us with these rights."[66] This assertion that evangelical ideology inform governance only continued to grow, especially as the country was trending more liberal and secular in the years following the Reagan administration and Falwell's influence within it. During an episode of the *700 Club* in the aftermath of the September 11 attacks, Falwell blamed the tragedy on various liberal groups he believed were trying to secularize Americans through alternative lifestyles, such as feminists, gays, and abortionists, saying "you helped this happen." The reason for this, according to Falwell, was because God had been successfully thrown out of the federal court system, public square, and schools, all of which were social institutions that reflected the nation's increasing plurality.[67]

Unfortunately, as a direct result of the evangelical movement having been emboldened over the decades since the heyday of the Moral Majority, the America depicted in *Joe's Garage*, one in which personal freedoms can be rescinded, has become less a warning and more a reality. While Zappa's rock opera is largely centered on the criminalization of music, it is an allegory about what could happen if the very idea that personal freedoms can be revoked through religious-influenced government is legitimized or even enforced, despite lack of public support and popular opinion. Since the album's release in 1979, the evangelical movement has been increasingly mobilizing to influence legislation to reflect their religious beliefs. For several decades, the number-one item on the evangelical wish list was to dismantle the 1973 Supreme Court's *Roe v. Wade* decision that provided constitutional protections for people seeking abortions. After being upheld for nearly half a century, a conservative-packed Supreme Court would strike down the ruling in June 2022, thus eliminating a constitutional protection for Americans.[68] Offering an opinion in support of the ruling being overturned, Justice Clarence Thomas said the court should reexamine other rights that, like abortion, were protected under the due process clause of the Fourteenth Amendment, such as previous rulings that "protect contraception access, same-sex relationships, and same-sex marriage."[69] A year later, in 2023, more prior court rulings would be overturned, which signaled the power the evangelical right had accrued within government, including decisions that race-conscious admissions practices within universities were unlawful and that businesses could discriminate against clients based on sexual orientation.[70] These decisions align with the goals and values of white Christian nationalists and motivate them to continue the systemic dismantling of individual freedoms from the federal level through state and local governments, such as conservative states enacting "trigger laws" that would automatically ban abortion access once the Supreme Court overturned the ruling.[71]

Rescinding a long-standing right by the judicial branch of the federal government due to the disproportionate influence of an extremist religious minority creates an environment that can facilitate the revocation of other rights and liberties. Religious fundamentalists and white Christian nationalists have been fighting for a long time to fulfill their vision of a more conservative and evangelical America, one that violates constitutional protections in order to suppress marginalized voices, and they have successfully gained momentum in shifting the ideological map of the United States since then. With the modern political landscape now, as opposed to the pre-Reagan years when *Joe's Garage* was released, the fervor of a strengthened and inflamed evangelical voting bloc has shifted the tone, with ethically and politically aligned government leaders now comfortable enough to say the quiet part of their plans out loud, such as Senator Mitch McConnell's strategy to "cement a conservative majority on the Supreme Court for decades to come" and "holding open vacancies that Trump then filled with conservative federal judges at a breakneck pace."[72]

Without the support or even approval of voters, these actions illustrate how the intertwined machinations of government and religion can create an antidemocratic atmosphere that caters to one select group: white Christian men. This has always been the strategy, to criticize the federal government for representing a pluralistic society while at the same time manipulating the system to use that very same government infrastructure to carry out totalitarianism. The culture wars that these ideological soldiers fight, from generation to generation and issue to issue, represent an endless conflict that is meant to distract the populace from the real work being done, which is building and reinforcing a societal dominance legitimized by institutional power. In 1989, when speaking to conservative evangelical attendees of the annual Southern Baptist Convention, Falwell said the Moral Majority had accomplished its mission as "the agent to train, mobilize and electrify the Religious Right." After a decade, Falwell felt it was time to disband the Moral Majority, saying, "I feel that I have performed the task to which I was called in 1979. The religious right is solidly in place and, like the galvanizing of the black church as a political force a generation ago, the religious conservatives in America are now in for the duration."[73] This meant, as Zappa warned in *Joe's Garage*, that it can happen here and, over the course of the ensuing decades, it has.

Zappa's inherent messaging within the narrative of *Joe's Garage*, specifically how various institutions work together to ensure the legitimacy and advancement of their own interests when perverted by religious influence, can be rather difficult to ascertain on first listen. It depends on the angle from which you approach it and the contextual knowledge you have coming into the experience—especially when you consider the album as a statement when released in its time and juxtaposed with evolving modern ideas on taste and art. It would be too easy, as well as do Zappa and his commentary a huge disservice, to just dismiss *Joe's Garage* as a relic from its era with no lessons to glean from it in the present. As with all art, and certainly provocative art, something about the human condition can be revealed to help us understand complex modern cultural and social issues. Fostering an inclusive understanding of human creativity, which involves accurately contextualizing art in its time while assessing its reverberating impact on culture, is essential in deepening our collective humanity.[74]

As a supporter of the Constitution, Zappa believed the ideas conveyed in *Joe's Garage* were protected speech; he was free to take his ideas and test the limits of taste and the First Amendment. So, when news reports surfaced about Khomeini's consolidation of power and what it meant for the individual freedoms of the Iranian people, specifically their inability to hear music, this was a personal matter for him because music was how he earned his living. He exhibited a prescient outlook in how the tide of American politics and culture could change, in not so obvious ways, to elevate the rights of a fundamentalist religious minority over the rights of the majority through the systemic compromising and dismantling of constitutional freedoms. In essence, because those freedoms existed on paper, they could be easily erased.

Joe's Garage is certainly a work of satire from Zappa's perspective, but with an added sense of urgency. If we consider the concept of satire in a modern sense, specifically the idea that what makes good satire is the act of "punching up versus punching down," as the debate over it has currently categorized the issue, we can see how effectively Zappa uses satire to punch up and condemn institutions and those with power in them. The album certainly shines a light on how major institutions implicitly contribute to the weakening, or even erasure, of artistic and individual freedoms. In act 1, Joe's musical ambitions are cut down by law enforcement, and he's encouraged to participate in religious activities as a warning for his societal improprieties. In act 2, Joe is financially taken advantage of by a fringe religious movement and acts in accordance with their doctrine amid deep feelings of exposure and vulnerability before being subjected to inhumane treatment in prison. In act 3, after Joe is released into a world where music has been made illegal, the institutional powers have completely subverted individuality, with Joe becoming another automaton providing labor to keep the gears of industry moving.[75]

Through that modern lens of satire, we can also see how elements within *Joe's Garage* may be lacking, even seemingly outrightly punching down. Within *Joe's Garage*, which features continuing ideas of provocative social and cultural commentary seen throughout Zappa's work up to that point, we see elements where humor is made at the expense of marginalized groups through the use of often sexist, racist, and homophobic language and tropes. "Catholic Girls," "Crew Slut," and "Fembot in a Wet T-Shirt" contain lyrics that objectify young women as sexual objects whose purpose is to fulfill the desire of the male gaze. The character of Father Riley, a Catholic priest, is described as a "fairy" in "Catholic Girls" and the word "faggot" is used in "Dong Work for Yuda," relying on language and stereotypes that have negatively impacted the gay community. Prison rape drives the narrative of "Keep It Greasy." And, of course, there is the cover of *Joe's Garage* itself, which features Zappa's face darkened with grease. It can be understandably construed as him performing in blackface, a peculiar creative move considering that Ike Willis, who plays Joe on the album and was a regular player in Zappa's band, is Black. The question becomes, when does satire cease being effective before it contributes to the systemic issues that reinforce racism, sexism, and homophobia?

When considering the provocative elements of *Joe's Garage* at face value, it can become difficult to rationalize their effectiveness as satire. It would be too easy, and rather intellectually lazy, to just consider these tropes as products of their time and therefore grant them a pass for that. While they may not be appealing at face value when examined through a modern lens, it is just as lazy to throw *Joe's Garage* into the dustbin of history as a cultural relic. To properly analyze the satire of the album and its effectiveness, one has to consider larger social and political factors from when the album was released and now.

Zappa was disturbed by the rise of this new brand of conservative evangelicalism. It conflicted with his politics, which prioritized individual freedoms. With the news coming from Iran about a fundamentalist religious minority enforcing their ideology of traditional cultural and social values on a majority population, Zappa saw the connection and how the systems of the United States could be manipulated in the same way. With that context in mind, and the political shift in the United States that would occur during the late 1970s and throughout the 1980s, it becomes a matter of determining whether and how using instances of offensive tropes to make broader political statements on powerful institutions can elevate or hinder the quality of satire if the implication of the satire is to address concerns and fears about increasingly accelerated efforts to rescind freedoms for all people regardless of their background.[76]

It is a complex topic, one in which many factors have to be taken into account, including not just Zappa's artistic intent but also his identity. It is a constructive dialogue to have because it forces us to evaluate our priorities within a pluralistic and multicultural society, even if disagreements do happen. While Zappa's attitude is largely centered on his unwavering belief that he had the freedom to say whatever he wanted, it does not mean he is not susceptible to criticism when evaluating the relevancy of his work. Certainly, there are some uncomfortable moments, as with any older work of art, but the very fact that it has complications does not immediately diminish the quality of its satire, especially if what makes that satire of a higher quality has to do with its purpose and who is really the target of its subtext.

I wanted to address the concept of satire in relation to *Joe's Garage* not just for what the album represents as an artistic statement, but also the place it occupies within Zappa's canon. *Joe's Garage* is not an album you typically find on lists chronicling the best albums of its period or genre, with Zappa instead largely represented by 1969's *Hot Rats* as a solo artist or as part of the Mothers of Invention by 1966's *Freak Out!* and 1968's *We're Only in It for the Money.* (This is certainly the case in my edition of *1001 Albums You Must Hear Before You Die.*)[77] For many fans who are first treading the musical waters of Frank Zappa, those albums are usually their introductions. *Joe's Garage,* along with other works such as *Sheik Yerbouti, Apostrophe ('), Over-Nite Sensation,* and *Zoot Allures,* are albums typically discovered as next steps for new listeners, primarily because they surface a lot less frequently in music histories than his more critically revered albums. That is certainly not to say those albums provide lesser quality listening experiences. With a catalog as vast and varied as Zappa's, there are many ways to begin familiarizing oneself with his work, but there are certainly trends in terms of engagement.

I count myself as one of the lucky ones to have had *Joe's Garage* be their first experience with Zappa's music. Though I do not recall exactly how the album came into my purview, it certainly cemented in me early on some of my long-held feelings about Zappa and his music. Everything that is great about Zappa is on this album. Musically, it is diligently crafted with a style that showcases Zappa's pop sensibilities, resulting in songs that are catchy and incredibly fun to listen to. The themes of the album are deeply rich and complex, with its portrayal of totalitarianism as evergreen a topic now as it was nearly five decades earlier. It is incredibly funny, proving that lowbrow humor can serve as highbrow commentary. *Joe's Garage* may not be everyone's cup of tea and may arguably even be an acquired taste, as with most anything else in Zappa's discography, but the album represents Zappa in peak performance as a musician, artist, and commentator. All the qualities that speak to Zappa's brilliance and mastership of his craft, as well as all the prickly parts of his persona that complicate his image, fall into place to present a work of art that radiates deep political convictions about a more just society in which the sanctity of individual liberties for all people is upheld. It is as powerful a social and cultural statement on the United States as any other, but with a tone and style that asks tough questions about the prejudices and biases that we can hold onto when it comes to collectively agreeing on the role and function of art in society. *Joe's Garage* is a microcosm of all the things that make Zappa "Zappa."

Still, *Joe's Garage* is more than just a great album on its own. Beyond being a clever satire that features some of Zappa's most accessible work in terms of aesthetic and style, the place it occupies within his legacy represents a major change for Zappa as an artist. While Zappa had addressed issues concerning religion and politics at various points throughout his career up to the release of *Joe's Garage,* his groundbreaking rock opera presented a creative Big Bang. As the early signs of a mobilized evangelical movement infiltrating government were becoming clearer, *Joe's Garage* set Zappa down an artistic path that he would embark on for the rest of his life. It is the earliest iteration in which his attitudes toward white Christian nationalism would combine to form a cohesive narrative, which Zappa would progressively double down on during the years following. While earlier songs and albums were conceptual documents of their time, with their own meticulous commentary, *Joe's Garage* takes things to a whole new level by becoming a public service announcement, a creative direction to which Zappa would frequently return to as the scourge of Christian fascism and supremacy grew more pervasive. The garage of the album's namesake may not have been a real place, but that does not matter. What matters is what the idea of the garage represents, as a place unburdened by the oppressiveness of theocracy. It is a place that welcomes all sounds, and the voices that make them, that would otherwise be silenced by the tokens of an extreme America. Down in Joe's garage, everyone gets to jam.

THE MEEK SHALL INHERIT NOTHING

Ronald Reagan's victory over Jimmy Carter in the 1980 presidential election did more than oust an unpopular incumbent candidate. It represented a monumental paradigm shift happening across the United States. By carrying an astounding forty-four states, with nearly nine million more votes in the popular count, Reagan's successful campaign not only signified that a rejuvenation of conservative ideology was popular among voters, but that also the election was a direct referendum on, and arguably a rebuke of, Carter's brand of progressive politics. Frustrations over stagflation, an energy crisis resulting in gas shortages, the Soviet war in Afghanistan, and the prolonged Iranian hostage crisis ushered in a wave of support for a platform focused on pushing back against those perceived circumstantial failures. Instead, what voters wanted from their government, as outlined by the Republican Party's official 1980 platform, was a focus on cutting taxes, increasing defense spending, deregulation across multiple industries, a hard-line approach to communism, a robust military, and commitment to family values.[1]

This conservative approach to governing opened up the door for many Americans to embrace self-centered individualization and the prioritization of profits over people, resulting in the popular notion that the obsession over wealth and greed dominated the ethos of the 1980s. By incentivizing success in the form of allowing people to keep more of their money as a result of lower taxes and cuts to federal programs, Reagan's commitment to supply-side economics, popularly known as "trickle-down" economics, was designed to jump-start the economy for a new era of American society where businesses were not hindered by the burdens of taxes and regulations. However, the policies failed to cascade downward and instead disproportionately favored wealthy corporations, their investors, and those motivated to get an even bigger slice of the American pie.

Along with the shifting of the political winds and the increasing prevalence of avarice in American society, changes in the communications industry and the arrival of new media platforms also had an outsized effect on how Americans engaged with and reflected their culture. Deregulation of the telecommunications industry would result in the consolidation of numerous local and regional television and radio stations under the umbrella of media conglomerates, thus limiting the variety of voices that could be heard across the broadcast spectrum, while cable television would become an increasing presence in homes across the country. In entertainment media, MTV, the music-video channel launched in 1981, would go on to "revolutionize the music industry and become an influential source of pop culture and entertainment in the United States and other parts of the world."[2] From the outset, the Reagan administration's policies would result in a media landscape where more and more Americans were exposed to less and less diversity.

Helping to drive the efforts to decrease the presence of diversity in American culture was a rising faction of religious advocates that sought to shape American society through their commitments to principles focused on family values influenced by conservative Christian morality. A major voting bloc that helped secure Reagan the presidency were social conservatives and evangelicals who opposed abortion, secularism, homosexuality, and feminism, all ideas representative of liberal and progressive politics. Increasingly, and unfoundedly, fearful of becoming a marginalized class of citizens based on their beliefs, religious conservatives made sure their grassroots efforts reverberated across the rest of the nation. Emboldened by their champion they elected into the highest office, the religious fundamentalist faction of the Republican Party would push back against an existential nightmare they believed would consume the United States.

As all these changes were sweeping across the country, Frank Zappa would release his thirty-fourth album, *You Are What You Is*, in September 1981. An album that "revolved around state sponsored greed, teenage indifference and the perverted power of religious fanaticism,"[3] *You Are What You Is* became

Zappa's first concerted effort to address the impending disaster of a Reagan presidency and its impact. It was Zappa entering the dawn of the MTV era, an iconoclast ideologically averse to the greed and religiosity of this new decade, as he traversed a new cultural and technological landscape that was becoming more out of step with his beliefs and musical stylings.

As rock music became an essential component in the increasing conditioning of whiteness in America by the time Reagan was elected,[4] Zappa shaped the album to reflect his attitudes on how and why the country was moving in the direction in which it was heading, with several songs speaking to different, but interconnected, issues. Opening the album, "Teenage Wind" continued Zappa's tradition of satirizing the immaturity and ineptitude of America's youth, featuring Bob Harris on lead vocals, portraying a whiny male adolescent complaining about not being able to go to a Grateful Dead concert, while Zappa lambasts youthful notions of freedom equating to nothing more than the desire to not have to do or pay for anything. Zappa then carries this theme further across a sequence of songs that includes commentaries on Reagan's policies and their destructive impact on the lower middle class;[5] the power of old money in small towns ("Society Pages"), a slam against "the sort of brainless coke-headed rich kid Zappa was increasingly encountering at his concerts" ("I'm a Beautiful Guy"), and the devastating consequences of drugs and the pursuit of vanity ("Charlie's Enormous Mouth," "Any Downers?").[6]

You Are What You Is also contains several tracks where Zappa infused humor into other aspects of his social critique, including topics such as popular culture ("Conehead") and the pleasurable perversions of the nightlife scene ("Mudd Club"), as well as tracks more aligned with Zappa's typical musical and lyrical aesthetic ("Goblin Girl," "Doreen"). As Zappa was known for using shocking imagery to convey certain ideas as part of his music's social commentary, several songs toward the end of the album delve into darker lyrical territory. Zappa remains true to form in his ongoing satirizing of destructive and privileged young white men in his music, with the album including a mini-suite of segueing songs featuring a narrative involving a teenage boy feigning suicide for attention, with Zappa encouraging the boy to go through with it, until an overweight teenage girl rescues him from his illusory brink ("Suicide Chump"). As the narrative progresses, the boy becomes disgusted with the girl, insulting her weight and smell before committing physical violence against her ("Jumbo Go Away," "If Only She Woulda"). At the album's conclusion, the young man, disillusioned by religion and media, then gets drafted into the military, where his violent tendencies are encouraged ("Drafted Again"). While the themes in these songs are meant to ridicule the systems and ideas that perpetuate toxic masculinity, they can understandably discourage some listeners from following the point Zappa is trying to make in them. While Zappa was often abrasive in his lyrics when dishing out his brand of satire, the lyrics pertaining to suicidal victim-blaming and gender-based violence elevate the status of these songs as being some of the most conceptually difficult in Zappa's canon for most average listeners. There is a nuance inherent in the messaging that can often be lost in the density of Zappa's music.

Nevertheless, *You Are What You Is* is most notable for how Zappa addressed the issue of race in Reagan's America. The title track, released as the album's second single, features a complex narrative on racial dynamics that continues to be relevant today. "You Are What You Is" is a pointed social commentary on the appropriation of racial identity and its resulting political discourse, offering a candid look into how Zappa perceived the inherent conflict and tension within racial politics in the United States. It sets the tone for much of the narrative flow and themes throughout the second half of the album, such as the violence committed by young white men, directing how Zappa would go on to convey ideas on the extremes the ideology supporting Reagan can manifest.

As part of the narrative within the lyrics, we follow the journey of two misguided young men as they attempt to navigate the complexities of a cultural landscape that exploits their insecurities. One of the men is a white guy from a middle-class family who starts singing blues music because of his belief that doing so would make him more of a man in society's eyes. This pursuit to achieve a maligned sense of manliness has evolved from merely appropriating Black culture to actively embodying a damaging racist caricature with him mimicking the character of Kingfish from the *Amos 'n' Andy Show*, an American radio and television program featuring white actors with minstrel-show backgrounds performing as Black characters, a shameful product of American broadcast history that had already become a cultural relic by the time Zappa reached his formative teenage years. The white man's pursuit of appropriating dangerous racial tropes then continues with his self-proclaiming that he understands what it is like to be Black because he uses Nivea lotion, wears Royal Crown pomade, and says chitlins taste just like candy, all of which are based on and perpetuate stereotypes that are harmful to Black identities and lives.

With Zappa flipping the script, and drawing upon similar tropes as with what the song's white character appropriates, the other man within the track's narrative is a Black guy who devotes his life to becoming white. He quits eating pork and greens while also throwing out his dashiki in favor of Jordache jeans, a style of denim pants popular throughout the 1970s and 1980s. Not just satisfied with looking the part, he also begins to act it out by becoming a proficient golfer, a sport that endures as a white bastion with a racist legacy of Black exclusion that has continued for decades after the song's release.[7] Now confident in himself that he has fully assimilated into whiteness, the Black man reassures himself that he is no longer Black, with Zappa interrupting the vocals to cartoonishly convey this transition through the use of a racist slur.

At the core of its narrative, "You Are What You Is" is a mocking critique of one's inability, or arguably even refusal, to ostensibly accept oneself and others within the framework of American society. The insecurity both men feel over their own identity results in each of them appropriating elements from the other to reclaim some semblance of self-worth.[8]

Despite coming from a place of privilege, the white man convinces himself he is being emasculated by society, which has an adverse effect on his self-esteem. Turning to and appropriating the culture and experience of Black people becomes a means for him to transform his own fragility into a manufactured feeling of victimization that he mistakenly believes he can personally benefit from. In other words, intentionally or not, he exhibits a failure to understand the concept of hierarchical power imbalance within American society when it comes to race, with him seeking validation from a level of oppression that has historically undermined and undervalued the actual people within the culture he targets. This dynamic in the critique that exists within "You Are What You Is" would begin to enter the broader public consciousness a decade later in the early 1990s when, as rap became a more commercial and mainstream genre, "a generation of white teenagers" began adopting "the culture associated with rap music, and claiming it for themselves," with many

Black Americans feeling uncomfortable with such "feckless an invasion into their culture" by white teenagers "perpetuating a fraud by being something they're not." Rock-and-roll music has no shortage of white men, Zappa included, who have either appropriated or outright stolen from Black culture. After all, it is a musical form that comes from the merging of gospel, blues, jazz, and other Black musical styles. Even the genre's conceptual pioneering founder, a queer Black woman named Sister Rosetta Tharpe, has until recently fallen to the wayside in the historical whitewashing of the art form.[9]

In an article for the *New York Times Magazine,* Wesley Morris, drawing connections between white musicians and the varying degrees to which they incorporate Blackness in their music, writes that Americans are invested politically in the myth of racial separateness which promotes the "idea that art forms can be either 'white' or 'black' in character when aspects of many are at least both." Morris elaborates further, saying that Black musical expression, in particular, centers elevating individual creativity because "music is the architecture to create a means by which singers and musicians can be completely free, free in the only way that would have been possible on a plantation: through art, through music—music no one 'composed' (because enslaved people were denied literacy), music born of feeling, of play, of exhaustion, of hope."

Acknowledging perceived freedom within rock music requires an understanding that the freedom being expressed in the music does not come from an equitable place. It historically comes from the bondage and subjugation of Black people, enslaved and indentured way before the advent of rock and roll, with the improvised musical stylings that came from that building the foundation for much of the musical forms that would later be appropriated by white musicians. As Morris writes, without that improvisation, the "listener is seduced into the composition of the song itself and not the distorting or deviating elements that noise creates." This then becomes a means for which white artists and audiences can feign Blackness or render Black people and voices unnecessary entirely through erasure.[10]

In 1973, eight years before the release of *You Are What You Is,* writer and academic Margo Jefferson published an essay in *Harper's* magazine entitled "Ripping Off Black Music," providing a critique of how white people have historically appropriated Black musical forms. At the closing of her essay, Jefferson discussed having a dream following the death of Jimi Hendrix that represented her concerns over the erasure of Black people from rock music, revealing that future generations would "be taught that while rock may have had its beginnings among blacks, it had its true flowering among whites. The best black artists will thus be studied as remarkable primitives who unconsciously foreshadowed future developments."[11]

Awareness of the ways in which rock music has undervalued and erased Black innovations and voices is key to understanding the desire of the white man in "You Are What You Is" to become Black. He feels that the life afforded to him by his privilege is not enough for him to feel secure with himself, but by appropriating what Jefferson referred to as a "remarkable primitive," he can ultimately find that security by exerting the same power afforded to him by his whiteness. By being able to take elements of Black culture, as well as the racist stereotypes white people applied to it, he can achieve a sense of power that he feels is otherwise missing from his mundane milquetoast existence.

Regardless of the reason, the white man feels like a victim because, in his mind, society has failed to validate how he feels he should be perceived by other people. The emasculation makes him feel like he is powerless to live up to their standards. By relying on his exposure to music and entertainment that have both misrepresented and erased Black influences, this white man builds an *identikit*, a mash of cultural tropes and stereotypes, to turn this self-imposed victimhood into something he believes will be perceived as something worthy of respect by those he feels are oppressing him.

For that to happen, he must first commoditize the bodies and experiences of Black people for his own benefit. The idea that he feels he can selectively curate this self-image to boost his self-esteem is a reflection that, despite his belief, the white man actually has a lot of disproportionate power. He has the power to reduce an already marginalized human being into something he can mold and use at will. To attain the feelings of manliness he seeks, by assembling this collection of misinformed notions of Blackness, he can not only align himself with an oppressed group to hopefully achieve the validation he craves, but he can also position himself to be seen as something far greater that, as Jefferson feared, foreshadows the future of how Black people are seen and represented in our culture. It is a power that exploits the myth of racial separateness Morris writes about. It is not only the power to reinforce that myth, but it is also the power to determine how that myth is constructed and how it is told.

In the spring of 1981, prior to the release of *You Are What You Is*, Zappa had written an article that was originally slated to be published in *Newsweek*, but it was rejected for being too idiosyncratic before ultimately finding publication within the liner notes of his forthcoming album. The article was an opportunity for Zappa to air his critique about "the limits of dissent in a society dedicated to the pursuit of profit."[12] It signified the beginnings of how he was addressing the influence of Reagan's brand of conservative politics, with its trend toward motivating Americans to go "on a consumption binge, growing more self-absorbed and less interested in the welfare of others," a phenomenon that political commentator Kevin Phillips refers to as "conspicuous opulence."[13]

Referring to materialist and mass-consumerist desires as "cheese" in the article, Zappa opens by proclaiming that future historians will come to the conclusion that modern-day Americans prioritized cheese based on the relics of the poorly designed and manufactured goods they left behind. This for Zappa reflects a weirdness that many Americans embody which has a direct impact on their intelligence and behavior, as if they were deformities that must be hidden by being, as he puts it, cosmeticized. Zappa claims that American mental health is in a "semi-wretched condition" because, besides choosing cheese as their leading priority, the United States has earned the status of being the most dishonest nation on the planet because its people and institutions invested a lot of resources to perpetuate the societal myth that such a way of life built on mindless consumption and consumerism is "moral, sane, and wholesome."

Throughout the rest of the article, Zappa explores his ideas about where all this cheese comes from. Americans value the concept of fun, a word Zappa uses though he is likely referring to entertainment content as distractions, but he says Americans have no idea that these distractions are not actually fun as they do not really enjoy or benefit from them. Television seems to be an obvious culprit at first, but Zappa recognizes that it is the people who run the operations and business of television that are responsible because they deliver what American audiences want. Zappa recognizes that those in power within television have created complex and pervasive systems that will continue to provide future audiences and consumers more of the cheese that modern-day Americans already enjoy in abundance.[14]

However, for Zappa, the television industry was not the sole reason for the state of modern Americans' unhealthy relationship with consumerism. Television, an arm of the institution of media, was just one facet of an amorphous system of various establishments that worked together to perpetuate a value system that he believed kept American consumers ignorant and complacent. Blaming committees and unions, Zappa decries the ways in which these system enforcers have repressed the emotional and biological needs and urges of the American public through their influence in legislation, the courts, and public spaces, and that they profit from the repression.

Zappa sees the interconnectedness of how these systems work together to influence the American public by saying, emphasis his, that "It is manufactured by people who *count money,* endorsed as *nutritionally sound* by Civic Leaders, and delivered by The Media *door to door.*" Zappa believes that the inevitable outcome of this relationship between the public and their institutions is that, while Americans are only being offered things that negatively impact their culture by these powerful systems, there is a freezing effect on the ability to create and distribute works of high art because of limited to no public interest or commercial viability. He warns that this festering ooze will continue to influence every outlet it can.[15]

While Zappa's commentary in this article echoes the themes of his earlier hit from 1973, "I'm the Slime," within the context of the album *You Are What You Is* and its song's namesake, there is an added urgency. Zappa is not just saying that the white man in the song is an ignorant racist at face value, but that he represents a concern that the commoditization of Black bodies through cultural appropriation across media can accelerate prejudices and racial biases into something far worse and dangerous. The emphasis on the racist tropes and stereotypes the white man claims for himself in the song "You Are What You Is" is not just that he appropriates them at all, but rather it is exactly what he appropriates: the things that reinforce the myth of racial separateness that the powerful leaders in media, business, and government have convinced him is accurate and of malleable value to him.

Zappa exhibits a clear understanding of how he believes these systems reinforce racist stereotypes and other socially and culturally dangerous ideas. In a 1991 interview with Florindo Volpacchio of *Telos*, a quarterly journal that publishes forums on social and cultural change, Zappa discussed his views on the weakening of institutions as a result of standards of living breaking down. He draws a connection between the deterioration of the American education system and mass media consumerism. He explains that, along with crumbling education standards and inflated work schedules that prevent parents from raising their children, television becomes the primary method to keep kids engaged, where they are subjected to conditioning from advertisers that prevents their intellectual development.[16]

Pressed further by Volpacchio on whether these problems caused by the media and culture industries are primarily urban in nature, Zappa acknowledges that they presently are but, however, are designed with an underlying dynamic that promotes the decline of the country's overall mental health. He claims that the entertainment produced and distributed by television networks in urban areas is created specifically to appeal to audiences in rural areas, who Zappa suggests are often thought of as country yokels by these networks. This is how Zappa explains the public's depreciation of what is artistically beautiful and valuable in society—the opposite of cheese. The public consumes the cheese because the cheese is the only thing the people in power at the networks feed them.[17]

As the interview continues, Zappa remains clear in his ideas on how these bad cultural values fester. Volpacchio implies that many communities in rural America have a past that is littered with ethnic and racial hatred, due to a systemic breakdown that impacts how moral and ethical decisions are made, which leads to communities becoming more homogenized. Zappa, perhaps as a recognition of the dynamic in how media produced in urban areas may influence rural prejudices, responds that what is happening in the cities is not any worse or better. As there are more people living in urban areas, Zappa says, then there are more outlets for media, speeches, and hypocrisy, and that what they say is the same form of racism as the kind found in rural areas.

When asked if racism was the biggest problem the United States faces, or if there is a kind exclusive to the country, Zappa said:

> It is a problem, but it is certainly part of the raw material of the American society. I think you've got the pigmentation racism . . . you've got the class-based racism . . . and you've got a kind of politically based racism too. And one of the things that, if you're trying to arrive at an assessment of whether or not the American strain of racism is more virulent than in other societies, you might point out that we probably have more racists rubbing up against each other in this country than people in other countries.[18]

Over three decades since these comments were made, and over four since the release of *You Are What You Is,* Zappa's commentary sounds prescient as we consider more recent issues that reinforce the substance behind his ideas. Since Donald Trump announced his presidential candidacy in 2015, and throughout his first term in office from 2017 through 2021, his rhetoric and administration policies emboldened a faction of young white men to aggressively and violently act out to compensate for their own personal grievances. The influence and impact of the first Trump presidency demonstrates how the institutions Zappa criticized reinforce and profit from maintaining and perpetuating power structures that further divide the American public.

In his article "Media Failures in the Age of Trump," Victor Pickard demonstrates how Trump "exposed structural pathologies" within American media and outlines three distinct ways in which the media industry showed inherent structural faults that imperiled democracy. The first was that the media constantly covered Trump because it provided them with commercial capital, with the cable news industry reportedly breaking records by earning $2.5 billion during the 2016 election cycle, which "normalized a fascistic politics that never warranted such legitimacy." The second puts the blame on social media companies like Facebook (now Meta) for developing algorithms that wielded incredible power in widely disseminating misinformation, a notion that was only gaining steam in 2016 when this article was published but which has since grown in scope within public debate.[19] And the third failure was an existential crisis within journalism itself because of changes in the industry, including the decline in newspaper circulation, an overreliance on ad revenue–generating models, and gaps left behind by the closure of local, independent journalism.[20] What all this means is that large media conglomerates financially benefited from allowing a controversial political figure to spew dangerous ideas on their platforms because that is what their audiences wanted; they got the foul-smelling cheese they thought they needed because that was the only thing being served to them.

With the rise of 24/7 cable news networks since the launch of CNN in 1980, one year before the release of *You Are What You Is,* the act of watching or reading news has transformed from merely staying informed about current affairs to one where biases and prejudices are reinforced by a profit-driven model where the type and quality of information content one receives can vary based on the intended audience. According to Regina Lawrence, a political communications expert and the executive director for the University of Oregon's School of Journalism and Communication, journalists working for major cable news networks can reduce complex political and social issues and simplify them in ways that reinforce and expand ideological biases. This ultimately exacerbates polarization within an increasingly divided nation because major news networks can cater to partisan viewers by reflecting their audience's biases through a business model that prioritizes opinion-driven contextual analyses over straight news.[21]

Further explaining how major news networks reflect biases, Lawrence also says, "Selective exposure is the tendency many of us have to seek out news sources that don't fundamentally challenge what we believe about the world." Furthermore, "We know there's a relationship between selective exposure and the growing divide in political attitudes in this country. And that gap is clearly related to the rise of more partisan media sources."[22]

While some news outlets may have an implicit bias, the growth of viewership among those networks with more explicit biases has significantly grown. Fox News is an example of a major network that has, with the aid of social media, spread misinformation and is emblematic of an "unregulated news monopoly, one that is governed solely by profit imperatives."[23] In 2014, according to data from the Pew Research Center, conservatives only accounted for 46 percent of Fox News's audience.[24] By 2019, the Pew Research Center would find that among viewers of Fox News, 93 percent identified as Republican.[25] In addition to increasing the percentage of conservative and Republican-leaning viewers, Fox News, as of 2021 through the time of this writing in 2023, would become the network with the most-watched cable news programming.[26] These changes in viewership reflect Lawrence's comments on selective exposure and signify that audiences will seek out partisan news sources that confirm their own biases.

Still, Zappa did not recognize any delineation between biases within the varying cable news outlets, instead seeing them all as contributors to the same problem: media companies representing a cultural institution where a small number of elites control programming and content in order to influence public and policy opinion in exchange for favors from those in power within government.[27] In his autobiography, published in 1989, Zappa would even challenge CNN, a network typically associated with liberal and Democratic audiences,[28] for the role they played in shaping public discourse through opinion-shaping content presented as hard news.[29]

During an interview with Elin Wilder for *High Times* magazine published in 1989, Zappa explains this viewpoint:

> The way the racket works is this: A right-wing guy who owns the license creates the myth of liberal media bias—with no proof that such a bias actually exists—then demands in the name of fairness that more balance be added into a news story. That buys him the chance to add even more right-wing ideological content into every news story and everything that goes on the air—as if there wasn't enough already. So in the name of fairness and balance, news stories must always contain an extra helping of right-wing agenda. And that's the reason for this whole myth about liberal media bias. It was just a promotion started during the Reagan administration. A very clever manipulation.[30]

When you consider the intersection of Zappa's commentary on the media perpetuating racial biases with the inherent structural faults of media institutions that perpetuate partisanship for profit, you gain a critical understanding of the underlying concern Zappa has about the white man in "You Are What You Is." Specifically, Zappa sees the raw material that is America's inherent systemic racism within media exploiting aggrieved white men to the point where their acts of cultural appropriation, as in commoditization of an other, can potentially snowball into racial violence and white supremacy. As Zappa told *Hot Flash* in 1974, "I think that to a great extent the media victimizes those who consume it. But then again I guess that's the price you pay for an exchange of a certain amount of information."[31]

There are, however, some challenges to Zappa's position toward being disinclined to see an ideological difference between media outlets labeled as liberal or conservative. In "Activating Animus: The Uniquely Social Roots of Trump Support," published in 2021, Lilliana Mason, Julie Wronski, and John V. Kane reviewed data that sought to determine how people in 2011 would feel about Trump's first presidency several years later, "finding them before Trump really existed on the political scene," using a "data set that starts in 2011 and interviews the same people in 2011 and then again multiple years after that." While Trump has often been blamed, rightfully, for generating a lot of hatred in American politics, the study revealed that people who already held animosity towards marginalized groups previously had since gathered and aligned themselves with Trump during his campaign and even well into his presidency. Proving that this faction of Americans with racial grievances had already existed prior to Trump, the authors of the study concluded that while the Republican Party was not necessarily to blame for this rise in racial animus, it did allow aggrieved people to "hide within the party in order to make American politics be focused more on the party and not on this faction of people who are feeling a lot of hatred towards marginalized outgroups." When reviewing data and information pertaining to Democrats and their feelings towards white people and Christians, the authors did not find any anti-white bias equivalent to the anti-Black bias driving support for Trump, adding, "There isn't an equivalent figure on the Democratic side. And, in fact, Trump is unique on the right."[32]

The animosity toward marginalized groups and the anti-Black bias that made up a significant portion of Trump's support would further be emboldened throughout Trump's first presidency. While many voters pledged their support for Trump over concerns such as America's place in the global economy, the creation and prioritization of a domestic labor force, or whether spending on federal programs was generating waste, a deciding factor for a large faction of his base was determined by Trump's stance on culture-war issues. Much like the authors of "Activating Animus" prove, this particular faction aligned themselves with Trump because he validated their grievances. With policy positions on curtailing foreigners from entering the United States through strict immigration reforms, including building a wall along the southern border, ending birthright citizenship, urging national cultural assimilation, establishing a commission on radical Islam that would surveil mosques, and barring refugees entry into the country,[33] Trump was primed to lock down a voting bloc with no loyalties to any particular party but rather to a strict ideology that prioritized whiteness. Trump became successful in his candidacy as a figure that these voters could be loyal to because he shared their grievances, validating their inherent hatred of marginalized groups and the perceived threat they posed to the sanctity of their version of American culture. In short, ever the salesman, Trump sold to this base the idea that they were victims despite their power otherwise to weaponize whiteness through their support of his presidency.

From declaring that Mexico intentionally sends rapists into the United States to suggesting that the white supremacists who marched through the University of Virginia were very fine people and from decrying mail-in ballots as voter fraud in order to suppress Black voters to referring to the insurrectionists that stormed the U.S. Capitol as peaceful people that he loved, Trump had consistently stoked fears within his white voters that ultimately led many to feel victimized. Through these actions and more, Trump's first presidency and influence within the Republican Party has since, according to the *Washington Post*, "wielded their own definition of racism, one that disregards the country's history of racial exclusion that gives White people a monopoly on power and wealth. To make America more equitable, they argue, everyone must be treated equally and, therefore, White men must not in any way be disadvantaged."[34] The effect from this is, because these things are being said by a president, media outlets feel compelled, or even obligated, to cover and analyze such invective at the risk of platforming and popularizing it.

Zappa understood that media can perpetuate feelings of victimization for those who seek it, which can potentially lead to violent consequences. Americans who make up a portion of the voting bloc that supports Trump and his allies for prioritizing their racial biases seek out news and content that further affirm their beliefs. This potentially leads some of them down rabbit holes of conspiracy theories that reinforce biases to the point where their racial grievances are expressed through hate crimes. Several mass shootings in recent years, such as the racially motivated one at a Buffalo supermarket in 2022, have been carried out by disaffected and aggrieved young white men over their belief in replacement theory, a white supremacist viewpoint that proposes the idea that white people are being systematically replaced by immigrants and minority groups.

Replacement theory is not an isolated concept generated within a vacuum or in one person's mind. It has been promoted and popularized by outwardly conservative media. Figures like Tucker Carlson, who was ousted from his position at Fox News in 2023 over text messages that amplified white supremacy, can leverage their platforms to promote inflammatory viewpoints that eventually get legitimized by elected officials, such as Republican congressional representative Scott Perry, who said, "For many Americans, what seems to be happening or what they believe right now is happening is what appears to them is we're replacing national-born American—native-born Americans to permanently transform the landscape of this very nation."[35] With this legitimization by a leader within government amplified by a mainstream media outlet, replacement theory becomes a convenient method for which a white man can place a value over a Black body. This presents the possibility of an extreme outcome of a white man feeling like a victim within society despite wielding more societal power than non-white people. The first step to get there, though, through the lens of "You Are What You Is," is to first place an initial value on marginalized persons by reducing them to their stereotypes—ones dictated in the first place by media that profit from perpetuating racial myths.

The Black man in "You Are What You Is" contains a deeply rooted tragedy within his narrative, which is why it becomes critical to explore how white victimization both fuels and is fueled by racial myths that cultural and social institutions systematically uphold and reinforce. While both he and the white man in the song refuse to accept their own race and find ways to distance themselves from their skin color, the circumstances behind their motivations and the consequences of their desired transformation are unequivocally unequal. While the white man's racial transformation is rooted in grievance despite the power behind it, the Black man's transformation is a fruitless Sisyphean endeavor because he can never achieve the power and status the song's white counterpart takes for granted.

Though the country's original sin of slavery is well documented and is, generally, understood and accepted as factual, what has become a point of contention within American society in the twenty-first century is just how much that sin still reverberates into our lives. For a significant portion of the country, typically self-identified as conservatives or aligned with the Republican Party, slavery is a historical relic and Black people gained equal footing with white Americans when the Civil Rights Act and Voting Rights Act were passed in the mid-1960s, and have remained equal ever since. Any criticism coming from non-white or liberal Americans over the last sixty years, in their view, is nothing more than an extremist outlier agenda because the nation's founding documents claim the inherent equality of all men. This strict adherence to national myths to reinforce a misinformed viewpoint relies on a complete dissociation from historical reality, guided by willful ignorance, that inevitably lays the groundwork for an ideology that not only upholds those national myths but also results in actions that can, with the help of national politicians and media outlets, reverse and even eliminate cultural and social progress.

A lot of great and essential work has been done in recent years to examine and contextualize the ongoing societal issues that stem from America's history with slavery. *The 1619 Project*, a long-form piece of journalism developed by *New York Times* journalist Nikole Hannah-Jones commemorating the four-hundredth anniversary of the first enslaved Africans arriving in colonial America, explains that no aspect of American culture over the last four centuries "has been untouched by the years of slavery that followed." It also explores how "America holds onto an undemocratic assumption from its founding: that some people deserve more power than others."[36] By examining the scourge of slavery and its history on the North American continent before the founding of the United States, we can trace how its influence affected the development of the myths foundational to the nation's formation and how these myths have since been woven into the fabric of the lives of everyday Americans.

"Critical race theory," an academic perspective that examines "America's history through the lens of racism," has become a major culture-war issue in recent years because many Republicans view that it "rewrite[s] American history and convince[s] white people that they are inherently racist and should feel guilty because of their advantages." However, as a result of mainstream media outlets providing opinion-based context and analysis, critical race theory "also has become somewhat of a catchall phrase to describe racial concepts some conservatives find objectionable, such as white privilege, systemic inequality and inherent bias." Ultimately, because the concept behind critical race theory centers the idea that the nation's institutions "function to maintain the dominance of white people in society," legislators within the state and national levels have fought vigorously to quash it.[37]

This social and historical context makes it clear why the Black man's desired transformation in "You Are What You Is" is in vain. Grievances rooted within white supremacist principles have allowed American myths to endure, structuring and evolving institutions to ensure their power and pervasiveness over the lives of Americans, including the subjugation of minority groups. Even sixty years after the civil rights movement ended, a period many Americans believe to have been the end of inequality in the United States, grievances continue to uphold myths based on white supremacy.

Robert Pape, a political science professor at the University of Chicago, reviewed data and information on insurrectionists who were being prosecuted, or risked prosecution, for their involvement in the January 6, 2021, siege of the U.S. Capitol. Of these profiled insurrectionists, Pape not only determined that 92 percent of them were white and 86 percent were male, but that only 14 percent had ties to extremist groups. Instead, what Pape found in his research was that, among these insurrectionists, more than half had come from counties where Joe Biden won the 2020 presidential election. He also found that, if a county had experienced a decline in the white population, it was more likely that someone from that county would riot at the Capitol. Explaining the motivations for the Capitol insurrectionists, Pape said, "Race is the primary factor" representing "as much as 75 percent of the energy underneath the insurrectionist movement." For Pape, it was less that the insurrectionists were fooled by Trump, but rather that Trump provided a voice that validated their concerns. "It's about demographic change," said Pape, "and whether you're afraid of it or not."

While many media personalities and political leaders have debated, and continue to debate, the reason insurrectionists attempted to overthrow the government by disrupting the congressional process to validate a secure and legitimate election, Pape's research recognizes that the real reason social and cultural progress is not being made is because too many people are distracted by the notion that Trump's lies and disinformation caused the insurrection. Instead, as Anthony Conwright explores in his article for *Mother Jones* that contextualizes Pape's research, this emphasis that Trump is largely to blame for weaponizing supporters and militia groups to overturn an election ignores how those groups' social and cultural grievances reinforce marginalization of non-white groups. "It would do history a disservice," says Conwright, "if we were to portray the insurrectionists as race-neutral victims of Trump's swindle rather than what they are: junior partners of white supremacy." Conwright goes on to say that "America remains menaced by our collective lack of honest self-reflection. If a significant segment of the populace goes unchallenged in rooting its identity in myths of the immaculacy of whiteness, and is willing to preserve that identity through violent acts, we perpetuate the lie—and the violence. If present-day domestic threats cannot move our society to confront itself, perhaps remembering those from the past might."[38]

The ending of "You Are What You Is" summarizes the destructive power of these American myths. During the song's out-chorus, Ike Willis and Ray White, both Black men in Zappa's band at the time, join Zappa in a call-and-response vocal segment that foretells the dangers of cultural appropriation while evoking a musical style with roots in Black churches and gospel.[39] Amid references to other songs and in-jokes from the rest of the album as well as Zappa's lore and discography, the song concludes with a warning about shedding your race as a means of denying your own identity in America. By dropping whatever part of you that you do not like and letting it rot on the ground, someone else can come along and assume it as part of themselves with no cost or consequence. This creates a cultural dynamic, as the out-chorus continues, where someone can completely lose their sense of self because the parts of their identity they leave behind can become lost and unrecognizable, potentially being reshaped and repurposed for intentions that could undermine their original owner. For the white man, it is to achieve validation of his grievances. For the Black man, it is a goal that is currently impossible in America, one that resulted in James Baldwin to ask the question, *Do I really* want *to be integrated into a burning house?*[40]

Zappa's proclivity to push the societal limits of taste and obscenity never slowed down throughout his career, but there were increasing ways in which his music faced obstacles which informed his outlook on how institutions influence the culture. With the poor album sales and concert attendance supporting *You Are What You Is,* Zappa felt as though he was getting squeezed out of commercial radio because only two stations—one in Connecticut and one in New York—played the album, which confirmed for him his outlook on the intertwining of politics and business in radio. "Today radio is not like it used to be," Zappa told Bill Milkowski in a 1981 interview with *Good Times.* "Most of the stations that matter are programmed by five people who are not even located in the same town where the radio stations are broadcasting from."[41]

With two decades of experience in the music industry at this point, Zappa had clearly seen how special interests could move the needle of cultural taste to determine what many Americans had access to. While his albums and concerts sold well in international markets, much of his artistic output never made the airwaves in the United States, something Zappa considered a type of censorship because of the political machinations influencing the industry. In a 1984 interview with the *Pitt News,* Zappa explained his outlook on the difficulty of getting his music on American radio:

> The musical outlook of the country, in the broadest sense, is determined by all media. First of all, what do you hear on the radio? You only hear what is formatted. What do you read in the papers? It is what is connected to what will sell because the rock 'n' roll business is like any other business. . . . Anybody today can have a hit record if they pay out the right bribes to the right people. That's what the rock 'n' roll business is. . . . It's back to the same payola that existed during the '50s.[42]

Zappa's complaints about why American radio stations refused to play his music were not just based on his own resentment for the business or even unsubstantiated conspiracy theories, but are supported by changes that had occurred within the industry during this time. The Telecommunications Act of 1934 established the Federal Communications Commission (FCC) as an independent government agency designed to regulate nongovernmental use of the radio spectrum. Not only did the FCC establish regulations with regard to radio broadcasting, it also established public interest standards which, with convenience and necessity for the public in mind as a priority, required that "a certain percentage of all broadcast time be devoted to news and public service content," and it established a fairness doctrine that prevented "a station from operating as a mouthpiece for any single ideology."[43] Following sweeping deregulation of the telecommunications industry in the 1980s during Reagan's presidency, which relaxed station-ownership rules that would pave the way for the rise of media monopolies, "the deregulation of the commercial radio industry was predicated on a reinterpretation of the 'public interest' clause—a reinterpretation supported by the language of the 1934 Radio Act—equating the public interest with the health of the industry rather than the public well-being."[44]

The Reagan administration's deregulation resulted in a media landscape where only a few members of the wealthy elite could own a majority of the broadcasting licenses and, therefore, could dictate the type and quality of programming on their stations. This was how Zappa rationalized why he felt censored on American radio. However, even beyond radio, with the arrival of MTV in 1981, Zappa still found his aesthetic style to be incompatible with the profit-driven model of this new entertainment platform when his music video for "You Are What You Is," produced and released three years after the album in 1984, was banned for featuring a caricature of Reagan strapped to an electric chair. Echoing his complaints about radio, Zappa told *Spin* in 1991:

> Before MTV if you wanted to have a hit record, there were probably 10,000 stations in America where you could break something regionally and have it spread. Now there is one MTV with a short playlist, and because of that the record companies put their own balls into the bear trap and sprung it on themselves, now they can't make a move without calling MTV and getting permission, they call up in advance to say we are getting ready to make a video, we are going to have such and such pictures in it, what do

> you think, and MTV is a total censorship organization and it has all the major record companies at its mercy.[45]

While Zappa's insight into the media industry is valid, his own provocative styling is what kept him from breaking through this new landscape. Not just for frying a president, "You Are What You Is" was also banned from MTV and received nearly zero support because of Zappa's use of a racial slur in the song. While Zappa's justification for the use of the slur is in service to a larger idea about race in American society, it is still a taboo that elicits strong negative reactions—though this was something Zappa relished. In *Frank Zappa: The Negative Dialectics of Poodle Play,* Ben Watson says Zappa exhibited a severe disdain for superficial elements in society that he felt hindered people's intellectual development, so Zappa pushed taboos while shouldering the consequences, such as allegations of being sexist and racist. Watson continues: "Rather than inveigh in the abstract against 'bad thoughts,' [Zappa] documents the distortions and disasters brought about by oppression and exploitation. By keeping to specific instances Zappa saves himself from the utterance of empty pieties; it explains the shocking intensity of his words and stories."[46]

While Watson makes a compelling point about Zappa's contextual use of taboo language, it still does not negate that these utterances require constant examination as our culture continues to grapple with reconciling its difficult history and the ways in which white supremacist myths remain firmly rooted. My understanding of this is limited because it is impossible for me to know what it is like being Black in America. My path toward understanding this dynamic is based on education and empathy. I can learn that cultural and social systems can be inherently racist and how they work together to dehumanize a human being, but I cannot claim that I know what it feels like to hear Zappa use a racial slur.

I spent so much time breaking down the narrative of "You Are What You Is" and tying it into concepts that expose the white supremacist framework underpinning American society because I believe the song's inherent themes are incredibly important. As evidenced by the ongoing culture-war debate on how to educate people on America's history with race, these are still radical ideas decades after the song was released. It is a song that remains powerfully relevant because it provides context to the dangers of how systems exploit race and reinforce white supremacy.

As an album, *You Are What You Is* is the first in which Zappa shifts his provocative form of satire to directly challenge the systemic forces that keep Americans racist and stupid in a profoundly significant way. While individual songs that speak truth to power through political and social commentary are peppered throughout Zappa's discography, "You Are What You Is" is a poignant linchpin that signifies Zappa's direction as an acerbic commentator. It is only one song, but the themes and ideas within it resonate not only throughout the rest of the album, but Zappa's discography as well. Specifically, its resonance is reflected in Zappa's commentary on how fundamentalist Christianity manipulates media, business, and government to reinforce racist and fascist ideals. Zappa would spend much of the remainder of his career exposing how white supremacy is foundational to fundamentalist Christianity. It seems necessary, therefore, to break down the racial concepts in this song in order to set the framework for addressing Zappa's criticisms of extremist theology.

Within the second half of the album, there is a trio of songs that segue into each other to form a mini-suite that thematically crystallizes the beginning of Zappa's concerted efforts to directly address fundamentalist religion's impact on society: "The Meek Shall Inherit Nothing," "Dumb All Over," and "Heavenly Bank Account." Together, these songs represent the convergence of several ideas of Zappa's that express fear and concern about the societal impact of Christian fundamentalism.[47] As part of the social critique in these songs, Zappa not only jabs at the powerful figures that drive the fundamentalist movement, but he does not even hold back punches when it comes to the American citizens complicit in their own exploitation, reflecting his animosity toward the cheese being fed to the masses. It is a direct and abrasive approach that acknowledges that the way powerful systems remain powerful is through the action, and even inaction, of people who remain ambivalent to the negative effects of these systems largely because of their belief that they themselves can gain something from those systems, often for ideological reasons.

The first song in the suite is "The Meek Shall Inherit Nothing," the title being a play on a notable tenet of Christianity found in Matthew 5:5 that reads, "Blessed are the meek, for they shall inherit the earth." The idea behind this is that those who rebuff worldly power will be awarded entry into the kingdom of Heaven. The meek are followers of Jesus who have humbled themselves in his presence. They do not represent any particular personality based on reticence, and their meekness is rooted in strength rather than weakness.[48] With "The Meek Shall Inherit Nothing" following "Mudd Club" on the album, as well as opening with some of its lyrics, the song takes on a satirical tone about how some evangelicals find perverse pleasure at being abused by religion.

In Zappa's song, the meek represent victims of a false hope that promises to advocate for the poor. The song's opening features Zappa directly suggesting that religious fundamentalists who take their Bible at its word when it says the meek shall inherit the Earth actually end up getting nothing in return. Blending his critique of Christianity with references to a sheik buying real estate in New Jersey and reciting the mantra of Hare Rama leading to wandering around with a bell on a stick, Zappa is brushing with broad strokes in his condemnation of the ways vulnerable followers are exploited by religious fundamentalism for financial gain. Zappa is expressing contempt for the hypocrisy of church leaders who preach compassion for the poor while spending millions of dollars on lavish expenses like private planes, houses, and megachurches.[49] As Zappa told *WLIR Free Flight* in 1981, "It's a matter of taking money from people who don't have any money; telling them they're going to go some place when they die and use the money to build a peer base and the peer base is then used to control the lives of the people they took the money from."[50]

In the song's bridge, Zappa personally addresses listeners, telling them the bad deal they have gotten in life is not even a deal to begin with because the powerful figures who run the government in Washington, DC, only look out for themselves and their own interests. Their own needs are their number-one priority while the listener is not even number two. Part of the reason for this, as Zappa continues in the next verse, is that these fundamentalist followers are closed-minded and do not care that the church financially exploits them. So, in turn, he mocks them, telling them to just eat their pork and ham while they choke on the empty promises of televangelist Billy Graham; their exaltations are a waste of time, and they are the ones most at risk of suffering the consequences of their fundamentalism.

The meek in "The Meek Shall Inherit Nothing" are also a sardonic reflection of the hippies of the 1960s who transformed into Christian fundamentalists throughout the 1970s. In *Dangerous Kitchen: The Subversive World of Zappa*, Kevin Courrier notes that the hippie counterculture's captivation with messianic figures is based on the symbolism applied to Jesus as an ill-fated hippie who was crucified by the power of the state. This song exposes the falsehood of romantic hippie ideals that got bought out by a yuppie version of Jesus Christ who preaches that you can be born again through salvation found in the almighty dollar.[51] As the song closes, Zappa sings that these yuppie Christians are free to do whatever they want so as long as it does not affect the lives of people who may not believe as they do, going as far as to call them out by suggesting they use a little bit of their holy buying power to help those who are less financially blessed.

Closing out this mini-suite is "Heavenly Bank Account." It is a song where Zappa expands upon his criticism of the followers of religious fundamentalism who are complicit in their own exploitation, including a castigating satire of the evangelical television preachers who gain enormous wealth due to their powerful connections in government. Zappa's lyrics get right to the point as Ray White, vocally evoking a church-choir leader, warns that men claiming a godly need will financially take advantage of you before Zappa gets on the mic to inform the listener of the fundamental difference between kneeling down for worship and bending over for the interests of hypocritical church leaders, implying anal sex for a bit of humorous flair.

The song then profiles the television preacher who drives its narrative. With twenty million dollars stashed away in the church coffers, given to him directly by his followers seeking spiritual salvation through prosperity gospel, he is a guy whose standard of living takes the idea of heaven on earth and imbues it with unworldly luxury. He has over half a dozen limousines, and a private plane, that he shares with his powerful friends in government, including members of Congress, governors, and even the president himself. With their full support for securing them a sizable voting bloc, as well as the help of a team of lawyers to make sure everything is nice and legal, the preacher can bleed his flock dry of all their money by putting the fear of God into them.

Though "Heavenly Bank Account" does not directly name any specific church leader, the subject of the narrative is based on and alludes to several preachers who popularized and stewarded the television evangelical movement of the late 1970s and early 1980s such as Jerry Falwell, Jim Bakker, Pat Robertson, and Jimmy Swaggart. Here is when Zappa starts to take aim at the figures behind the Moral Majority in a fight that he would wage through the rest of his life.

Falwell, in rationalizing church influence on the state through groups like the Moral Majority, said the nation's founding leaders "established America's laws and precepts on the principles recorded in the laws of God, including the Ten Commandments . . . [and any] diligent student of American history finds that our great nation was founded by godly men and godly principles to be a Christian nation." This historical misinterpretation from Falwell, and others like it from his fellow televangelists, is why Andrew L. Seidel, a constitutional attorney at the Freedom from Religion Foundation, declares in his book *The Founding Myth: Why Christian Nationalism Is Un-American* that religious leaders are the most vocal Christian nationalists. Seidel adds that Christian nationalism is not entirely about religious ideas but rather represents "an unholy alliance, an incestuous marriage of conservative politics and conservative Christianity."[52] This unholy alliance was what Zappa warned listeners about in "Heavenly Bank Account" that would leave Americans to pay the bill for the incestuous marriage's reception party.

A key point Zappa makes in "Heavenly Bank Account," furthering his criticism of the cozy relationship between television preachers and government leaders, is that the reason this wealth is able to be accumulated in the first place is because of tax loopholes that religious organizations can exploit. The preacher is dealing all the cards, the Internal Revenue Service cannot figure out how he cheats his way through the game, and the federal authorities will never end up prosecuting him for financially exploiting American citizens because of the influence he has with the White House. Zappa's sarcastic recommendation then, in the song, is to just play dumb because television turns religion into a branch of the entertainment industry.

This was a theme Zappa echoed throughout the rest of his life. Even in his autobiography, Zappa addresses the issue of church tax exemptions, citing Robert Drinan's 1979 statement that the Republican Party made deals to alter their platform to gain "financial and logistical support of The Religious Right."

Zappa suggests that Reagan entered the Oval Office because of support from the National Religious Broadcasters, an association of conservative Christian media leaders, that encouraged their followers, through television sermons and direct mail fundraising campaigns, to support the cause of keeping their tax-exempt status. Zappa then quotes the entirety of the 501(c)(3) tax code to further illustrate his incredulousness over the Reagan administration's, and by extension the Republican Party's, "license to pillage and plunder" through their lobbying of political candidates and legislation.[53]

In her article, "Religion, Politics, and the IRS: Defining the Limits of Tax Law Controls on Political Expression by Churches," Anne Berrill Carroll explains that one of the reasons why "the issue of the federal tax code's prohibition against campaign speech and activity by exempt churches" became a major public interest story was because of "the emergence of the so-called 'New Christian Right' as a potent political force" during the 1980 election, which brought "the debate about the role of religion in American political life to the forefront of public consciousness." Carroll says the Christian evangelical movement, which identified as having a "pro-family, pro-life, pro-morality" agenda, was not just motivated to elect Reagan to the office of the presidency, but also mobilized its partisan supporters resulting in the "defeat of numerous incumbent federal and state officeholders viewed as unsympathetic to its goals." Many critics of this movement believed this new Christian right was espousing rhetoric that stoked religious intolerance, endangered religious liberty, and threatened the separation of church and state. Allegations from the press suggested that political action committees with a tax status that permitted intervening in elections had been openly encouraging political activism within evangelical churches, and that funds collected from those churches would end up in the movement's political treasury.[54]

Zappa in his autobiography also called out James Baker III, named as secretary of the treasury in 1985 during Reagan's second presidential term, and chastised him for failing to audit the "multibillion-dollar con game" that was tax-exempt status for politically active churches. Speculating on why Baker's inaction was a "case of selective nonenforcement," including allegations of Baker's intentions based on his connections within the Christian evangelical movement, Zappa said Drinan's promise to alter the Republican Party platform was paid with "legislative initiatives against abortion, in favor of school prayer, against homosexuals—all to be upheld by a bouquet of handpicked 'trustworthy' conservatives—in an atmosphere of total immunity from IRS interference."[55]

The accusations from Zappa regarding Baker's and the Reagan administration's selective nonenforcement of Section 501(c)(3) of the IRS tax code were valid and not based on partisan observations about a significant cultural shift happening in the United States at the time, but rather on real world events. One of the leading figures of the emerging Christian right movement during the late 1970s through the mid-1980s was televangelist Jim Bakker, who, along with his wife Tammy Faye, built a media enterprise through a satellite network that carried their flagship program, the *PTL Club* ("*Praise The Lord*" *Club*). The *PTL Club* connected viewers with an array of religious programming, including sermons, musical performances, talk-show conversations, and telethons, which allowed the Bakkers to raise financial support for their organization and its mission. These donations from viewers not only went on to support political causes championed by the Christian right, but also the Bakkers' opulent lifestyle, which included several mansions, luxurious cars, and even a *PTL Club* amusement park called "Heritage USA," thus symbolizing the greed of televangelists in the public eye.[56]

In 1985, a confidential IRS report recommended that Bakker and the *PTL Club* be stripped of their tax-exempt status. However, it was not until 1988 that Bakker would be "indicted on federal charges of mail and wire fraud and of conspiring to defraud the public." Michael Isikoff and Art Harris, in a 1987 investigative article for the *Washington Post,* speculated that the reason the Reagan administration was so slow to take action against Bakker was because doing so would have had a negative impact on support from the president's evangelical base,[57] a connection that Zappa notes in his autobiography as he derides Reagan for giving Bakker a humanitarian award in 1983.[58]

While Zappa makes a compelling argument to listeners about the abuse of the tax code in "Heavenly Bank Account," he is also aware that, as he sings in "The Meek Shall Inherit Nothing," many evangelicals do not care if the church skims funds. This is an important acknowledgment on Zappa's part because it contains so much truth. While a handful of televangelists over the last few decades since Bakker's indictment have faced criminal prosecution over financial fraud charges, the business and political reach of ministry media empires has grown exponentially since the 1980s. While a part of this growth can be traced back to the FCC deregulation during Reagan's presidency, the Christian right movement experienced a boon in the 2000s during the administration of George W. Bush, who bolstered evangelicals with symbolic rhetoric over the decline of morality and rewarded them with White House programs like the Office of Faith-Based Initiatives,[59] solidifying a renewed sense of zealotry at a time when more and more people were connecting online. A far cry from the days of holding telethons as their primary source of income, current-day celebrity preachers like Joel Osteen, T. D. Jakes, and Kenneth Copeland can engage with bigger audiences through streaming platforms and social media, further accumulating enormous wealth more quickly through their tax-exempt status. Copeland, who is America's wealthiest pastor, as of 2021 had not paid any taxes on his $7 million mansion in Texas and has an estimated net worth of $750 million,[60] a nearly 3,700 percent increase on the figure Zappa criticizes in "Heavenly Bank Account."

If there is any doubt to Zappa's claims that many Christian evangelicals are complicit with hypocritical religious and political leaders exploiting systems of power so they could have a disproportionate voice in American culture, then look no further than the campaign and presidency of Donald Trump. Throughout both of his campaigns and first presidential term, Trump not only refused to release his tax returns, a practice that had been customary among presidential candidates since the early 1970s, but he had also lied about his finances, which conflicted with the image of a smart, successful, and savvy businessman that he projected which appealed to many of his supporters. Once investigative journalists were able to review Trump's financial records in 2020, the final year of Trump's first term in office, they found the documents revealed Trump "had paid no income taxes at all in 10 of the previous 15 years—largely because he reported losing much more money than he made," and that he only paid $750 in federal taxes during the few years he did pay income taxes, including "the year he won the presidency."[61]

Even beyond the controversy over his taxes, Trump's first presidency was an endless celebration of malfeasance that included scandals involving his paying hush money to hide an affair with a pornographic film star, pressuring a state-level secretary of state to illegally generate fake votes, and encouraging supporters to seize the nation's Capitol to void a valid election, all of which contain complex layers of moral and ethical violations that could result in a former president facing criminal prosecution. However, for many of his evangelical supporters, if they accepted the idea that Trump might have been responsible, even if only in part, for these scandals, the reality is that none of those things matter. These evangelicals vindicate Trump for these issues, or even ignore them altogether, because they see him as a leader who not only prioritizes their worldview, but also that Trump will rid the world of the evil they see as society's ills which reinforce their own sense of victimhood.

Laura Gifford, an independent historian of modern American political history, told the Organization of American Historians that Trump acted "upon evangelicals' desires on a scale at least equivalent to George W. Bush's administration," which made pro-Trump evangelicals willing "to forgive behavior that would get one kicked out of Sunday School if the leader of their party will articulate their policy priorities—and nominate conservative candidates to the Supreme Court."[62] The reason goals like Supreme Court nominations are so important to evangelical voters is because the core identity of part of their movement is white supremacy, which can influence policy priorities under the guise of religious exemptions and undermine the freedoms and rights of many Americans. In essence, many evangelical voters rationalized that supporting Trump, despite his behaviors being antithetical to their religious doctrine, was justified if it meant their policies on abortion and sexuality could come to fruition.

According to Lerone A. Martin, associate professor of religion and politics in the John C. Danforth Center on Religion and Politics at Washington University, Trump's adoption of Reagan's campaign slogan "Let's Make America Great Again" afforded evangelicals an opportunity to revive traditional moral rhetoric in an America they felt was experiencing a moral and cultural decline. This traditional rhetoric has its roots in white evangelical movements that "endorsed and flirted with racist ideals" and included "anti-miscegenation, endorsements for legal segregation, and opposition to civil and human rights protests." The reasoning behind opposing civil rights legislation and desegregation varied among evangelicals. Some believed they were communist plots while others argued those ideals represented an unnatural evil. However, as Martin explains, the common element threading all these ideas together was that "permitting such things would topple the country's Christian foundations."[63]

As long as white evangelicals could incorporate white supremacist ideas to influence the larger evangelical movement's support of Trump's first presidency, Martin says, Trump could "continue to lobby explicit and thinly veiled arguments concerning how the very presence and growth of 'ethnic' or religious others, especially Islam, possesses the potential to destroy America's (white) Christian foundation" while also passively accepting "the endorsements of known white supremacist organizations and officials." On the support received by white evangelicals that contributed to Trump's 2016 election victory, Martin says Trump could be seen as "revealing, more than causing, the (re)-acceleration of a number of existing trends within the white evangelical community." Martin puts the blame on modern white evangelicals for downplaying the role racism plays in modern society, specifically their claiming "colorblindness" while "their religious and policy positions and decisions consistently privilege white male heterosexual subjects while marginalizing others."[64]

Anthea Butler, author of *White Evangelical Racism: The Politics of Morality in America*, says that, up until their embrace of Trump, "evangelicals had cloaked themselves in morality, respectability, and power. . . . The racism that underlay their religious movement could be waved away through belief, theology, and denial." However, since Trump's first election and the ensuing influence he has had in our culture, Butler said, "Evangelical grievances, anger, and disappointment in the wake of 9/11, as well as the election of America's first Black president, pushed believers into an open, belligerent racism that culminated in their wholesale embrace of the man they would call 'King Cyrus': Donald Trump. The journey to Trump is a story of how whiteness and racism combined to make evangelicals a potent voting bloc awash in racism and racial animus."[65]

The socially and culturally oppressive intersection of Christian evangelicalism and white supremacy was something Zappa clearly understood while recording *You Are What You Is*, and no song on the album illustrates that more than "Dumb All Over," the middle section of the album's mini-suite addressing the hypocrisy of religious leaders. With Zappa on lead vocals, he rap sings through an electronic voice filter, sounding almost as if he is interrupting his own album via a pirate broadcast system, breaking away from regularly scheduled programming to warn listeners about the sinister extremes of religious fundamentalism. It is Zappa in very sincere and serious form, unironically taking to proselytizing in the middle of a suite of songs, bookended by "The Meek Shall Inherit Nothing" and "Heavenly Bank Account," that makes fun of people who do that for a living under the guise of religion. However, Zappa's sobering tone is meant to convey deeply uncomfortable feelings about the nightmare that could befall society if evangelical leaders, with ideology rooted in white supremacy, are allowed to take their preaching to its severe conclusion. "It's frightening," Zappa told *Good Times* in 1981. "We're looking at the prelude to the New Dark Ages here. If you know anything about history, the Dark Ages we're going into now is gonna make the first one look like a company picnic."[66]

According to Kelly Fisher Lowe in *The Words and Music of Frank Zappa*, "Dumb All Over" features Zappa revisiting his belief "that, throughout history, war and conflict seem to be based on differing interpretations of what their book says and argues that bad things will happen."[67] From the very beginning of the song, Zappa makes it clear that the inherent danger that threatens all of humanity is people collectively behaving stupidly everywhere, and so, resolving this crisis of intelligence requires transcending artificial divisions within our society, like those that result in racial genocide, if we have any hope for a safe and secure future for all people. Zappa places the blame for perpetuating this deadly foolishness directly on religious fundamentalists who use their media platforms to instill fear in their followers through violent rhetoric designed to dehumanize people who do not share their beliefs or look like them. These fire-and-brimstone orations from the safety of broadcast studios encourage listeners to seek revenge against and destroy unbelievers, exterminating them for the sole purpose of stealing their land, upon which to build their own holy temples.

While the theme of "Dumb All Over" can be applied to any branch and denomination of religious fundamentalism, several lyrics in the song directly address extreme positions from evangelical Christian leaders. Zappa calls out Christian televangelists, who sit behind their desks with humble white hair and glasses, for promoting themselves as servants of God because they can leverage their institutional power to promote the idea that God demands these actions if their followers want to go to heaven, and only under the condition that their version of Christianity is the morally and ethically superior one. Zappa turns this logic against fundamentalists, challenging them to look into the mirror to reflect their own ugly stupidity back at them. He cynically mocks the notion that they cannot really be dumb if they are just following God's orders, but Zappa does not let them off the hook. He tells them to get serious about their own ignorance, suggesting that God knows what he is doing and that we have to carry out the orders he outlined in the Bible because he made us all in his image, which is dumb and ugly. Although harsh and abrasive in tone, "Dumb All Over" features a necessary commentary as Zappa channels his deepest fears into a blistering guitar solo while Ike Willis and Ray White repeatedly sing the chorus outro "Dumb all over / A little ugly on the side."

"Dumb All Over" expresses Zappa's fear of how the nascent evangelical movement of the early 1980s could evolve into an existential threat to humanity, largely because of how white evangelicals appropriated Christian ideology to rationalize their racism and xenophobia against non-white and non-Christian people. Zappa's concerns seem prophetic when we consider how that threat has grown to reflect a real danger to democracy in the United States. In December 2022, the House Oversight Subcommittee on Civil Rights and Civil Liberties finished the last of seven hearings exploring the dangers of white nationalism. As part of these hearings, Amanda Tyler, a co-organizer for Christians Against Christian Nationalism, testified that "Christian nationalism seeks to manipulate religious devotion into giving unquestioning moral support for its political goals." In the wake of the 2024 presidential election, the 2025 Presidential Transition Project, commonly known as Project 2025, is a political initiative playbook that "calls for far-reaching changes in government, including rolling back protections for the LGBTQ community and infusing Christianity more deeply into society." The aim of Project 2025, and by and large the goal of the Heritage Foundation, who published it, is to advocate for conservative right-wing policies to dramatically restructure and reshape the federal government in service of consolidating executive power during a second presidential term for Donald Trump.[68]

These political goals, when combined with the concept of American exceptionalism, reinforce in evangelicals the belief that Americans are more valuable in God's eyes than non-Americans. Furthermore, for many of them,

America's social and cultural progress as a pluralist nation presents enough of an existential threat that they weaponize their ideology to distinguish between "real" Americans and "fake" Americans. As Joseph Wiinikka-Lydon writes for the Southern Poverty Law Center, which has monitored the threat of white nationalism as part of its Intelligence Project, "large segments of the U.S. population are seen as un-American. Some leaders of this movement uphold the racist idea that white Americans are the image of sacred Americanness. Civil rights advocates who struggle for a pluralist, multiracial, equitable democracy are often smeared as Marxists, communists and even pedophiles by this movement." These positions by white evangelicals, fueled by their religious beliefs, motivate them to disrupt community services and resources they believe are championing un-American values such as local elections and school board meetings, with special attention paid to organizations focused on inclusive education.[69]

What drives these beliefs, as Zappa asserts in "Dumb All Over," is that many evangelicals believe a biblical apocalypse will befall the United States unless radical efforts are carried out to stem the tide of what they believe is ushering in the country's fall from grace into eternal damnation. Miles T. Armaly, David T. Buckley, and Adam M. Enders, the authors of "Christian Nationalism and Political Violence: Victimhood, Racial Identity, Conspiracy, and Support for the Capitol Attacks," published in *Political Behavior,* say that Christian nationalism "blends a religious understanding of America's origins with nearly 'apocalyptic' views on future threats to that Christian heritage." Indeed, "Christian nationalism not only affirms a uniquely American Christian history, but also highlights the alleged danger to that heritage from rapid demographic, legal, and political change." The way in which people perceive their own victimhood connects with the level of violence they encourage, and "the combination of Christian nationalism with white identity, feelings of victimhood, and conspiratorial information sources may produce violent action, or at least support for it, where religious belief may not do so absent those other conditions."[70]

In *Preparing for War: The Extremist History of White Christian Nationalism—and What Comes Next,* Bradley Onishi confirms these ideas as someone who spent much of his life surrounded by the confluence of right-wing politics and religion, including attending an evangelical megachurch and handing out anti-abortion materials to other students before becoming a youth minister. From his experience, the Christian nationalist movement "provides a window into the political forces shaping the American right as a whole."[71] Onishi explains:

> There is a sense of acceleration in today's movement. In the Obama years, you had somebody who really embodied the fears of the counter-revolution of the '60s: a mixed-race man with a Black family, a Muslim dad, an immigrant dad, somebody who grew up in Hawaii, that far-away corner of the Union. And then during his presidency, through the *Obergefell* decision, same-sex marriage is made legal. So in the wake of that presidency, there is a real sense [among white Christian nationalists] that the apocalypse is coming for this country if we don't do something radical. The idea that they would continue in ways that are standard—campaign, voting drives, national renewal through ecumenical movements—that went by the wayside.[72]

Much like the song "You Are What You Is," "Dumb All Over" addresses the commoditization of non-white bodies. Zappa delivers some clever wordplay to twist a call to arms, as in preparation for violence, into arms as body parts, while adding a level of gallows humor by throwing in legs and ears to the mix. It is a macabre level of satire that ridicules the notion that religious fundamentalists can be reasoned with using humanistic logic, dismissing claims of equality since they can just toss these parts into a box or keep them as souvenirs. Their holy book gives them permission to do this because the other group, who are of a different race, do not believe in the same holy book. It is a facet of the song that is easy to miss because of Zappa's rapid delivery, but it draws clear connections between the confluence of racial identity and religious fundamentalism. Zappa is saying that white Christian evangelicals place a value, by placing no value, on non-white lives because the other's existence prevents them from carrying out their own vision of society based on their devotional dogma.

Anthea Butler echoes similar sentiments in *White Evangelical Racism*, noting how evangelicals differentiate their own identities from others because they feel that "'Christian race,' America, and belief are synonymous." Further,

"Christianity is whiteness as well as belief. It is this conflation that causes evangelicals to ignore their racism. They truly believe that their Christianity is a race, and this comprises an all-encompassing identity. That is why when some evangelicals say they don't see color, they really mean it. They just see whiteness. No color but the dominant one."[73] Butler continues: "Evangelicalism is synonymous with whiteness. It is not only a cultural whiteness but also a political whiteness. The presupposition of the whiteness of evangelicalism has come to define evangelicalism, and it is the definition that the media, the general public, and politicians agree on."[74]

Despite the spooky vocal effect, stinging lines, and ferocious delivery, Zappa's comments about the bleakness of our collective future is devoid of any real sensationalism. The advancement and legitimization of Christian nationalism as a key component of a major political party's platform over the last four decades has proven that Zappa's concerns were clearheaded and based on real trends. In "Dumb All Over," Zappa offers a measured view of the consequences of religious fanaticism. While he sings that joggers and dogwalkers may not have a street to walk on if zealots take over, he makes a point to say that he does not mean that life will end as part of some fiery and explosive holocaust but rather that everything will just look ugly for a millennium.

This is the most poignant line of the song, and arguably the whole of *You Are What You Is*, because it reflects what Zappa truly feared. Zappa considered himself a very serious musician, which requires standards of judgment when it comes to aesthetics. He was a creative person with a creative vision who dedicated his life to the pursuit of that vision through music. As much as Zappa opposed religious fundamentalism for its racism and xenophobia, the extreme effects of those beliefs on culture, including the kind of art that would reflect that culture, might be distilled into something he would find completely and utterly ugly. The world he feared was one devoid of art and the ability to create it.

You Are What You Is, as an album, contained an essential political and social commentary that ushered in a new phase of Zappa's career by shifting the direction of his artistry and how he used it. While he continued musical and lyrical traditions that had often isolated him throughout his career, mainly his penchant for taboo and offensive subjects, Zappa recognized that the American cultural landscape was changing, and for the worse. While Zappa had called truth to power in his music throughout his career, such as addressing media exploitation of racial violence in "Trouble Every Day," the threat of religious fundamentalism was proving to be more insidious. By exposing the ways in which religious fundamentalists manipulated and misused major institutions like media, business, and government, Zappa had hoped to open the eyes, ears, and minds of audiences to the idea that their leaders did not have their best interests at heart, with the consequence of their civil rights and individual freedoms being rescinded becoming an ever-increasing possibility. Even when a changing entertainment landscape was impacting how his music could be heard, Zappa refused to compromise the integrity of his art by bending to the will of people he believed were ruining America. While Zappa had remained true to his principles in his music up to this point, *You Are What You Is* reaffirmed exactly why he had those principles to begin with and what they were for. For the remainder of his life, Zappa would continue to prove one thing: He is what he is.

THE "TORCHUM" NEVER STOPS

During his first term as president, turning around the economy became one of Ronald Reagan's primary goals. His administration set forth to implement an economic policy, popularly known as "Reaganomics," that prioritized industry deregulation as well as reducing government spending and taxes, such as the federal income tax and capital gains tax. Reagan's economic policy was in lockstep with the prevailing conservative ideology of the 1980s, which he had been emboldened to pursue after evangelical support had secured his ascent to the White House through an astounding victory during the 1980 election. This political ideology advocated for the decreased presence of government institutions and reducing the impact they had on citizens. This led to many domestic government programs facing significant budget cuts, such as Social Security and education, while other areas of the government, such as military defense, received boosts in federal funding. Medical programs would also experience significant cuts during this time. The Reagan administration cut Medicaid funding by 18 percent while also slashing a quarter of the budget for the Department of Health and Human Services, which resulted in the elimination of several public-health programs.

For conservatives who supported these policies, Reagan had been a godsend. With another election just around the corner in 1984, the Reagan administration would remain committed to these values, thus instilling confidence in conservatives, and especially evangelicals, about the future of their country. Nevertheless, the cuts in government spending would ultimately have disastrous consequences for the marginalized populations who relied on those programs for their health and safety, which fueled intense grassroots opposition to the president and his policies. With a burgeoning public health crisis unfolding, one that still reverberates nearly a half-century later, the ensuing national conversation would reveal some of the deepest cultural divides within the country. As people grappled with the chaos of government, business, and religious leaders attempting to adequately address the crisis, at a time when the media landscape was rapidly changing due to deregulation, these cultural divides continued to widen, furthering a progressively divisive atmosphere in which extremist positions could be encouraged. Despite all the noise, as evangelical voices were becoming louder and critics of the president were having difficulty being heard, the message coming from the White House was clear: Reagan's silence was deafening.

In 1981, the U.S. Centers for Disease Control (CDC) reported that five young, previously healthy homosexual men around Los Angeles had been diagnosed with Pneumocystis carinii pneumonia, a rare lung infection. The men had also exhibited symptoms of other infections, which indicated that their immune systems were not functional, and two of them would die before the report was officially published. This would mark the first official reporting on what the public would come to understand was Acquired Immunodeficiency Syndrome (AIDS), which the CDC would term as a new disease a year later in 1982. During the early years of the epidemic, the response from the gay community was swift but still vastly under-resourced and underrepresented, with writer Larry Kramer raising only $6,635 from a group of over eighty men he hosted in his apartment in New York City, "the only new money, public or private, that will be raised to fight the epidemic for the remainder of the year."[1]

The next year, in 1982, the response to and awareness of the epidemic were growing, even if only slowly. New organizations were founded in order to slow the spread of the disease by providing medical services and prevention resources to the members of the communities most at risk. The Gay Men's Health Crisis became the first community-based AIDS service in the United States and had received over one hundred phone calls during the first night its counseling hotline was operational. That year also saw the first responses from the federal government. In April, Henry Waxman, a U.S. representative from California, organized the first congressional hearing on AIDS. A few months later, in September, the first congressional legislation to allocate funding for

AIDS research was introduced by Ohio representative Philip Burton and New York representative Ted Weiss, though it failed to pass through the committee, and funding for AIDS research and treatment would not be approved by Congress until July 1983.[2]

Some progress toward developing resources for the treatment of AIDS was made by 1983. At that point, the disease had affected more than one thousand Americans. The world's first outpatient clinic dedicated to treating AIDS, Ward 86, opened at San Francisco General Hospital. The CDC that year also established the National AIDS Hotline and reported "that most cases of AIDS have been among gay men, injection drug users, Haitians and people with hemophilia."[3] National media outlets had also begun reporting on the epidemic during this time: the *New York Times* ran its first front-page story on AIDS in May, and *Newsweek* hosted AIDS activist Bobbi Campbell and his partner Bobby Hilliard on the cover of their August 8 issue, which became "the first time two gay men are pictured embracing one another on the cover of a U.S. mainstream national magazine." Global recognition of the AIDS epidemic would arrive at the end of the year, in November, when the World Health Organization held its first meeting to discuss the public health crisis and its potential impact on the international community.[4]

By 1984, a reelection year for Reagan, the AIDS epidemic was now at the forefront of the national conversation, although there was still much confusion surrounding the issue. AIDS activists had already been working tirelessly to educate the public in order to increase funding and access for medical services and treatments, but their mission was consistently hindered by political and religious leaders who spread ideologically driven misinformation to advance their agenda by complicating the general public's understanding of and reaction to the epidemic. Many had denigrated AIDS as being a "gay disease," which had motivated their opposition to its treatment and funding. Bill Dannemeyer, a Republican representative from California, delivered a speech called "What Homosexuals Do" on the House floor, which formalized his depictions of graphic sexual acts into the *Congressional Record*. Dannemeyer also advocated for the federal government to create a national register of "AIDS patients, quarantines, and deportation, the fear of which made it more difficult for public health researchers to get access to gay men." Other members of Congress, such as Indiana Republican representative Dan Burton, further exacerbated the public's fears and misunderstanding of AIDS transmission by saying he brought his own scissors to the barbershop so as not to get infected with AIDS.[5] Misinformation like this fueled the stigma surrounding the epidemic, especially among conservatives and evangelicals, but with the potential to influence the broader American public.

When an AIDS patient in Los Angeles became a Christian and wanted to be baptized, members of the church refused because of fears that the virus would spread through the baptismal water. Church leaders eventually relented after a doctor not only assured them that AIDS could not be transmitted that way, but that he would also drain and sterilize the basin after the baptism, a practice the young man would be the last to go through as a precautionary measure. Reactions like this from the religious community were not uncommon as most AIDS sufferers had often experienced rejection from that community even before their diagnosis because "the perceived moral issue of its transmission through homosexual behavior makes the AIDS crisis especially difficult for the religious community."[6]

Beyond the ways in which the epidemic was exacerbated due to misinformation, there were also leading political figures who used the crisis to fan the flames of bigotry through scaremongering and divisive language rooted in evangelical conservative attitudes. In a June 1983 column, Pat Buchanan, who would later become White House communications director during Reagan's second term, said that homosexuals had "declared war on nature, and now nature is exacting an awful retribution."[7] This in turn fueled rhetoric among evangelical conservatives that AIDS was a punishment from God for the country's moral decline, a narrative that had an outsized impact on the national conversation surrounding the disease but did not represent what most people believed. Cardinal Bernard Law of the Roman Catholic Archdiocese of Boston called AIDS "a tragically divisive disease" and observed that "What is obviously a human health problem has become electrically charged with fear, outrage and suspicion."[8] However, despite all the confusion, misinformation, and ideological rhetoric contributing to the national dialogue, the leader of the country remained silent.

During the early 1980s, Reagan's response to the AIDS epidemic was poor. Since victims of the disease were viewed as being primarily homosexuals and intravenous drug users, the administration framed its official response to the epidemic from the perspective that solving the issue had to come from moral reforms. As a result, little was done to offer the public any health or policy information that would educate them on AIDS, including its effects and transmission, which resulted in an inconsistent response to concerns from the public. Reagan moved slowly in properly addressing the crisis, almost to an adversarial degree. C. Everett Koop, who served two terms as surgeon general during the Reagan administration, was barred from publicly addressing AIDS "for reasons he insisted were never fully clear to him but that were no doubt political." Edward Brandt, Reagan's assistant secretary of health, informed journalists that they could not ask questions about the epidemic during press conferences in the White House Briefing Room. Though the Reagan administration did provide some funding to sponsor research, their official silence during those early years prevented a response that might have saved the lives of many people and fueled criticism that AIDS was being ignored as a public health crisis.[9] Reagan would not even mention AIDS publicly until September 1985, well into his second term and several years after the epidemic had been raging; his first speech on the subject given two years later, in 1987.[10]

In 1986, Reagan finally assigned Surgeon General Koop the task of preparing a report on AIDS. With support from groups such as the National Hemophilia Foundation and the National Coalition of Black Lesbians and Gays, Koop worked to ensure that "he remained careful to treat AIDS not as a moral but as a public health issue, and to preserve his independence from any of the groups he consulted—as well as from the White House."[11] Koop's report, the *Surgeon General's Report on Acquired Immune Deficiency Syndrome*, "provided accurate, nonjudgmental, and comprehensive information on the HIV/AIDS epidemic, educating Americans in plain language about how the virus could and could not be spread and how individuals could protect themselves."[12] As part of his recommendations, Koop ruled that the most effective way to protect oneself from the virus was to practice abstinence and monogamy, with condoms as a precautionary measure if neither of those options were preferred. To have the biggest impact to limit the spread of the virus, Koop issued twenty million copies of the report, as well as additional AIDS education materials, and had them "distributed to the public by members of Congress, public health organizations, and Parent-Teacher Associations."

Koop's plan to distribute his report and materials had also taken into account his concerns over the Reagan administration and the politics of moralization in which they framed the epidemic. In order to prevent an outcome where the Reagan administration could redact crucial public health information, such as his recommendations for proper condom use, Koop drafted the report from his home basement and submitted numbered copies to the Domestic Policy Council that he would then re-collect under the guise of avoiding information being leaked to the media. This was done to ensure the most productive and safest results in slowing the transmission of AIDS, with Koop telling conservatives that "science and traditional morality reinforced one another,"[13] in an effort to reverse the impact of extremist positions on the administration's response to the epidemic. Koop's resistance to the pressures he faced from evangelical conservatives can be seen in how he cautioned against the stigma surrounding the disease in the foreword of the report, saying, "At the beginning of the AIDS epidemic many Americans had little sympathy for people with AIDS. The feeling was that somehow people from certain groups 'deserved' their illness. Let us put those feelings behind us. We are fighting a disease, not people. Those who are already afflicted are sick people and need our care as do all sick patients. The country must face this epidemic as a unified society. We must prevent the spread of AIDS while at the same time preserving our humanity and intimacy."[14]

The response, or lack thereof, to the AIDS epidemic by the government and religious leaders, amplified by their presence in the media, rang alarm bells for Zappa and made him suspicious about the information being shared with the public. As evangelical conservatives were gaining a bigger foothold in American culture, strengthened by the coziness between Reagan and televangelists such as Jerry Falwell, Zappa was incredulous toward the idea that a virus, which had surfaced in the popular consciousness as primarily having an impact in the gay community, could have natural origins. Given Zappa's record of distrusting authority figures, the increased presence and mobilization of fundamentalists across various cultural and social institutions had convinced him that something much bigger was going on. So, in the way he knew best, Zappa took to music to convey his ideas about public health crises and the role government plays in them.

Thing-Fish, released in December 1984, was an album composed for a proposed Broadway musical that Zappa would fail to produce and which served as his artistic response to Reagan's mishandling of the AIDS epidemic. A much maligned entry in Zappa's catalog, it presented a confusing and labyrinthian narrative that drew parallels between one of the biggest medical travesties of the early twentieth century and his perception of the one that was currently unfolding. Split into two acts, *Thing-Fish* tells the story of a government conspiracy to carry out a genocide for the benefit of Christian fundamentalists. It is a work that has a complicated legacy built on accusations of racism, with the core of Zappa's intended social and cultural commentary largely forgotten or ignored since its release. However, it serves as a key to understanding Zappa's evolution as an artist and how he channeled that art to criticize systems of power.

The album's "Prologue" opens with its titular narrator, portrayed by Ike Willis, a figure whose speech and characterization come from the satirizing of tropes based on minstrel shows, establishing the exposition and setting the scene for the rest of the story. Within a secret underground laboratory in Virginia, on the outskirts of Washington, DC, an Evil Prince, portrayed by Napoleon Murphy Brock, with a side hustle as a musical theater critic, is working on a diabolical scheme to concoct a special potion designed to eliminate all non-white people and homosexuals from the general population. With full cooperation from government authorities, the Evil Prince visits San Quentin to test his experimental substance on prisoners who were previously exposed to syphilis by sprinkling it on the mashed potatoes in the prison kitchen, resulting in no immediate effect, much to the dismay of the Evil Prince. So, as an alternate plan, it gets added to a shipment of Galoot Cologne, pronounced in a racial affectation as "Galoot Co-log-nuh" by the Thing-Fish, which results in the unexplained deaths of several gay and Black men. However, for the inmates at San Quentin, due to its potency being reduced when blended with the mashed potatoes which resulted in delayed effects, the potion makes them uglier and more aggressive, with some of the homeliest prisoners mutating into a Mammy Nun—a giant potato-headed, duck-lipped creature with huge hands, one of which can be seen on the album's cover.

Opening the first act of the musical, these strange creatures get their own introduction in "The Mammy Nuns," singing as an ensemble about how their shoes talk through dancing, that their level of importance is newsworthy, and how they have a lot of fun doing the buck-and-wing, a type of dance that had evolved from the blending of African and Irish flat-footed dance-stepping traditions from the early 1800s into a form of tap during Black Vaudeville acts of the late 1800s through the early 1900s. The Thing-Fish then introduces the Mammy Nuns to the audience, warning the audience they have no voluntary control of their urinary functions. Two members of the audience, a waspy white husband and wife named Harry and Rhonda, are shocked by the production and that they were urinated on by the Mammy Nuns. Rhonda, an uptight and self-absorbed Italian American woman, portrayed by Dale Bozzio, complains about the urine staining her fox fur while lamenting how much Broadway entertainment has been degraded, with its milquetoast allure of sequined fairy costumes and uplifting musical score replaced by Black performers and music stylings. Harry, Rhonda's timid and naive husband, played by Terry Bozzio, attempts to reassure his wife that they will get the traditional Broadway-show experience they paid for, one that better matches their skin tone and its respective theatrical aesthetic. Instead, the Thing-Fish ties Harry and Rhonda up with chains in order to fully immerse them in the show ("Harry & Rhonda").

The Thing-Fish then introduces Mammy Nun Sister Ob'dewlla X, also portrayed by Ike Willis, to help him provide an update on the Mammy Nuns' response to the situation involving the deadly shipment of Galoot Cologne, which had been successful in killing off a considerable number of homosexuals and non-white people just before the election. With support from religious organizations, the government became excited about the prospect of moving the Galoot Cologne project forward as all these deaths could be explained as being determined by God's will through Biblical retribution, and a lot of white people were believing it. As the Thing-Fish further explains, the Mammy Nuns were all up for parole at the same time after their heads turned into giant potatoes, and they were soon met with difficulties during a depression and were unable to find janitorial or assembly line work. However, despite this setback, the conditions which they endured had made the Mammy Nuns indestructible to societal oppression, saying that whatever was done to them before no longer has an effect on them now, thus making them the only ones strong enough to survive the Galoot Cologne mystery disease, a subtle nod that acknowledges Black women and infers their historical legacy of being the most marginalized group in the United States because of the intersectionality of their identities ("Galoot Up-Date").

Meanwhile, the Evil Prince, first introduced in the musical's prologue, is working in his laboratory on a potion that will make him immortal while also raising an army of the dead. In this reimagining of "The Torture Never Stops" from Zappa's 1976 album *Zoot Allures,* the Evil Prince holds traditional Broadway performers and theatergoers captive as he injects them with this potion, turning them into zombies who will reclaim Broadway for white people. With racist and ethnocentric intentions, the Evil Prince is manifesting a master plan to turn musical theater bland and lame by using his zombies to displace queer, Black, and other "creative" people through the spread of the Evil Prince's scientifically engineered disease, really turning Broadway back into the Great White Way. Only by making theatrical musical entertainment as bland as he is could the Evil Prince become a successful, full-time theater critic ("The 'Torchum' Never Stops"). Harry and Rhonda watch the Evil Prince unveil his plan with awe and amazement, with the Thing-Fish disgusted by the Evil Prince eating raw chitlins, which the Evil Prince uses to test his immortality ("That Evil Prince").

Thing-Fish, with its narrative and dialogue, did not directly address the AIDS crisis in any clear or straightforward way, with Zappa instead crafting "a very complex narrative that mixes up aspects of the government's poor reaction to the AIDS epidemic with the government's use of African Americans as unwitting test subjects for syphilis studies."[15] In 1992, Zappa told Neil Slaven, author of *Zappa: Electric Don Quixote,* about the origin and messaging of the album:

> The simple thought behind the album is that somebody manufactured a disease called AIDS. They were developing it as a weapon and they tested it on convicts, the same way as they used to give syphilis to black inmates

> in US prisons. That's documented, that's fact. So we take it one step further and they're concocting this special disease which is genetically specific to get rid of all "highly rhythmic individuals and sissy boys." So I postulate that they do this test in a prison, and part of the test backfires, and these mutants are created. I could show you a book which has an extract from the 1971 or 1972 Congressional Record, where a man is asking the Congress for money to develop a biological weapon that would be genetically specific. This is not fiction.[16]

For forty years, between 1932 and 1972, the U.S. Public Health Service conducted an experiment at Tuskegee University in Macon County, Alabama, to "record the natural history of syphilis in Black people." When the test was initiated, there was no known cure for syphilis and the white supremacist thinking that permeated the culture of the southern United States at the time believed that the sexually transmitted disease had a different effect on Black people than it did on white people. Over six hundred Black men enrolled in the study, with most being "poor and illiterate sharecroppers from the county" and were enticed with incentives such as free food and medical examinations; they were led to believe they were being treated for "bad blood," a local expression that could be applied to any number of illnesses.[17] Without their knowledge or consent, some of them were treated with toxic substances such as arsenic and mercury. For others who did not receive any treatments for their syphilis as part of the study, they experienced the disease's debilitating effects, including blindness, paralysis, mental illness, and organ damage. Though penicillin emerged in 1947 as an effective and readily available cure for syphilis, "the medicine was withheld as a part of the treatment for both the experimental group and control group."

The study would come to a close in 1972 after Jean Heller, a journalist for the Associated Press, uncovered the truth behind "a 40-year nontherapeutic experiment called 'a study' on the effects of untreated syphilis on Black men in the rural south." A panel was soon organized by the assistant secretary for health and scientific affairs, including experts from fields such as medicine, law, education, and religion. Though the panel had come to their own conclusion that the participants had freely consented to the treatments, "there was evidence that scientific research protocol routinely applied to human subjects was either ignored or deeply flawed" because the participants were not provided informed consent, including researchers not even informing the men that the study was called the "Tuskegee Study of Untreated Syphilis in the Negro Male." Ultimately, the panel's final opinion of the study was that it was "ethically unjustified."[18] The Tuskegee syphilis study is not only one of the country's most regrettable and shameful events of the twentieth century, revealing another instance of the United States' history of systemically harming Black people, its legacy has also continued to endure well beyond the AIDS epidemic and Zappa's commentary of its effects on that population. The specter of the study continues to haunt the nation, with its reverberations having most recently fueled hesitancy for Black Americans in getting vaccinated against COVID-19, thus furthering the disparity in medical treatments for marginalized communities.[19]

Zappa already had a longstanding distrust of government, which he was not afraid to discuss whenever the topic came up, but he was becoming more vocal about his grievances as more instances of evangelical influence could be seen having direct results within the Reagan administration. As he was not satisfied with the information coming out of the White House about the origin and extent of the AIDS crisis, Zappa could not be dissuaded from speaking out against the evangelical conservatives who were echoing the very same ideas. He felt they were hiding a truth from the general public that could potentially cast them, and by extension their ideology, in a negative light. In his 1989 autobiography, Zappa accuses Koop of spreading misinformation through unscientific data skewed by fundamentalist doctrine, including the surgeon general's assertion that heroin and cocaine have the exact same pharmacological effects on users. Regarding the information being officially dispensed to the American public by Koop and the Reagan administration, Zappa ridicules them for proposing that AIDS could have originated from an indigenous person cutting his finger while skinning a sick monkey and becoming infected by its blood.[20] He goes further by saying, "Folks, it is far more likely that the disease was spread in Africa (and Haiti) as the result of injections administered by evangelical 'medical missionaries'—either on purpose (as part of 'God's Republican Plan For The Advancement Of Rich American White People') or through incompetence (using dirty needles for multiple injections without sterilization). How did it get back to the U.S.? Is it possible that some of those nice little missionaries share Jim Bakker's blessed sexual preferences?"[21]

With this comment, Zappa is not just merely suggesting that AIDS could have been spread locally where evangelical missionaries were practicing, but he suspects that their intentions were likely illegitimate by normal medical standards. He also uses that notion to imply that one possible explanation for the spread of AIDS in the United States could be that evangelical missionaries were having sexual relations with sex workers, throwing in a jab at televangelist Jim Bakker over his then-recent sex scandal for good measure. As Zappa was not assuaged by the explanation coming from Reagan's surgeon general, given what seemed to him like an overcompensation by government and religious leaders to uphold that position, he felt there was enough evidence for him to be vocally skeptical and offer dissenting ideas. Specifically, he thought AIDS might have been created by the government or, on the chance it was not, then the disease's transmission rate was exacerbated by religious intervention. These thoughts would fuse together to create the impression that it may be plausible, at least as far as Zappa was concerned, that the religiously conservative administration overseeing the federal government's response to an increasingly volatile health crisis might have nefarious purposes.

When asked by *High Times* during a December 1989 interview about suggesting in his autobiography that evangelical missionaries were likely performing medical treatments with unsanitized needles, thus accelerating AIDS transmission, Zappa says he heard that from someone else so he could not claim it as his own theory. Zappa discusses the first time he had heard about AIDS, in a report that suggested "700 people of a certain persuasion in a certain city had died in the month of November,"[22] implying that the deaths of metropolitan homosexuals were timed to reduce their impact on the election cycle. Since his father "was a mathematician and chemist who worked in the defence industry,"[23] Zappa proposed that his tangential knowledge of germ warfare and poisonous gas when growing up alerted him to the possibility that AIDS was a scientific experiment in which American citizens were the lab rats. In essence, Zappa believed AIDS might be a chemical weapon tested on civilians. Zappa illustrates his reasoning by saying there are plenty of other events in recent history where private citizens were being experimented on without their consent or knowledge by the government, citing the Army's experiments testing LSD on soldiers as a form of enhanced interrogation.[24] As an advocate for personal freedoms and liberties, Zappa believed that American citizens were not obligated to "participate unwillingly in chemical and biological warfare experiments."[25]

Though Zappa's comments sound like conspiracy theory, especially at that time during the early days of the AIDS crisis, it would seem that some of the dissenting ideas he proposed in opposition to the government's narrative may have been more grounded in reality than many were willing to accept back then. In their 2020 essay, "Sex and the Mission: The Conflicting Effects of Early Christian Missions on HIV in Sub-Saharan Africa," published in the *Journal of Demographic Economics*, Julia Cagé and Valeria Rueda investigated the breadth and scope of missionary activity pertaining to HIV treatments in sub-Saharan Africa. Their research explored how missionaries performing medical treatments brought a budding modern medical infrastructure to the region while at the same time allowing their religious ideology to influence sexual health beliefs in a way that would magnify the impact of the virus. Through a geocoded dataset they built, Cagé and Rueda found "that historical missionary presence is associated with higher probability of being tested positive for HIV,"[26] a trend that seemed to be "driven by the Christian population" and that "missionary presence and conversion are also relevant historical determinants of HIV."[27]

Cagé and Rueda say, "the history of modern medicine in sub-Saharan Africa is closely linked to the development of missionary activity."[28] With their main goal being to convert local and indigenous populations to Christianity, the missionaries consider administering medicine as an integral component of that plan. Their religious beliefs suggest that "healing the body and soul is indeed deeply rooted in the Christian dogma," as illustrated by the Gospel of Matthew 10:1: "Jesus called his twelve disciples to him and gave them authority to drive out impure spirits and to heal every disease and sickness."[29] This dogma that motivates them to practice missionary medicine is "a part of a larger conversion enterprise," which Cagé and Rueda suggest presents an unstable dialogue about modern medicine that "illustrates the tension between the Christian and the scientific response to these diseases."[30]

Cagé and Rueda attribute the increased risk of HIV around missions to two things. First is the number of religious groups and programs that utilized abstinence-only sex education, preaching to locals that they should refrain from having sex until marriage. Missionaries who promoted abstinence-only sex education inadvertently created a boom in the "commercial sex work sector,"[31] which resulted in the increased risk of HIV for a community. Missionaries also "pushed hard for the emancipation of women and the abolition of polygamy, directly and through the colonial authorities, while nuns developed activities aimed at improving the status of women," with one of the effects being that, when they were "No longer forced to have sexual relations with a man selected by their kin, some women opted for something that was easier to attain than the proposed idealistic monogamous union based on love and the Ten Commandments: the trade of sexual services."[32] As part of the influence evangelicalism had on the region, the disruption caused to the traditional societal framework of these communities resulted in a higher risk of contagion for both the locals and the missionaries. As the number of sex workers rose during this period, so did the number of opportunities for people in these regions to become infected with HIV. For Zappa to suggest the likelihood of some missionaries having transmitted the disease back to the United States through sexual intercourse, we can see with this data that such a scenario is indeed within the realm of possibility.

The second thing that Cagé and Rueda attribute to the increasing of HIV transmission in regions with missionary medical centers, as Zappa also suggested in his autobiography, was "health campaigns where frequent use of unsterilized needles facilitated iatrogenic diffusion,"[33] which "occurs when the deleterious effects of the therapeutic or diagnostic regimen causes pathology independent of the condition for which the regimen is advised."[34] This would describe the reaction a patient could have when administered a variety of treatments or drugs in which their combined effects would result in worse symptoms, not unlike all the negative side-effects the voiceover in pharmaceutical commercials reads through quickly when advertising the merits of a drug.

In order to halt the spread of HIV, especially within the marginalized communities most at risk, various government and nonprofit organizations established programs and initiatives to inform the public about the dangers of HIV and the reality of its transmissibility, primarily through needles and syringes which come in contact with potentially infected blood. In 1984, the Centers for Disease Control and Prevention issued recommendations discouraging intravenous drug injection and sharing needles. A decade later, in 1994, syringe exchange programs were determined by the National Academy of Sciences as being effective in their efforts to prevent and limit the transmission of HIV and AIDS.[35] As these programs were championed and proven to be effective in slowing the spread of HIV in the United States, it would not be unreasonable to suggest that religious programs with limited medical experience, motivated by ideological concerns, could have accelerated the spread of the disease. With this in mind, we can see how Zappa came to speculate on the intentions and purposes of medical missionaries, questioning whether their actions were the product of ineptitude and poor training or if they were indeed part of a grander scheme to make the United States whiter and more conservative. The latter possibility fueled the conspiratorial idea that AIDS was meant to medically eradicate queer and non-white people, which Zappa adhered to because it seemed to him to be a more plausible explanation than the disease originating from an ill monkey in Africa.

Nearly five decades later, though, it is still the prevailing attitude within the medical community that HIV originated from a species of chimpanzee in Central Africa, with the CDC citing the likely first transmission to humans occurring during the late 1800s. It is speculated that the species-specific version of the virus, called simian immunodeficiency virus (SIV), transmitted to humans through the consumption of infected meat, initiating a slow spread across the African continent until the human version of the virus became discoverable during the latter half of the twentieth century.[36] As someone born in the late 1980s, I missed the hysteria surrounding the AIDS crisis and was taught this longstanding theory that the disease came from a sub-Saharan primate, so I was spared being bombarded by conspiracy theories disproven by years of medical and scientific research since its discovery. However, when I think about the early days of the AIDS crisis, when accurate information was sparse, I can empathize with how people came to believe the conspiracy theories, especially when compounded by what seemed to many as a slow and inefficient response by the Reagan administration. With hindsight, it is not difficult to see how Zappa came to his conclusions—not just from researching his comments on the issue and the context in which they were made, but also having witnessed how COVID-19, the biggest public health crisis since AIDS, fueled its own conspiracy theories based on the government response and misinformation spread across social media.

You do not have to look too far to see how much confirmation bias, meaning one's inclination to interpret new evidence in a way that structurally reinforces existing pre-determined beliefs and ideas, plays a role in how conspiracy theories spread. By saying all this, my purpose is not to rationalize any misinformed outlook Zappa may have had but rather to add context to the art in which he channeled these ideas. *Thing-Fish* was not intended to cause increased harm for the communities most at risk of HIV infection. The purpose of its narrative was to shed light on how the United States had historically abused marginalized communities through medical experimentation, specifically the Tuskegee syphilis study. Knowing that history, it was not a stretch for Zappa to come to the conclusion that AIDS could have resulted from a similar program. Given that his motivations for the musical were to make the United States confront its ugly past by reflecting the condition of its considerably unattractive present, we can see how confirmation bias affected the quality of Zappa's musical. While Zappa's aim may have come from a progressive attitude that called out systems of power for abusing marginalized communities, even well-intentioned misinformation and conspiracy theories can still complicate public attitudes. *Thing-Fish* is a prime example of how that balance between artistic intent and audience perception can be disrupted, resulting in a work that is culturally maligned and misunderstood, particularly when its provocative nature makes it difficult for that intent to be understood.

The AIDS crisis was further complicated by the confirmation biases resulting from the poor government response. Between 1981 and 1983, religious groups did not officially respond to the AIDS crisis, primarily because members of the evangelical community believed the disease only affected homosexual people, which presented little to no opportunity for evangelicals to encounter AIDS sufferers because the two groups occupied different spaces within society. As a result of this social dynamic, the devastation within the gay community was not fully appreciated enough to necessitate a response from these religious groups. For evangelicals, AIDS was a gay issue. It was not until 1983 when a religious group officially recognized the crisis. The National Council of Churches of Christ began advocating for gay and lesbian groups in order to motivate increased spending on AIDS research and education. A year later, in 1984, the Roman Catholic Diocese of San Jose, California, would become the first religious group to issue a statement formally recognizing the scope of AIDS and its impact on the gay community, saying in its literature that "Ministry to the sick, dying and bereaved requires special attention and sensitivity in this context because the misunderstanding and hostility surrounding homosexuality has been grievously aggravated by the uncertainty and fear surrounding Acquired Immune Deficiency Syndrome," with victims of the disease and their families having a "special claim on the ministry of the church."[37]

Anthony Petro, assistant professor of religion at Boston University and author of *After the Wrath of God: AIDS, Sexuality, and American Religion*, confirms the slow response to AIDS by religious groups, saying that mainstream voices within the Christian community did not call attention to the public health crisis until the mid-1980s. Though most religious groups by the end of the decade would publicly call for the compassionate treatment of people diagnosed with HIV or AIDS, the evangelical conservative factions proclaimed that God spread the disease to punish society for its immoral sexuality. Petro says of the origin for this rhetoric that, during the medieval period, "Christian writers reinterpreted biblical passages about the destruction of the city of Sodom as descriptions of sexual sin, namely, the sin of 'sodomy' (which would become the sin of homosexual acts in the 20th century)."[38]

Petro also said that "Conservative Christians, in the decades preceding AIDS, worried about an epidemic of immorality tied to the sexual revolution of the 1960s."[39] R. Marie Griffith, director of the John C. Danforth Center on Religion and Politics at Washington University, explores this history in *Moral Combat: How Sex Divided American Christians and Fractured American Politics*, analyzing how American Christians broke into two ideologically separate identities, progressives and traditionalists, and how the politics surrounding the sexual revolution and women's rights divided them. Griffith says:

> Until the early 20th century, most Americans believed that sexual morality consists of a system of values that must be guarded and preserved for the

> greater social good as well as for one's personal salvation. While people disagreed about any number of issues—slavery, states' rights, labor laws, alcohol use, etc.—most believed in, and took for granted as natural and divinely ordained, a sexual order in which men were heads of households, wives must submit to husbands' authority, and monogamous heterosexual marriage was the only proper site for sexual relations. Those who broke the rules were punished or shunned.[40]

This would become the theological basis in which the fracture between religiously progressive and traditional groups would grow, prompting many evangelicals to believe that feminism would dismantle the social and cultural hierarchy they upheld through their beliefs. By the 1960s, evangelical fundamentalists championed the idea that such notions would corrupt American youth and that such debauchery was a communist plot to subvert American principles.[41] When the AIDS crisis was accelerating and public attention to it was growing, a 1985 study measuring intolerance of AIDS victims revealed "that only 'failure to recognize the contributions of Christian Fundamentalists' related significantly and independently to intolerance of persons with AIDS." The author of the study continued: "The Christian Right sees such people as secular humanists, abortionists and homosexuals, not only as deviants but their activities as being major causes of the breakdown in America's moral standards. Thus, homosexuals, and by association AIDS victims, may serve as scapegoats for conservative Fundamentalists, so that they might blame someone for the moral decay they see all around them."[42]

Andrew Greely, a former priest and sociologist at the University of Chicago's National Opinion Research Center, echoed these sentiments. In his review of *General Social Survey* data collected in 1988, which included numerous questions about the intersection of AIDS and religion, Greely said:

> The religious correlation with negative attitudes toward AIDS victims or AIDS education is the result of moral and religious narrowness among certain members of the more devout population. . . . this finding establishes that it is not religion as such but a certain highly specific type of religious orientation which tends to induce hostility on the subject of AIDS. While

> this religious orientation represents a strong component of American culture and society (38 percent of Americans believe in the strict literal interpretation of the Bible), it is not a majority orientation; and even among fundamentalists the majority support AIDS education programs. . . . One would predict that the greatest resistance to attitudinal change . . . would come from those with rigid religious orientations and the highest likelihood of attitudinal change from those with the most gracious images of God.[43]

Another point Petro makes about evangelical conservatives' response to AIDS was that their rhetoric "characterized AIDS as God's wrath" and "was overrepresented in the media and in national consciousness."[44] In her essay, "AIDS and the News Media," published in the *Millbank Quarterly*, Dorothy Nelkin said that "news coverage of AIDS can be viewed as a genre of risk reporting," with public concern "reflected in extended media coverage, frequent controversies about the nature and causes of risk, and a veritable industry of risk assessment." This had led to a culture where "communicating information about AIDS has been especially divisive" because many groups "want[ed] to communicate through the media in order to change people's behavior" for reasons including "economic or personal stakes, professional ideologies . . . and moral beliefs" which "all have influenced perceptions of this disease, interpretations of evidence, and views on appropriate modes of risk communication."[45] Nelkin claims that, since media outlets had labeled AIDS as a sexually transmitted disease as opposed to being a viral disease, they had inadvertently "clearly laid the blame on immorality," with many articles emphasizing the homosexual narrative as journalists "provided rather little critical analysis that might have called early attention to the growing number of intravenous drug users and women with AIDS."[46] Though done in the spirit of increasing public awareness about the AIDS crisis, Nelkin says, "media coverage may exaggerate the problem of risks, but . . . it may also elicit the support that is essential to bring risks under control."[47] This dynamic can result in the polarization of facts within the media, which can be leveraged to achieve a certain outcome by manipulating public opinion. "Conservatives have encouraged the tone of reprobation as a way to further their moral agendas," says Nelkin. "Attracted by extreme positions, the press reiterated Jerry Falwell's comments that AIDS was God's will, that a 'man reaps as he sows,' and William Buckley's proposal to tattoo seropositive men on their forearms or buttocks."[48]

The role that evangelical conservatives played in shaping the public discourse on AIDS cannot be overstated. By leveraging the systemic advantages of a large presence within the national media landscape as well as their close proximity to powerful figures in the federal government, the leaders of the fundamentalist movement gave outsized power to their extremist followers in order to subvert popular opinion built on factual legitimacy. Falwell, one of the leading personages in the televangelist industry, who had outsized influence within the Reagan administration due to his mobilizing the Moral Majority to support his presidency, used AIDS "to craft new fundraising appeals" because "conservatives like Falwell found the punitive manifestation for homosexual behavior for which they had been searching."[49]

This ability to shape the popular consciousness over a public health crisis can result in situations where ideology is held in higher regard than universal morality, which can affect professional responses to public health issues due to the increasing pervasiveness of fundamentalist conservative ideology in health-care practices. In 1987, some doctors had made public statements that they would not treat HIV-positive people, resulting in the American Medical Association issuing a statement that it was unethical for medical professionals to deny care.[50] Twenty years later, in 2007, a survey published in the *New England Journal of Medicine* revealed that 63 percent of doctors said "it is acceptable to tell patients they have moral objections to treatments," with 5 percent of survey respondents saying "their doctors had refused to treat them for moral, ethical or religious reasons."[51] In 2023, with recent Supreme Court rulings that have prioritized religious freedom, "more than 1 in 8 LGBTQ people now live in states where doctors, nurses and other health care professionals can legally refuse to treat them" due to the expansion of religious rights that provide guidelines to license legal discrimination, particularly for transgender people.[52] With the context of how media can influence popular dialogue through the oversaturation of evangelical conservative ideology, especially when the dominant fundamentalist figures espousing that ideology have the ear of the president, it becomes easier to understand how Zappa viewed the

AIDS crisis through a conspiratorial lens. Zappa would summarize this viewpoint during a 1987 interview on *Today:*

> We have a batch of religious fanatics now in the United States who believe that Armageddon is a Biblical necessity. . . . in an event called the Rapture, God would scoop his chosen people into the clouds just before the bomb went off. . . . After all, fundamentalists believe that sex is a sin, especially the way that gay guys do it. Weird? Well, I don't think so. Especially after the rhetoric flying around when AIDS was first "discovered." Religious leaders like Pat Buchanan and Jerry Falwell were gleefully claiming that it was divine retribution from God—it gets rid of gays, prostitutes and intravenous drug users.[53]

The opening tracks of *Thing-Fish* present the most cogent look into the themes of the album as well as an opportunity to discuss the historical context behind those themes. Though you would not know on a first listen without context that it was about the AIDS epidemic, there are enough elements within the narrative to get a sense of the basic story: an evil prince works with the government to poison and kill Black and gay people so he can make American culture whiter and heteronormative, which requires the listener to get past the uncomfortable and shocking tone of the characters and their dialogue to even understand that. However, the narrative does take a turn in which the story becomes less and less clear, making it increasingly difficult for the listener to comprehend the album's concept and inherent meaning. It is a juncture in the listening experience where a seemingly coherent story breaks down into a convoluted mess that does very little to build up the purpose behind Zappa's artistic intent for the album.

At this point in the musical, the story jumps back several years into the past. The next three songs are reimagined tracks from the album *You Are What You Is,* released a few years prior in 1981, featuring lyrical and production updates to fit the narrative of *Thing-Fish.* The Thing-Fish and the Mammy Nuns explain chitlins to Harry and Rhonda, as they are both ignorant white people, while also informing them that the mashed potatoes tainted by the Evil Prince are what mutated an average prisoner at San Quentin into the Thing-Fish ("You Are What You Is"). As the Mammy Nuns explain to the white people that butchering a cow does not make ham, as a metaphor to describe that they are what they are and nothing will change that, the scene turns into a dance club where people engage in bondage and sadomasochistic sex play ("Mudd Club"). One of the club goers, a fundamentalist Christian preacher with a giant pompadour named Quentin Robert DeNameland, making a reappearance after first philosophizing in "The Adventures of Greggery Peccary" from 1978's *Studio Tan*, welcomes the Mammy Nuns to his video chapel. There the Mammy Nuns reject the budding televangelist's proselytizing and instead comment on how the business of religion is creating a societal disparity in which only government leaders, with the support of evangelical voters, maintain wealth and power ("The Meek Shall Inherit Nothing").

Unable to get any action at the Mudd Club, Quentin flies out to Las Vegas, a destination the Thing-Fish refers to as a paradise for hypocritical Jesus jerks, looking for a sexual release since the only type of people who can stand him are the nameless, faceless sex objects he can find roaming the Strip. He ultimately settles on an ugly blow-up doll waitress. Meanwhile, back at the hotel, Quentin's television wife, Opal, is having a sultry affair with a bellboy who is later revealed to be Harry-As-A-Boy, a younger Harry portrayed by Bob Harris, and also the illegitimate son of Quentin ("Clowns on Velvet"). This boyhood version of Harry is asked by the Thing-Fish about his plans for the future, with Harry-As-A-Boy hopeful that he will live a life of homosexual depravity, drugs, and getting his heart broken. When pressed by the Thing-Fish about how the young man figured out this was the way he wanted to grow up, Harry-As-A-Boy informs him that he lost all sexual desire for women after they started to enter the workforce because it would be too traumatic to have intercourse with someone who resembled a more curvaceous and full-figured version of someone's father. Harry-As-A-Boy says he is too preoccupied with his own desires to be distracted by reproduction, referring to the Women's Liberation Movement as a government population-control program and that his homosexuality is a business decision ("Harry-As-A-Boy"). As the Mammy Nuns sing about Harry-As-A-Boy's dalliances with underground homosexual fetishism, Brown Moses, a religious figure portrayed by Johnny "Guitar" Watson, provides commentary on all the ways in which Harry-As-A-Boy is exploring his newfound sexual liberation ("He's So Gay").

The blow-up doll waitress, who is now revealed to be a mechanized version of Rhonda, falls in love with the young Harry. However, the adult Harry offers his protests to the Thing-Fish over his younger self reciprocating those feelings for Artificial Rhonda, with adult Rhonda excitedly egging him on and telling Harry how his standing up for himself excuses any homosexual fling he might have. Harry then suddenly realizes he has sexual urges for the Mammy Nuns, with the Thing-Fish encouraging him to lustfully pursue any of the bland Broadway zombies instead ("The Massive Improve'lence"). In a reimagining of "Ms. Pinky" from *Zoot Allures*, Harry-As-A-Boy complains that his older self should not have sex with any of the Mammy Nuns until he has had a chance to fall in love himself. He awkwardly asks the blow-up doll version of Rhonda for a dance before succumbing to the allure of her artificial anatomy, with the Mammy Nuns singing ensemble about how a rubberized woman may be the only suitable partner this ignorant, pathetic white boy needs or even deserves ("Artificial Rhonda").

The second act of the musical opens with Harry-As-A-Boy and Artificial Rhonda gathered as part of a nativity scene staged in the front yard of a middle-class suburban New Jersey home owned by an Italian man named Francesco, together with their mechanical child, the Crab-Grass Baby, taking the place of the infant Jesus. Sporting the features of Artificial Rhonda's face and Quentin Robert DeNameland's white pompadour, the Crab-Grass Baby speaks in a computerized voice about problems he has been experiencing with his girlfriend and car and asks Harry-As-A-Boy, whom he calls father, to buy him a new one. The young father is amazed by his son being so intelligent as the Crab-Grass Baby repeatedly tells him that he soiled himself, with Harry-As-A-Boy too distracted by the size of his son's penis to even pay attention ("The Crab-Grass Baby"). The Mammy Nun ensemble, led by Sister Owl-Gonkwin-Jane Cowhoon, as portrayed by Ray White, sing a blues lamenting the automobile and relationship burdens of the little white Crab-Grass-Baby. Though Harry-As-A-Boy claims he is incredibly happy for how his life turned out and is thankful for his son, job, and romantic partner, he is mystified by how Artificial Rhonda became pregnant, a question accentuated by the nativity setting. The Thing-Fish informs the young Harry that it was the television preacher Quentin who impregnated Artificial Rhonda, and warns Harry-As-A-Boy that things are going to get a lot worse now that Artificial Rhonda is attending consciousness-raising seminars and is looking to get a professional career ("The White Boy Troubles"). In a reimagined version of a track from Zappa's 1982 album, *Ship Arriving Too Late to Save a Drowning Witch,* Harry-As-A-Boy becomes a semi–trailer truck driver hauling string beans to Utah while Artificial Rhonda takes on work as a waitress in a local diner, where she encounters Quentin looking to rekindle their former relationship ("No Not Now").

The setting then jumps forward to the present with Harry and Rhonda back on the front lawn of Francesco's home in suburban New Jersey. Harry is now in full leather bondage gear, sexually fondling Sister Ob'dewlla X, ignoring the vexed Rhonda who is livid with Harry's sexual predilections. Failing to distract Harry from his desired Mammy Nun by showing off her breasts, Rhonda verbally degrades Harry by calling him a worm. She shows off her vagina to Harry, as an attempt to tease him with it, and grinds on her briefcase while sticking a fountain pen up her ass for sexual gratification, all the while yelling at Harry to urge him to watch her achieve carnal pleasure without him ("Briefcase Boogie"). All of the action stops in a freeze-frame as Brown Moses returns, relying on his religious proclivities, to criticize and condemn Harry and Rhonda for their sexual promiscuity and abandoning their child, the Crab-Grass Baby ("Brown Moses").

The Evil Prince returns for the final scenes, but he has since turned himself into a Mammy Nun following his last appearance. Attempting to build an immunity to his own diseased potion, he ingested too much Galoot Cologne from the inside of a butchered pig, which became the catalysis for his mutation. Now a Broadway zombie himself, he makes one last attempt to secure Broadway's identity to reflect his own mundane musical preferences by glorifying the enduring legacy of musical theater, staying true to its white-washed traditions ("Wistful Wit a Fist-Full"). Following the Evil Prince's finale, Harry exults in his theatrical experience and the sexual liberation that came with it while Rhonda demeans him for being a male chauvinist and tells him to eat shit. Rhonda then delivers a feminist speech about the uselessness of the all-

American "Man-Worm," exalting women as the future of society since they are able to perpetually sustain their own joy and independence. Rhonda then takes the pen from her ass and demands that Harry smell it, telling him the stinky pen represents deep and meaningful Broadway symbolism about how all men will die off because their weak and submissive minds kept them from evolving, with Rhonda proclaiming that women have been able to reproduce by having sex with their briefcases ("Drop Dead").

During the finale, the lights dim with only a single spotlight held on Rhonda, which Harry crawls into, begging like a dog to sniff the pen. The Thing-Fish urges Harry to get a big whiff of the pen while also encouraging the Mammy Nuns to dance with the Broadway zombies and for the Evil Prince to forget about the Galoot Cologne. The scene descends into chaos as the Mammy Nuns tango with the zombies before throwing them offstage, while characters from earlier scenes join in on the mayhem onstage. The Evil Prince starts anally penetrating Rhonda, unbeknownst to her, as she distractedly continues to tease Harry with the fountain pen, yelling at him about its symbolism. The Thing-Fish then grabs both the Crab-Grass Baby and Sister Ob'dewlla X and dances around, shaking them like maracas. Harry-As-A-Boy and Artificial Rhonda reappear to chase their infant around, Quentin the televangelist has anal sex with Brown Moses, and Quentin's wife Opal is given an enema from Francesco the Italian New Jersey homeowner, all while Dutch Midgets erupt from the nativity scene to offer onions to theatergoers in the audience. Before the curtain falls on this bizarre display of fetishized hypersexuality, the Thing-Fish addresses the audience, offering a kernel of philosophical wisdom, by telling them that what they have just witnessed was based on a true story and that the musical was a public service announcement about the danger of ingesting Galoot Cologne.[54]

The rest of *Thing-Fish,* once the story jumps to the past, seems to become less a commentary about the ways the government has historically abused marginalized populations and more an airing of Zappa's grievances about America during the Reagan years. The surrealism of the lyrics and music blend ideas on a variety of topics that are interesting on their own, such as yuppie culture, sexual liberation, and religious hypocrisy, but the result is an experience that becomes difficult to understand without added context, and even then it still largely goes over listeners' heads. I know this can be said about much of Zappa's music because his concepts, lyrics, and production could be rather dense at times, but *Thing-Fish* stands out on its own in that regard. As opposed to Zappa's other works, this was intended to become a staged musical production, but it never happened. Zappa tried to raise money to stage the show on Broadway, but was not able to secure funding, telling *Songwriter Connection* in 1984 that, "If the show had a more boring plot, it would have been okay, but it had a real controversial plot. It has stuff in it that has never been on Broadway before."[55] The album had even generated controversy before it was released when an employee at MCA's record-pressing plant "objected to the lyrics and corporate panic ensued," resulting in Zappa's record deal being cancelled. In response, Zappa put a label on the cover of *Thing-Fish* warning that political and religious organizations were violating constitutionally protected free speech, a move that would foreshadow his crusade against parents' rights groups the following year.[56]

If Zappa had been able to raise the funds for a staged production, then perhaps the more confusing elements of *Thing-Fish*, as an album, could have benefited from being portrayed visually and thus more easily convey Zappa's ideas. *Thing-Fish* would eventually be adapted for a limited production in 2003, but much of the album could not be fully brought to the stage due to the small budget for the production.[57] Still, Zappa had prepared publicity stills for a staged production which were reprinted in the April 1984 issue of *Hustler*, featuring graphic depictions of the album's finale with Harry dressed in leather bondage gear fondling a Mammy Nun puppet while a nude Rhonda has sex with her briefcase and has a giant pen shoved up her ass.[58] Looking at these photos, one wonders whether Zappa considered his Broadway aspirations to be realistic. Given the reception of the album and the inability to produce it for Broadway, one can ask the question whether *Thing-Fish* missed its moment or if its moment was ever possible to begin with. When Bill Templeton interviewed Zappa for *Music* in 1985 and told him he still did not know what *Thing-Fish* meant after listening to it, Zappa said, "The general release schedule is four months apart, OK? If you wait longer to release *Thing-Fish*, then the whole business about AIDS, and the references to the mystery disease that is in there gets farther and farther away from the initial impact of when it was in the news."[59]

Of all the songs on the album, "He's So Gay" is the one that usually elicits the strongest critical reactions. Released as one of the singles in support of the album, collected on the maxi-single *True Glove* along with another *Thing-Fish* cut ("Won Ton On") and two other tracks featuring subversive sexual commentary ("In France," "Be in My Video"), "He's So Gay" is about how people will degrade themselves regardless of their sexuality, with Zappa disagreeing with the notion that "North American society was undergoing a sexual revolution designed to free the individual."[60] The song offended several gay rights groups,[61] as it was released at a time when they were under attack by a life-threatening disease and the ideological reactions to it. The song represents certain ideas Zappa had about the feminization of culture, a theme he had revisited throughout his career, often communicating nuanced observations with such a corrosive tone that can make it difficult for first-time listeners to get past surface-level assumptions about Zappa's music. It is certainly a song that references its own time, ending with the band recalling the title of Culture Club's hit "Do You Really Want to Hurt Me?" which represented Zappa's idea of the type of MTV band whose "proud allegiance to homosexuality" signified that "being gay was a quick way to corporate success."[62] As much as it is an example of Zappa's ability to record a fun satirical pop song, its best qualities become murkier when experienced in relation to the rest of *Thing-Fish* than on its own as a single.

But just how much was rock and pop music being scapegoated because of the AIDS crisis? The answer to that question might give clarity to some of Zappa's complicated ideas about homosexuality in entertainment. In a December 1989 interview with *High Times*, Zappa recalls being invited onto the CNN show *Crossfire* to debate the topic "Does Rock Music Cause AIDS?" On the program, he was paired against Reverend Jeff Ling of the Parents Music Resource Center, who proposed the idea that listening to rock music makes people want to have sex and, since unprotected sex was one way AIDS could be transmitted, it was plausible that listening to rock music increased the risk of AIDS exposure. When Zappa was asked the question if rock music was a path to an AIDS diagnosis, he plainly said "No" and was met with silence.[63]

The main criticism of *Thing-Fish* is that the musical is racist and damaging to Black people—primarily because the titular character is based on Kingfish from the *Amos 'n' Andy Show*, a character whose dialect the National Association for the Advancement of Colored People had declared as racist.[64] *Thing-Fish* also appropriated other tropes, such as the case with the Mammy Nuns, whose clothing and appearance were based on the Aunt Jemima breakfast-brand mascot who in turn perpetuated stereotypes harmful to Black women by insinuating their servitude to white people. For Zappa, these details were meant to be in service to a larger idea, one that challenged white institutions for exploiting Black people. Zappa used these tropes to convey a broader message through a "'theory of excess' that results in 'verbal confrontations'"[65] by addressing "themes that were hotly debated in the early 80s." Continuing his crusade "against the dumbing down of the culture," Zappa viewed Broadway as being the biggest offender of this phenomenon, with *Thing-Fish* representing "a virulent trashing of the condescension and racism of Broadway's association of entertainment with happy all-singing all-dancing black folk."[66] In this view, the presence of the Thing-Fish, even as a caricature based on racist tropes, adds political context to the narrative through its spin on Broadway tradition. This is taken even further when juxtaposed against the characters of Harry and Rhonda, who "stand in for the worst excuses of white people in the early eighties."[67]

In response to the accusations of racism against *Thing-Fish*, Ben Watson, in *Frank Zappa: The Complete Guide to His Music*, cites noted Zappa scholar Ian Stonehouse's analysis of the problematic dialect used in the album, saying that Stonehouse bridged "this fascination with sabotaged lingo to a suppressed tradition of *artgotique*, or mockery of authority." Watson claims that people who accused Zappa of racism were just projecting their "own snobbish value systems." Watson also notes that several of the key contributors on the album, including Ray White and Napoleon Murphy Brock, who portrayed characters, were Black and "highly sensitive to these issues." Based on Zappa's artistic intent, coupled with the direct contributions of several Black men during the creative process, Watson calls *Thing-Fish* an "anti-racist satire at the cutting edge, vilifying the 'political correctness' that expresses the condescension of the rich and powerful."[68]

The album's star also dismissed the accusations that *Thing-Fish* was racist, saying he had been involved with the creative process early on in a way that dictated the tone and direction of the musical. Ike Willis, who portrayed the Thing-Fish, joined Zappa's studio and touring bands in 1978, just a few years prior to the release of his character's Broadway musical namesake. Willis considered the *Thing-Fish* album to be the most challenging project he worked on as a vocalist for Zappa's band, recalling that there were script changes daily, which necessitated his having to rerecord parts to accommodate the new ideas that were coming in. Zappa would give Willis some basic instructions and guidance for the songs, and then allowed him to offer his own interpretation of the materials, with Zappa calling it "the Ike Willis show."

On his character's controversial dialect, Willis said it originated from an inside joke between him and his mother, a former jazz singer, where the two would have conversations mimicking the dialect that the Black poet Paul Laurence Dunbar would use in his poetry. Willis considered the dialect hilarious and would later tell Zappa about it and how Dunbar's poems would inspire the linguistic characteristics of the infamous Kingfish, with Willis thinking of himself as coinventor of the album narrator's language. When asked during a 1996 interview with *T'Mershi Duween*, a now defunct Zappa fanzine, about whether *Thing-Fish* mocked Black speech, Willis said it did not at all and that everyone involved with the album were just trying to be funny. Willis even denied that the potato-headed characters were specifically meant to represent Black people, suggesting instead that the mashed potatoes that mutated the prisoners in the musical was based on how prisoners were actually treated in the United States: "They put things like saltpetre in the food to lower their sex drive and they mix it with the mashed potato so it will keep them calm and non-violent. That's why Thing-Fish became a potato-headed mutant because of all the mystery chemicals in the mashed potato." Though *Thing-Fish* has earned an infamous reputation for its subject matter and lyrical content, Willis expressed that he personally never had an issue with the lyrics except for one moment in which it seemed like he could have a problem with them. After considering what criticisms could come from the government and the general public, Willis decided that he "didn't really care as we had a statement to make."

When asked about what the message of *Thing-Fish* was, Willis said, "Basically it has several messages. It was part of a government thing that we'd found out about. AIDS suddenly appeared out of nowhere back around 1983 and there were rumours that the government had something to do with it. Secondly, how they tried to manipulate people and put them in prison—that's another message. And the main message is 'Don't trust everything the government says because they're not always right.' Very seldom are they always right."[69]

The fact that Willis was integral to the development of *Thing-Fish,* and that other Black musicians contributed to it, supporting the album's messaging, is something that should be considered when evaluating the album's merits and legacy. However, it is important to also not treat them as token monoliths when criticisms surface over Zappa's work, especially with this album. Though they were young Black men recording that album, with all the life experience that came with that identity during that time in American history, they do not speak on behalf of all Black people. I know they were involved in other controversial works throughout Zappa's career, but *Thing-Fish* stands out from the rest because of the specificity of its complicated legacy. Regardless of their input, it is Zappa's name on the cover. As much as they collaborated, he was the one in charge. This dynamic brings to mind the conversation President Barack Obama had with Bruce Springsteen on their podcast, *Renegades: Born in the USA,* with Obama commenting on the interracial dynamic between Springsteen and his bandmate Clarence Clemons, who was a defining presence in the E Street Band. "Here's an older Black man who's been hustling out there for a long time," Obama says, "and he's gotta hook up with a young white guy . . . who is less experienced than him. Now, it works out beautifully for the both of you. But there's also complications, right? To that whole relationship." With those comments, Springsteen replies by saying, "He had to give more than I had to give. . . . Clarence was the only Black man in the room a lot of the time. He had to swim in white culture for most of his work life, you know?"[70] That relationship does not exactly mirror the dynamic between Zappa and Willis, or between Zappa and any of the other Black men on the album, but with Zappa being the one leading a project that contains such a deeply complicated narrative about race, it does force one to confront the tough questions surrounding this album.

Zappa was attempting to draw parallels between the AIDS crisis and the Tuskegee study, making the argument that the United States continues to leverage its power to harm marginalized people. I do not think many people would disagree with that, but the question regarding the album becomes whether this white musician is the right voice when the commentary is rooted in Black tragedy. Even the tone in which the narrative was presented, recalling racist tropes from America's past, begs the question of just how effective *Thing-Fish* is as a work of art with a compelling commentary. Lowe, in his book on Zappa, makes the case that one of the signs of "African American progress had been the use by African Americans of racist language for their own political purposes."[71] While some Black artists have reclaimed the most tragic elements of their history, like Spike Lee did with his 2000 film *Bamboozled*, in which Black actors donned blackface for a modern minstrel show, it is a more complicated matter when white artists attempt the same for a history that is not their own. *Thing-Fish* was Zappa's album, so he owns the messaging and, therefore, bears the brunt of the responsibility regarding its criticism.

When I was in the earliest stages of writing this book, I posted in social media groups and fan forums, asking if there were any critiques of Zappa written by women and people of color. While some of the responses were helpful and pointed me to resources that included quotes and interviews from people who knew and worked with him, including women and Black people, several of the responses came off as abrasive, questioning my motives. All I wanted was to read some non-male and non-white perspectives about Zappa to help me with my research, especially over his more culturally complicated work. *Thing-Fish* is certainly one of those complicated works—with criticisms that would make me think, *OK, I get that.* It is an album with an admirable intent, one in which Zappa speaks up against systems of power and the harmful effects they have on the most vulnerable populations, but with a creative execution that has yet to be satisfactorily dealt with by writers on Zappa's music. While some of its players were people of color, Zappa listeners are largely not, and that presents a monumental gap in appreciating and assessing his work as an artist. An album with such a deep, rich message deserves a reevaluation of its merits. However, I firmly believe, because of its more incendiary qualities, such a reevaluation needs to come from someone who is not a white man. After all, it is an album that has had a complicated legacy for forty years, and it has yet to see a reappraisal worthy enough to reverse that, despite the efforts of a whole lot of white guys writing about it, including myself. It may or may not very well be an album of great musical quality with commentary ahead of its time, but for now it occupies a space in Zappa's back catalog as a musical oddity, as seemingly unappealing as the lead character who graces its cover: the Thing-Fish as both himself and a recurring symbol of America's future repeating the past. For Zappa, America was a place where the torture never stopped.

PORN WARS

In 1984, the presidential election results would show that, not only did most Americans approve of the conservative influence of the Ronald Reagan administration, but that it was more popular than ever. By platforming the growing evangelical movement during his first term in office, Reagan was able to secure a second in what would become the biggest landslide victory in modern American history since Franklin D. Roosevelt's first reelection in 1936.[1] Winning nearly 98 percent of the electoral votes against his opponent, Walter Mondale, and earning a 10.5 million vote increase in the popular count as compared to his first election, Reagan secured a voting bloc that would not only promise to slow the growth of liberalism that had been taking root since the New Frontier vision of John F. Kennedy through the progressive compassion of the Jimmy Carter administration, but seek to stamp it out completely. With a stranglehold on the executive branch, as well as maintaining a majority in the Senate while picking up seats in the House of Representatives, conservatives were now poised to use their near total power in federal government to shift the battle for the soul of America to the front line of the culture war.

That year, the National Parent Teacher Association (PTA) would prepare formal proposals for record companies to enact self-policed, internal protocols that would grade the music they distributed. The proposals requested that labels be placed on the covers of albums, displaying a rating that would inform consumers of the content of the music if its themes and lyrics were violent, profane, or vulgar.[2] Advocates for these PTA groups believed that unfettered access to music with this type of content would invariably traumatize children by psychologically and emotionally damaging them, stunting the development of their young minds in ways that could have lifelong consequences or drive them to self-harm. By implementing a rating system, in their view, children could be protected from ideas that would otherwise make them grow up to be maladjusted adults.

It was a modern crusade that continued the practice of limiting artistic expression, one many decades in the making, from when police frequently raided stores in the 1940s and 1950s to destroy "race records" they found obscene to the weaponization of the Federal Communications Commission over a 1978 Supreme Court ruling giving it the authority to regulate indecency because of what George Carlin identified as the "seven dirty words,"[3] the legendary comedian's bit from 1972 about words you can never say on television. One of the groups to carry on this tradition would be the Parents Music Resource Center (PMRC), a coalition of mostly activist women known for their powerful and affluent connections in Washington politics. Derogatorily dubbed the "Washington Wives," they could hold sway over the national dialogue regarding obscenity in rock music, or "porn rock," by relying on high-powered spouses for political support.

As the parents' rights movement grew in its quest to regulate music labels by increasing public pressure, so did a movement that opposed their proposal. Many opponents of the PMRC throughout the music industry, and elsewhere, vocalized their opposition with claims that the PMRC's proposal for a rating system was in fact a coded ultimatum designed to suppress free expression. As this discourse over the role and limitations of the government in matters concerning censorship became a barrage of media appearances on news debate and talk programs by advocates on both sides, the American public's understanding of the issue would be obfuscated. As record companies were beginning to fold under the weight of the pressure from the PMRC by agreeing to put warning labels on their albums, the U.S. Senate sought to hold a hearing to publicly address the growing national concern.

On September 19, 1985, before the Senate Commerce, Science and Transportation Committee, testimony was conducted and broadcast to explore "the subject of the content of certain sound recordings and suggestions that recording packages be labeled to provide a warning to prospective purchasers of sexually explicit or other potentially offensive content."[4] Supporters of the proposals to implement warning labels made their case by showing several album covers and music videos they had identified as being the most harmful to children. As with the media blitz that had propelled their cause into being one of the most discussed public health issues of the Reagan era, the hearings before members of the Senate became another platform in which the PMRC's advocates would seek to legitimize their appeal to the public watching at home.

However, on the opposing side were members of the music industry that believed their art was being unfairly stigmatized in a way that would ultimately restrict the rights of all citizens. Among those who testified on the inherent danger to civil liberties that a rating system for music would present, Zappa was deeply disturbed by what the PMRC represented on several levels. Not only did they, in Zappa's view, embody another faction of the Reagan administration's emboldening of evangelicals to dictate the rights of other Americans, but he saw the PMRC as a lobbying group working to influence legislation that penalized American taxpayers with a private tax that had their culturally conservative ideology baked in. No stranger to the microphone, Zappa stepped out of the studio and in front of U.S. senators to deliver one of the biggest hits of his career—not a song, but a speech that cemented his legacy as an advocate for free expression.

As the hearings were a major news story and involved several high-profile representatives of the music industry, including Zappa, there was an increased potential that international news media and entertainment outlets would cover the testimony. Before formally delivering his statement to the Senate committee, Zappa begins by reading the First Amendment of the U.S. Constitution, which in addition to protecting free speech also prevented Congress from making laws respecting religious establishments or prohibiting its free exercise, so as to provide context to members of the foreign press regarding his concerns and objections over the PMRC's actions and goals. Zappa then states that he only represents himself and is not speaking on behalf of any group or organization. With that preamble, Zappa sets the tone for a speech that would become one of the most significant cultural touchstones of his career.

Opening his statement, Zappa declares the PMRC's proposal to be ludicrously absurd. He states it provides no measurable positive impact on a child's well-being, increases the risk in which a citizen's civil liberties could be violated, and suggests an inevitable outcome where courts will be too backlogged with cases to deal with the granular details of the proposal's implementation. Such circumstances do not align with his understanding of the legal interpretation that First Amendment issues are decided with a preference for the least constraining option; in contrast, the PMRC's position is "the equivalent of treating dandruff by decapitation."[5] Zappa criticizes the members of the PMRC, specifically naming Susan Baker and Tipper Gore, for demanding that composers and performers alter their art in order to appeal to the "Washington Wives'" cultural tastes. While they are free to purchase whatever forms of music they want as consumers, Zappa says they are not entitled to more than what is on that particular album, and their concerns over a select few artists will have an unfair and unconstitutional impact on the rest of the music industry.

Zappa's comment that it was only a few artists whose music earned the PMRC's ire and contempt is an important one. Not that these artists deserved to be censored or have their music subjected to restrictive regulations, but rather the PMRC cherry-picked examples to reflect their biases. These particular artists would become cultural boogeymen to instill fear in the American public and encourage the support of authoritarian principles and ideas that would ultimately have a freezing effect on the creative process of artists who were not among the ones being targeted. Dubbed the "Filthy Fifteen," these were a select group of songs specifically identified by the PMRC to rationalize their rating system. The fifteen were:

- "Darling Nikki" by Prince
- "Sugar Walls" by Sheena Easton
- "Eat Me Alive" by Judas Priest
- "Strap On 'Robbie Baby'" by Vanity
- "Bastard" by Mötley Crüe
- "Let Me Put My Love into You" by AC/DC
- "We're Not Gonna Take It" by Twisted Sister
- "Dress You Up" by Madonna
- "Animal (Fuck Like a Beast)" by WASP
- "High 'n' Dry" by Def Leppard
- "Into the Coven" by Mercyful Fate

- "Trashed" by Black Sabbath
- "In My House" by Mary Jane Girls
- "Possessed" by Venom
- "She Bop" by Cyndi Lauper[6]

This playlist, compiled by the PMRC, conveyed their view of the worst examples of pure filth excreted by the music industry, rationalizing why music should be assessed by a rating system similar to the way the Motion Picture Association of America (MPAA) rated movies. Ratings proposed for the music content were: "X" for sexually explicit lyrics, "O" for occult references, "D/A" for lyrics about drugs and alcohol, and "V" for violence.[7] There are a few interesting things about the PMRC's list of the "Filthy Fifteen." The first speaks to the specific artists mentioned. Some, like Cyndi Lauper and Madonna, were contemporary artists wildly popular during the time of the Senate hearing. The songs by AC/DC and Def Leppard were already a few years old and were no longer featured in regular rotation on commercial radio. Also, some of the artists, like WASP, did not release music that was ever heard on commercial radio nor was easily accessible for purchase. With artistic material like that, there was already a social contract between the consumer and the artist. By the PMRC including WASP in the mainstream conversation, they then became subject to the scrutiny of an audience their music was never intended to be marketed to.

The other interesting thing about the list concerns the story of how one of the songs directly inspired Tipper Gore to form the PMRC. "Darling Nikki," from Prince's 1984 soundtrack to the film *Purple Rain*, but not released as a single, sparked Gore's crusade against the music industry after she listened to the song with her eleven-year-old daughter. Gore considered the song's references to masturbation to be incredibly offensive and damaging to her child. Writing in her 1987 book, *Raising PG Kids in an X-Rated Society*, Gore said of the song: "The vulgar lyrics embarrassed both of us. At first, I was stunned—then I got mad! Millions of Americans were buying *Purple Rain* with no idea what to expect. Thousands of parents were giving the album to their children—many even younger than my daughter."[8] Zappa, in his 1989 autobiography, calls Gore out for feigning ignorance and shock in her reaction to *Purple Rain* by pointing out that the film was rated R by the MPAA and had already by then generated a lot of controversy in the media for its sexual content.[9] Gore's experience, along with a similar one by Reagan treasury secretary James Baker III's wife Susan Baker over her seven-year-old daughter singing the lyrics to Madonna's classic hit "Like a Virgin," would lead to the formal creation of the PMRC in 1985.[10] Even though these were isolated experiences, and based on conjecture, they would hold outweighed influence in the public discourse in ways that would damage other artists.

At this point in his statement, Zappa puts the blame for the PMRC's proposal on the major record labels. He specifically criticizes them over their support of H.R. 2911, also known as the Home Audio Recording Act, which proposed a private tax, generally referred to as the "blank tape tax," which would be "levied by an industry on consumers for the benefit of a select group within that industry."[11] Zappa conveys his belief that the proposal put forth by the PMRC represents a consumer issue, referencing bill 2911 within the House of Representatives which, with the support of the Recording Industry Association of America (RIAA), proposed "the imposition of a 10–25% surtax on the sale of all tape recorders and a tax on blank tape of a penny-per-minute."[12] This was intended to be a measure to offset the loss of revenue resulting from music consumers using blank cassette tapes to record songs from the radio as opposed to buying the album directly from a music retailer. As both an artist and the owner of a record label, Zappa had a nuanced outlook on the benefits and losses of home recording: "The trick involved is that they say it's needed legislation in order to compensate copyright owners for the revenue lost when a person tapes a record at home. . . . If a person is taping a record at home in order to cheat someone from earning their living of making music, I don't approve: but, if a person is taping a record at home in self defense because he can't buy a good quality cassette manufactured by the record company. . . . That's why a lot of people do it at home. . . . That doesn't bother me as an artist or a record company owner."[13] Zappa's argument, being that he was a copyright owner himself, requires an insider level of industry knowledge in order to discern the refined points of his argument over copyright law, specifically the royalty split between performance copyright and registered copyright, the basis for much of his concern over the proposal. He recognized that such a surcharge would only benefit the record company as opposed to the retailer, songwriter, or artist. The structure of the bill, in which Zappa recognized the inherent copyright complications, then becomes fundamentally flawed as he draws connections between the PMRC and Congress, including specifically naming in his testimony Senator Strom Thurmond's relationship with the PMRC through his wife Nancy Janice Moore's affiliation with the organization.

This part of Zappa's statement illustrates the probability of a conflict of interest within the PMRC, specifically that several members were either married to senators or to men who otherwise had close ties to Congress. These included Susan Baker, wife of James Baker III, who served as both treasury secretary and chief of staff to President Reagan; Tipper Gore, wife of then senator from Tennessee, Al Gore; Pam Howar, wife of a prominent realty contractor in Washington, DC; and Sally Nevius, wife of Washington City Council chairman John Nevius.[14] On these spousal relationships, Zappa said in an interview with *Gallery* that an organization consisting of the wives of government officials would have the potential to leverage their fury toward the recording industry through committees that included their husbands. This would then perpetuate the biased Christian notion that anything dealing with sexuality could be denigrated as sinful, making it impossible for such an organization to be trusted with assigning ratings given the amount of recorded material released each year, far more than could be handled in an objective way. Zappa designated this cultural quagmire as "the Beige Zone," where the country's music culture would exist "somewhere between the Salem witchcraft trials and the McCarthy era."[15]

Zappa in his statement then relays that he was told by the PMRC's receptionist that the organization is only made up of founders and has no members, a distinction that Zappa found hard to believe due to the organization's fundraising efforts and tax exemption. With little to no transparency regarding the organizational structure and its membership, Zappa calls out the PMRC for generating a confusing culture-war issue within the public discourse through drawing inaccurate connections between different artistic media within the music industry, including song lyrics, music labels, and album covers, as well as the music presented via broadcast and in concert. Doubtful whether the

PMRC's concerns were rooted in constructive dialogue surrounding mental health, public safety, or morality issues, Zappa makes the claim that the organization's actions are meant to coalesce support for the bill containing the blank tape tax, with the public largely ill-informed about the legislation, which would unduly restrict fair business practices due to the distraction over the PMRC's crusade on pornography in rock music. In essence, Zappa is saying that senatorial spouses of those affiliated with the PMRC cannot be trusted to vote on music-business tax legislation due to a conflict of interest, especially if such tax legislation comes at the expense of the First Amendment's guarantee of freedom of speech.

To understand the finer points of Zappa's testimony over the PMRC legitimizing their culture-war issue through government legislation, consider the organization's history, using its influence in the media as a lobbying strategy. Early meetings between Gore, Baker, as well as others, including Kandie Stroud, a journalist and spokesperson for the PMRC, were focused on conversations about the music their children were listening to and their reactions to it. In order to bolster their impact, they each circulated their Christmas-card lists to find influential contacts sympathetic to their cause. From there, they began to send out press releases outlining their concerns as parents and consumers. They would even go as far as to engage with the music industry directly, sending out a letter to over fifty record labels with the stated purpose of asking them to "either cease the production of music with violent and sexually charged lyrics or develop a motion picture–style ratings system for albums."[16] As Sis Levin, the executive director of the PMRC, said, what was primarily driving the organization's concern was "that the music is a form of violence in our children."[17]

The PMRC's initial goal, according to Baker, was to raise awareness over the content of the music, and they felt a rating system similar to that of the film industry would contribute to that awareness. After several months of engagement with the RIAA and its president, Stan Gortikov, the PMRC was assured a solution would be put into place. After a year, the PMRC was unsatisfied with the RIAA's results, which involved small, barely legible warnings. However, by this time, the PMRC had garnered a lot of support through coverage in the media, using appearances on talk news and daytime television programs to influence the public discourse on popular music. This media saturation elevated the organization's profile and allowed it to take its message on the road, meeting Parent Teacher Associations and other parents' rights groups to warn about the inappropriate music harming their children by exposing them to sexual and violent content.[18]

In her essay, "Parental Advisory: Tipper Gore and the PMRC," published in the journal *Women Leading Change: Case Studies on Women, Gender, and Feminism,* Avery Anderson says the PMRC had to effectively create a robust media strategy in order to center the conversation on "porn rock" in a way that would gain traction. By securing a place on panels, both in conferences and on television, the PMRC could wield cultural power and influence against executives in the music industry in order to continue "to distribute abundant anti-obscenity literature, attracting factional support and more media attention."[19]

This lobbying in the media produced a cultural behemoth that concerned the music industry. In an article for the *Village Voice* in 1985, Dave Marsh printed a memo written by Gortikov on June 7 that, in response to the PMRC's demands, stated the RIAA's position that "Non-response by companies to this emerging problem can have serious negative backlash effects." Initial warning labels the PMRC felt to be inadequate were also rejected by factions within the music industry, including the National Association of Record Merchandisers. Insiders throughout the industry believed the RIAA "originally endorsed a plan calling for warning labels on potentially offensive albums, because they wanted to show Congress they're accommodating enough to deserve the financial break that home-taping legislation . . . would give them."[20] Danny Goldberg, founder of the Musical Majority, the anti-censorship group that countered the PMRC's demands to place warning labels on albums, said: "Our opinion is that the pressure groups, led by the wives of the senators and the secretary of the Treasury, have tried to use the impending home-taping legislation to intimidate the record companies into instituting an '80s-style blacklisting that they call record rating. . . . There's no question that the message was sent to the RIAA, by whatever means, that failure to compromise with the PMRC would affect the views of certain senators on the home-taping bill."[21]

Gortikov dismissed notions that there was a connection between music ratings and the home-taping legislation. However, his memo suggested otherwise, saying, "Our legislative and national/international antipiracy enforcement projects and priorities can be diluted or jeopardized." In response, Gortikov said in the *Washington Post*, "Certainly, it's important to us to have Washington, both legislators and administrators, look favorably on our industry."[22]

Zappa in his testimony before the Senate committee then pointed out the connection between the tax and the PMRC's mission, using it as a means of commenting on the United States' substandard education system and the lack of funding for music and arts education in public schools. He notes that children have an instinctive appreciation for music, and he calls upon parents to be the ones responsible for what music their children have access to. He challenges the PMRC by saying that, if parents have any objections to what is playing on popular radio, then they should support music-appreciation programs in schools which not only expand the musical options for children but are also much less expensive than sports programs. He asks the Senate committee whether the PMRC's desire for a government-sanctioned sanitization of music is a reflection of the organization's own cultural preferences or if their lobbying advocacy represents another example of the Reagan administration placing a low priority on arts education, answering himself that neither is the case and that the whole discourse on ratings in music is a distraction to pass an arbitrary tax in lieu of education reforms. As Zappa points out, the only way the PMRC could have been successful at this was by focusing on salacious content.

It is worth noting that several of the songs on the PMRC's "Filthy Fifteen" list never played on commercial radio and were fairly obscure to most of the general public. According to Cerphe Colwell, a radio personality in Washington, DC, who testified at the hearing, "Ironically, most of the heavy metal songs that they listed at the time were virtually unknown to the public. Heavy metal as a music format hadn't really blossomed. I truly believe to this day that one of the reasons that metal took off so much in the 1980s as a successful format is that the PMRC brought attention to what they thought was unacceptable, and of course that made it very much in the spotlight."[23]

Even the artists who were targeted by the PMRC were confused about why their songs were under the microscope. Cronos, the singer for Venom, thought a prank was being pulled on him when he was told about the PMRC during a recording session. Cronos was in disbelief at the ignorance of the PMRC's culture war, telling *Newsweek* that most people in rock music have children and did not need the lobbying group to help them protect their children from harm. Joanne McDuffie, singer for the Mary Jane Girls, felt the PMRC had unfairly misrepresented her work, saying that, while their song was about sex, it was composed tastefully and would not motivate children to learn more about sex. On the immediate impact of the PMRC, McDuffie said, "I think it was a blacklist. Or a modern-day witch hunt. Or an attempt at censorship for certain artists and certain songs. When I look at what happened, it didn't stop the airplay. . . . What it did stop was our consideration for the awards that I think any other artist of our stature or our popularity would have gotten."[24]

Dee Snider, lead singer of the band Twisted Sister, which had been targeted by the PMRC, also testified in front of the Senate committee, saying he did not support the RIAA's decision to place warning labels on albums, believing that his music had been unfairly misrepresented by the public discourse generated by the PMRC. Twisted Sister's 1984 hit, "We're Not Gonna Take It," which was included on the "Filthy Fifteen" list, was accused by the PMRC of promoting violence while another song of theirs, "Under the Blade," which was about the fear one feels before surgery, was accused of promoting sadomasochism, bondage, and rape. Snider told the senators that if Tipper Gore were so intent on looking for bondage, then she would indeed find it, much in the same way that someone looking for references to surgeries would find those as well, implying that Gore's singling out his music was an act of confirmation bias. Snider, much in the same way that Zappa felt about music consumerism being a parent's responsibility, said in his testimony that only his wife and he were responsible for their children and that no one else had the authority to make judgments on how they raised them.[25] Snider was concerned that the PMRC's proposal for a warning label on albums was not about informing parents in order to make them more knowledgeable consumers, but rather that they would be used to segregate art by keeping certain works inaccessible to the public.[26]

This was the basis upon which many artists believed their music would be censored. With the implementation of a warning label on albums, whether resulting from government legislation or self-imposed industry standards, the fear was that music retailers would refuse to carry albums with such labels, which would have a direct impact on sales and royalties for everyone involved in the production of the album, from the producer to the composer to the songwriter. Zappa, in an interview with *Relix*, said retailers like Sears and JCPenney told the RIAA that they would not buy or rack any albums with warning labels on them. Even music retailers who agreed to rack albums with the labels faced undue pressure, such as Camelot Records, threatened by its landlord, Shopping Mall Owners Associations, that the stores would lose their lease if they carried albums with warning labels. Zappa then tells *Relix* that the amount the record industry was expected to lose as a result of this, somewhere between $200 million and $250 million per year, was roughly the amount of money the blank tape tax bill was expected to generate.[27]

Zappa shared the same concerns as many others in the music industry, believing that the morality standards the PMRC advocated for reflected a predominantly white Christian ideology that would result in a freezing effect on artists and their work that did not share the same religious and political values. In his Senate testimony, Zappa said the ratings standards the PMRC proposed, whether voluntarily enforced by the RIAA or through government legislation, would create a slippery slope where special interest groups, largely Christian in nature, could increasingly create federally supported social and cultural programs that policed standards for others. He rhetorically asked the Senate committee what would happen if future iterations of the PMRC demanded labeling for artistic material created by Jews, an obvious dig at the value systems of the PMRC with Zappa equating their tactics to those of the Third Reich.

Zappa then makes a compelling point about the relationship between the PMRC's proposal and how the public responded to it. He had already said that the only way the PMRC could have been successful was by framing the cultural dialogue around the controversial topics of sex and violence. Zappa did not believe the PMRC's assertions that a ratings system for the music industry would have the same effect as it did for the film industry, largely because of how differently the public responds to both mediums. He asserts an actor's reputation and public profile would not be negatively impacted by a film's rating, while a rating on an album then becomes a scarlet letter upon which the public would project their prejudices and biases onto the artist. Since an artist is largely responsible for the material on the album, Zappa believed that any musicians standing up for their art would be condemned in the court of public opinion.

For Zappa, the facts surrounding the public discourse on rock lyrics were presented in ways that were one-sided and inaccurate, potentially creating a circumstance in which legislation could irreversibly damage the First Amendment right of free speech, as well as the Fourteenth Amendment's due process clause. Gail Zappa, Frank's wife, said in an oral history for *Newsweek* on the thirtieth anniversary of the hearings that Frank was upset about the hearings because he felt they would be "a waste of resources and expenses to get involved in censorship of people's artwork, apart from everything else. He was pissed."[28] Zappa remained consistent, explaining exactly how the PMRC would create a confusing and cumbersome approach to moderating music content that would have an adverse effect on creative and artistic expression. During an interview on ABC's *Nightline*, Zappa told Ted Koppel:

> [The PMRC's] proposals are really dumb if you take away the aroma and look at the mechanics of what they are, and they're also very dangerous in terms of what they can lead to for violating your right to free speech, your right to assemble, because they want to apply the same ratings to live concerts, and the right to due process for people—for example, if you're a songwriter and you have a song included on an album that gets an X, and through no fault of your own the album is banned from stores, or the sales of it are impinged on in some way, you don't have a chance.[29]

While it was easy for parents' rights groups and their supporters to dismiss Zappa's and Snider's criticisms of the PMRC because they represented the type of rock music that was being labeled as damaging to America's youth, it was harder to do the same to the other artist whose testimony before the Senate committee would have a significant impact, folk-rock icon John Denver. Many were surprised when Denver revealed in his testimony that not only did he consider the PMRC's proposal for warning labels as being censorship, but that he was a strong anti-censorship advocate. Like both Zappa and Snider, Denver personally understood the ways in which people could misinterpret music because his song "Rocky Mountain High" was incorrectly believed to be about drug use as opposed to the way one feels when communing with nature. He discussed the song being banned by some radio stations to share his experience with censorship.

Much like Zappa's warning that the PMRC's proposals could snowball into other situations in which Christians target social and cultural ideals they do not approve of, Denver implied similarities between the PMRC's motives with those of the Third Reich, saying, "the suppression of the people of a society begins, in my mind, with the censorship of the written or spoken word. It was so in Nazi Germany. It is so in many places today where those in power are afraid of the consequences of an informed and educated people." Since Denver had an image and made music that was aesthetically different from the artists the proposals would have an outsized negative effect on, many had assumed that Denver would back the PMRC—even Zappa and Snider were unsure of which side Denver was on. Recalling Denver's testimony in an oral history for *Newsweek*, Snider described it as scathing and how shocked many at the hearings were because they had believed he would have supported the proposals because of his all-American image. Snider said that, when Denver made the connection to the Nazi book burnings, the members of the committee were "running for the hills."[30]

The 1980s were a turbulent decade for artistic expression. Religious ideology, emboldened by its growing influence within government, was weaponized to enforce censorship within the culture. According to Judith Krug, director of the Office for Intellectual Freedom at the American Library Association, her office received more than one thousand incident reports claiming censorship in 1982, a significant jump from the annual average of three hundred at the beginning of the decade. Most incidents stemmed from debates over banned books in schools and libraries, but there was also an upward trend of incidents regarding the broadcasting and visual arts, such as the Federal Communications Commission fining radio and television stations "found to be 'patently offensive' to the listening or viewing public." Krug attributed this increase in the number of reports to "a confluence of moralistic social ferment driven by values dictated by fundamentalist Christianity and a not-unrelated conservative political agenda that demands that government get off of the backs of the citizenry but at the same time require conformity with stricter and more subjective moral standards." This trend "parallels a combination of political and social developments that have . . . resulted in an ironic reality: The conservative tide that washed Reagan into the presidency precipitated a still-growing trend toward government and societal pressure on freedom of speech and expression."[31]

Early in Reagan's presidency, his administration proved it was no friend to the liberal arts. According to Livingston Biddle, former chair of the National Endowment for the Arts, in his book, *Our Government and the Arts: A Perspective from the Inside*, Reagan's team had a plan to abolish the endowment when they entered the White House in 1981. They had put together a task force specifically focused on investigating the arts before it was dissolved when they "discovered 'the needs involved and the benefits of past assistance,'" and that federal support was still needed. Biddle became aware of the task force and its plan after piecing together information from congressional contacts over a three-year period. The rumors circulating around Biddle proved to be true after meeting with Barnabas McHenry, who was soon to be appointed as the task force's vice chairman, and he confirmed that "some people in the coming administration wanted the endowment to 'disappear.'" While the endowment was not completely abolished, the administration was successful in cutting its budget by half.[32]

Zappa understood that the Venn diagram of faith and politics between the PMRC and the rest of the initiatives organized by the Moral Majority–influenced Reagan administration was a complete circle. In a 1986 panel debate on CNN's *Crossfire*, Zappa debated the conservative *Washington Times* columnist John Lofton about the outsized power religious ideology has on the censorship of free speech. In that debate, in response to Lofton's accusation that American families are under direct assault from obscene rock lyrics, Zappa declared that the Reagan administration was stewarding the United States toward becoming a fascist theocracy, which he felt was a bigger threat to the nation than the administration's purported concerns over communism. When asked by cohost Tom Braden to deliver an example supporting his claim, Zappa responds by saying that, when a far-right conservative ideology adopts its values based on a particular religion in order to create legislation, it is designed to benefit the believers of that religion. As Lofton interrupts

Zappa's response, calling him an anarchist and insisting that moral values are foundational to government, Zappa quickly shoots back that such a system of morals should be based on acceptable social behavior as opposed to religious ideology.[33]

Zappa would continue to speak out on how minority extremist religious groups, with institutional cultural and political support, perpetuated baseless fears to directly impact the public's perception of art. In a 1988 interview for *East Coast Rocker,* referencing the Satanic Panic controversy in which religious groups spread misinformation about devil-worshipping cults harming children through music, Zappa said, "The fact of the matter is that the rhetoric of the PMRC is the rhetoric of the fundamentalist right. They can deny it until they're blue in the face, but all this stuff about the devil and backwards masking and all of the rest of this hocus-pocus is right out of Jimmy Swaggart. The PMRC *is* like Jimmy Swaggart, the PMRC *is* like Jim and Tammy Bakker, and we've seen what those people have turned out to be."[34]

Zappa would even satirize the whole cultural debate over backward masking by releasing his own backward-masked music. On his 1984 album *Them or Us,* Zappa took earlier records and reversed the vocals, resulting in the album's track "Ya Hozna." In a September 1984 interview with BBC Radio, Zappa said of the album and its concept, "Now, the name of this album is *Them or Us,* and in America, as far as I'm concerned, it means US, the Pagans, versus THEM, those hideous Christians. And if they want to have a law in Congress that says you can't put anything backwards on a record, well, then how about a record that's got it all backwards?"[35]

Since the heyday of the PMRC in the mid-1980s, we have seen how the discourse on censorship has evolved and how it was shaped by conservative religious and political ideology. In 1990, a city council ordinance in Rhode Island was deemed unconstitutional for executing prior restraint when censoring a 2 Live Crew concert, the same year three members of the group were arrested following a concert in Florida after a local retailer was arrested for selling an undercover police officer their album *As Nasty as They Wanna Be*, with the group ruled as not obscene in 1992 when the "appeals court overturns the obscenity ruling, and the case ends when the US Supreme Court denies further appeals." Those incidents occurred within a year in which the legislatures in twenty-one states introduced bills preventing the sale of albums with warning labels to minors, none of which passed.[36]

Following the September 11, 2001, attacks, the Clear Channel radio network issued an internal memo to all of its stations featuring a list of 160 songs not to play, which were believed would cause offense to listeners still recovering from a collective national trauma. While some songs on the list were labeled as "lyrically questionable" for having language that would trigger post-traumatic stress, others were there for political reasons. The entirety of Rage Against the Machine's catalog was "deemed unacceptable, apparently because the band had been critical of America and capitalism," while John Lennon's iconic peace song "Imagine" was also banned from airplay "because envisioning a world where we all got along was at odds with the public demand for bloody justice."[37] The Dixie Chicks (now the Chicks) would experience the fervor of the public's lust for revenge in the wake of the United States' 2003 invasion of Iraq after the band was blacklisted from radio over Natalie Maines's comment that she was ashamed President George W. Bush was also from Texas.[38]

Throughout their advocacy efforts, the PMRC consistently denied that they were a lobbying group or that they were there to police people's political views or speech. During a 1985 interview with the *Metro Times* just eight days before the Senate hearings, Susan Baker, when asked if the PMRC's next steps were to propose standards on political expression, Baker said, "That's OK. In this country we are free to have differing opinions. I happen to have differing ones than the ones in the music industry and as a citizen I have a right to express that. We are asking the industry to give us consumer information. Political ideas are different."[39]

Kandie Stroud, a guest on *Nightline* alongside Zappa several weeks after the hearings, reiterated Baker's point that the PMRC was not interested in censoring anyone's right to free speech. However, in this discussion, she makes comments on the subtext of the PMRC's mission that are worthy of noting. She admits that any rating system is inherently flawed, and its enforcement only works if parents are engaged in what content their children are exposed to, and if parents allow their children to consume any media they want, then they are not upholding their duties as parents. Stroud uses this logic to declare that a child's education is the sole responsibility of the parents as opposed to rock stars, who she believes have subpar moral standards that will damage and corrupt young minds. Zappa retorts that he does not speak on behalf of any group or organization within the music industry, but rather as a parent who has concerns that his children's speech is being involuntarily restricted. As a father who happens to be a musician, Zappa understands the implicit power the PMRC and their advocates have on making artists capitulate to their will through the stigmatizing power of a warning label.[40]

The majority of the artists targeted by the PMRC performed rock music, which was influenced by rhythm and blues and other genres with roots in Black expression. While most of the artists caught in the crosshairs of the PMRC were white and represented an industry that disproportionately favored white artists, the intended effect of the proposals would reverberate across all genres that threatened white Christian evangelical sensibilities, which would lead to outsized impact on Black artists. In 1985, when the Senate hearing was held, rap music was in the early stages of becoming a worldwide cultural phenomenon, striving to find a secure place in the musical landscape where ownership had consolidated as a result of the Reagan administration's deregulation, which "allowed for an increasingly smaller number of people to impact what forms of Black cultural production become popular and then re-disseminated back to Black audiences here and around the world."[41]

While rap music would be unfairly accused of corrupting America's youth not long after the Senate hearing, country music was suspiciously absent from any of the PMRC materials and ensuing cultural discourse. Country music, a genre that to this day has systems in place to limit the popularity of Black expression while reinforcing dominantly white Christian views, contained all the same types of lyrical content as rock music but inspired none of the contempt the PMRC leveraged against other forms of artistic expression in their crusade against the culturally subversive and depraved forces destroying the minds of American children. As one anonymous vice president of a West Coast–based record label told the *Los Angeles Times* in 1986, "You have to wonder if its just a coincidence why the PMRC, which has a key leader whose husband is a

Senator from Tennessee, hasn't touched any Nashville country records. If they want to find explicit lyrics, they should try country music. They'd find lots of records to keep 'em busy."[42]

Zappa also noted this discrepancy. In a September 1985 interview with the *Metro Times*, he cites the legal definition of pornography as "material designed to arouse prurient interest," commenting that whatever qualifies as prurient is determined by members of the community through agreed-upon social and cultural guidelines. "I don't think there has ever been nor will there ever be any lyric or piece of music that qualifies under the law as porn rock or porn country or porn classical or porn anything else. It's not designed to arouse prurient interest," said Zappa. He adds that the PMRC had not requested any labeling on country albums despite the genre's many allusions to subjects the PMRC found exceptionally deviant in rock, including references to sex, substance abuse, violence, and Satan. Echoing the sentiment of the anonymous record label executive, Zappa furthers his claim that the PMRC is a lobbying group because country music plays a major role in Tennessee's economy, where these albums can be proudly displayed in stores while rock albums are kept in protective packaging behind the counter.[43] Relying on his experience in the music industry, Zappa proposes the practical question of how many rock musicians have actually been imprisoned for their lifestyles, while noting his personal interactions with country-and-western musicians who have bragged about building a career on an outlaw identity stemming from serving time in prison. "Meanwhile, the country and western covers have American flags and pictures of nice things on them," said Zappa, "but inside is the same kind of stuff these people are complaining about. So what's going on here?"[44]

In the essay "Parental Advisory," Avery Anderson says "the PMRC's gendered criticism of female musicians reflected the dominant cultural attitude of the time," because men's tastes had been historically indulged, which led to female musicians being undervalued. In order to compete in an overwhelmingly male-dominated field, these women were "forced to contend with reactionary discrimination" because of the framework of cultural and social traditions built into the foundation of Western society. Anderson notes that the arrival of MTV as a cultural medium reinvigorated "patterns of suppression and dominance" where musicians who were white men were prioritized, leaving women to be ridiculed and underappreciated for their contributions to the art form. Anderson said women could not "simply create music because they are forced to contend with the constricting and ingrained sexism of the industry itself."[45]

Anderson also explores how the PMRC's concern over their children's innocence, specifically that of one of its founders, Tipper Gore, comes from a parenting philosophy "rooted in historical notions of moral motherhood," which she connects to the American Revolution as a pivotal moment in which the role of women in colonial society was transformed. "The birth of America coincided with the creation of republican motherhood," says Anderson, "an alternative form of maternal citizenship that designated women as the moral protectors of their children." This occurred alongside changes within the Protestant church that afforded "American women greater cultural influence," which motivated "increased involvement in religious activism as they began to create church-led voluntary associations dedicated to the protection and betterment of American society" as a direct response to the fear that "the commercialization of American society would cause men to lose their moral compass, increasing the need for devout women who could preserve the virtue of the republic."[46]

Anderson expands on this idea, saying that censorship has historically been used as a form of "cultural protection," often based on ideals championed by those whose specific inclinations are informed by their religion or politics.[47] Zappa claimed that the PMRC had an inherent religious bias because they relied on Christian ideology as part of their media campaign. Anderson says the PMRC was inextricably linked to evangelical principles by using language that evoked rock music as being a religion filled with false prophets determined to irreversibly damage young people, potentially converting fragile minds into adopting ethical standards not aligned with conservative Christian values. Anderson points out that, despite the PMRC's assertions that they did not outwardly express an allegiance to any particular system of religious beliefs, they were connected to church leaders who evangelized their talking points on obscenity in rock music, including youth minister Jeff Ling, who would host slideshows depicting extreme examples of the stereotypically debauched lifestyles of rock musicians, and Bob DeMoss, who produced a promotional video for the PMRC and was affiliated with the conservative religious organization Focus on the Family.[48]

The implicit agenda of the PMRC was to silence specific types of voices, ones that did not adhere to their distinctive brand of religious and political ideology. They may have preached about the important role parents should play in raising their children, but they were resistant to the child-rearing philosophies of other parents, who were as equally invested in the safety and health of their own kids, because those parents had a different system of beliefs. Though they continuously vocalized that their only goal was to educate parents through consumer information so they could make informed decisions about what media access their children should have, the PMRC leveraged their lobbying power through institutional access in order to systematically, via the culture war and legislation, enforce their dogmatic faith-based virtues over the will and consent of many Americans. They recognized the media as a powerful tool for people to be exposed to new ideas, and these ideas reflected cultural and social principles that not only conflicted with theirs but were becoming increasingly popular. As Zappa explained to *Music Connection* in December 1985, three months after the Senate hearing:

> TV picked up on the story because they could illustrate it with rock videos. It had everything: sex, violence, devil worship. If it weren't for the availability of music videos, I doubt the issue would have gotten the kind of coverage it did. But remember: The original complaint was about words, not images. When the PMRC took over the debate from the PTA, it was broadened to include the visual. And reference to live concerts. To understand the truth, go back to the first PMRC press release. One of the main things that they were concerned about was that these songs "cause rebellion." That was a little item which was dropped from their rhetoric during the ensuing months.[49]

Four decades since the Senate hearing on porn rock, we have seen how much power conservative and religious groups have gained in their crusade to control the lives of other people. A 2023 report by PEN America, an organization that champions and protects free expression through literature, said that "the 2022–2023 school year shows expanded censorship of themes centered on race, history, sexual orientation and gender," including "the effects of new state laws that censor ideas and materials in public schools, an extension of the book banning movement initiated in 2021 by local citizens and advocacy groups. Broad efforts to label certain books 'harmful' and 'explicit' are expanding the type of content suppressed in schools."[50]

Despite a poll conducted by the American Library Association showing that more than 70 percent of parents oppose book bans while also having confidence in libraries as a public education resource, nearly fifteen hundred book titles had been banned by the end of the 2022–23 school year, doubling the number from the previous year. Most of these bans came from states whose electoral votes went to Trump in the 2020 presidential election, including Texas, Florida, Missouri, Utah, and South Carolina. Thirty percent of the bans in these states concerned titles "about race, racism, or" which "feature characters of color," while 26 percent of the banned titles "have LGBTQ+ characters or themes."[51] "This is much bigger than you can really count," said PEN America's director of free expression and education, Jonathan Friedman. "People need to understand that it's not a single book being removed in a single school district, it's a set of ideas that are under threat just about everywhere."[52]

Much like how the PMRC found a boogeyman in the lyrics of Prince or Sheena Easton, conservative and religious parents' rights groups advocating for book banning today began coalescing their efforts to target school curriculums and library resources because they found some content pertaining to different identities to be objectionable. While several advocacy groups initially established themselves to oppose the COVID-19 restrictions their local and state governments had enforced on schools, their demands to have increased oversight into how their children were educated shifted from merely demanding reopening schools so their children could have access to their educational resources to having an outsized opinion in what their children were taught. Groups like Moms for Liberty and Utah Parents United developed materials detailing titles they found objectionable, which excessively focused on books that contained themes of LGBTQ issues or racial inequality, further enflaming the culture war to dangerous new levels as "librarians and teachers have been accused of promoting pedophilia, and some have lost their jobs or quit under pressure after refusing to remove books."[53] The movement is continuing to expand, with membership in Moms for Liberty exceeding 120,000 people across three hundred chapters in forty-five states, becoming "the most consequential education advocacy organization since Teach for America."[54]

PEN America notes in its 2023 report that these book bans increasingly affect a more varied range of titles, including those that cover sensitive topics such as domestic violence, personal health, and grieving. Part of this trend of broadly blanketing book titles stems from unclear legislation with hazy guidelines that implicates books without any standardized review process, with some titles being removed without even being read. By condemning titles as pornographic or obscene, labels that are being applied comprehensively and indiscriminately with little to no oversight, wholesale bans on books are being implemented that block student access to information that could be beneficial to their health and well-being "in ways that are impossible to track or quantify."[55]

Though Zappa and others in the music industry called the PMRC out for masquerading faith-based morality under the guise of protecting children, these modern parents' rights groups that have followed in the wake of the PMRC have evolved in a way that centers their conservative religious convictions as political, cultural, and social capital to blatantly endorse and advance legislation that would systematically prioritize their ideals. Tennessee, a state whose leaders Zappa called out for their hypocrisy over country music being judged by different standards than rock, passed a bill in 2023 "that would subject book publishers and distributors to criminal prosecution and hefty fines for providing public schools with material that is deemed to be obscene."[56] Four decades prior, Zappa was fearful that the PMRC's proposals would criminalize artists for their albums and concerts, and now we are seeing that fear fully realized as political leaders continue to target marginalized voices with harmful legislation by criminalizing educators and library workers.

The purpose of these recent book bans, like the efforts of the PMRC, is to silence voices that are not rooted in white Christian nationalism, specifically Black and LGBTQ voices. In December 2021, Florida governor Ron DeSantis announced the Stop the Wrongs to Our Kids and Employees [W.O.K.E.] Act, a piece of legislation that would "give businesses, employees, children and families tools to fight back against woke indoctrination." The press release announcing this effort touted it as the "strongest legislation of its kind in the nation" and builds upon previous actions by DeSantis "to ban Critical Race Theory and the *New York Times*' 1619 project in Florida's schools." DeSantis, on announcing this proposed legislation, which went into effect July 2022, said, "We won't allow Florida tax dollars to be spent teaching kids to hate our country or hate each other. We also have a responsibility to ensure that parents have the means to vindicate their rights when it comes to enforcing standards."[57]

Just as the PMRC pushed to protect children from obscenity in rock music, current initiatives aim to make children ignorant by shielding them from learning about slavery and the civil rights movement, thus weaponizing government authority to reinforce dangerous principles surrounding white Christian nationalism that are built into the American mythos. This intense commitment to historically whitewash America's role in the subjugation of an entire race, through banning educational resources like *The 1619 Project*, has extended to reversing civil liberties for other groups like LGBTQ people, with DeSantis, as well as leaders in other conservative-leaning states, moving forward legislation that endangers the lives and safety of queer and transgender people, all under the guise of protecting children, whom the legislation would ultimately harm anyway by denying them access to health-care information to such a dangerous degree that the American Medical Association considers such restrictions as being child abuse.[58] From the PMRC to Moms for Liberty, and all the tangential iterations in between, the members of these parents' rights groups have increasingly become more emboldened in their advocacy to the point where the previously quiet part is now being blared through a bullhorn, signifying the threat of a culturally dystopic nation where anyone unlike them is criminalized, punished, and worse.

The reason the stated goal of the PMRC, and subsequent parents' rights groups, is to protect children is because children can be utilized as an effective propaganda tool. Nicole Hemmer, author of *Messengers of the Right: Conservative Media and the Transformation of American Politics*, says conservative political and cultural leaders use children to advance their interests in facilitating "the emergence of a full-on right-wing children's entertainment complex. Its sole mission: to fight what the right sees as liberal indoctrination with some indoctrination of its own." By banning access to books featuring Black and LGBTQ voices, and filling the gap with material and entertainment designed to promote conservative moral values, these figures are able to rationalize to the American public their "argument that mainstream media and educational institutions were already indoctrinating consumers—whether students or readers or audiences—with liberal values" with the goal of disconnecting "conservatives' children off from a broader culture."[59] This intersection of various institutions, involving government, business, and media, after decades of advocacy and deregulation, reveals how white Christian nationalism has grown to become an entire industry, brandishing its cultural and social power in more overtly destructive ways than the founders of the PMRC ever imagined with their comparatively modest proposals, but whose intended outcome has since become fully realized.

Zappa understood the long-term consequences of the PMRC and its mission. While the underlying theme of his Senate testimony was the effect religious and political ideology was having on artistic expression and constitutionally protected free speech, his argument against the PMRC proposals extended beyond the culture war. He was concerned with the methods by which culture-war issues get legitimized into legislation, which is why he questioned the efficacy of the blank tape tax, asking in his testimony if lining the pockets of leaders in the music industry was worth forfeiting the right to free speech. It was a decision being made by an elite few instead of being voted on by the American public, who would ultimately pay the bill for a corporate subsidy beyond their understanding—all due to a lobbying organization that sensationalized the national conversation and had personal, and dubiously ethical, ties to political leaders who would vote on the tax.

Zappa had even proposed a compromise in his statement, one he believed would satisfy all parties involved. Met with criticism that he was unwilling to empathize with the concerns of the PMRC, Zappa actually agreed with the idea of providing parents with informational resources to aid them in becoming better consumers, such as having the lyrics of an album printed and featured prominently as part of the packaging so they could make more informed decisions on what their children were being exposed to. The only caveat, and what Zappa addressed was an effect of the PMRC's proposal as it stood, was that externally displaying the lyrics should not stigmatize musicians or anyone else involved with the recording, production, and distribution of the album. However, the inherent problem with this plan was that the financial aspects of implementing it were complex, a topic the PMRC seemed ill-equipped, and perhaps even outright uninterested, in addressing. Zappa explained that the record company could not automatically print lyrics because they were the property of their respective publishing companies, and that the record company would have to pay a licensing fee in order to print those lyrics for inclusion in an album's packaging. Zappa suggested that the government print these sheets, thus reducing the burden placed on the music industry, since the government seemed interested in addressing the controversy as a consumer-education issue. Zappa ended his statement outlining the way in which this system of printing lyrics could potentially provide a resolution to the PMRC's proposal, and that there would be no need to accelerate the issue further by elevating the rhetoric surrounding music albums to apply similar ratings to concert performances.

Zappa's testimony can be heard on the spoken-word album *Congress Shall Make No Law . . .* , released posthumously in 2010 to mark the twenty-fifth anniversary of the Senate hearing. As the title track of the album, the complete testimony can be heard, as well as featuring members of the committee responding to Zappa's statement. Committee chairman John Danforth, a Republican senator from Missouri, opens the dialogue by suggesting no one is seeking to enact legislation to censor rock lyrics, with Zappa responding that the tactics used by advocates of the PMRC proposals seem to indicate misinformation about the law. Zappa engages with Al Gore as the Tennessee senator asks questions to assess how seriously Zappa considered the concerns from parents over provocative rock lyrics, with Zappa responding that he saw the PMRC's lobbying and media advocacy as being rife with hidden agendas. Noting that he is a parent of four children, two of whom attended the hearing, Moon and Dweezil, Zappa expresses he is more concerned about government authority determining how they can think and live their lives. Following the questions from Gore, Jim Exon, a Democratic senator from Nebraska, praised the women of the PMRC who escalated the issue of morality in rock music as he addressed the finer points of Zappa's statement concerning the printing of lyrics and the stigmatizing effect it could have on artists, noting that he did not see the purpose of convening the committee unless legislation was on the table but that it could be eventually. Next, Ernest Hollings, the conservative Democratic senator from South Carolina, voiced his approval of the idea of printing lyrics as potentially being a better solution than a ratings system. Toward the end of Zappa's part of the hearings, and the track "Congress Shall Make No Law," was Republican Florida senator Paula Hawkins probing Zappa on what toys had been purchased for his family and whether as a parent he had objections to the age recommendation featured on the box, to which Zappa suggested he could object because it would mean some executive in the toy industry was making a judgment call on his children's intelligence. When Hawkins facetiously says she would be interested in seeing what toys the Zappa children played with, Zappa surprises her by offering an open invite to his house to come see, with Hawkins responding that she might consider it, amid laughs from the committee and the audience. Zappa's testimony concludes when, after confirming to Hawkins that he does earn a profit from the sale of rock records, Hawkins implies that Zappa's answer has informed the committee of everything they need to know about Zappa's bias as a member of the music industry. At the end of the track "Congress Shall Make No Law," Senator Hollings can be heard speaking candidly of Zappa off-mic, saying, "We haven't got 'em whipped on this one yet. You got a bear by the tail here, hm? Jesus!"

Congress Shall Make No Law . . . includes other spoken-word tracks, altogether comprising what Frank's widow, Gail, calls "an educational project, representing Zappa's tireless commitment to the First Amendment which he felt his duty to protect by providing (in his words) 'stimulating digital audio entertainment' in the form of 'material which a truly free society would neither fear nor suppress.'"[60] The album's next track, "Perhaps in Maryland," features a speech by Zappa to the Senate Judicial Proceedings Committee of the Maryland state legislature to oppose a bill that would "prohibit the distribution or sale of obscene records, tapes and compact discs to minors."[61] Also included on the album are ten tracks of interview excerpts, titled after the Ten Commandments ("Thou Shalt Have No Other Gods Before Me," "Thou Shalt Not Commit Adultery," "Though Shalt Not Steal," and so forth), which feature Zappa elucidating his opinions on the effects warning labels and the PMRC's lobbying efforts would have on free expression. The final track, "Reagan at Bitburg Some More," is a shortened alternate version of "Reagan at Bitburg" (both versions inspired by Reagan's controversial decision not to visit a concentration camp during a ceremonial visit to a German military cemetery), an instrumental composition completed right before Zappa's death for the 1994 posthumous album *Civilization Phaze III*, "a complex and vivid dialogue about modern music" in which, as Ben Watson says in *Frank Zappa: The Complete Guide to His Music*, Zappa does not explore musical inspiration within "ideas or philosophy or faiths, but in restless curiosity about the actual, material world."[62] With that album featuring Zappa "dealing with civilization on the grand scale,"[63] the inclusion of an alternate version of one of its tracks adds gravitas to the educational curation of *Congress Shall Make No Law . . .*, in which Zappa's statement to the Senate committee serves as an enduring cultural touchstone in the advocacy for free expression.

Zappa also reflected the spirit and themes of his testimony through his music. Released in November 1985, just two months after Zappa spoke before the committee, *Frank Zappa Meets the Mothers of Prevention* is an experimental album consisting of mostly instrumental tracks and which has a title that parodies the name of his old band, the Mothers of Invention, to criticize the PMRC. Two of the tracks are musical compositions that directly address the PMRC and serve to continue Frank's argument via the art form he knew best, his music. The haunting "H.R. 2911" refers to the House of Representatives' blank tape tax bill, utilizing sinister grunts and prickly sounds overlaid on a disturbing musical foundation that evokes the feeling of living in a culturally myopic landscape that the bill's passage Zappa feared could bring to fruition. The other track, "One Man, One Vote," is a soaring and energetic synthesizer composition with an enthusiastic, get-up-and-go flair that conveys the importance of playing an active role in a participatory democracy.

The Senate hearing made its way onto another track on *Frank Zappa Meets the Mothers of Prevention*, quite literally. "Porn Wars" is a sprawling twelve-minute musique concrète sound collage where Zappa slices, dices, and splices audio from the hearing, as well as soundbites from PMRC news reports and press conferences, "using the latest technology to make extremely apt points about power, repression and self-serving witch hunts."[64] By distorting the original audio to such absurdist lengths, such as speeding up soundbites to rapid chipmunk levels or repeating them ad nauseum with various filters and effects, the track takes the panic over moralist condemnations against "sex" and "outrageous filth" and heightens its effects to the point where the bombardment of the senators' own words can make the listener feel like they stepped off a carnival Tilt-A-Whirl with the kind of dazed and queasy feeling one might get at the prospect of a world where speech can be censored or even penalized. Zappa, through the repetition of these comments, makes a point about how it is actually the PMRC that is responsible for putting content it deems to be outrageous filth into mainstream media.

There are a couple of instances where the original sampled audio is left unaltered in "Porn Wars," revealing the underlying message. The first of these is at the beginning of the track, with no music, opening with a clip from committee chairman Danforth stating that the purpose of the hearings are not to promote any legislation but rather to facilitate a public forum where the topic of obscenity in rock music can be addressed. Chairman Danforth then introduces Senator Hollings, who says he was briefed before the hearings with a presentation that demonstrated various examples of music the PMRC identified as "porn rock." Commenting on the legal parameters of pornographic content as being defined as having no redeeming social value, Hollings jokes that rock music could be an exception since he found it difficult to understand. He then doubles down on the humor by suggesting he could have made a good rock star since his constituents could not understand him, after which he immediately becomes dour and says that he does believe the content he was shown was "outrageous filth" and that he would indeed explore options to include provisions to the Constitution that would restrict the type of content he was shown. Five minutes into the track, Chairman Danforth is heard reiterating, despite Hollings's statement, that no one at the hearings is proposing legislation.

The second unaltered segment, mixed into the composition nine-and-a-half minutes in, features Republican Washington senator Slade Gorton responding to an earlier statement from Senator Gore professing his admiration for Zappa's music while noting that he disagrees with his statement, which can be heard in "Porn Wars" just after the five-minute mark. In this response,

Gorton says he is shocked by Gore's good-natured comments because he found Zappa's statement to be boorish and offensive. Gorton even says that Zappa would tarnish the reputation of the U.S. Constitution if anything he said had actual merit, stating explicitly that Zappa has no understanding of the difference between government and private action before informing the committee that he believed Zappa had destroyed his own credibility with his statement. Zappa replies by asking if the issue is private action. The use of these clips at length is Zappa highlighting the hypocrisy of the committee, using the senators' own words to illustrate the "reality of Washington power-mongering."[65]

The titular narrator from *Thing-Fish* also makes an abrupt appearance shortly after the track's eight-minute mark, interrupting to poll the listeners regarding their thoughts on the state of America, while addressing those who might be displeased with the Thing-Fish's intrusion on their listening experience as he delivers his public service announcement. The Thing-Fish first asks listeners who believe he speaks the truth to raise their hands and then asks listeners who believe he is crazy to raise theirs. Then, continuing in the uncomfortable trope dialect the character is known for, he asks how many of the listeners actually believe the government is apathetic toward the increase in the number of "undesirable tenants" taking up residence within the country's condominium class, cleverly phrasing the fear white Christian nationalists have over the changing demographics of the country. The final question the Thing-Fish proposes in this interlude concerns how many listeners feel secure with their own place in society, asking whether they firmly believe they won't be targeted next when the wind starts blowing from the East, lyrically evoking the cardinal direction as an allegory of the encroaching presence of extremist ideology from the right. The Thing-Fish then, as the grotesque avant-garde expression of America's original sin, tells the listeners that they need to come to terms with the fact that he represents their future, an idea suggesting that the white Christian nationalists who are methodically shifting the balance of power in America ultimately will see their fellow citizens as monsters. The closing of "Porn Wars" features audio from the hearings introducing John Denver as the next witness, alluding to the notion that even Denver's all-American sensibilities and image won't be enough to dissuade white Christian nationalists' pursuit of total cultural and social supremacy, all because he dared to join

Zappa in standing up for principles that championed the voices they wished to silence.

In a December 1985 interview with the *Los Angeles Times,* when asked if the satire on "Porn Wars" was arbitrarily biased, Zappa said, "Not at all. You could (just read their remarks in) the Congressional Record and have gotten the same charge. I just did a little grunt work to dig up some of the more amusing lines and stick them in a package that will hopefully make sense to a rock 'n' roll consumer, and maybe make them concerned about what kind of people there are in Washington."[66] He would reiterate this point a month later when, in January 1986, he responded to *Music* interviewer Bill Templeton's question whether "Porn Wars" was meant to profit from the publicity he received from the hearings by asking, "Why is this capitalizing on a situation? I'm doing the public a service for people who would never pay attention to what they really do in Washington. On this record they get to hear them . . . to smell them."[67] Even though Zappa had been consistent with his principles on the matter of free expression when it came to the PMRC, he was still challenged by the institutions of media and government regarding the authenticity and legitimacy of his arguments, further solidifying his distrust of the people in power within those institutions. After all, the PMRC came into power by relying on connections in both to get their word out.

To further elevate the themes within *Frank Zappa Meets the Mothers of Prevention,* Zappa included his own warning label on the cover of the album as a scornfully sardonic satire of the labels proposed by the PMRC. On Zappa's label is a warning, plus a guarantee, that his album contains material that would not be repressed in a fully free democratic society. It continues by saying that certain areas of the country that have been culturally and socially overrun by political and religious conservative groups are actively working to dismantle the American public's First Amendment rights through the unconstitutional censoring of rock music. He promises that the material contained therein is of a high quality and that anyone listening would outgrow programs enacted by the government that otherwise keep Americans compliant and stupid. He offers a guarantee to the listener that the album's compositions and lyrics will not cause them to go to hell, cautioning the listener that the label is as useless

WARNING /GUARANTEE: These concerts contain material which a truly free society would neither fear nor suppress.

In some socially repressed areas, religious fanatics and ultra-conservative political organizations violate your First Amendment Rights by attempting to censor rock & roll. We feel that this is un-Constitutional and un-American.

As an alternative to these government-supported programs (designed to keep you docile and ignorant), we are pleased to provide stimulating audiovisual and holographic entertainment for those of you who have outgrown *the ordinary.*

The language and concepts contained herein are GUARANTEED NOT TO CAUSE ETERNAL TORMENT IN THE PLACE WHERE THE GUY WITH THE HORNS AND POINTED STICK CONDUCTS HIS BUSINESS.

This guarantee is as real as the threats of the video fundamentalists who use attacks on rock music in their attempt to transform America into a nation of check-mailing nincompoops (in the name of Jesus Christ). If there is a hell, its fires wait for them, not us.

Warning/Guarantee Label. Courtesy of Zappa.com and Universal Music Group.

as those offered up by fundamentalist evangelicals who aim to alter the structure of the nation to suit their own faith. Zappa's warning label concludes by saying that hell awaits those Christian fundamentalists, if it even exists at all.

One of Zappa's concerns was that artists would be stigmatized by the actions of the PMRC, and he was proof of that. Gail said her husband's contract was canceled after the hearings concluded. The warning label for *Frank Zappa Meets the Mothers of Prevention*, albeit a product of Zappa's cynical brand of humor, was his compromise with the PMRC's demands, but MCA Records was not satisfied and would ultimately cancel his contract. The hearing and the media dialogues over warning labels would result in a strange circumstance that proved the questionable efficacy of the PMRC's proposal when Zappa would win a Grammy award for "Best Rock Instrumental Performance" in 1988 for *Jazz from Hell*, an entirely instrumental album from 1986 recorded using primarily the Synclavier digital synthesizer. In *Newsweek*'s oral history of the PMRC, Gail said the voting committees had asked why *Jazz from Hell* did not have a warning label, even though it was entirely instrumental, and suggested that nobody had even listened to it.[68] Such inane moments make one wonder how fundamentalist conservatives could get away with this madness, a question Zappa musically explores on the album with "The Beltway Bandits," a composition that gives rise to the idea that the whole movement is one big con game to distract the American public.

I believe Zappa's statement before the Senate committee was prescient, speaking to the same issues we are still addressing four decades later. Increasingly emboldened over that time, white Christian nationalists have been driving culture-war issues where the voices of marginalized groups are scapegoated and silenced under the guise of an insincere concern over the health and safety of children. The reason their argument is insincere is because it has done nothing to actually keep children healthy and safe. Whether it's rock lyrics or library books, these white Christian nationalists are only interested in an agenda that ultimately further harms children. They believe content they do not approve of will psychologically and emotionally damage children, making them antisocial and ill-equipped to properly function in society. However, mass shootings have grown into a major problem in the decades since the PMRC phenomenon. The Gun Violence Archive documented 648 mass shootings in 2022 alone,[69] many carried out by young white men (some of whom are actual children murdering other children). The outlets of free expression that parents' rights groups oppose have become convenient targets for them to espouse their agenda, designed to restrict the civil liberties of all Americans. Instead of addressing the failures within the education system, the systemic privilege of toxic masculinity, and substandard access to adequate mental health services, as well as other factors that contribute to this problem, they instead blame the artistic expression of those who are not like-minded. Though Zappa's statement before the Senate committee did not address how censorship would indirectly contribute to this specific problem in modern-day America, his words about the intent behind that censorship reveal the insidious ideals that enabled its rise at the expense of free expression.

Just as in the mid-1980s, the goal of these parents' rights groups now is to systematically alter how government and society function in order to manifest their fundamentalist will over the American public, which requires dismantling the foundational elements of a pluralist society. Democracy is a cornerstone of that foundation, requiring all voices to be heard. The PMRC and the culture war it waged on free expression became a defining moment in Zappa's life and career, one that would signal a shift in his art and how he expressed it. Though Zappa would create work that directly addressed the people and policies that facilitated the rise of censorship through the imposition of faith-based principles, he also used music to push the limits of taste as pressure tests to safeguard the constitutional guarantee of the right of free speech, further cementing his reputation as a figure unwilling to bow down to commercial or critical pressures. However, pushing back against the fundamentalist evangelical forces aiming to silence a whole swath of Americans requires more than just making music. In order to fight the porn wars, and whatever future culture wars followed, the real way to secure democracy was getting people to vote. With the next election just a couple of years away, Zappa would stand his ground regarding the best strategy to defeat the enemy of free speech: "one man, one vote."

JESUS THINKS YOU'RE A JERK

With Ronald Reagan's presidency winding down, not untarnished due to several controversies throughout his second term, the 1988 presidential election was shaping up to be a contest that was anyone's to lose. Since Reagan was constitutionally prohibited from running for a third term, the playing field was wide open for anyone from either party to try to sway voters into letting them occupy the Oval Office. However, both Democrats and Republicans seemed unsure of who could lead the charge and secure a victory. The Democratic contenders, including future president Joe Biden and future vice president Al Gore, as well as an assortment of other candidates, were derisively mocked in the media by political commentators. Republicans were also unsure that their purported candidate, Reagan's vice president, George H. W. Bush, would be able to overcome his wimpish reputation to achieve victory. By the time for the national conventions, it would be Bush against Massachusetts governor Michael Dukakis competing as their respective parties' nominees, before Bush ultimately won the election thanks to a better-organized campaign rather than with any particular vision for the country.[1] For Zappa, in the lead-up to the election, the race represented a far more heinous juncture, one in which ideology would set the tone for how America would venture into a new decade.

Not only would Zappa continue to make music that challenged the Reagan administration and his conservative evangelical supporters, but he would also work tirelessly to build and mobilize a voting bloc that would prevent them from continuing to shape America's future and whitewashing its history. Zappa, while on tour, organized a voter-registration campaign that he hoped would turn the tide of religious ideology that had infiltrated one of the country's two major political parties. "During the last seven years, we've seen an incredible blurring of the distinction between church and state and that's got to be cleared up," Zappa told the *Register-Pajaronian* in April 1988. "So what I'm trying to do on this tour is get as many people as possible to register."[2]

Partnering with various citizen action groups, including local chapters of the League of Women Voters in cities where his band was performing, Zappa's voter-registration campaign resulted in approximately eleven-thousand sign-ups, "most of them first-time voters between the ages of 18 and 25."[3] To give you an idea of the significance of that number, only Jesse Jackson was able to register more young voters that year,[4] which is quite remarkable, especially considering Zappa was not even running for political office. For Zappa, the matter at hand was more than just the prestige and power that comes from amassing enough votes to secure office. He was deeply disturbed by the trends he was witnessing, and he feared the country could face an existential crisis of democracy. "If you don't register," Zappa warned voters, "you can't vote, and if you don't vote, democracy doesn't work."[5]

Zappa's concert voter-advocacy work is documented on the 2021 live album *Zappa '88: The Last U.S. Show,* which opens with a track called "'We Are Doing Voter Registration Here,'" in which Zappa actively registers someone to vote onstage during a concert at the Nassau Coliseum in Uniondale, New York, on March 25, 1988, the final show of the American leg of the tour. At the beginning of the concert, Josh Reuben and Alice Chef, volunteers with the League of Women Voters, join Zappa onstage to register a local fan named Greg Bolognese to vote. As Greg fills out the registration form, Alice conveys to the audience her hope that they will do their civic duty to vote while Josh tells them that it is very easy to vote as long as they know their name and where they live, with Zappa poking fun at Greg for registering for a local minor anti-abortion party called Right to Life. They are soon joined by Ben Waxman, a staffer from New York governor Mario Cuomo's office, who reads a statement from the governor commending Zappa for his work in registering people to vote, noting that their participation in the democratic process is crucial to making "our democracy stronger, our government better, and our future more secure."[6] Zappa had shared this sentiment before, but with a much harsher tone, summarizing his outlook on the 1987 home-video release *Video from Hell,* with a note saying "Register to vote and read the Constitution before it's void where prohibited by law."[7]

On his voter-advocacy work, in a posthumously published interview for a December 1993 edition of *Humo,* a radio-and-television magazine published weekly in Belgium, Zappa said:

> I'm still doing my best to wake up young people. In America there is no obligation to vote, and the only reason an idiot like Reagan got to power is because most of the young people didn't go out to vote. So during the "Broadway the Hard Way" tour, I put up voting booths in every concert hall, where young people could go to register to vote. Of course, it's still hard to motivate them to vote if they only have a choice between two nitwits. The choice in the American two-party system is between Tweedledee and Tweedledum; between earwax and toecheeze: you don't want either one to be running the country.[8]

Zappa's work as a voting-rights advocate, and the issues in which he hoped voting could be leveraged to resist, can be heard throughout *Broadway the Hard Way,* his 1988 live album showcasing an assortment of new songs and his new twelve-piece band, offering an introspective look at the state of modern America on the eve of the 1988 presidential election.[9] At the tail end of Reagan's second term in the White House, Zappa had a lot on his mind to channel into music. It is an album in which Zappa captures a slice of life for the average American during the late 1980s, a twisted Rockwellian portrait of a nation whose fabric had begun to fray, revealing the threads that could be pulled to accelerate its decline as a democracy. It contains a multitude of themes, all intersecting to provide a thought-provoking critical response through which Zappa shares keen insights as a social and cultural commentator. With songs that address the rise of the evangelical faction of the Republican Party, preacher sex scandals, voting advocacy, the country's widening wealth gap, the devastating AIDS crisis, and the creeping fascism shaping American politics and society, Zappa drops a Rolodex of those responsible for these issues. *Broadway the Hard Way* is a bold satirical stand against the country Zappa feared America was becoming.

Broadway the Hard Way contains several songs that criticize the culture of greed and self-obsessed individualism that Reagan's administration fostered in many Americans. "Planet of the Baritone Women" is a gender-bending satire of yuppie culture, presenting a confusing narrative that blends the themes of women entering the workforce with the feminization of men. Although the song appears to be about women becoming more like the power- and money-hungry men who have historically been at the helm of American enterprise, thus uprooting the patriarchy's power imbalance within corporate office culture, Zappa was insistent that the song was about men. Ben Watson, in his book *Frank Zappa: The Negative Dialectics of Poodle Play*, illustrates this juxtaposition between the lyrics and Zappa's intentions, saying that "Planet of the Baritone Women" could represent "underclass resentment at feminism as the ideology of the new middle class," a social critique on consumerist and corporatization culture not unlike the one more famously explored in the 1996 Chuck Palahniuk novel *Fight Club*.

"Any Kind of Pain" is Zappa's response to critics who claim his lyrics are misogynistic,[10] featuring a narrative that criticizes public relations firms that hire conventionally attractive yet dubiously intelligent women to go on talk shows and regurgitate talking points on behalf of their political and business clients in order to manufacture consent among the American voting public.[11] A rewritten version of "Tell Me You Love Me" from 1970's *Chunga's Revenge*, "Why Don't You Like Me?" is a commentary on celebrity culture through the lens of Michael Jackson's bizarre public persona. "Murder by Numbers," a cover of the 1983 song by the Police, features an appearance by Sting as he recounts how televangelist Jimmy Swaggart claimed that his band and song were products of Satan. Pulling double duty in its satire, "Elvis Has Just Left the Building" symbolizes Zappa's departure from rock music,[12] while also commenting on how different styles of music were reflecting the cultural and political ideology of their listeners.[13]

Broadway the Hard Way also features songs with narrative themes that centered the people and policies facilitating the rise of nationalism and authoritarianism within American institutions. They include a complex array of ideas that sometimes seemed to border on the fringe, but would ultimately reveal how accurate Zappa could be with his social commentary. For a decade up to this point, since the release of *Joe's Garage* in 1979, Zappa was building upon these ideas in his music in order to sound the alarm of what he was witnessing: the increasing mobilization of a fundamentalist religious minority to effectively change how American society was structured and operated in order to prioritize their system of beliefs over any other. Now, in the waning months of a presidency that emboldened and accelerated that cause, the frontlines of the culture war Zappa was fighting against had shifted, signaling that his evangelical adversaries were making headway in every aspect of American life. With a new decade looming, even as Zappa's album and concert sales shrunk, the stakes were becoming bigger. Undeterred, *Broadway the Hard Way* was a kiss-off to a fascistic ideology, setting the tone for how Zappa would venture into a new presidential term that would irreversibly shape the direction of the 1990s.

"Dickie's Such an Asshole," a bluesy anti–Richard Nixon jam sporadically performed by the Mothers in the early 1970s,[14] gets updated for the Reagan era, with Zappa drawing criminal parallels between the two administrations. The track opens with Zappa mocking the special committee in charge of investigating the Watergate scandal, expressing his skepticism over the government's sincerity in holding Nixon accountable for his criminal activity and delivered with a lyrical pun on the former president's nickname, "Tricky Dick." Ike Willis lends his backing vocal support as Zappa lists how much evidence the Federal Bureau of Investigation has against Nixon's coconspirators, setting up a moment for Zappa to comment that there is nowhere in the United States where one can have a private conversation. Not just a slam on Nixon for having his staff install a secret audio-recording system in the White House, his private office in the Old Executive Office Building, and Camp David, Zappa's remark also reflects his outlook on the dwindling illusion of individual privacy, singing that people elsewhere in the world will find out that their "confinement loaf" tastes just the same as it does in the United States. A term to describe "a blend of several different kinds of food mashed together and baked into a flavorless, brick-like loaf that meets all of a person's daily nutritional needs" provided as "punishment food served to misbehaving inmates,"[15] confinement loaf in this case refers to manipulative mistruths from government leaders that they force upon the public to accept as reality, a "disturbing symbol for life under capitalism."[16] It is a reference Zappa uses at several points throughout *Broadway the Hard Way,* sometimes to represent bullshit fed to voters and other times as actual shit for added nuggets of scatological humor. On the track "Bacon Fat," a brief interlude based on a song by blues singer Andre Williams and Dorothy Brown, confinement loaf is what Zappa sings that his critics in Washington, DC, want to feed him over his voter advocacy. It is a reminder, as Kelly Fisher Lowe says in *The Words and Music of Frank Zappa,* "that presidential administrations, especially Republican presidential administrations, have a fine history of trying to pull fast ones on the American people."[17]

The influence of Nixon's criminality and its reverberating effects get highlighted by Ike Willis in a vocal rap from the perspective of the former president. Riffing on public comments famously attributed to Nixon wanting to make himself "perfectly clear,"[18] Willis as Nixon claims there was no wrongdoing because he was elected by the American public and that he cannot remember what happened to his secret audio tapes, alleging some went to his personal friends—Bebe Rebozo who accepted secret payments on behalf of Nixon, Pat Boone who was a singer who appropriated Black music, and Ronald Reagan. Willis then references Nixon's famous line about not being a crook within a dig at Reagan's military intervention in Nicaragua, with Zappa calling Reagan a "cocksucker by proxy" for his connections to Nixon. By the end of the track, Zappa questions how either man could ever have been elected president, addressing them both by name. It is a sentiment he echoed four years later in a 1992 interview with *Record Hunter* on the election of George H. W. Bush, saying, "The damage that has been done to this country since Reagan took office . . . actually, the shit hit the fan with Richard Nixon. It's been truly a downhill slide since Nixon, the first major Imperial presidency."[19]

Republicans are not the only ones subject to Zappa's satirical sneers on *Broadway the Hard Way.* "Rhymin' Man" is a nonpartisan takedown of Jesse Jackson, who campaigned twice for the Democratic Party nomination, in 1984 and 1988, delivered as a novelty country-western tune with Mike Keneally on lead vocal ridiculing Jackson's relish for rhymes.[20] The song opens by responding to Jackson's claim that he held civil rights leader Dr. Martin Luther King Jr. during his final moments after he was shot by James Earl Ray at the Lorraine Motel in Memphis, Tennessee. The first verse sets the scene with Jackson scheming to fool the press by insisting he held a dying King in his arms, dipping his hands in his friend's blood and smearing it on his shirt for dramatic effect. Zappa told *Playboy* in 1993 that "Rhymin' Man" was a song about "the idea of communicating through nursery rhymes, as Jackson is prone to do" because he rubbed him the wrong way for not taking off his bloodied shirt after King's assassination,[21] a reference to Jackson still wearing the shirt for a Chicago television station interview the day after. Zappa was not the only person to call Jackson out for allegedly misleading voters during the election. During New York's Democratic presidential primary, New York City mayor Ed Koch said Jackson had been lying about his presence during King's assassination for twenty years "in a way that was false and to feather his own nest."[22]

The second verse explores Jackson's campaign controversies. Keneally sings that Jackson was made to look like a clown by Louis Farrakhan, the leader of the Black nationalist organization, the Nation of Islam, for the anti-Semitism that dominated the discourse over their shared political associations as civil rights activists since meeting in the early 1970s. As Jackson was preparing for his first presidential campaign in 1984, Farrakhan supported Jackson's candidacy by accompanying him to Syria to provide translation and diplomatic support during the negotiations to release captured Navy pilot Lt. Robert O. Goodman Jr., and Farrakhan even offered to leverage the Nation of Islam's private security force, the Fruit of Islam, while Jackson was a candidate. Relations between the two men came to a head after the *Washington Post* reported that Jackson had used the anti-Semitic slur "hymie" to describe Jews, while also referring to New York as "Hymietown," with Jackson later apologizing. The fallout from this caused Farrakhan to condemn Jackson's critics with a veiled threat evoking Allah if the controversy negatively impacted the campaign. When the opportunity for Jackson to speak at the Democratic National Convention was jeopardized, the "Hymietown" issue, as well as others such as Farrakhan's remarks that Adolf Hitler was a "great man" and that Judaism was a "dirty religion," resulted in Jackson publicly cutting ties with him. At the end of the campaign, as indicated in the song, the voters rejected Jackson.[23]

The final verse addresses Jackson's candidacy during the 1988 election, with Jackson's claim of being a friend to voters mocked in the lyrics. Keneally sings that anyone can make a rhyme, noting that it is something cowboys do rather frequently, drawing on the legacy of cowboy poetry and tall tales of the

American West to drive home the satirical commentary of the song, dismissing Jackson's self-proclaimed personal growth as being nothing more than horseshit with the lyrics rhyming "mature" and "manure" for comedic effect. As Zappa told *Mother People* in 1988, "Jesse Jackson is a demagogue, who's interested in only one thing, Jesse Jackson."[24]

"*Broadway the Hard Way* was very very specific. . . . in the long term it may be an interesting historical document the same way *We're Only in It for the Money* is," Zappa told Q magazine in 1989.[25] Zappa connecting the themes behind the two albums, separated by twenty years, speaks to larger ideas he had about the role of his music in American culture at the time when each was released. *We're Only in It for the Money,* released in 1968, was a critical look at the counterculture of the era with Zappa expressing skepticism of the flower power movement. The album is an artistic statement Zappa thought of as seemingly redundant at the time of its release because of the cultural pervasiveness of the hippies and their ideals, so much so that its inherent themes would not be heard as obvious until much later when listened to at a distance. Zappa seemed to view the commentary on *Broadway the Hard Way* in much the same way, with his critical outlook on both the left and the right potentially overlooked amid the general chaos and saturation of election politics perpetuated by the increasing prevalence of 24/7 news media. As elsewhere throughout Zappa's discography, *Broadway the Hard Way* becomes a mirror in which Zappa reflects the nation's true face in that moment, a visage easily lost in a crowd where everyone is driven by the individualist consumerism of Reagan's America.

Conveying his distrust in political party systems in general, "Hot Plate Heaven at the Green Hotel" is Zappa's condemnation of the failures of America's two major political parties to reconcile the shrinking of the country's middle class. In a narrative about losing his job amid an economic depression, Zappa's narrator now cooks his meals on a hot plate at the Green Hotel, a setting that represents America's problems with wealth disparity and income inequality. Blaming both Republicans and Democrats, Zappa calls them out for not really caring about the poor because they themselves never had to stay at the Green Hotel, encouraging them to visit and listen to the people who live there. The track ends with Zappa criticizing Reagan for his trickle-down economic policy and jelly-bean etiquette, a reference to the president giving up pipe smoking for a vice more conservatively wholesome, commenting that his presidency has aged about as well as the rags worn by the people living in the Green Hotel. In *The Words and Music of Frank Zappa,* Kelly Fisher Lowe describes the track as one that reveals just how ugly American government can be over this disconnect between political leaders and the public.[26]

Although the lyrical skewering of Democrats in "Rhymin' Man" and "Hot Plate Heaven at the Green Hotel" reflected his wariness and suspicion of the party's representatives and policies, Zappa did exhibit a reasonably nuanced outlook on not only his personal politics but also his relationship between both sides of the political spectrum. Though Zappa was a registered Democrat and a supporter of Michael Dukakis during the 1988 election, he also positioned himself as both a traditional conservative and a "social commentarist, advocate for certain causes, and unashamed Democrat."[27] Zappa self-described as a practical conservative because he supported lower taxes and a smaller government that did not intrude on the individual freedoms of Americans.[28] This was an outlook influenced by his central belief that people own themselves and have the agency to make their own decisions, and that the democratic process only allows for government to exist on the condition it operates to enact the will of the people, a dynamic in which the people own the government and not the other way around.[29]

Zappa's claim that he was a conservative was based on a traditional philosophy at odds with contemporary Republican policies, but he understood that the political label had a different meaning within the context of Reagan's America. In his 1989 autobiography, Zappa expressed his belief that American citizens are entitled to several large-scale national programs and services that the federal government is obligated to deliver, including Social Security and national defense. However, as Zappa says, these services must be paid for by the federal government at a reasonable rate and be as efficient as possible. The only people who would protest these services, according to Zappa, were those who asserted their conservatism through moralism based on fundamentalist religious doctrine, eager to have their views "certified by bizarre judicial decisions, legislated by semantic chicanery . . . , maintained by 'emergency policy measures' and, occasionally, implemented by selective enforcement of the tax code."[30] In other words, the Reagan conservatives leveraged religion to tip the scales of power away from voters in favor of a more intrusive form of government, one that prioritized their politics.

Zappa told *Society Pages* in 1988 that, while he felt less sympathy toward Republicans, he was unsure whether the Democratic Party had the best solutions to fix the problems in the United States.[31] Zappa believed Republicans represented "raw, unbridled evil and greed and ignorance,"[32] but also that "the Democrats have no agenda, and when they speak on any topic, they want to sound as Republican as possible while still finding a way to retain the pork."[33] These comments from Zappa provide an insight into the underlying ideas within "Rhymin' Man" and "Hot Plate Heaven at the Green Hotel." In *Frank Zappa: The Negative Dialectics of Poodle Play*, Ben Watson says that Jackson's foreign policy positions represented the first instance in decades where progressive ideas were elevated within the discourse of mainstream politics,[34] such as his meetings between Egyptian president Anwar Sadat and chairman of the Palestine Liberation Organization, Yasser Arafat, regarding peace negotiations to end conflict with Israeli settlements in occupied territories.[35] Central to Jackson's foreign policy was reducing military spending and transferring those funds to facilitate systemic changes regarding how low-income and marginalized communities received economic support, but Jackson would later feel compelled to concede certain principles of his campaign in order to align with the Democratic Party platform. However, despite these pragmatic efforts to persuade voters, Watson says that Jackson's defeat as a presidential candidate revealed much about the priorities of white and economically secure voters.[36] This cultural disconnect in the Reagan era represented for Zappa the problems interwoven between the two political parties, with the Republicans compromising their original platform because they were overtaken by evangelicals and the Democrats championing complex social programs with little understanding of how to fund them.[37]

On first listen, it might seem like that the songs compiled on *Broadway the Hard Way* represent a slapdash airing of Zappa's personal grievances about the political establishment during the mid- to late 1980s, especially with a track like "The Untouchables," which features Ike Willis, evoking the Chicago 1920s Prohibition agent Eliot Ness, cheekily referencing various prominent Republicans involved with the Reagan administration. However, the album does not just convey Zappa's overall political and social stance, but rather his ideas that the people and policies he challenges on these songs pose a direct threat to the health and safety of the American public. "Promiscuous" is a funny, yet corny, rap fashioned after Public Enemy that addresses Reagan's surgeon general, C. Everett Koop, and his management of the AIDS crisis,[38] with Ike Willis on the mic mocking him for his spurious "Dr. God" outfit when he delivered comments on C-SPAN regarding AIDS transmission via anal sex. The track further connects Koop's faith with the evangelical influence that permeated the Reagan administration, with Willis suggesting Koop's medical credentials are based on preaching that sexual activity is the handiwork of Satan while Jesus would practice medicine the same way as Koop.

Koop's integrity as a medical doctor is then questioned because he was a Reagan appointee, with Willis comparing him to fellow appointee Ed Meese. In 1988, the same year that *Broadway the Hard Way* was released, Meese resigned as attorney general from the Reagan administration as a result of his involvement in the Iran-Contra affair, a secret arms deal that the United States orchestrated in order to free American hostages held captive by terrorists in Lebanon. Meese admitted that the funds that resulted from the arms deal then went on to support military intervention in Nicaragua, where the communist Sandinista government was engaged in bloody conflict with the insurgent anti-communist Contras, the latter having received support from Reagan, who described them as "the moral equivalent of the Founding Fathers." It was a scandal that tarnished Reagan's legacy and threatened to bring his presidency to a screeching halt.[39]

Reagan's involvement with the Contras stuck in Zappa's craw. In 1986, on the topic of Meese, Zappa was quoted in the *Duckberg Times*, saying, with reference to Reagan's comment about the Founding Fathers, that "If we must interpret everything in the Constitution in terms of the intent of the writers (who were slave holders and anti-women), then Reagan's so-called conservative government is the most radical administration ever in Washington."[40] As part of Reagan's State of the Union address delivered in 1985, the foundation of his doctrine was supporting anti-communist freedom fighters through militant self-defense: "Freedom is not the sole prerogative of a chosen few; it is the universal right of all God's children." Believing that it was America's divine mission to "nourish and defend freedom and democracy," Reagan said, "We must stand by all our democratic allies. And we must not break faith with those who are risking their lives—on every continent, from Afghanistan to Nicaragua—to defy Soviet-supported aggression and secure rights which have been ours from birth."[41] Zappa questioned this in his autobiography, asking, "Did these fine statesmen really think Nicaragua was a menace to our national security? Yeah? Then why the fuck did they hire an amateur army to look after our 'interests' down there? Wait a minute—what are our 'interests' down there?" He then challenges Reagan's doctrine by offering his own outlook on what he believed were the best methods toward protecting American interests abroad, including convincing potential global adversaries that America is an ally, brokering fair and reasonable diplomatic agreements that the United States will uphold, and developing a strategy that fosters economic growth for developing nations based on fair trade instead of exploitation of foreign labor.[42]

Besides connecting Meese with this distrust over Koop being part of the Reagan administration as its surgeon general, "Promiscuous" also calls out the American Medical Association for their dishonesty. Zappa believed the AMA to be a monopoly because of a publicity campaign aimed to discredit alternative medicine, saying the health-care organization was "certainly nothing to brag about."[43] The claim of falsehood in the song comes from the federal antitrust case *Wilk v. American Medical Association*, in which the AMA was believed to have leveraged its organizational and lobbying power to "contain and eliminate the chiropractic profession" because of a 1983 medical ethics policy decision to consider any chiropractor as an "unscientific practitioner" and chiropractic medicine as "an unscientific cult."[44]

With these ideas concerning the lack of faith in American establishments, the closing of "Promiscuous" directly questions Koop on his origin story for AIDS and asks whether the American public is being intentionally misled. These lines recall Zappa's conspiratorial views on *Thing-Fish*, but they resurface on *Broadway the Hard Way*, doubling down on those views as Willis cross-examines Koop. He asks the surgeon general if he is leaving crucial information out of the national dialogue, something about which the medical establishment discourages public discussion—the conspiracy theory that

AIDS may have been developed by the Central Intelligence Agency as opposed to originating from a chimpanzee in Central Africa. In the closing lines, Willis posits the notion that it is the CIA that has been promiscuous, defying Koop's morally religious stance to suppress sexuality by weaponizing it through a disease.

At the center of Zappa's criticism of Koop's influence on the Reagan administration and the medical establishment in "Promiscuous," and which also explains his outlook on other songs throughout *Broadway the Hard Way,* is an ever-increasing distrust of establishment institutions that had evolved throughout his career up to this point in 1988. During the mid- to late 1960s, Zappa pushed antiestablishment views that proposed the elimination of a binary political party system,[45] rejected the influence of religion in society because "pop music is the real religion of young people today,"[46] advocated for people to self-educate at libraries because America's education system was failing,[47] and encouraged leftist radicals to join police and military forces to change the system from within.[48] Plus his views on the institution of media, such as the music business and its influence on cultural taste and accessibility, came from personal and professional experience that framed how broadly Zappa applied his free-speech philosophy. During the 1970s, as elements within these institutions began to monopolize, Zappa kept up with these cultural and social changes and addressed them directly in his songwriting. In a 1975 concert review in the Duke University student newspaper, *The Chronicle,* Bill Gardner says Zappa's "music took a backseat to his lyrics. His lyrics began to satirize sacred or cherished social institutions. . . . But the institutions which he parodied tended to be those which had become socially acceptable to satirize, e.g., television in 'I'm the Slime.'"[49]

As the power and influence of these monopolies began to grow due to a variety of industry deregulations during the 1980s, evangelical fundamentalism found legitimacy within the media and political arenas, and Zappa's musical commentary expanded to condemn the escalating ways these institutions supported and reinforced each other. His outlook grew to convince him that perhaps the best way to democratize these institutions, in order to fight back against their negative influence on society, was to effectively dismantle them. Just a few months before his passing, when asked by *Playboy* in 1993 if he had a method for determining who and what became a target of his musical lashings, Zappa answered with "most institutions," including America's government and education system, and even elaborated on the topic of the 1992 presidential election, saying, "America has to be completely restructured. We have to question every institution in terms of efficiency. I'm serious about abandoning the federal system."[50]

As much as Zappa distrusted these establishment institutions, and those complacent in upholding them without concern for the consequences, he had some semblance of faith that the voting public would come to his view that they were being played by the powerful heads of those institutions, which is why he dedicated so much time advocating that people vote. Speaking to *Playboy* on the nuance of this position, and illustrating the way in which he framed this advocacy, Zappa said, "Even if you don't like the candidates, there are issues that affect your life. Bond issues affect your pocketbook. That's the only real reason for voting. As far as the rest of government is concerned, forget it."

Zappa did not have much faith in the government itself, referring to its projected sense of self-importance as "science fiction" because of the waste it generated through inefficient programs that did nothing for the people. The problem, Zappa believed, behind his perception of the government's self-imposed grandiosity stemmed from major media outlets, like CNN, which he believed were distributing propaganda in the form of talk shows that turned political discourse into entertainment, referring to panelists like President George H. W. Bush's chief of staff John Sununu and President Reagan's National Security Council staff member Oliver North as criminals and asking, "Why do we need to be presented with them as voices of authority whose opinions are something we should even waste our time with?" Zappa then explains that the goal of the government is to control the news, something he attributed to Reagan's domestic policy, which he believed resulted in the firing of journalists and news stories being inundated with spin.[51]

While this attitude does convey a high level of cynicism, it was something Zappa only dealt out to people who abused power. Zappa's pessimism about the government was not enough for him to give up trying to change it, because he understood there had to be some element of cooperation with establishment institutions in order to effect real change through voting. Projecting broad cynicism would not have been effective in getting people, whose lives were impacted by powerful systems, motivated to leverage voting as a tool to restructure those systems of power. A complete restructuring of the American federal system, in Zappa's view, required that change to come from within through voting. This outlook reveals a degree of subtlety to Zappa's brand of cynicism, one recognizing the elements that perpetuated an imbalance of power between the people and the government but also which sought to resolve it. In a 2003 interview with Avo Raup in Estonia, Allan Zavod, who had played with Zappa from July through December 1984, said:

> He was very politically minded. . . . He had good relations with the establishment, the police and with the mayor. He used to advise the audience to vote for Democrats. He was a Democrat. He said: There are voting polls out in the lobby, fill in the papers and vote! In 1990, I think, President Bush objected to recordings that had obscene lyrics, keeping them in record stores but not on display. That was wonderful for Frank. He just got up and spoke in front of 200,000 people. He talked about abortion and drugs; he said: George, stay out of their bush. Frank was heavily into politics. I tell you, he didn't want any drug records because if he had drug problems he would never have a chance of having the same cooperation from the establishment.[52]

At first listen, one might dismiss the song "Promiscuous" because of its ideas about AIDS that sound a bit like conspiracy theories to criticize Koop's influence on the Reagan administration. However, that attitude comes with the benefit of hindsight, so understanding the context of how Zappa viewed the overlapping interests of establishment institutions is crucial. He may have been wrong in this particular case, but it does not necessarily destroy his credibility when looking at the bigger picture of fundamentalist religious influence in politics and health care. In his article "Doctor, Not Chaplain: How a Deeply Religious Surgeon General Taught a Nation about HIV," published in *The Atlantic* in 2013, twenty-five years after the release of *Broadway the Hard Way*, John-Manuel Andriote profiles Koop upon his death as a "deeply religious Presbyterian and the author of a book opposing abortion" who "also brought the evangelical Christian credentials Reagan wanted to reward the religious right wing that had helped elect him." Zappa was not alone in his attitude toward Koop. Andriote said that "Liberal Democrats in Congress worried Koop would use the surgeon general's bully pulpit on public health issues as a de facto church pulpit to push a conservative religious agenda on the nation." Koop's appointment was lobbied against by "public health groups, women's and gay rights group and medical associations."

Koop was also prevented from publicly addressing the AIDS crisis for the first few years of his appointment, until he formally issued a report, the *Surgeon General's Report on Acquired Immune Deficiency Syndrome*, in 1986. Anthony Fauci, who tutored Koop on the AIDS epidemic, said Koop was "deeply driven by principle when it came to public health, not by any ideology," and that Koop would say "this thing about AIDS is very troubling, and I want to make the right impression on public awareness. He got it in his mind that we as the federal government need to be explicit about this—oral and anal sex, commercial sex. He was hell-bent on doing it. When it came out, it shocked a lot of people because of its explicitness."[53] Koop's report "offended his fellow evangelicals in the Reagan administration who preferred to see AIDS as 'God's punishment' for people of whose very existence they disapproved."[54]

Much to the surprise of his critics, Koop bucked against the moralism of the evangelicals by applying a pragmatic view to the treatment of AIDS, focusing on the facts of how the disease spread, not just through anal and vaginal intercourse but also intravenous drug use, even going as far as to educate the public by mailing informational flyers to American citizens, conveying the message that "knowledge and understanding are the best weapons we have against the disease" and encouraging the American public to discuss health and safety in "schools, synagogues, and community groups [that] offer AIDS education activities."[55] It was an approach that succeeded "in at least chipping at the wall of evangelical resistance to Christian charity."[56] This work amid mounting pressure would go on to elevate Koop's legacy as a compassionate health-care professional who responded to a crisis with principles defined by the tenets of his faith, and not the politicization of it.

While it can be easy to fault Zappa for his obstinance regarding his beliefs on the AIDS epidemic, especially after the publication of Koop's report,

"Promiscuous" is just one element within the larger context of the themes addressed in *Broadway the Hard Way*, the major one being the overreach of evangelical Christianity in American politics. The role of conservative Christian values in politicizing a major health crisis would resurface over three decades later when Donald Trump's administration mishandled the response to the COVID-19 pandemic during the final year of his first presidency. In his article, "Donald Trump, the Christian Right and COVID-19: The Politics of Religious Freedom," Jeffrey Haynes of London Metropolitan University says that, as a result of Trump being unwilling or unable to effectively manage the COVID-19 pandemic, many state governors "shut religious places of worship to the chagrin of many Christian conservatives: to them, this was an intolerable reduction of their religious freedom."[57]

Haynes added further:

> The Christian Right was alarmed that their religious freedoms were being curtailed—albeit temporarily—in order to fight the pandemic. Many did not accept the medical reasons behind the closures of places of religious worship; instead, some regarded the closures as sinister: an aspect of the toxic process of secularisation whose purpose, they believed, was to undermine and eventually remove the right of religious believers to exercise their faith without control by secular state authorities. Others refused to believe that COVID-19 was "real," contending instead that it was a "phantom plague."[58]

The passion and intensity of the conservative response to the COVID-19 pandemic, especially in states with liberal or Democratic governors such as Michigan, where armed protestors stormed the state capitol,[59] elevated the crisis to the point where the social discourse contained a partisan dichotomy. Preventive measures like getting vaccinated or wearing cloth masks were associated with liberal ideology while opposing those very same things was seen as an expression of conservative principles, with the polarization between the two points of view exacerbated by hyper-partisan news media. As the origin of the COVID-19 pandemic is still being investigated, and will likely be debated for many years to come, even the topic of the virus's source splits the room between liberals and conservatives. The ensuing discourse offers some insight into the danger threatening American citizens when religious fundamentalism influences the nation's politics, especially if the media establishment has a symbiotic role to play in the crisis.

I bring up the politicization of COVID-19 to provide some understanding as to why Zappa might have had the view he did regarding Koop and his AIDS response. Considering the context of the pandemic, it becomes clear how easily ideological battle lines can be drawn over something like health care, especially when there are media outlets, and now social media—which was not the case during Zappa's time—which can profit from that conflict. Zappa's views on AIDS were developed as a result of his distrust in the coziness between establishment institutions and religious ideology at the time, much in the same way many conservatives viewed governors' responses to the COVID-19 pandemic. However, this is not to say that Zappa would have shared the same views (largely because he is not alive and we cannot ascertain how he would feel). Zappa's opinions on AIDS, albeit misinformed, were held in the interest of speaking truth to power against an administration influenced by evangelical politics, while the conservative response to COVID-19 was in service to an administration that catered to their evangelical politics. Therein lies the nuanced difference, which does not rationalize Zappa's view, but rather frames it within its proper context. The motivations behind those misconceptions are vastly different, and that should be taken into consideration when we talk about Zappa's politics.

In keeping with the album's overall theme, many of the remaining tracks from *Broadway the Hard Way* contain messaging and ideas that expose the hypocrisy and violence of religious fundamentalists and their political enablers. While Zappa had addressed these before at various points throughout his career, in some ways rather directly while at other times with a bit more subtlety, the songs on the album form a cohesive cultural statement that drives an urgent message: these people do not hold themselves to the same legal, social, and cultural standards they demand of everyone else and, all the while, they connive and conspire to steal individual freedoms and civil rights through legislative means. Zappa was always ahead of his time, both as a musician and a cultural commentator, but *Broadway the Hard Way* especially reveals just how prescient he could be.

"Jezebel Boy" is a track about an esteemed conservative district attorney soliciting oral sex from a male sex worker, featuring a collection of strange musical sounds to convey the feeling that this whole exchange is rather gross. In my research, I could not find any references in the song that pointed to a specific person, event, or controversy. Zappa's lyrics could be rather dense at times, often containing overlapping and self-referential inside jokes that allude to any number of things based in reality or within the musical lore of his catalog. For one, there's a comment referencing Ernest F. Hollings, the Democratic senator from South Carolina notable for his involvement with the PMRC Senate hearing, but he never experienced such a scandal as is portrayed in the song. Or it could be Zappa and the band having a laugh poking fun at hypocritical conservatives. Certainly, there has been no shortage of conservative politicians who, while advancing or preaching religious family values, have been caught covertly soliciting gay sex from men. Mark Foley, Jon Hinson, Robert Bauman, Larry Craig, and Ed Schrock are just a few of those conservative politicians who were exposed in high-profile gay sex scandals,[60] and that is not even to mention those implicated in other types of salacious extramarital misconduct. Though not a particularly strong source of political commentary, the song is a piece of set dressing that speaks to the grander politics of the time.

While "Jezebel Boy" is presumably fictional in origin, "What Kind of Girl?" comes from real events. Though based on "What Kind of Girl Do You Think We Are?" from the live album *Fillmore East, June 1971*, a song about the members of Zappa's band and their dalliances with groupies while touring, the iteration on *Broadway the Hard Way* gets modernized with a satirical slant as a parody of the 1988 scandal involving televangelist Jimmy Swaggart soliciting a sex worker. In an issue of *Penthouse* magazine, a sex worker named Debra Murphree claimed she engaged in twenty separate sexual encounters with Swaggart over the course of a year. The story broke after Marvin Gorman, a preacher at the center of a $90 million defamation lawsuit after he was defrocked by the Assemblies of God following Swaggart accusing him of adultery, received photographic evidence of Swaggart entering a Louisiana motel room with a sex worker.[61] After the scandal broke and an internal investigation within his church was being conducted, Swaggart delivered a tearful confession to the seven thousand congregants of his megachurch, as well as to his live television audience, begging for their forgiveness: "I do not plan in any way to whitewash my sin. I do not call it a mistake, a mendacity; I call it sin."[62] Despite the apology to his flock, Swaggart would later be caught in the company of another sex worker in a separate scandal in 1991.[63]

"What Kind of Girl?" as it appears on *Broadway the Hard Way* is a bawdy duet featuring the two figures at the center of the controversy, with both Zappa and Ike Willis playing Swaggart and Mike Keneally as the sex worker meeting at the Texas Motel in Louisiana to engage in acts of evangelical promiscuity. Various references to the Swaggart scandal find their way into the narrative, setting the tone of the song as a satirical commentary about the fraudulent morality of evangelical politics and their influence on the Republican Party. Willis briefly takes over the Swaggart role from Zappa, as he mimics the disgraced televangelist's denial of the affair during a segment parodying the melody for the Beatles' "Strawberry Fields Forever." A week after the Swaggart scandal broke in February 1988, Zappa rewrote the lyrics for three classic songs by the Beatles to reflect the affair in a medley performed during the tour as "The Beatles Medley" (née "The Texas Medley"): "Norwegian Jim" ("Norwegian Wood"), "Louisiana Hooker with Herpes" ("Lucy in the Sky With Diamonds"), and "Texas Motel" ("Strawberry Fields Forever"), which would not receive an official release until the 2021 live album *Zappa '88: The Last U.S. Show.*

Zappa had a lot of fun with the Swaggart scandal, the subject of which he returned to many times during the tour for a bit of humorous levity amid his starker critique of the influence of Christian evangelicalism on American politics. He would take existing compositions of his own and add Swaggart for comedic effect, such as on the live album *Make a Jazz Noise Here,* recorded in 1988 and released in 1991.[64] As with "What Kind of Girl?" the point for Zappa regarding these Swaggart versions was to reflect their timeliness through modernizing their lyrics to address contemporary issues. For a 1988 interview with *New Paper,* Zappa said of these updates: "Well, there's a lot of material in America, just turn on the TV and you've got it. There's so much stupid stuff going on, that you can't even keep track of it. The Jimmy Swaggart stuff is hilarious. We had an old song from '71 called 'What's a Girl Like You Doing in a Place Like This?' Now I've changed the words: 'What's a Girl Like You Doing in a Church Like This?' It's got all the appropriate lyrics for Swaggart."[65]

While "What Kind of Girl?" references a high-profile televangelist abusing his power, it is also one of those songs that makes it tougher to rationalize Zappa's music for modern audiences. Though the song, and the reworked versions of others during the 1988 tour, lyrically center Swaggart as the punching bag, "What Kind of Girl?" does use extreme sexual imagery that also puts blame on the sex worker and refers to her as a "lazy prostitute." There are times when Zappa's humor can be insensitive and cruel, and the rhetoric of "What Kind of Girl?" is one of those instances where Zappa fails, or one could argue even outright refuses, to see the power imbalance within gender issues. He spends time in the song questioning the values of the sex worker, as if her decision to engage with Swaggart was based on personal preference. Even as of this writing in 2024, the issue of the legal and social protections of sex workers has yet to experience mainstream consideration, with sex workers disproportionately "vulnerable to sexual assault, stalking, harassment, and other forms of abuse from law enforcement."[66]

Much of Zappa's view of the sex worker character can be traced to his attitude toward groupies, which the song's original version addressed. Zappa told *Record Mirror* in 1971: "To me groupies are girls that you meet on the road. Some are nice, some are nasty, some have a sense of humour, some have none, some are smart and some are dumb. They're just people!"[67] This outlook reflects limitations in Zappa's commentary because he was a white man who exhibited an absolutist attitude about gender equality, especially with him being a rock star with the power and status that is often associated with that line of work. However, despite the archaic attitude attributed to the sex worker on this track, Zappa is largely targeting Swaggart, as evidenced by the frequency in which he appeared in reworked compositions; the central issue for Zappa was the absurdity of those preaching moral standards that they do not practice.

Zappa considered Swaggart himself to be a joke, but not what he represented. While Swaggart's sex scandal and subsequent apologetic blubbering on television were great satirical fodder that allowed Zappa to modernize the deeper social and political commentary that underpinned much of his music, the evangelical principles Swaggart espoused presented an existential threat to American democracy. When asked by *Cash Box*, shortly after the 1988 election, why he dedicated so much material on *Broadway the Hard Way* to address the increasing threat of religious fundamentalism, Zappa said, "Unless you happen to be the kind of person who enjoys being told when to kneel down, these people should be feared. There are some who believe that certain beliefs should be forced on them through legislation. That's bad. And as far as I can tell through the constitution, it's against the law. Reagan was put in power partially by men of God, who turned out to be men of commerce."[68]

Of all the wealthy televangelists with a special connection to the president's ear, none represented a bigger danger for Zappa than Pat Robertson. Robertson, who founded the Christian Broadcasting Network in 1960 and its flagship talk program the *700 Club* a few years later, would go on to do more than anyone else to change the label "evangelical" in a way political scientist Ryan Burge would suggest was "less a theological identity now than a political one tied to the Republican party." Coalescing a voting bloc that he cultivated as he grew his media empire, Robertson would eventually leverage the political power of his built-in audience to support his presidential campaign for the 1988 election.[69]

Following two terms of a Republican administration that prioritized the needs and values of white evangelicals over other groups, Zappa feared that a Robertson presidency would build upon that mobilized support to legitimize fascist ideology through legislation. Zappa elaborated on this concern, speaking with *Gallery* in 1989: "I'm talking about the evil influence the radical right has had on the Republican Party. If Abraham Lincoln came back today, he would not recognize the Republican Party as he knew it. If Jesus came back today, he would not recognize what is being said [in his name] as Christianity. A lot of the negative things the Republican Party has become I blame on Pat Robertson and the religious fundamentalists who have flocked to the party. I think their influence is undermining American democracy."[70]

By the time he became a presidential candidate, Robertson was no stranger to controversy due to his views about the liberalization of America, which were based on bigotry and white Christian nationalism. Robertson was a known opponent of women's rights and equality, having referred to feminism as a "socialist, anti-family, political movement that encourages women to leave their husbands, kill their children, practice witchcraft, destroy capitalism, and become lesbians."[71] Two years prior to his election bid, Robertson said in a 1986 interview, "The great builders of our nation almost to a man have been Christian," referring to other groups as termites that are "destroying institutions that have been built by Christians." In language that invokes supremacy and genocide as a means of eradicating liberalism, Robertson's solution was for a "godly fumigation" to deal with the termites that were in charge of American institutions because "that is not the way it ought to be."[72]

Even years after his campaign for president, Robertson would continue espousing bigoted views under the guise of evangelical teachings, making comments in the wake of the September 11 attacks denouncing Islam as a violent "political system," saying Muslims and members of the queer community should "kill themselves" following the 2016 Pulse nightclub shooting in Orlando, and predicting the marital union of homosexual couples would only bring forth disease. As Jay Michaelson said about the televangelist in a commentary for *Rolling Stone* following his death, "More than anyone, Pat Robertson succeeded at mainstreaming the craziest fringes of Christian fundamentalism, and his descendants are, today, the base of the Republican Party: religious extremists motivated by rage, fear, and conspiracy theories."[73]

"When the Lie's So Big" is one of two songs on *Broadway the Hard Way* where Zappa clearly illustrates his outlook on how one of the two dominant political parties has emboldened fascist, nationalist, and white supremacist rhetoric under the guise of religious ideology. He sings that prominent evangelicals, with the support of conservative politicians, tell lies of such great magnitude that they do not even make a noise, implying that the insidious nature of these outrageous lies come with the effect that their reverberations across society are felt so gradually, but deeply, that they result in a numbness that makes one unaware that systemic social and cultural change is happening at all. Evoking the concept of the Big Lie, a term coined by Adolf Hitler to describe "an extreme distortion of the truth, used for the purpose of spreading propaganda,"[74] Zappa warns listeners that Robertson relies on his media empire to advance and normalize his own particularly dangerous brand of fundamentalist Christianity. Zappa fears that those Americans who are non-white and non-Christian will face violence, abuse, and torture from evangelicals who feel empowered by what Robertson preaches.

Zappa demonstrates a clear understanding of how Robertson and other televangelists are able to get their message across. By reducing party-platform politics into recognizable iconography, such as a mother holding a pie and a Bible in front of the American flag, people who project value onto those things as representative ideas associated with a particular ideology, whether they be political or faith-based, are more amenable to persuasion by those who use the ideas behind those icons to slowly introduce dangerous rhetoric. In essence, Zappa is saying that people will listen to anything if it is presented in a certain way, especially if it reinforces their already existing biases and prejudices. In this case, Zappa is criticizing Robertson's linking of fundamentalist Christianity with American identity that aims to push an agenda defining an American from an evangelical perspective, in which being American is synonymous with being white and Christian. Zappa questions how all this came to be, asking whether the nation was so dumb as to have let this religious dogma establish a stranglehold on the culture.

Zappa is not so much concerned with religion as personal practice, but rather the widespread implications of forcing it on other groups, a hallmark of fundamentalism. He was especially concerned that fundamentalism was having a direct impact on legislation, representing to him such a blatant manipulation that he goes as far as to refer to Robertson as being anti-Christian himself.[75] Speaking with the *Register-Pajaronian* in 1988, Zappa said, "Every person has the right to believe what they want, but they do not have the right under the U.S. Constitution to inflict their religious beliefs on legislature. I describe Robertson's campaign as the effort to elevate superstition to the level of legislative enforceability, and that is something everybody ought to be concerned about."[76]

This yearning for people to be concerned can be heard throughout "When the Lie's So Big," especially when Zappa calls out Republicans for conveniently disappearing facts and logic while orchestrating a fog of confusion to spread the Big Lie. He urges listeners to recognize that religious zealots have infiltrated all three branches of the government—the courts, Congress, and the White House—and are using them to fulfill their "heavenly mission." Zappa cleverly alludes to their criminality in enchanting an entire nation with religious extremism, notably at the beginning of the song with a reference to "confinement loaf," suggesting the ingredients that make up the Big Lie have been baked into the ideology and fed to the public. It is a dynamic that frustrates Zappa so much that not once, but twice, the question is asked when the country will be free from these men who are facilitating the homogenization of a white Christian America.

The influence of Robertson on American conservative and evangelical politics has been so great, we are still experiencing the effects of it nearly four decades after the release of *Broadway the Hard Way*. In particular, the Donald Trump administration represented for evangelical Christians their ultimate manifestation of a political and cultural savior. Leah Payne, an associate professor of theology at George Fox University and Portland Seminary, said of Trump that his "presidency is, in many ways, a triumph of Robertson's life and work. He wasn't alone, but he was one of the most prominent mass media moguls of the late twentieth century who said, 'We are going to mobilize toward specific ends: abortion, heterosexual marriage, prayer in public schools'—the laundry list of all these things. He did a lot to get white charismatics and Pentecostals on the national political agenda."[77]

This is something Sarah Posner echoes in her book *Unholy: Why White Evangelicals Worship at the Altar of Donald Trump:*

> For decades, the Christian right has successfully used the mechanisms of democracy, such as voter registration and mobilization, citizen lobbying, and energetic recruitment of religious candidates to run for office, to advance its agenda. In these efforts, conservative evangelicals are driven not by a commitment to liberal democracy but rather by a politicized theology demanding that they seize control of government to protect it from the demonic influences of liberalism and secularism. Previous presidents pandered to evangelicals, but Donald Trump constitutes the culmination of a movement that has for decades searched for a leader willing to join forces in this battle without cowering to shifting political winds. In Trump, the Christian right see more than a politician who delivers on promises; they see a savior from the excesses of liberalism.[78]

The Christian right's crusade for a savior who will fight the forces championing liberal ideals sheds light on one particular line in "When the Lie's So Big." Within the final minute of the song, at 2:52, Zappa, using a silly voice to sound like a character that has been brainwashed, asks listeners if they believe in the "invisible army." Between the cartoonish voice and its quick appearance before the band continues with a circus-like flourish, the implications of the line can easily be missed. It is meant to represent one of the most dangerous ideas at the heart of Christian nationalism: that an element of the rhetoric encouraging the Christian right to fight liberalism inherently implies violent action. This rhetoric comes in the form of reframing evangelicals as an Army of God, in essence playing the role of Christian soldiers to enforce a narrative through rising up and waging spiritual warfare against those they see as enemies to their establishment of white nationalist principles in mainstream American culture.

Carter Heyward, an American feminist theologian and priest in the Episcopal Church, in her book, *The Seven Deadly Sins of White Christian Nationalism: A Call to Action*, says of this violence that it "is believed by many Christians to be sanctioned by God."[79] To convey the gravity of that and how it came to be, Heyward outlines three specific tenets that many Christians have taken for granted as violence increasingly became a bigger part of the American culture and consciousness: (1) that the enemies of God must be fought against in his name because they are viewed as God's enemies, (2) that Christians practice charity more than working together to put a stop to the root cause of poverty which engenders systemic cycles of violence, and (3) that nonviolence is too rooted in idealism to be an effective response to the inevitability of violence in our culture.[80] Heyward is clear about how this culture of hate is cultivated, saying of this violent rhetoric among white Christian nationalists:

> In truth, to even present violence as a deadly sin in America, one fully (if often apologetically) supported by Christianity, is redundant. . . . No one paying attention in America or in American churches could fail to notice that our national culture centers around a pride strengthened over time by the fondness of many white Christian American men (and some women) for wars, guns, conquests, police and military readiness,

> and scapegoating—whether onto Jews, Muslims, or people of other nations, cultures, or religious traditions; Native Americans; Black people and other racial-ethnic populations; women (especially successful professional women and feminists); LGBTQ people; and all "others" deemed alien, unpatriotic, or dangerous to the white Christian "all-American way."[81]

White Christian nationalism, along with its intended consequences, becomes the central point of the other song on *Broadway the Hard Way* in which Zappa examines how the Republican Party thrives on stoking fear among white evangelicals, the final track, "Jesus Thinks You're a Jerk." It is a sprawling satire of a song, clocking in at over nine minutes, dedicated to the televangelists Zappa believes are ushering in a dangerous vision of America, specifically Jim Bakker and his wife Tammy Faye, Swaggart, and Robertson, the latter of whom gets special attention for leveraging his presidential campaign to popularize ideas with the potential to "lead us all into the Twilight Zone."[82] By focusing much of the song's narrative on Robertson's presidential ambitions, Zappa imbues the listening experience with a dire sense of seriousness that reveals the real-world fear Zappa had of what a Robertson presidency would mean. Zappa told the *Chicago Sun-Times* in 1988: "It seems to me, because of the theology he preaches, that the risk is greater for nuclear war with a man who believes that Jesus will not come back until there is a final conflict . . . And that the faithful, the good guys, won't suffer at all because they will be assumed into heaven, and they get to watch all the sinners roasting and toasting. If a man who has that theology is sitting next to anything that resembles a red button, we're in big trouble here."[83] "Jesus Thinks You're a Jerk" captures a rawness in Zappa's spirit that seemed so radical at the time, but sadly predicts the tightening grip that white Christian nationalism would come to have on the platform of one of the nation's two leading political parties.

The first several minutes of the song, with a comical yet tight horn-filled musical arrangement, feature Zappa poking fun at Jim and Tammy Faye Bakker over their involvement in "a scandal encompassing embezzlement, adultery, and homosexuality,"[84] the latter stemming from Jerry Falwell publicly accusing Jim Bakker of being secretly gay.[85] The lyrics compare the Bakkers to various types of rodents for manipulating their followers by stealing funds intended for their church. Robertson also gets called out for his relationship with the Bakkers, specifically his using them to swindle evangelical followers to enrich church coffers. Without any hint of subtlety, Zappa makes several jokes about the scandal at their expense, suggesting Robertson and Jim Bakker should be on the receiving end of some very uncomfortable anal sex while they also get tarred and feathered. While the jokes and comments referencing the salacious elements of the Bakker scandal may sound like they are at the expense of the gay community, the intended effect is to illustrate the hypocrisy of the two televangelists. Zappa specifically says in the song the punishment he recommends be inflicted upon them is exactly what they want to do to people who do not think like them because they are incensed by the increasing prevalence of liberalism in American culture, such as prayer being removed from schools.

By the bridge, the tone of "Jesus Thinks You're a Jerk" begins to shift, revealing particularly disturbing trends regarding white Christian nationalists. Zappa warns that this group considers itself to be chosen by God, while noting that its constituents are card-carrying members of the National Rifle Association who pray while keeping their finger on the trigger. The message in the image Zappa is crafting is simple and obvious: these people will take violent action to enforce the will of their ideology. This critique is more than just the low-hanging fruit of understanding that the Republican Party is largely made up of white conservative Christians who have an affinity for guns. It is saying that the gun is a symbol, a representation of the commitment to carry out a vision of America in God's name through violence. "Many Americans condone [violent gun culture] in the name of the Christian God," says Carter Heyward, noting that the typical targets of this violence are people who are non-white, immigrant, LGTBQ, women, and Democrats. "These groups of Americans are portrayed as seeking to overthrow the American family, the American way, America's capitalist spirituality, and America's Christian devotion to an historically white male Father God."[86]

Zappa understood that the legacy of white Christian nationalist hatred of other groups is a tale as old as their holy book, as evidenced by the verse immediately following the gun messaging in the bridge. Here Zappa, very clearly and unequivocally, implies that the American nationalist faction of Christian evangelicalism has elements of white supremacy built into the foundation of the ideology, singing they even have Ku Klux Klan attire in their trucks. This comment sets up the rest of Zappa's stinging rebuke as he critiques the hypocrisy of white Christian nationalist beliefs. While their anti-abortion stance advocates for the right to life, he expresses skepticism in their unwavering belief regarding the sanctity of life by raising the question of what it is he sees hanging in the neighbor's tree, before revealing that the answer looks to him like a lynched Black person. This allusion to Billie Holiday's 1938 song "Strange Fruit" acknowledges that white Christian nationalists have historically facilitated the murder of Black people in America for many years, and they have no intention of stopping as they more broadly apply their fundamentalist wrath to other groups they deem as un-American.

Zappa's critique of the moral and ethical hypocrisy of televangelists and their gun-loving evangelical followers within the first half of "Jesus Thinks You're a Jerk" characterizes the people and ideas that help establish the underlying theme of the second half of the song: how they play a role in Robertson's vision for the presidency and what that could mean for Americans if he were to be elected. Eric Buxton, a Zappa superfan who followed the band during the East Coast leg of the tour, kicks off the second half by dynamically reciting a monologue detailing controversial elements of Robertson's life and career. The monologue makes several claims, including that Robertson's senator father pulled his son out of active duty in Korea, that he is unqualified to practice law despite having studied it, that he fathered a child out of wedlock, that he has been under investigation by the Internal Revenue Service for tax evasion, and that he is a close and personal friend of Reagan with ambitions of following in his steps as president. At the end of Buxton's monologue, Zappa returns to describe Robertson's version of America as being reminiscent of *The Twilight Zone,* referencing the classic science-fiction series to make the point that America could become a scary place for many people. "Well, let's say you subtract all the religious content from what Robertson says," Zappa told *Society Pages* in 1990. "Just from an ethical and moral standpoint, I believe what he preaches is questionable. He's really a situational ethics kinda guy. He's a stinker."[87]

Following the monologue, kicking off the third and final part of the song, Ike Willis joins Zappa as the two hypothesize on what the consequences of a Robertson presidency might be. Willis notes that, if elected to the presidency,

Robertson's administration would systematically take away the civil liberties and rights of the marginalized groups who would be most at risk from policies rooted in the principles of white Christian nationalism. This very idea, that American citizens could be stripped of their freedoms by a government imposing a fundamentalist religious dogma, Zappa describes as a national tragedy. Here Zappa sheds his cynical veneer, worried about the future of his country and the direction it seems to be going, declaring his hope that such a dark day will never arrive. However, Zappa remains grounded, though unsure of his own confidence, by questioning whether it could still happen in the coming years as the 1980s close and new elections await in the 1990s, at which point the nation could cross a troubling threshold.

Zappa's gazing into the near future reveals the sense of urgency he feels within himself. As someone who observed the increasing influence of religious fundamentalism within the culture over the previous decade, which informed the outlook and messaging in the music he wrote and performed, Zappa exhibits a rare moment of personal introspection in "Jesus Thinks You're a Jerk" that is not only fascinating on its own but especially when framed within his entire career. He sings that, if the audience is still unaware of what he has been saying through his music after all these years, then he must have failed in his mission as an artist. He repeats the notion of his failure several times, displaying a rather uncharacteristic level of humility, given his reputation as a cynic. It is movingly powerful with the messaging and delivery suggesting that Zappa was aware of the limitations of his own art as satire, so much so that he questions his own effectiveness. It is a poignant moment at the tail end of a career filled with provocative lyrics accused of being pornographic and obscene. The feeling stays with you even after Zappa returns with a sense of levity by saying that then Jesus will think he is a jerk, especially if his listeners still find themselves manipulated and fooled by televangelists.

In the final moments of "Jesus Thinks You're a Jerk," Zappa captures the vision of what a white Christian nationalist version of America would look like in a single image: a cross burning on the lawn, evoking a method that white supremacists and white nationalists have historically used to instill fear in Black people and others whose very existence threaten their myopic view of the nation. As the band finishes and the audience erupts in applause, Zappa closes the song, urging the audience to register to vote during the band's intermission, a fitting end to *Broadway the Hard Way* that reinforces the weight and importance of the album's themes.

"Jesus Thinks You're a Jerk" is not only a crowning achievement on *Broadway the Hard Way,* but I also consider it to be Zappa's masterpiece. The song perfectly encapsulates not only the brilliance of his satirical humor, but reveals that his core message as an artist contains a relevancy that continues to resonate decades later: we need to stop the dangerous people with dangerous ideas who will systematically take away the rights and freedoms of non-white and non-Christian Americans. The song is a prime counterpoint to critics of Zappa who believe his ideas were antithetical to liberalism. With lyrics that clearly state the danger facing marginalized groups, "Jesus Thinks You're a Jerk" is Zappa ringing the alarm bell of not only what could happen if the country became a fascist theocracy but also of such a possibility being closer to becoming reality than many realize. That was in 1988. Nearly forty years later, we can see how white Christian nationalism has evolved, mutating from a fringe element to representing more than half of Republicans and nearly a third of all Americans as of 2023,[88] thus securing its increasing role as a significant feature of American politics in the twenty-first century. Of all the criticisms one could possibly apply to Zappa, no one can doubt the accuracy of his concern over the power and domination of white Christian nationalism. Considering how much time and energy he dedicated to that cause through his music and political advocacy, all other complaints based on taste and presentist judgment seem trivial.

Broadway the Hard Way, despite its flaws, presents some of the most politically and socially compelling music of Zappa's career, especially since his pioneering countercultural work of the 1960s. As a snapshot of American life in the late 1980s, the album contains material and references that are intrinsically linked to that era, something that occurs with any work of art so rooted in capturing the topical issues of its time. However, the underlying themes lift the album up from being just a bric-a-brac collection of songs. Beyond the elements that are forever frozen as relics of their day, there is a forward-thinking spirit driving the album. Zappa's critique of the maligned values of American life, such as mass consumerism and corporatization, still rings true four decades later as the country's wealth disparity continues to grow. And the dangers of religious fundamentalism, emboldened by white supremacist and white nationalist ideology, continue to present an existential threat to American democracy, a disturbing reality that elevates *Broadway the Hard Way* as being not just a statement of its time but an enduring commentary on the conditions that foster such a crisis. Certainly, Zappa never made it easy on himself, knowing the difficulty of fighting back through his art while powerful business, media, and government interests worked to increasingly limit avenues for free expression and thought. Nothing worth fighting for is ever accomplished easily. The only way to win back the soul of the nation from the grasp of white Christian nationalists would be the Zappa way, the hard way.

AMNERIKA

As the 1988 election came and went, Ronald Reagan's influence would linger, even though the conservative firebrand no longer sat behind the Resolute desk after meeting the constitutional limit of his executive branch duties. Despite his wimpish characterizations in the media, an image to which Zappa had contributed through his music, George H. W. Bush would win the election with a solid majority, showing that many Americans were just as enthralled with the conservative direction of the country as they were when they voted Carter out of office eight years earlier. Though Bush carried fewer states and earned fewer electoral votes than his Republican lodestar predecessor, but not resulting in an election that could be considered close by any means, Bush's victory represented something larger than a third consecutive conservative term. With the United States experiencing a good economy and a significant reputation on the world stage, as well as the momentum from Reagan's presidency, Bush "confirmed the Republican Party as the dominant force in Presidential politics and reflected the country's satisfaction with eight years of Republican government under Ronald Reagan."[1] However, due to the overwhelming support from fundamentalist evangelical Christians, the contest between Bush and Michael Dukakis would come down to an ideological referendum, with Dukakis defeated due to his being a liberal during a time when conservative social issues were a priority for American voters.[2] The new decade that was coming would begin as a continuation of the same forces Zappa had rallied against in the previous one, and he would kick off the 1990s with a renewed vigor that would further confirm his reputation as an advocate for civil liberties. With eyes on a new horizon, one that not only transcended his legacy as a rock-and-roll iconoclast but also allowed him to forge new pathways to share his messaging, Zappa remained focused and committed to speaking his truth through his music and beyond.

Zappa was concerned about how socially effective a Bush presidency could be. In March 1988, eight months before the presidential election, Zappa told the *Monroe Doctrine,* the student newspaper for Monroe Community College in Rochester, New York, that he did not want to see another administration continue the damage Reagan had caused during both terms of his presidency. Zappa said that most people were not better off now than they were before Reagan, with only an elite few having prospered during that time, and Bush continuing the same policies for another four years would only worsen that divide.[3]

Not only was Zappa embittered over the prospect of what would effectively be a third term advancing the Reagan Doctrine, he was also frustrated with how the Bush candidacy was being covered during the campaign. In the weeks prior to the election, during an interview with Bob Marshall, a broadcaster for Canadian radio CKLN, Zappa chastised pundits and election watchdogs for using their platforms to prematurely declare Bush as the winner of the election. Asking why Bush was still actively campaigning if he was assuredly going to be elected, he criticized a $46 million payment made out to both Bush and Dukakis for use toward their campaigns.[4] Zappa was referring to payments provided by the U.S. Treasury in which each candidate would get "$46 million in public funds to run their campaigns," and despite that, "the amount spent on the presidential race" could still double by the fall. The *Washington Post* reported that "Much of the additional money will be in the form of unregulated and often unreported contributions from wealthy individuals, corporations and labor unions not permitted to contribute directly to the campaigns."[5] In response to these payments, within the context of the media narrative surrounding the inevitability of Bush's victory, Zappa said, "If he's won the election, then why is he still spending that money? Shouldn't he give it back? I think that if he insists on spending that money, then he's committing some kind of fraud."[6]

Zappa also criticized pollsters during his interview with Marshall, referring to them as "pollstergeists." When Marshall told Zappa that many voters were frustrated with election polling, Zappa said those were people who were too intelligent to be fooled by the polls while the ones who would be the most deluded by them he believed would vote for Bush anyway. Zappa explained, "It's the whole idea that Americans think a winner is so terrific, and if you put the little winner's crown on one guy before the election, the day after the election, you want to make sure you voted for the guy who won. Because when you talk to your buddies when they slap each other on the back drinking Miller Lite in the bar after the election, you want to have been on the team. And that's part of the peer pressure to move the votes around."[7]

The main sticking point for Zappa about Bush as president was that he was not convinced Bush had policies, or even the interest, to support people in poverty or otherwise disadvantaged by income inequality. He told *Gallery* in a June 1989 interview how repulsed he was by Bush's inauguration, rebuffing Ron Chepesiuk's comments regarding Bush promising to be a kinder and gentler president, saying it bothered him that $27 million was spent on the pageantry of an inauguration while Washington, DC, could not reconcile with its rising homelessness issue. Bush had to "literally . . . step over the homeless and poor who are starving in Washington to get to the podium."

Zappa also said that Reagan, during his two terms in office, "had the gall to say poor people were poor because they chose to live that way." If Bush was actually going to get anything done in office that was practical and beneficial to the real social issues facing the United States, according to Zappa, he would "have to go beyond the hocus-pocus that Reagan fooled the American people with and do something concrete." This was Zappa addressing the media narratives surrounding the two presidents, with Bush viewed as a pragmatic moderate while Reagan was seen in hindsight as an unyielding ideologue, offering a sound outlook on how Bush could separate himself from the previous eight years. However, Zappa was cynical about Bush being successful in doing that, saying that his support as a candidate was bolstered by evangelicals who were committed to leveraging their cultural and financial capital toward fundamentalist conservative principles such as eliminating abortion access. "I think the next four years are going to comprise a critical period in American history," said Zappa.[8]

Zappa even continued his voter advocacy work during this time, expanding his reach in ways other than through his music. In 1991, Zappa narrated and hosted a half-hour educational special called *Your Vote* for The Learning Channel, informing viewers that, while American citizens have the constitutional right to register and vote for the candidate of their choice, that has not historically been the case for many people, including women, immigrants, and people of color. Supported with interview clips featuring an array of historians and academics, as well as political leaders such as former Dwight Eisenhower attorney general Herbert Brownell, former senator George McGovern, and Georgia representative and civil rights activist John Lewis, Zappa details the nation's history of voter suppression and how those rights were expanded through legislation and suffrage movements. "Two centuries of legal and individual struggle has brought universal suffrage to all Americans over eighteen," Zappa narrates, "but today one massive obstacle remains and that is apathy." Closing the program, after clips from Lewis and McGovern emphasizing the importance of young people voting, Zappa says, "It's your vote and only you can use it. Each election brings you the chance to help change the world around you. In the past, ballots have been cast to set the driving age, the minimum wage, federal funding for your high school or college. Even the quality standards for the water you drink and the air you breathe is determined by the people you vote into office. Your vote counts. It's your right and your responsibility to use it. So use it!"[9]

As Bush's term in office progressed, and Bill Clinton would become his challenger for the 1992 election, Zappa was skeptical that either would be an effective leader. He said he did not trust either candidate, diminishing the race as a "choice between Tweedledee and Tweedledum."[10] Still, Zappa did not truly see the two as equal, and he recognized which one of them would result in an administration more damaging to the United States. "Even if Clinton and his people just stood still for the next four years," Zappa told *Pulse!* in 1993, "it would be better than what we had the four previous years under President Nero, which is what Dennis Miller calls Bush." However, as an absolutist when it came to civil liberties, Zappa did have his complaints about what a Clinton presidency represented. Zappa, who was an avid cigarette smoker, chided Clinton for banning smoking in the White House, saying, "What kind of symbolism is this? It's a social-engineering program by the Health Nazis in the White House against people who like tobacco." Reigniting his longstanding disdain for the healthcare industry and its proponents in government, Zappa wished "people would get off this I'm-gonna-live-forever kick and dispel the myth perpetrated by Reagan's evil Surgeon General C. Everett Koop, who said that second-hand smoke is the most dangerous thing Americans confront in their everyday lives. This is from the same guy who told us that green monkeys gave us AIDS."[11]

Frustrated by how the U.S. government was functioning, Zappa entertained an idea about his own path to the White House. In 1991, he announced his intention to run for president, having previously turned down a spot as vice president on the Libertarian Party ticket for the 1988 election.[12] As part of a ticket for the 1992 election, Zappa contemplated running on a third-party platform, while seriously considering Ross Perot to be his running mate, describing his main qualifications were "that I don't play golf, I don't take vacations and I do think the U.S. Constitution is one hell of a document and that this country would work better if peopled adhered to it more closely."[13]

Zappa explained that his goals as president if elected would have been to present plans to dismantle the government and have the voters decide on its operation, believing that Americans living outside of the Beltway would have at least been receptive to the idea since one of the attractive aspects of such an endeavor would have been eliminating federal income taxes, resulting in citizens receiving bigger paychecks. When pressed if dismantling the federal government would mean he would be out of a job as an elected official, Zappa rejected the notion, suggesting many people would recognize that some aspects of the government would still need to be operational, such as those departments overseeing infrastructure like roads, drinkable water, and clean air. Zappa elaborated that the components of the federal government that should be dismantled were programs and departments where funding was wasted, suggesting their only supporters were the "universe of political talk shows," like CNN, responsible for the "fiction of the theoretical value of the thoughts and words of these inferior human specimens who manage to become Beltway insiders."[14] After twelve years of Republican rule in the White House, Zappa was not so optimistic about the future of the country. "Things are getting worse in the United States," Zappa told *Music Express* in 1992. "The whole mood is on the verge of becoming a police state."[15]

Zappa's presidential ambitions, though, were short-lived. In 1990, Zappa received a diagnosis of prostate cancer after several years of repeated medical examinations to treat urinary problems. When the cancer was discovered, doctors informed Zappa that it was inoperable after having been present for quite some time, with their prognosis that he did not have much time left.[16] When asked by *Playboy* in 1993 if he was serious about running for president, Zappa said that he wanted to do it but that having a cancer diagnosis made it difficult to launch an election campaign, commenting that he had received phone calls and mail from "squadrons of volunteers."[17] Following her husband's death, Gail Zappa would become more active in politics, often appearing at fundraising events for President Clinton and Vice President Gore. According to a January 1999 profile in the *New Yorker*, Gail began thinking about becoming more involved in the political process a few years after Frank's death, motivated by her husband's "frustration at failing to fulfill his ambition." On her growing support of Clinton, Gail said, "It appeared that he had a sense of humor and didn't take himself too seriously. And he reminded me of Frank, in that he was really smart and perceptive and inclusive."[18]

As Zappa passed away before Clinton could even complete his first year in office, we are left with the unanswerable question of how Zappa's music, as American cultural and social commentary, would have evolved and what impact it might have had on the country's politics. Some of the music released since then has given us insight into what could have been. Released as a response to the "spirit of the dramatic 2016 presidential election" between Hillary Clinton and Donald Trump, *Frank Zappa for President* is a posthumous compilation of "unreleased material composed on the Synclavier, along with other unheard tracks that relate to the uniting political thread that ties it all together."[19] Tracks featured on the album are a remix of "Brown Shoes Don't Make It," a "litmus test on the freedoms of his audience and his society;"[20] two instrumental pieces ("Overture to 'Uncle Sam'" and "Medieval Ensemble"); and live versions of "When the Lie's So Big" and "America the Beautiful," which would both be rereleased on 2021's *Zappa '88: The Last U.S. Show.*

Also included on the album is "'If I Was President . . .'," an interview clip overdubbed onto an instrumental track in which Zappa discusses his presidential outlook. He says he would do the job well because he doesn't owe anybody and that he doesn't believe in any political platforms, which would motivate him to figure things out as he went, unworried whether he would please everyone in the country. Zappa then outlines what he would do, including filing as a candidate unaffiliated with any party and raising enough money to earn a spot on election ballots without any campaigning whatsoever. With this approach, Zappa believed the media would contact him to ask about his policy positions while he would sit back and let the other candidates spend vast amounts of money to debate publicly. He reasoned he could get his information out to the voting public via the marketplace of ideas through the appeal of being an outsider. His purpose as a candidate would be to provide an alternative to the traditional system of politics. Zappa describes the current system as unfair and expensive, with neither trend reversing but rather maintained as the status quo. The current process of electing leaders to public office Zappa describes as a system that offers no real choice, which necessitates the need for someone outside of the system to enter the fray to offer an alternative to the binary he believes the majority of Americans find to be insincere and unreal. The album was issued to provide "a glimpse into what could have been."[21]

Though Zappa would never fulfill his presidential ambitions, he would very nearly achieve a role in government. In January 1990, Zappa visited Prague to meet with Václav Havel, the Czechoslovakian activist and writer. Havel was a founding member of a group of dissidents, artists, and cultural leaders who would establish Charter 77, a civic initiative based on a document detailing collective injustices over the Czechoslovakian government's failure to fulfill civil and human rights obligations established in several national and international documents, including the 1960 Constitution of Czechoslovakia, the 1975 Conference on Security and Cooperation in Europe, and commitments to freedoms outlined by the United Nations in 1966.[22] Havel's 1978 essay, "The Power of the Powerless," criticized the politicization of a trial against a rock group called the Plastic People of the Universe, whose name was borrowed from Zappa's song "Plastic People" on 1967's *Absolutely Free*.[23] The band, through their music, protested their government's "intense censorship and blacklisting of western culture" through actions designed "to stop subversive ideas from taking hold among the youth."[24]

In 1974, the members of the Plastic People of the Universe went into hiding after police arrested students who were visiting Prague to see them perform. Two years later, members of the band were put on trial and ultimately convicted for the crime of "organized disturbance of the peace" by the Czechoslovakian government, receiving prison sentences of eight to eighteen months. After completing their sentences, the Plastic People of the Universe would continue to make music that challenged their oppressors for suppressing their art and the right to express it, working underground until the Velvet Revolution in 1989, when the communist government was overthrown through nonviolent action.[25] Havel proclaimed that the mistreatment of the Plastic People of the Universe, as well as other groups in the Czech musical underground, represented the government's abuse of human freedoms, noting that one's individual freedom to perform rock music was "the freedom to engage in philosophical and political reflection, the freedom to write, the freedom to express and defend the various social and political interests of society." Havel said the band's "trial was not a confrontation of two differing political forces or conceptions, but two differing conceptions of life. On the one hand, there was the sterile puritanism of the post-totalitarian establishment and, on the other hand, unknown young people who wanted no more than to be able to live within the truth, to play the music they enjoyed, to sing songs that were relevant to their lives, and to live freely in dignity and partnership."[26]

After successfully leading the Velvet Revolution, Havel would become president of Czechoslovakia until 1992, then becoming president of the Czech Republic from 1993 through 2003 after the country separated from Slovakia. Michael Kocáb, a leader within Havel's Civic Forum Party and a member of the acclaimed Czech band Pražský Výběr, made the arrangements for Zappa to meet the president. When Zappa landed at the Ruzyne Airport in Prague, he was surprised to find five thousand people cheering for him when he came off the plane. Zappa was touched by the reception of the Czech people, expressing that he had never experienced anything like it during his quarter of a century working as a musician. Until the Velvet Revolution, his music had never been legally sold in Czechoslovakia, with fans circulating his music through underground markets because it "represented a freedom of expression that was irresistible to the younger generation of Czechs."[27] Zappa told *Playboy* in 1993 that he had met a young man at the Ministry of Culture in Moscow who told him that he paid his school tuition by bootlegging tapes of Zappa's music from Yugoslavia.[28] By bootlegging and distributing those tapes, that young man Zappa met in Moscow had risked his life for Zappa's music because Zappa, as well as President Jimmy Carter, were considered the two biggest enemies of Czechoslovakia's communist government. On his records being distributed throughout the Soviet Union, Zappa told *Billboard* in 1990:

> They've always been illegal. Also, the people that purchased them, or acquired them, or even possessed transcripts of the lyrics were beaten by the secret police. On one of the occasions, when we were doing kind of a question-and-answer thing in a club in Prague, there were two guys who said that they had been grabbed by the secret police and before they were beaten, the guy said, "We are now going to beat the Zappa music out of you." And nobody in the audience seemed too surprised about it, because apparently it has happened to a lot of people.[29]

Meeting with Havel at Hradčany Castle, Zappa came prepared with ideas he believed could help Czechoslovakia jump-start its economic independence through implementing systems focused on tourism, trade, and the manufacturing and distribution of cell phones and magnetodynamic technology.[30] Prior to meeting with Havel, Zappa was in the Soviet Union to conduct interviews for a talk show offered to him by the Financial News Network, and his meeting with Havel would have been part of that until network executives cancelled the show out of concern for running a disclaimer before the program noting that Zappa's opinions were his own.[31] Zappa asked Havel what types of foreign investments his government was seeking, but he was told that such questions should be discussed with his finance ministers. Over lunch, Zappa and Havel would be joined by Havel's wife, Olga, and Richard Wagner, Havel's adviser on economic and ecological matters, to discuss how to increase the country's national income. Later in the day, the Czech minister of culture, Milan Lukeš, joined the discussions. He would appear on television that evening to announce that Zappa would represent "Czechoslovakia on trade, tourism and cultural matters." Zappa told David Corn for the *Nation* in March 1990, two months after his meeting with Havel, that "Havel and his ministers know they need some Western investment, but they don't want all the ugliness that often invades a country with Western investment. The easiest way to keep the lid on that is to have someone involved whose primary concern is culture, who can reject or modify a project if it is going to have a negative impact on society. Hence my request for the involvement of the Minister of Culture."[32]

Zappa understood how culture, as an articulation of civil liberties such as artistic expression, could be restrained or even revoked outright having witnessed how the U.S. government was empowering religious fundamentalism. His experience advocating against the PMRC revealed to him that the United States was on its way to resemble the kind of system he was hearing about during his visit to the Soviet Union, a society in which being exposed to ideas through music could be met with state-sponsored violence. Kevin Courrier, in *Dangerous Kitchen: The Subversive World of Zappa*, said: "Americans took their democracy for granted, flirting with rock-music censorship and allowing Christian fundamentalism to stage a 20th-century witchhunt. While America denounced Zappa as a perverted freak, here were people who had literally taken beatings to hear what Frank Zappa recorded. He suddenly encountered a hideous irony, something that always lurked somewhere in his compositions—those deprived of freedom learn to understand and value it; those who have it, as in America, fail to embrace it."[33]

The morning after his meeting with Havel, Zappa received a letter from Valtr Komárek, the economic team's deputy prime minister, asking if he would manage "negotiations with foreign partners for preparation of preliminary projects," including drafts of trade agreements.[34] However, Zappa's tenure as a cultural emissary was extremely short-lived as the Bush administration interfered and pressured Havel to distance himself from Zappa or suffer consequences such as economic sanctions.[35] When Havel had mentioned to Zappa that Vice President Dan Quayle would soon visit him, Zappa told him that it would be regrettable for Havel to spend any amount of time, even if just a few moments, around someone he believed to be so incredibly stupid. Instead, U.S. secretary of state James Baker III, husband of PMRC cofounder Susan Baker, would intervene and "literally lay down the law" in what Zappa thought of as an act of sabotage through government interference.[36] Baker would minimize Zappa's role as a cultural emissary by declaring it as unofficial. In a statement issued by Havel's press secretary, while opening it by confirming that they liked him, Zappa was declared as being unauthorized to "negotiate any trade agreements with our government."[37] As Ben Watson notes in *Frank Zappa: The Negative Dialectics of Poodle Play,* "Havel and his country simply did not have the clout to offend the US. As Zappa burned his fingers in his attempts at nurturing free enterprise in Eastern Europe, it became clear that his politics are valuable as iconographic rupture rather than as practical intervention."[38]

Despite the revocation of his cultural emissary status, Zappa's impact was deeply felt and reverberated throughout the country. In a tribute published in the *New Yorker* on December 20, 1993, sixteen days after Zappa's death, Havel called Zappa "one of the gods of the Czech underground during the nineteen-seventies and eighties" and that his music signified that "Western rock was far more than just a form of music." Havel described Zappa's visit as occurring during a time when Czechoslovakia was "still vibrant with revolutionary energy." Zappa was remembered by Havel as being excited by the idea of how artists could be active participants in politics, offering cultural and economic assistance with such sincerity that it made a lasting impression on him. Havel called Zappa a friend and said, "Meeting him was like entering a different world from the one I live in as President. Whenever I feel like escaping from that world—in my mind, at least—I think of him."[39]

Europe would play a significant role in Zappa's life after the collapse of the Soviet Union, culminating in the last album he would release during his lifetime. *The Yellow Shark,* released in 1993, would feature modern orchestral arrangements of earlier compositions as well as some new material for the first time since 1988's *Broadway the Hard Way.* The genesis of this album came from a 1991 meeting between Zappa and Dieter Rexroth, director of the Frankfurt Festival, and Andreas Mölich-Zebhauser, head of the Ensemble Modern whose mission was to elevate the works of modern composers. Their goal was to convince Zappa "to contribute scores for an evening of concert music."[40] Along with John Cage, Karlheinz Stockhausen, and Alexander Knaifel as featured composers, Zappa would participate in the 1992 iteration of the festival. In a 1993 interview with *Pulse!* when asked by interviewer Dan Ouellette how he had managed to maintain considerable relevance throughout a career that spanned three decades, Zappa answered with an uncharacteristic modesty: "I don't know how it's happened. How have I survived? I guess by word of mouth, but I don't know. I got lucky."[41] With rock music behind him, Zappa's sights were set on the future where his orchestral work would be taken seriously, with the Ensemble Modern being the group that would best represent the complexity and vastness of his music.

Rehearsals for a series of concerts with the Ensemble Modern lasted for two weeks, and included modernized arrangements of classic Zappa compositions, including "Dog Breath Variations," "Pound for a Brown," "Be-Bop Tango," and "Uncle Meat." More recent pieces were also rehearsed. Among the works selected to be rearranged for the show in Frankfurt was "G-Spot Tornado," an instrumental composed on the Synclavier for Zappa's 1986 album *Jazz from Hell* that was "considered impossible for the group to play."[42] "Outrage at Valdez," originally composed as the soundtrack for the 1990 Jacques Cousteau documentary *Alaska: Outrage at Valdez*, documenting the 1989 oil tanker disaster in Prince William Sound, would also be added to the program. The day before his final tour, on the subject of rearranging his music, Zappa said:

> The thing to stress is what the musical ideas are and what the structural ideas are. I regard the differences in performing entities as textural differences. If I'm writing for the instrumentation of the original Mothers Of Invention, that's me writing for the specific limitations of that format. If I write for the symphony orchestra, that's me writing for those limitations. If you step back and look at the whole picture, at some point the differences in the performing liabilities dissolve and you realise what could happen if there was one thing that could do it all. There is no one thing, of course.[43]

Though his cancer had a direct impact on his ability to compose and record music, Zappa remained enthusiastic about the forthcoming concerts with the Ensemble Modern, telling journalists the shows would be filmed and recorded. With the goal of having his music be heard the way he had intended, the venues for the concerts were chosen for their ability "to accommodate Zappa's six-channel surround-sound system, which would provide a unique aural experience for an audience not used to such technical means at a classical concert."[44] The concerts were held in three cities—Frankfurt, Berlin, and

Vienna—with several performances scheduled for each. The Frankfurt shows, held at the Alte Oper on September 17 and 19, were hugely successful, with over twenty-four hundred people in attendance. Zappa would go on to say that the extended applause from the Frankfurt audience left musicians and organizers stunned. Due to his ailing health, Zappa's only involvement in the program was as host and to conduct improvisational pieces, as well as conducting the finale, "G-Spot Tornado." He would be too unwell to attend the remaining shows at the Philharmonie in Berlin on September 22 and 23, as well as the shows in Vienna at Wiener Konzerthaus from September 26 through 28.[45]

Compiling recordings from these shows, *The Yellow Shark* would be Zappa's final artistic statement as a living composer, released one month before his death. Though the album was an opportunity to present his work as he had intended it to be heard, and included older material, Zappa's worsening health did not deter him from still making profound cultural, social, and political statements in his music. "Times Beach II" is a composition about one of the most devastating environmental disasters in U.S. history,[46] in which the town of Times Beach in Missouri experienced a flood in 1982 that spread dioxin, an extremely toxic substance that had been used to suppress dust on its roads.[47] "Pentagon Afternoon," with plastic ray-gun sound effects, is a tone poem dedicated to the military brass that Zappa referred to as "the dealers in death."[48]

Among the tracks on *The Yellow Shark,* two stand out as distinctly stark and bleak statements about the United States and the direction in which Zappa believed the country was heading. "Food Gathering in Post-Industrial America, 1992" is a musical dramatic reading performed by Hilary Sturt, a violist for the Ensemble Modern. Sturt visualizes Zappa's outlook on the future of America, a postapocalyptic environmental nightmare in which, after all the factories have finally finished poisoning the water supply with their pollution and industrial waste, we find the last remaining inhabitants of a New America dining on rats and foam packing pellets floating in raw sewage. Punctuated with a myriad of different cues from the ensemble, including a siren at its beginning, vocal responses from performers, and various sound effects and musical snippets that convey the toxicity of this new, perfect postindustrial America, it is a startlingly sober piece that, at the time, seemed to blend fiction with reality as a cautionary tale. However, over the last three decades as the climate change crisis has worsened, with the 2023 Intergovernmental Panel on Climate Change's report warning that humanity will cross the environmental threshold by 2030, when it is believed the remaining carbon budget will be depleted,[49] Zappa's warning instills an existential fear exponentially more severe now than with audiences in 1992. In an interview for *Oor* in September 1992, Zappa said of the track: "The idea behind that is that we are evolving toward a postindustrial society, a country where everyone is occupied with rendering services to each other and consuming products that have been made by others. This composition is built around the small acts of desperation of people looking for food. Everytime somebody finds something eatable, the musicians shout: Wooo."[50]

Zappa's portrait of a nation collapsing from industrial devastation is not just a warning at face value about the extreme consequences of not caring about the planet. It also contains a subtext about the people responsible for this decline. Seeking the few remaining food sources, the denizens of this toxic wasteland feed on the diseased body parts of feral children, who have grown in number because of a complete ban on abortion a few years earlier. This final line, read with barely tempered anger by Sturt, is a gut punch, made even worse since the Supreme Court's overturning of the constitutionally protected right for people to seek safe and accessible abortion in 2022. For five decades, evangelical Christians and pro-life advocates made eliminating abortion access their most important goal, their strategies shifting to influence state governments to interfere with the bodily autonomy of people without their consent now that national protections have vanished. For Zappa, eliminating abortion rights was an affront to civil liberties at the hands of religious fundamentalists shaping government to enforce their will on other Americans.

In a September 1989 piece for *Tuttifrutti*, an Italian magazine, Zappa said the cultural argument involving abortion failed to take account of the larger issue. For Zappa, the subject of abortion was not a matter of being pro-choice or pro-life. The country had to decide whether it wanted to be a "pro-choice nation" or a "no-choice nation," with Zappa rhetorically asking the question if Americans truly wanted democracy while he also placed the blame on religious fundamentalists for championing the notion that government built on democratic principles should be eradicated. Zappa then describes a subversive agenda of religious fundamentalists viewing themselves as, emphasis his,

"GOD'S CHOSEN PEOPLE" and "THE ALL-AMERICAN MASTER RACE," while everyone else that is part of the democratic majority will burn in hell. Therefore, they believe that most of the country has to be controlled because doing so is not only honoring God, but betters their own lives as well. Viewing the democratic process of voting as an "evil tool," they have implemented programs and initiatives "designed to strangle freedom of choice at every level of American life" with "ideological kamikazes" nestled within numerous facets of the American government, including the Supreme Court. Zappa, in closing, says, "These assholes are a bigger threat to Democracy than any KGB agent ever could be."[51]

Immediately following "Food Gathering in Post-Industrial America, 1992" on *The Yellow Shark* is "Welcome to the United States," a chillingly surreal reading inspired by immigration forms issued by the U.S. Department of Justice. The track opens with a Germanic-sounding orchestral fanfare as Rainer Römer, a percussionist for the Ensemble Modern, speaks in German as conductor Peter Rundel leaves the stage, with Zappa as Rundel's guest replacement. Römer then introduces Ensemble Modern pianist Hermann Kretschmar as other players from the ensemble laugh on cue. Kretschmar, in a comically booming German voice over grim orchestration, welcomes everyone and informs them that immigration forms must be filled out by nonimmigrants who have not already acquired a visitor's visa, urging them to write legibly in capitalized English. Kretschmar then guides the players through the various questions on the form. The first couple of questions concern how the individual arrived in the United States. Next, Kretschmar asks the questions that cover the visitor's health, including whether they have been diagnosed with a communicable disease or otherwise suffer from any other physical or mental illness. As Kretschmar continues, moving on to vice questions, he asks the players if they have ever been convicted of a crime involving illegal and controlled substances, whether they have been sentenced to prison on drug-related charges for more than five years, or if they are traffickers seeking to commit drug-related offenses in the country.

As Kretschmar goes through his reading, the players in the ensemble react with a variety of sounds, either giving comical answers to the questions or performing quick improvisational musical snippets. "Welcome to the United

States" seems rather farcical, an easy notion given the rehearsed laughs coming from the musicians as participants in the reading. The improvisational moments in the piece also add a layer of levity, elevating the overall piece to absurd heights. Kretschmar asks if anyone completing the form has ever been an active participant in acts of terrorism, including espionage, sabotage, or genocide. In response to each of the crimes, Zappa conducts the ensemble through these improvisational snippets, like a rearrangement of the Kingsmen's hit "Louie Louie" following the question concerning terroristic activities.[52]

However, as Kretschmar prepares to ask the final question on the form, the mood immediately turns dark. With a militaristic snare drum coming in on the onset of the question, Kretschmar asks if anyone present was involved in persecutions involving Nazi Germany and its allies between 1933 and 1945. He reads the question as a rising dissonant orchestral noise erupts from the ensemble, and Kretschmar yells over the sound, a dark specter ushering the listener into the depraved madness of human sin evoking the Holocaust as it creeps steadily into the frame, no longer content to be in the rearview mirror of history. As the music quickly fades away, Kretschmar is left in silence to solemnly instruct people to answer either yes or no to the question. As one single man answers yes, Kretschmar ecstatically thanks the lone voice and welcomes him to the United States.

Ben Watson interviewed Zappa for his book *Frank Zappa: The Negative Dialectics of Poodle Play,* mentioning that he could think only about the music from *The Yellow Shark* when recently reading an immigration form on an airplane. Zappa responded, referring to the World Trade Center bombing on February 26, 1993, by saying, "It's bizarre. Here you have all these Middle Eastern terrorists just flying in and blowing up the World Trade Center, and you have all that bureaucracy dealing with that form to find out if you're a Nazi. It's like, if you fill it out properly, what happens—you get a job in the cabinet?"[53] Zappa's response to Watson's anecdote is notable to me because these comments were made in the early 1990s, when politicians with neo-Nazi sympathies were gaining prominence throughout Europe. In September 1993, the British National Party, the United Kingdom's far-right fascist party, achieved its first electoral success when one of their candidates won a council seat during a by-election in East London.[54] Jean-Marie Le Pen, instrumental in founding

France's far-right National Front, was pulling in less than 1 percent of votes during elections in the 1970s, but would soon earn more than 15 percent by the early to mid-1990s.[55] Even in Germany, a nation that has in the decades since World War II worked tirelessly to reconcile with its troubling history, experienced a resurgence of neo-Nazi violence in the early 1990s, most notably through a series of hate crimes and murders committed against Turkish people that led to days of rioting.[56]

Even in the United States during this time, neo-Nazism was on the rise. The July 1990 issue of the *Nation* was entirely dedicated to printing journalist Elinor Langer's report, "The American Neo-Nazi Movement Today," which addressed the "long, slow re-emergence of racial thinking in the United States from its retreat after World War II to the point where it can once again energize action; of the gradual, tentative crystallization of a political movement openly aimed at white hegemony." Langer's report noted that, while activities by neo-Nazis were extreme in their ideological severity, "they exist along a racist continuum on which it is difficult to draw a line" and were advancing as a movement that had entered mainstream politics on issues such as immigration. Grappling with the existential crisis explored by Sinclair Lewis in his 1935 novel *It Can't Happen Here,* in a narrative in which an American politician becomes the first dictator of the United States in an allegory to the rise of Hitler, Langer says it is probably not likely for another Hitler to come into power, but "only because history does not literally repeat," going on to make the case that modern forms of fascist ideology resurface in subtler ways. "In a period of declining national authority manifested everywhere from our weakening social structure to our worsening economic position," said Langer, "a movement is stirring that explains it all, and people are starting to listen."[57]

Zappa was aware of the homegrown Nazi influence as it was something he had addressed at various points in his music, even as far back as 1967's "Plastic People." Unfortunately, as much as the rise of neo-Nazism was a concern in the early 1990s, and the track "Welcome to the United States" a pointed commentary on seemingly complicit attitudes toward it through faulty bureaucracy, it is deeply troubling how the trends of neo-Nazism and white supremacy have grown over the last three decades. Since 1979, the Anti-Defamation League, a nonprofit advocacy group dedicated to the preservation of Jewish civil rights, has published annual reports documenting the number of anti-Semitic incidents. In 2023, the ADL reported that the number of such incidents, including direct violence, increased by 36 percent over the previous year, a record high. Jonathan Greenblatt, the national director of the ADL, said, "We've seen antisemitism normalized in ways that would have been unimaginable a few years ago. If people see conspiracies behind every misfortune, it doesn't take long for them to look at the Jews and say they're the problem."[58] In the face of such record numbers of anti-Semitic incidents and rhetoric, President Joe Biden and his administration issued the U.S. National Strategy to Counter Antisemitism in May 2023, featuring a plan to direct "a whole-of-society effort to combat antisemitism, including unprecedented, coordinated, and bold actions that will be implemented across government agencies, as well as calls to action for public officials, private sector leaders, and Americans from every sector, industry, and walk of life," with the plan's strategy also serving "as a blueprint for tackling other forms of bigotry, hate, and bias that fuel toxic divisions in America."[59] With these types of hateful incidents on the rise, emboldened by neo-Nazis who have been infiltrating systems of power, including Republican members of Congress,[60] whose party is unanimously opposed to rooting out white supremacy within powerful institutions like the police and military,[61] the underlying sentiment of "Welcome to the United States" sounds less absurd with every listen. It is a manifestation of Zappa's apparent far-sightedness on the direction of America on the cusp of a new millennium, proclaiming that, yes, it can happen here.

One composition that premiered at the Frankfurt concert, but which was not included on *The Yellow Shark,* was "Amnerika." Blending the words "America" and "amnesia" to describe a particular state, either as an actual territory or a psychological frame of mind, both evoking a dystopian version of the United States, the composition would later appear as "Amnerika Goes Home" on the 1999 posthumous album *EIHN (Everything Is Healing Nicely),* which consists of recordings by the Ensemble Modern in preparation for *The Yellow Shark* concerts. The instrumentation sounds anxious, with the music syncopated and offbeat, featuring horns jarringly punctuated to pierce the fog of confusion suffusing a nightmarish vision of America. A rearrangement, "Amnerika (Vocal Version)," would appear on *Frank Zappa for President,* with lyrics that heighten the tension of the earlier instrumental version. Featuring vocals from the Evil Prince antagonist in *Thing-Fish*, we gain insight into the ideological framework of this vision of the country as a cultural amnesiac destined to forget and destroy whatever aspects of society that cannot be bought out. The prince monologues that artists and Indigenous people distress and anger the citizens of Amnerika, and his religious texts and ideology give him a moral pass to kill them without guilt or divine retribution.

While "Amnerika" would not be included on *The Yellow Shark*, it would make its debut on *Civilization Phaze III*, a 1994 posthumous release and the last album Zappa would complete before his death.[62] Zappa's first album of all new material since 1986's *Jazz from Hell*, *Civilization Phaze III* concluded a conceptual musical trilogy that began with *We're Only in It for the Money* and continued with *Lumpy Gravy*, both released in 1968. Composed on the Synclavier, and using sampled audio recorded by the Ensemble Modern, the album's narrative features a group of people who live inside a piano and struggle to come to terms with the dangerous and complex world outside. They sit in this piano in the dark, listening to it grow and discussing if it's their home and whether the piano playing hurts their ears. The piano dwellers speculate on what happens to a friend who left the piano and what kind of bugaboos they could find if they venture out, commenting on the viciousness of humans. They discuss music, animals that run the media, and cultural differences such as language barriers. The album's scenario, outlined in its liner notes, says this storyline originated from improvised dialogue based on random concepts, including livestock, music, nationalism, and personal isolation, all performed as opera pantomime,[63] continuing the musique concrète sound-collage tradition of the album's conceptual predecessors; "we get a few more clues about the lives of the piano dwellers and note that the external evils have only gotten worse since we first met them."[64] Zappa would tell Joe Jackson, in a 1993 interview for *Hot Press*, "There is very little, if any, singing in this opera. There is the human voice but most of the material is spoken and 90% of the musical accompaniment is done with computer. And the spoken text, though comprised of comprehensible sentences and paragraphs, when you hear what's said you're still left scratching your head in terms of what people are actually saying. Largely because it was created out of found objects, pieces of conversations that were edited together to produce the plot."[65]

In *Frank Zappa: The Complete Guide to His Music,* Ben Watson describes *Civilization Phaze III* as "Zappa's last great work," signaling that Zappa "was far too aware of the social implications of 'art' music to do anything so positivist." Even the album's final track, "Waffenspiel," which is German for "weapon play," features "a recording of homeowners in the San Fernando Valley shooting their automatic weapons skyward" during New Year's Eve revelry in 1987. "What should be celebratory fireworks has become a manifestation of property-owner paranoia and aggression," says Watson. "The pained expression on Zappa's face as he described these 'assholes' to me said everything about his art's relation to society: his music was always objective investigation, a telling of home truths."[66] A real-world manifestation of Amnerika.

Gail Zappa would go on to release *Civilization Phaze III* as a mail-order album only available through their label Barking Pumpkin Records, with no advertising or marketing support, as an experiment "to see who's really out there, and how much attention they're paying to the importance of having Frank's music in their lives."[67] Zappa told Don Menn and Matt Groening in an earlier 1992 interview with *Guitar Player,* in regard to the issues he had encountered distributing his music in recent years, that "as long as we have the current type of political and supposedly moral machinery of the United States, the way it is now, it's not likely that the music has much of a future in this country." Zappa believed there would be few composers left because writing music was becoming less and less profitable as a profession: "If you expect to have a future history of music, somebody's got to write it, and they can't write it unless they can survive while they're writing it," with Frank blaming the music industry for stripping away the rights of the composer.[68] When asked if defunding music education programs was signaling another cultural black hole for the future of America, Zappa said he believed it to be "the subtext for stamping out the arts. . . . In the realm of arts, you always have the possibility for creative thinking, which means deviation from the norm, the prescribed political norm that everybody is trying to cram down your throat. If they can stop creative thinking, then they've got a better chance of maintaining the stranglehold of stupidity on the entire population."[69]

Gail said she thought *Civilization Phaze III* was "perhaps the ultimate destiny" of this period of her husband's career, noting that Frank "worked so hard to finish it before he died" and that it resulted in "something a little different than he originally intended." Gail said her husband had realized there were many things he would not be able to do, so *Civilization Phaze III* became a pragmatic outlet, Frank's way of saying "thanks for the memories."[70] "I think it's very much about finishing his life," said Gail, recalling her husband telling her, "I've done everything I can."[71] At a July 1992 press conference in Frankfurt to promote the forthcoming concerts for *The Yellow Shark*, when asked about his future plans after the concerts were finished, Zappa said, "I have to finish the albums and see what happens then."[72] Zappa would succumb to his prostate cancer on December 4, 1993.

In 1990, Zappa was interviewed by Niles Lesh in what would come to be known among fans as "The Lost Interview." Lesh asks Zappa about his musical influences as well as a range of political topics, including the Bush administration, censorship, UFOs, and the state of American democracy. At the end of the interview, Lesh asks Zappa if he has a final message to deliver to people living in the year 3000. Zappa tells Lesh he does not believe humans will even exist in a thousand years. Suggesting that only bacteria and slugs will be left on the planet by that point, Zappa says he would try to speak to them using bacteria language, mouthing a noise like an organic theremin to deliver whatever coded message he has to offer to the last lingering lifeforms following in the wake of mankind's self-destruction.[73] This sentiment, as both a statement on humanity and a reflection of his perception of America's darkening future, would be continued in the only way Zappa could completely and honestly share the truth of his visions: through his music and what little time he had left to express it.

As the cancer motivated him to make music to say as much as he possibly could before the disease would have the final word, Zappa approached the topic of his legacy with complex emotions, viewing his music in the context of his own increasingly finite mortality. During a February 1991 interview for a BBC Radio documentary—unpublished until twenty-five years after Zappa's death—finally printed in the November 2018 issue of *Mojo*, Zappa jokingly said, "Few people know or even care that I exist. I don't think there'll be anything of what I do that will survive beyond my lifespan." Though, interviewer Pete Frame recognizes that, beneath Zappa's "superficial resignation, he hoped that his contribution would one day be recognised by the grisly breed (he continued to hold them in the lowest esteem) who write about rock music." Toward the end of the interview, in regard to a question about whether he draws any lines when it comes to pornographic lyrics, Zappa said, framing the answer to reflect critics of his musical cultural commentary over the years, "I don't think of those things as pornographic. Look at it this way: if I had a degree from a university and I was going into the jungle to study the behaviour of some unusual tribe, no matter what they did, pornographic or otherwise, it would be regarded as serious research. But I don't have a degree. However, I am writing songs about various tribes that exist in my country—their behaviour and their folklore. This is what they do and how they are. It's anthropology, pure and simple." When Frame responds by suggesting his work will be studied in two hundred years by scholars looking to trace the development of popular culture, Zappa replied, "Well, first of all, I don't think we are going to be around in a couple of hundred years and certainly there won't be any scholars—they'll be phased out. And curiosity? That'll be forbidden. So the usefulness of this research? For entertainment purposes only." Zappa then suggested that America is going to be worse than the society depicted in George Orwell's *1984*, and that Americans would prefer to live in such a dystopia.[74]

After three decades of being a groundbreaking and boundary-pushing musical visionary, Zappa's career would come to an end very much in the same way it began—as an artist dutifully dedicated to his craft. Despite his ever-worsening health, Zappa, until the very end of his life, developed his music with integrity and purpose. Regardless of commercial and critical pressure, he eschewed nearly every standard imaginable in order to present the most honest version of his art as social, cultural, and political commentary. Even while battling a terminal illness, Zappa remained committed to his convictions, based on principles that guaranteed civil liberties and personal freedoms for Americans of all backgrounds. By the sunset years of his life, he had a disturbing vision of America's future in which the lights of the shining city on the hill were dimming for those who were most at risk of the country's darkest impulses. The very fact that he remained steadfast in his dedication to this until the end of his life, leaving the impression that he could have offered so much more, suggests that Zappa was not the cynical misanthrope his most ardent critics would suggest he was. Instead, what he actually was, and what he attempted to express to audiences all over the world, was a musician with a capital "M," utilizing his art—from rock star to classical composer—to visualize a more equitable and just world. I don't believe this is something a true cynic would have been able to accomplish or even attempt, especially to the magnitude of how Zappa approached his music. Writing and composing his final musical works, with death lurking in the background, Zappa worked prodigiously to offer what would be his final artistic statements. With so much left to say and so little time to say it, the message Zappa would leave behind for listeners is one we have been grappling with for decades and will continue to do so for the foreseeable future. Whether as a sign of things to come or as a sign of the times, Zappa's vision of the coming phase of an amnesiac American civilization would not be a welcome, but rather a warning.

EPILOGUE

Have I Offended Someone?

The genesis for this book was an article I wrote for *PopMatters* in which I analyzed the origins of *Joe's Garage* as a response to the Ayatollah banning music in Iran; I recontextualized the album following the Supreme Court's overturning of *Roe v. Wade* in June 2022. When I initially pitched the essay to the editors, I was focused on drawing parallels between the two events as a commentary on the rising influence of Christian fascism in the United States since the election of Donald Trump in 2016. My goal was to address the similarities in order to demonstrate Zappa's prescience as an artist and commentator. When the pitch was accepted, I was excited to dive deep into this album that I had not listened to in quite some time. While I had remembered the album's overall narrative and subtext, I realized after relistening that I had largely forgotten about the lyrics and imagery on it that had contributed to Zappa's reputation as a provocative figure. As I was carefully listening to the words and thinking about the context in which they were said, it dawned upon me that this essay was going to be a more expansive project than I had pitched.

If I were going to move forward with praising this album for its cultural significance, I could not do so without also addressing the socially difficult aspects of the album. Not only was this essay going to be bigger in scope, but I also had to touch upon ideas and themes that some people, especially those in marginalized communities, might find offensive and inappropriate. For that reason, I had concerns that the editors would not publish the article. Of course, this was all based on assumptions and projections on my part, albeit based on real experiences and observations. Trump's ascent to the White

House had resulted in an endless deluge of toxicity that drove, and continues to drive, the national dialogue. Some of these conversations were absolutely necessary, shifting the focus of discussion to address how non-white and non-male groups were most at risk over the administration's dangerous policies. However, some of these conversations would devolve into ideologically based culture-war issues that complicated efforts to raise awareness over enacting real social change, and instead advanced polarization. In other words, as I was listening to *Joe's Garage*, I was thinking, *Is now really the time for Frank Zappa?* As the Central Scrutinizer, the album's narrator, asked, *Ultimately, who gives a fuck anyway?*

One thing I knew I did not want to do was to simply dismiss criticisms by saying that Zappa was a product of his time and that things were much different in the 1970s. I found that approach to be intellectually dishonest and, quite frankly, rather boring. Instead, what I did was examine the politics of the late 1970s to recall how a burgeoning evangelical movement would form in the waning days of a liberal administration before becoming a significant presence in 1980s culture and politics. With that, I was able to close my article, introducing ideas on how Zappa would evolve as an artist throughout the 1980s following the release of *Joe's Garage*. I was able to make a narrative through-line that showcased Zappa's ongoing commitment to channel progressive values through his music that challenged the undercurrent of white Christian nationalism that was a part of Ronald Reagan's evangelical base. Doing this got me to a point where I felt satisfied with the subtext of my article, and that paid off. Not only was the article published with support from the editors, I also felt validated when the article would go on to win an award from a professional journalism organization.[1] I had begun this journey unsure over whether the point I was making would be seen as having intellectual and artistic merit, especially considering how the Trump administration forced many Americans to take a long, hard look in the mirror and decide who we wanted to be in the new normal that was being created. By the end of it, I felt confident to move forward and champion the image I had of Zappa. With that article, so began this book to expand upon that narrative through-line that I argued had started with *Joe's Garage*.

In telling the story of how Zappa evolved his music to address white Christian nationalism despite ever-growing critical and commercial pressures, I knew I had to be careful in how I approached the subject and crafted the narrative if I wanted it to be effective. There were certain things I knew I did not want. The first was to speculate on what Zappa would say about American society now, many years after his death. This was a nonstarter for me because Zappa is dead and there is no way to know what he would say now. When people make assumptions about what dead people would say about modern society, it becomes a way to project their own biases and prejudices. Certainly, there is no shortage of that projection. Consider the legacy of George Carlin, another provocative but deceased cultural commentator. Since his death in 2008, his jokes and commentary have been appropriated in social media to rationalize views that Carlin would not have shared. Conservatives and far-right Republicans have shared clips of Carlin, devoid of context, in order to make some obfuscated point about liberals they see as opposition. Carlin's own daughter has publicly said, "It just always shocks me when these Trumpers wanna claim him" as one of their own.[2] Even beloved civil rights hero Martin Luther King Jr. gets the same treatment every January when white conservatives use the occasion of his birthday to misappropriate his messaging to rationalize their own destructive policies and behavior, weaponizing his words to advance an agenda that is antithetical to Dr. King's teachings.[3] As these people are unable to speak for themselves, they have no control of how their words are used. I did not want to speak on Zappa's behalf.

The second thing I did not want to do with this book was to rely on a narrative that addressed "cancel culture" or "woke," or what those terms represent in the collective consciousness today. Frankly, I find them to be meaningless. As of this writing in 2024, they have become politicized phrases that have furthered polarization in our society in ways that I believe are fundamentally dangerous. They either shut down conversations or remove nuance within them. The popular dialogue around them is too toxic to be effective. I did not rely on those concepts because I did not want my book on Zappa to be another white man whining about how you cannot say anything these days without some imaginary mob coming after you. I find that approach to be cowardly and not very interesting.

However, just like a stopped clock being right twice a day, those concepts are not entirely without merit. I believe there is something happening within our culture that is getting objectively worse, and it is no coincidence that it is happening at a time when white Christian nationalists are becoming more prominent. I am unsure that we have the language to adequately describe it yet, or at least language that we can use without it devolving into banal partisan rhetoric, but something is undeniably there. I've mentioned the concept of the panopticon, which has a built-in system of control that "allows a watchman to observe occupants without the occupants knowing whether or not they are being watched."[4] Whether anyone is actually occupying the guard tower does not matter. It is the prospect of their presence that enforces the rules. As a result, when we apply this concept broadly to culture, there is a freezing effect regarding self-expression. Many would suggest this is a system that prevents people from doing things and behaving in ways that are in bad faith. That does make sense when we are talking about things that directly oppress or subjugate human beings, but it becomes a complicated matter when we think about it from the perspective of the role art plays in society.

Consider the open letter that appeared in *Harper's* during July 2020. Signed by over 150 prominent cultural figures, including Salman Rushdie and Gloria Steinem, the letter argued "that stifled free speech is creating an 'intolerant climate' within society."[5] The letter not only addressed the recognition that "racial and social justice are leading to overdue demands for police reform, along with wider calls for greater equality and inclusion across our society," but its signatories also endorsed the notion that "this needed reckoning has also intensified a new set of moral attitudes and political commitments that tend to weaken our norms of open debate and toleration of differences in favor of ideological conformity."[6] This letter would receive mixed reviews from the public and through online feedback on social media, largely due to the controversial reputation of some of its signatories, such as J. K. Rowling, who "faced public condemnation for comments widely deemed to be anti-transgender."[7] Despite the reputation of some of those who signed the letter, there is validity to the overall arguments being made. One of the people who signed the letter was Noam Chomsky, who in 1988, along with Edward S. Herman, authored a book about the concept of "manufacturing consent." Chomsky and Herman make the argument that institutions in the United States use mass media as a "system-supportive propaganda function" that relies "on market forces, internalized assumptions, and self-censorship, and without significant overt coercion."[8] Powerful systems utilize propagandized media, implemented across capitalist channels, to change people's behavior in order to make them obedient and unquestioning. As a bookend to the prologue discussing the *Freedom Wall*, the *Harper's* letter can also be seen as a sort of cultural public display that attempts to capture the zeitgeist, with both pieces comprising a list of names, but conjuring different reactions as one attempts to explain its meaning while the other lets you come to your own conclusions with little to no controversy.

I bring up that *Harper's* letter and the response to it because they capture something I did want to do with this book. While the majority of the criticism lobbed against the letter was based on reactionary responses to the people whose reputations have some problematic qualities, that outlook tends to ignore the particular direction the letter took, which was to address these concerns on an institutional level. In its final paragraph, the letter reads: "The restriction of debate, whether by a repressive government or an intolerant society, invariably hurts those who lack power and makes everyone less capable of democratic participation."[9] That captures the essence of why I avoided writing a book about Zappa from a presentist perspective and instead commented on institutional and systemic power to make my case. I did this because Zappa also did this. While there are plenty of examples where Zappa makes cynical, emotional, or hyperbolic comments to reporters and interviewers, condemning certain elements of society, I found Zappa to be more interesting and effective in his commentary when he addressed institutions and how they function.

Zappa exhibited a deep knowledge of how various social and cultural institutions maintain their own power and authority, often at the expense of average citizens. This understanding fueled much of his outlook. Not only did he convey this understanding through his music, but he also utilized his platform to address these issues on a broader scale despite the risk and scrutiny. Consider as an example the argument he made over the PMRC's proposal to put warning labels on albums, one of the most enduring aspects of Zappa's legacy. While Zappa shared views similar to both John Denver's and Dee Snider's about the fascistic aspects of the proposal, much of his argument was centered on legal and tax-code structures. Or consider his explanation of how racism was perpetuated through the media, explaining how conservatives consume stereotypical tropes because governmental deregulation of telecommunications allowed for less cultural diversity in broadcast programming. This was an approach Zappa made throughout his career. While commenting on education standards, political reforms, cultural literacy, and so much more, Zappa framed his arguments to specifically state that these various institutions that dominate and control our lives are helmed by elites who wield an exorbitant amount of power, with the consequences of their decisions and actions having to be shouldered by those who do not share that power, with the effects disproportionately felt within marginalized communities. Seeing this pattern throughout his career allowed me to understand how relevant his messaging is because the issues he was addressing decades ago still reverberate today and, in many cases, have since grown in size and impact. This explains why Zappa pivoted in his career, going from just commenting on these issues through his music to actively engaging with and championing the democratic process. Just like the people who signed that letter for *Harper's*, Zappa was concerned that the foundational elements of democracy were at risk of crumbling.

Zappa's commitment to a participatory democracy as a response to the outsized power of social and cultural institutions is ultimately why I decided to write this book. This, after all, is how I came to realize that the messaging in his music still matters today and that the things he fought against are still active threats. When it comes to music, no one did more to advocate for the freedom of expression than Zappa. During a period in his career when he was experiencing a decline in album and ticket sales, he still fought for these values at great personal and professional expense. Though being music's greatest pitchman for democracy, he did come with a lot of baggage. Some of that I've done my best to address with nuance and sensitivity. Certainly, some of Zappa's musical output presents difficult listening for some modern listeners. Outdated ideas, sometimes jumbled with conceptual continuity in-jokes and references, can be quite difficult to relate to, especially if it requires so much context in order to understand the subtext. Though the period I focused on is often his most neglected, it contains ideas and a spirit that truly make Zappa a timeless figure. In analyzing this particular period, I was able not only to contribute a more complete understanding of him as a musical icon but also comment on how the modern culture-war issues are extensions of the ones he fought against decades ago, thus illustrating how dangerous ideologies can resurface with a new dance despite being the same old song.

Zappa's fan base has largely historically been white men, myself included. While there are many women and people of color who do enjoy Zappa's music, it is not unreasonable to suggest that many songs have not resonated widely among those groups. Much of this has to do with Zappa's own particular image and musical style as elements of his overall brand. He was a self-proclaimed ugly white guy who often made music that was difficult to access because it did not appeal to broad popular tastes. However, my purpose is not to make an aesthetic argument. If something does not connect with you and does not sound appealing on a sonic and musical level, then it is pointless to try to convince you otherwise. My goal instead is to analyze the inherent themes within Zappa's music to demonstrate that his catalog, as vast and diverse as it is, reflected a trajectory that increasingly spoke truth to power about the various machinations within society and culture that are objectively damaging, like having individual and personal freedoms be rescinded and nullified by overzealous religious fundamentalists influencing government and media. In doing that, I hope to make Zappa more accessible for new listeners.

The primary issue for many critics of Zappa's music is that his songs frequently contain sophomoric humor, with taboo subjects often at the center of these jokes. For many people with only a passing familiarity with Zappa, this notoriety may be all they associate with him. However, of the twelve hundred songs Zappa recorded, less than 10 percent of his music contains lyrics and themes that could be considered objectionable and risqué.[10] I think the best response to that kind of criticism comes from Ben Watson, from his January 1994 article for the *Socialist Review,* a monthly magazine for the British Socialist Workers Party, in which he says Zappa "showed that critical culture is not the preserve of highbrow forms." Closing his tribute, Watson says, "Not only a consistent irritant to moralists (in whatever guise), Frank Zappa is a hero for anyone who thinks that the class system, along with its cultural divide, needs dismantling."[11]

Zappa considered himself a free-speech absolutist, and the method he used to express his views on collective humanity was through his music, especially when it came to exposing hypocrisies within powerful systems. Much of this advocacy for free expression was informed by his experiences in the music business, which he felt had often excluded him for making music that clashed with the standards of taste as determined by the media business owners and their partners in government. The way these institutions complemented each other, in the interest of benefiting the elites at the top, was where Zappa witnessed the systemic hypocrisy he railed against in his music. So, instead of quieting down, he would fight back using language that challenged conservative evangelical policies and values. When interviewed for *Rockhead* in 1990, Zappa was asked about the relationship between politics and laws; the interviewer said laws did not necessarily reflect what American citizens actually think, and Zappa responded:

> Yeah, but what you're missing here is that in order to have any kind of control over the media, unless you own the media outright yourself, the only way that you can exert influence over the media is to be a president, because a president can make things happen. Not by laws but by force of personality. You can't really legislate beliefs, but if you are in some sort of political situation, you can guard against legislation that forbids free speech in that you could lobby against legislation that forbids it. And you publishing a newspaper or a magazine, you know, those things have impact. If they didn't have impact then why in every repressive regime do they try to shut them up?[12]

While Zappa's championing of free expression is certainly an admirable quality, I can understand why some people would be skeptical of him, especially in the wake of the Trump presidency's influence on public discourse concerning free speech. Many conservative leaders and alt-right supporters of Trump have taken up "free speech" as a pet cause, most notably as a response to their false and inaccurate claims that their voices are being censored online,[13] using these claims as a crutch to rationalize language and ideas that could harm marginalized groups by reinforcing dangerous systemic trends. Social media have no shortage of edgelord comedians and disingenuous political commentators who say offensive things, get criticized by other users, and then rely on the same old excuses of "but it was a joke" or "I'm just practicing my right to free speech." In those instances, with those kinds of trolls, there is no intellectual, artistic, or social value beyond a pathetic punchline. Zappa, in his unwavering attitude toward free speech, is completely separate from those kinds of people because of how he evolved as an artist and used provocative ideas to shed light on the real danger to society: the creeping influence of fundamentalist religious ideology and authoritarianism. Throughout his career, Zappa "railed against America's corporate complacency and political lurch to the right" and he "deplored racism and homophobia."[14] As a voting rights advocate, Zappa partnered with and hosted chapters of the League of Women Voters to conduct voting registration drives at most of his concerts.[15] Zappa even personally advocated for women's reproductive rights, including giving a speech at a pro-choice rally in 1989 at Rancho Park in Los Angeles, to which Zappa heard positive reports and feedback from feminists.[16] These are not the actions of a troll who uses free speech as a cover to suppress and harm women, queer people, and people of color.

Of course, Zappa's sometimes direct and abrasive attitude never did him any favors when it came to his harshest critics. He was his own worst enemy in that regard. However, perhaps that was the point: not to be liked by everyone, as a form of de rigueur antiestablishmentarianism toward popular culture, in pursuit of the freedom to embody individualism by making the music he wanted to make without resistance. When Alex Kershaw interviewed Zappa for the *Guardian Weekend* in 1993, Zappa said of political correctness, "I try not to be correct. It's just another manifestation of cowardice—when you're afraid to say what's on your mind. It's not even the language of niceness."[17] Though he was often criticized by feminist and gay rights groups, Zappa was a vocal supporter of everyone being entitled to equal rights—the caveat being, and what has ruffled the feathers of many who do not see him as more than just a sexist shock rocker, is that the equality should be total and every social standard should apply to everybody regardless of identity.[18] Speaking to the *Observer* in 1989 about such criticisms of his music, Zappa said, "If you looked at the number of songs that I've written and how many characters in the songs are men, most of the songs are about men. No men's group ever said, 'Hey, how come you're sayin' we're stoopid?' Women are sensitive if you say they're stupid. I like women: women are fine. But—men do bad stuff, women do bad stuff."[19]

While there are certainly aspects about Zappa's music that are not easy to love for some people, I believe his commitment to challenging systems of power and supporting civil liberties far outweigh any criticism that stems from a fundamental misunderstanding of his work based on projected biases. I did not come to this conclusion easily. While writing both the article and this book, I often thought about whether I could be wrong about Zappa. Since Trump entered the political arena, like a lot of other white men, I had to think about the power and responsibility that came with that identity. At a time when white male grievance was being legitimized by mainstream politics, it became increasingly easy for a specific type of white man to rationalize his frustration over feeling powerless in a country that was looking less like him. These men then created or sought out cultural silos, hidden within encrypted messaging apps or behind cartoon avatars on social media, where dangerous ideas could manifest and grow, and then latched onto chosen figures and their rhetoric that validated them and elevated their visibility among the public. Public figures and celebrities that grift for far-right conservative causes, such as Tucker Carlson, Alex Jones, and Steve Bannon, have made a lot of money off of these aggrieved and angry white men, thus not only profiting from them but also using that money to share their hateful messaging even further, reaching more and more audiences. These are the types of men whose ideas and influence were unequivocally designed to restrict and harm anyone that is not a straight white Christian male, and who have the platform and power to perpetuate them across our culture. With this, I kept asking myself if Zappa's critics were right. As I would listen to his music and read his lyrics, the thought would sometimes cross my mind whether Zappa was everything negative that I saw was said about him: if he were sexist, racist, homophobic, juvenile, a misogynist, or any other critical label that could be applied to him. I questioned whether my championing of Zappa meant I was sustaining harmful rhetoric and indirectly reinforcing my own power as a white man in America. After all, Zappa was seen as problematic by many for a reason, right?

Ultimately, I was having these thoughts because it was necessary for me to have them. While many white men would double down on grievance to claim power through victimhood, I did not want that—not if I truly believed in a pluralist democracy. I had to come to realize this introspection was important for any white man to understand his role in society, and the implicit power that comes with it. As I listened to Zappa over the years, as well as in preparation for this book, I had to understand just exactly what it was that drew me to his music. As his own career progressed, Zappa became frustrated that the audiences he was drawing were primarily young white men who not only did not understand his messaging but misappropriated it as well. How could I be sure I was not one of them? In order to answer that question, I had to understand both Zappa's music and my relationship with it. That is where this book comes in. By covering an aspect of Zappa's music and career that has often been overlooked, I was able to answer some deeper questions within myself. Understanding Zappa's commitment to democratic principles and how he relayed that through his music allowed me to grasp the underlying themes and subtexts that had existed in his music since his debut. In effect, I was answering my own question as to why Frank Zappa was included on the *Freedom Wall*.

At the center of all this is a complicated discussion about art because art is one of the most powerful things that exists. It is a way for people to express themselves and share ideas and values, and that is why it has always been a target. Whether it involves outrage that children could be exposed to allegedly pornographic lyrics or concerns about preserving harmful stereotypes, art and its inherent quality as an outlet of personal expression and individual freedom have always been in the crosshairs of those with political or ideological motives. Much of the discussion around art concerns the idea that it needs to reflect something greater in our society, that it "is often expected to say something about the various urgent injustices that define our world—and not just to say something but to be a conduit for change."[20] Art has served this purpose exceedingly well in countless ways. People who want to attack art essentially want to suppress the people behind it because of their views and self-expression that challenge the status quo.

There is also the argument that art can cause harm. There are innumerable instances in the past where art had become propagandized and what it expressed had abused marginalized communities by preserving stereotypes and tropes in ways that continued myths designed to exert power over those groups. This has since fueled discussion about representation and institutional power, and while many examples of this destructive ephemera exist as shameful relics of their time, some of their influence can still be felt. No one puts on minstrel shows now, but the feelings and attitudes they represented still linger in both direct and indirect ways. This forces us to face some uncomfortable truths about the concept of art and its malleability in society. Art is a product of human imagination, and there have been times when one person's imagination reflected another's nightmare. As Donald Preziosi, emeritus professor of art history and critical theory at the University of California, says:

> Art's dangers are at the same time the source of its powers for positive change and social advocacy. Art advocates and invokes as much as it revokes what you imagine yourself and your worlds to be. Those selves are porous: permeated by and defined relative to others, real or imagined. And, in fact, a close attention to the real powers of art makes the distinction itself between the real and the imaginary; between fact and fiction; circumstantial and conditional rather than fixed and permanent. Art is dangerous, in the end, because it brings to consciousness the reality of the fiction of reality—that what we take to be reality is a work of art: the finest of the fine arts; the supreme fiction.[21]

This debate about art is the reason I examined my relationship with Zappa's music. Like many others, I first learned about Zappa during college. Also, like many others who just discovered Zappa, at first I did not understand his work. College is often a time when people are exposed to new ideas that challenge their old ways of thinking, and Zappa was certainly challenging to me. I had not heard this kind of music before, and it was unlike anything else that was in heavy rotation on my iPod Mini. I did not initially understand it, but I knew I liked it. Plus, Zappa was diverse. There were many sounds to match my many moods. I could listen to complex orchestral compositions, which would eventually open doors for me to other avant-garde artists, or I could indulge in the absurdity of his abrasiveness, laughing to myself about the crassness of some of his lyrics because this type of music had been inaccessible to me before. Though there are some who discovered Zappa at similar points in their lives and have since moved on, largely because they felt they outgrew Zappa's particular brand of humor, I continued to listen. While over the years I have gone in and out of phases with Zappa, he has stayed with me. During all that time, and especially now, I have sought to understand why. If other people found Zappa offensive and quit listening to him, then why did I never stop?

Especially as I grew older and understood the world better, having experienced a lot of social change during that time that resulted in my having to think about complex questions about my role in society.

There could be a lot of answers to that question, and I cannot speak for anyone else. I can only speak for myself. As my understanding of the world changed, so did my understanding of Zappa and his music. Over the years, I came to appreciate his dedication to democracy and his advocacy for individual freedoms and liberties. The PMRC hearings and voter advocacy are among the defining highlights of his career, but it was a considerable journey for me to understand Zappa's subtexts within the scope of his music. My own level of education and cultural literacy changed and grew over time. Also, Zappa enjoyed being shocking, and he relished being confrontational and obstinate when faced with criticism. I recognize that this is a part of his reputation that continues to live on after his death. Even the title of this epilogue comes from a posthumously released compilation celebrating some of his most polarizing satire. None of this lessens the quality of his music and the artistic statements within it, but such considerations play a major role in his legacy—which has been shaped and warped over time.

In writing this book, I wanted to evaluate a complicated musical and cultural icon through the lens of his most underrated period. By focusing on his work that challenged white nationalism and Christian fundamentalism, I could contribute to Zappa's legacy and people's perception of it in a way that felt more complete, accurate, and representative. At the same time, I could also challenge the most enduring criticisms of Zappa's music and persona, which paint a skewed portrait of him and leave a blurry impression of his art and his contributions to our culture. I wanted to explore how his ideas and advocacy continue to be relevant as many of the issues he addressed have since grown more dangerous.

When I was in the early stages of conceptualizing the book, a friend I consulted with told me, "The people who should read this book won't." He is likely right. After all, we live in a society that, despite being more connected, has only grown smaller thanks to algorithms that curate our lives and show us only what we want to see, or what the social media companies think we want to or should see. Many people do not want their ideas to be challenged and therefore lack a type of curiosity that would allow them to avoid those situations. However, I do not worry about them. By focusing on Zappa's music from the perspective that his commentary addressed institutional power that could harm marginalized communities, my goal is to expand that part of his legacy. The majority of Zappa fans happen to be white men; it was my goal to adequately address that issue to make his music more broadly appealing and accessible because there are women and people of color who do listen to his music and enjoy it. And though I may not be able to convince Zappa's most fervid critics, if this book helps expand the understanding of Zappa and his work by making it more appealing to those communities and encourages them to contribute their voices in whatever way they see fit, then I will have accomplished what I set out to do.

As it always has been, art continues to be scapegoated. Society has changed since Zappa was alive, but there are systemic forces that continue to thrive on misinformation at the expense of creative expression. Over the last few years, I have observed situations and events that have allowed me to come to two general conclusions about the dialogue over the role of provocative art in society: (1) people often are not reacting to what is being said but rather who is saying it, and (2) people will often go to any length to rationalize their biases. The consequence of these is that they together can create chaotic conditions where misinformation and malfeasance can have a direct impact on self-expression, ultimately leading to conditions that are antidemocratic. Recognizing our own prejudices and biases, and the limitations that they can place on us, is a huge step toward enacting social and cultural change.

We know how deregulated and profit-driven media companies have contributed to the spread of misinformation. Take a look at the role they played in the outcome of the 2016 presidential election and in fanning the flames that led to the insurrection at the U.S. Capitol on January 6, 2021. Further compounding the issue of misinformation is that social media, besides being where the majority of people get their news, have shifted the concept of the public square to the point where it exists largely within digital spaces owned by private corporations. This misinformation has spread in ways that impact the lives of everyday citizens to the point where rights are being rescinded, such as safe and legal abortion access, and fascists and neo-Nazis are emboldened to demand that their views be normalized. All the while, business and government interests gain power from these developments, with disastrous effects. Education standards have drastically decreased, not just from lack of funding or public support, but because of the same forces that are spreading misinformation. While the Internet is a great educational tool, profit-driven models have advanced algorithms that reinforce biases and myths by curating the most popular or desired results over ones that are more accurate, leading to confirmation bias and further fueling the misinformation that is creating an existential threat to our democracy. This phenomenon continues with the mainstreaming of artificial intelligence, which scrapes inherently biased data that reinforces feedback loops.

These institutions that wield systemic power continue to increase the already outsized effect they have on citizens. If we are able to conclude that these forces are using misinformation to chip away at the foundation of democracy, then we can certainly conclude that misinformation can also be used to reinforce attitudes that limit other forms of self-expression. When I was writing this epilogue, news reports came out that a couple of anti-violence protests organized by a Baltimore-based musician named Imani Wj Wright were "likely funded by pro-Beijing operatives as part of a plan that is aimed at undermining American democracy and promoting China's economic interests," resembling tactics employed by Kremlin-linked groups in Russia designed to "influence American activist groups in a bid to exacerbate existing divisions in the US."[22]

The forces that are subverting democracy utilize the same systems and institutions as those that have a hand in degrading cultural standards and attitudes toward art. By reducing complex ideas to oversimplified, and sometimes intentionally misleading, bits of information that can fit in a meme or clickbait headline, the presentation of the narrative can be controlled, resulting in an incomplete understanding of a work of art and how it reflects what it is that makes us human. Using the same systems, someone could sow discord, distrust, and division over matters of creative expression in ways that can scapegoat art.

In a 1981 interview, when asked if he thought of himself as a true American, Zappa said:

> Absolutely. I'm 100% American. . . . I'm proud of this country. I just wish it would work a little bit better and I think that if everybody thought about America a little bit more and what its future might be, that they would probably reevaluate their own attitudes towards their country. A lot of people have been ashamed about being American because they keep reading bad things about themselves in the newspapers and it's like those same people who were smart and acted dumb in order to have friends, I think a lot of Americans pretend to act ashamed just so that they can wind up agreeing with something that somebody else said.[23]

At the end of the day, I am just one person trying to make sense of the world in which I live, and this is a life-long endeavor. Over the last several years, it has been hard to be optimistic about the future because it certainly does seem like things are getting worse. Sometimes, it can make one feel powerless. However, I ultimately have to believe that I am not powerless to help foster change. I am someone who believes in the unifying power of art to deepen our collective understanding of humanity, and I believe we all have an individual responsibility to make sure art continues to do that. If it could not do that, there would not be so many efforts to hinder creative self-expression.

Due to the seemingly endless barrage of threats against personal freedoms and civil liberties, it is imperative to elevate every voice that speaks to the tenets of democracy—even if that voice can be controversial at times. Every voice, especially from artists, promoting those ideals is worthy of being heard. Zappa was prescient in his commentary about art and freedom, and there is a lot we can learn from the messaging in his music today. Does this mean that the threats to democracy will end because more people are listening to Frank Zappa? No, of course not. But, by discussing his work, I hope to encourage people to think more critically about art and its role in our culture, and to realize that attacks against it come from institutional systems of power, and the incendiary instigators within them, that seek to deindividualize us through the enforcement of conformity. America is close to crossing a threshold that will be impossible to backtrack, and we need every voice that strengthens a collective resolve to not let that happen. If we as citizens cannot defend our right of freedom of expression through our own collective efforts, then we cannot be surprised when our systems fail us and we no longer have those rights.

Even though it has sometimes been difficult to be optimistic, I still am. Just as Zappa advocated for people to express themselves by being active members of a participatory democracy, so too do I believe in that very same process to pull us away from the unknown that is life after America. By relaying Zappa's own words, I hope it helps others feel more optimistic about the role and responsibility they have in a democratic society, and that they feel empowered to enact real social change. That is what his music does for me, and I hope it can do the same for others. In writing about this, have I offended someone? Then, in the words of Frank Zappa,[24] tough titties.

NOTES

PROLOGUE

1. Cardoza, "28 Years of Freedom."
2. Loerzel, "A Fresh Look."
3. "Aung San Suu Kyi."
4. Rand, "Objectivism."
5. Cardoza, "28 Years of Freedom."
6. Loerzel, "A Fresh Look."
7. Cardoza, "28 Years of Freedom."
8. "Frank Zappa."

1. IT CAN'T HAPPEN HERE

1. "The Legacy of JFK."
2. "JFK: The Legacy."
3. Murray, "Frank Zappa."
4. "Freak Out!"
5. "Freak Out!"
6. Courrier, *Dangerous Kitchen*, 93.
7. Marshall, "Frank Zappa Interview."
8. Murray, "How to Write," 41.
9. Lowe, *Words and Music*, 33.
10. Kofsky, "Frank Zappa (Part I)," 19.
11. "Freak Out!"
12. "Watts Rebellion."
13. Georgacopoulos and Poche, "Fake News."
14. Ouellette, "Frank Zappa," 49.
15. Zappa, "Absolutely Free: The Complete Libretto."
16. "Mother of Two."
17. Lewis, "The Life & Times of Frank Zappa," 1.
18. Penney, "Frank Zappa: The Early Albums," 40.

19. Kofsky, "Frank Zappa (Part I)," 17.
20. Mothers of Invention, *Absolutely Free.*
21. Zappa, "Absolutely Free: The Complete Libretto."
22. Zappa, "Absolutely Free: The Complete Libretto."
23. Watson, *Negative Dialectics*, 83.
24. Alterman, "If You Get Headache," 26.
25. Zappa, "Absolutely Free: The Complete Libretto."
26. Zappa, "Absolutely Free: The Complete Libretto."
27. Kofsky, "Frank Zappa (Part II)," 32.
28. Franz, "Mother-Images," 7.
29. Hopkins, "Frank Zappa," 13.
30. Zappa, "Absolutely Free: The Complete Libretto."
31. Salvo, "Dialogue: Frank Zappa," 94.
32. Paulsen, "Frank Zappa," 45; Zappa, "Absolutely Free: The Complete Libretto."
33. Sidey, "The Presidency."
34. "500 Songs That Shaped Rock and Roll."
35. Lowe, *Words and Music*, 42.
36. "Registry Titles."
37. Salvo and Salvo, "Mother in Lore," 40.
38. Bourne, "The Aesthetics of Freakery," 38.
39. Fox, "Owsley Stanley."
40. Zappa and Occhiogrosso, *Real Frank Zappa*, 229.
41. Fuller, "Zappa Shows Flair for Weirdness," 5.
42. Senoff, "A Bizarre Night," 11.
43. Kofsky, "Frank Zappa (Part I)," 16.
44. Lewis, "The Life & Times of Frank Zappa," 1.
45. Fricke, "Lumpy Money."
46. Lowe, *Words and Music*, 64.
47. Watson, *Complete Guide*, 38.
48. "Summary of Uncle Remus."
49. Baker, "The Grand Wazoo Speaks," 1.
50. Rense, "Frank Zappa—A Would-Be Chemist."
51. "Hollywood Is Losing."
52. Ulrich, *The Big Note*, 388.
53. Brown, Meldrum, and Pepperell, "The Zappa Interview," 12.
54. Martin, "Wielding Words," 7.
55. Courrier, *Dangerous Kitchen*, 239–40.
56. Demarest and Stanley, "Living: How To-dully Max Is Their Valley."
57. Courrier, *Dangerous Kitchen*, 419.

2. A TOKEN OF MY EXTREME

1. "1977–1981: The Presidency of Jimmy Carter."
2. Warburton, "Jimmy Carter's Biggest Challenges."
3. Warburton, "Jimmy Carter's Biggest Challenges."

4. Bender and Robinson, "25 Photos Show What Iran Looked Like"; Afary, "Iranian Revolution."
5. Bender and Robinson, "25 Photos Show What Iran Looked Like."
6. Bender and Robinson, "25 Photos Show What Iran Looked Like."
7. "White Revolution."
8. Bender and Robinson, "25 Photos Show What Iran Looked Like."
9. "Ruhollah Khomeini."
10. Bender and Robinson, "25 Photos Show What Iran Looked Like."
11. "Ruhollah Khomeini."
12. "Iran Hostage Crisis."
13. Warburton, "Jimmy Carter's Biggest Challenges."
14. Haltiwanger, "5 of the Most Controversial Choices."
15. "Examining Carter's 'Malaise Speech.'"
16. Carter, "Crisis of Confidence."
17. Carter, "Crisis of Confidence."
18. "Examining Carter's 'Malaise Speech.'"
19. Strong, "Jimmy Carter: Campaigns and Elections."
20. "Ronald Reagan Becomes President."
21. Daniel Williams, *God's Own Party*, 187, 197.
22. Haberman, "Religion and Right-Wing Politics."
23. Kifner, "Khomeini Bans Broadcast Music."
24. Askew, "What Happened When Iran Criminalized Music."
25. Courrier, *Dangerous Kitchen*, 331.
26. Morgan, "It's Time We Hung Out."
27. Morgan, "It's Time We Hung Out."
28. Morgan, "It's Time We Hung Out"; Zappa, *Joe's Garage*.
29. Swenson, "Frank Zappa: The Myth of 'Joe's Garage,'" 22.
30. Davis, "Zappa Busy as Ever," 7.
31. Swenson, "Frank Zappa: The Myth of 'Joe's Garage,'" 22.
32. Manilla, "Frank Zappa," 53.
33. Morgan, "It's Time We Hung Out."
34. Morgan, "It's Time We Hung Out."
35. Marshall, "Frank Zappa Interview."
36. "Warning! The Real Zappa," 4.
37. "Warning! The Real Zappa," 4.
38. John Swenson, "Frank Zappa: The Myth of 'Joe's Garage,'" 22.
39. Morgan, "It's Time We Hung Out."
40. Morgan, "It's Time We Hung Out"; Zappa, *Joe's Garage*.
41. Kalbacher, "When Confronting Frank Zappa."
42. "Jewish American Princess."
43. Gray, *Mother!* 178.
44. Gray, *Mother!* 178.
45. Lowe, *Words and Music*, 144.
46. Zappa and Occhiogrosso, *Real Frank Zappa*, 61.
47. Gray, *Mother!* 179.
48. Morgenstern, "Democracy's Pitchman."

49. Rothman, "A Conversation with Frank Zappa," 128.
50. Watson, *Negative Dialectics*, 377.
51. Gritter, "The Sanest Man," 29.
52. Marshall, "Frank Zappa Interview."
53. Mahon, "Frank Zappa Unveils Secrets," 10.
54. Goldberg, *Kingdom Coming*, 11.
55. Milkowski, "Zappa: He Are What He Is."
56. Goldberg, *Kingdom Coming*, 10.
57. "Moral Majority."
58. Falwell, "Sermon in Lynchburg," 91.
59. John Swenson, "Frank Zappa: America's Weirdest Rock Star," 41.
60. Lisa White, "Frank Zappa," 16.
61. Lisa White, "Frank Zappa," 16.
62. Mitgang, "Groups Aim to Counter Book Bans."
63. Falwell, "Listen America," 322.
64. Brady, "The History (and Present) of Banning Books."
65. Falwell, "Listen America," 321.
66. Falwell, "Listen America," 323.
67. Goodstein, "Falwell: Blame Abortionists, Feminists, and Gays."
68. McCammon and Totenberg, "Supreme Court Overturns Roe v. Wade."
69. Hall and Han, "As the Supreme Court Overturns Roe v. Wade."
70. Liptak and Murray, "The Major Supreme Court Decisions."
71. Kruesi, "Three More GOP-Led States Enact Abortion 'Trigger Laws.'"
72. Boghani and O'Donnell, "How McConnell's Bid to Reshape."
73. Steinfels, "Moral Majority to Dissolve."
74. Morgan, "It's Time We Hung Out."
75. Morgan, "It's Time We Hung Out."
76. Morgan, "It's Time We Hung Out."
77. Dimery, *1001 Albums*, 92, 156, 190.

3. THE MEEK SHALL INHERIT NOTHING

1. "Republican Party Platform of 1980."
2. "MTV Launches."
3. Templeton, "Frank Zappa's Revenge," 16.
4. Watson, *Negative Dialectics*, 389.
5. Lowe, *Words and Music*, 169.
6. Lowe, *Words and Music*, 170–72.
7. Pryor, "Golf's Historic Problems with Race."
8. Lowe, *Words and Music*, 172.
9. Blumenfeld, "Black Like Who?"; Usborne, "Wiggers Just Wannabe Black"; Hilbring, "The Pioneer."
10. Morris, "Why Is Everyone Always Stealing Black Music?"
11. Jefferson, "Ripping Off Black Music."

12. Watson, *Complete Guide*, 65.
13. McKenzie, "Was It a Decade of Greed?"
14. Zappa, Liner Notes for *You Are What You Is*.
15. Zappa, Liner Notes for *You Are What You Is*.
16. Volpacchio, "The Mother of All Interviews," 134.
17. Volpacchio, "The Mother of All Interviews," 135.
18. Volpacchio, "The Mother of All Interviews," 136.
19. Pickard, "Media Failures," 119.
20. Pickard, "Media Failures," 119.
21. Brichacek, "Six Ways the Media Influence Elections."
22. Brichacek, "Six Ways the Media Influence Elections."
23. Pickard, "Media Failures," 119.
24. Engel, "Here's How Liberal or Conservative."
25. Grieco, "Americans' Main Sources for Political News."
26. Joyella, "Fox News Hits 23rd Consecutive Month."
27. Zappa and Occhiogrosso, *Real Frank Zappa*, 350.
28. Engel, "Here's How Liberal or Conservative."
29. Zappa and Occhiogrosso, *Real Frank Zappa*, 349.
30. Wilder, "Frank Zappa: Somebody Up There," 36.
31. Baker, "The Grand Wazoo Speaks," 8.
32. Kurtzleben, "Study Looks at What Motivates."
33. Blake, "Trump Promised."
34. Wootson, "Trump and Allies."
35. Peters, Schmidt, and Rutenberg, "Carlson's Text"; Wolf, "'Replacement' Conspiracies."
36. Hannah-Jones, "The 1619 Project."
37. Bryan Anderson, "Critical Race Theory."
38. Conwright, "American Myths."
39. Lowe, *Words and Music*, 172.
40. Baldwin, *The Fire Next Time*, 93.
41. Milkowski, "Zappa: He Are What He Is."
42. Sewald, "I Stand Accused," 12.
43. Klaess, *Breaks in the Air*, 23.
44. Klaess, *Breaks in the Air*, 24–25.
45. Guccione, "Signs of the Times," 91.
46. Watson, *Negative Dialectics*, 393.
47. Watson, *Complete Guide*, 66.
48. Milton, "How Is It That the Meek."
49. Lowe, *Words and Music*, 173.
50. Manilla, "Frank Zappa," 51.
51. Courrier, *Dangerous Kitchen*, 360–61.
52. Seidel, *Founding Myth*, 8.
53. Zappa and Occhiogrosso, *Real Frank Zappa*, 298.
54. Carroll, "Religion, Politics, and the IRS," 220.
55. Zappa and Occhiogrosso, *Real Frank Zappa*, 299–300.

56. Effron, Paparella, and Taudte, "The Scandals That Brought Down."
57. "Televangelist Jim Bakker Is Indicted"; Harris and Isikoff, "PTL's Missing Millions."
58. Zappa and Occhiogrosso, *Real Frank Zappa*, 300.
59. John Green, "Bush and Evangelicals."
60. Bostock, "America's Richest Pastor."
61. Buettner, Craig, and McIntire, "Long-Concealed Records."
62. Fea et al., "Evangelicalism and Politics."
63. Fea et al., "Evangelicalism and Politics."
64. Fea et al., "Evangelicalism and Politics."
65. Butler, *White Evangelical Racism*, 98–99.
66. Milkowski, "Zappa: He Are What He Is."
67. Lowe, *Words and Music*, 173.
68. Wiinikka-Lydon, "Dangerous Devotion"; Ali Swenson, "Project 2025."
69. Wiinikka-Lydon, "Dangerous Devotion."
70. Armaly, Buckley, and Enders, "Christian Nationalism and Political Violence," 952.
71. Ward, "There Is a Real Sense."
72. Ward, "There Is a Real Sense."
73. Butler, *White Evangelical Racism*, 9.
74. Butler, *White Evangelical Racism*, 11.

4. THE "TORCHUM" NEVER STOPS

1. "Timeline of HIV and AIDS."
2. "Timeline of HIV and AIDS."
3. Cisneros, "40 Years of AIDS."
4. "Timeline of HIV and AIDS."
5. Joshua Green, "Heroic Story."
6. Chandler, "God's Wrath?"
7. "Pat Buchanan's Greatest Hits."
8. Chandler, "God's Wrath?"
9. "AIDS, the Surgeon General."
10. "Reagan's Response."
11. "AIDS, the Surgeon General."
12. Valdiserri, "In Memoriam: C. Everett Koop."
13. "AIDS, the Surgeon General."
14. "Surgeon General's Report."
15. Lowe, *Words and Music*, 192.
16. Slaven, *Electric Don Quixote*, 277.
17. "About the USPHS Syphilis Study."
18. "About the USPHS Syphilis Study."
19. Elliot, "In Tuskegee, Painful History."
20. Zappa and Occhiogrosso, *Real Frank Zappa*, 235.
21. Zappa and Occhiogrosso, *Real Frank Zappa*, 235–36.
22. Wilder, "Frank Zappa: Somebody Up There," 87.

23. Starkey, "Exploring the Unusual Childhood."
24. Khatchadourian, "High Anxiety."
25. Wilder, "Frank Zappa: Somebody Up There," 87.
26. Cagé and Rueda, "Sex and the Mission," 217.
27. Cagé and Rueda, "Sex and the Mission," 218.
28. Cagé and Rueda, "Sex and the Mission," 221.
29. Cagé and Rueda, "Sex and the Mission," 222.
30. Cagé and Rueda, "Sex and the Mission," 222.
31. Cagé and Rueda, "Sex and the Mission," 225.
32. Pepin, *The Origin of AIDS*, 98.
33. Cagé and Rueda, "Sex and the Mission," 225.
34. Kasthuri and Krishnan, "Iatrogenic Disorders," 2.
35. "AIDS Crisis Timeline."
36. "About HIV."
37. Jonsen and Stryker, "Religion and Religious Groups," 129–30.
38. Barlow, "How the AIDS Crisis."
39. Barlow, "How the AIDS Crisis."
40. Goudsouzian, "Moral Combat."
41. Goudsouzian, "Moral Combat."
42. Jonsen and Stryker, "Religion and Religious Groups," 132.
43. Jonsen and Stryker, "Religion and Religious Groups," 133.
44. Barlow, "AIDS Crisis."
45. Nelkin, "AIDS and the News Media," 294.
46. Nelkin, "AIDS and the News Media," 299.
47. Nelkin, "AIDS and the News Media," 305–6.
48. Nelkin, "AIDS and the News Media," 301.
49. Bull and Gallagher, *Perfect Enemies*, 25.
50. Parachini, "AMA Says It Is Unethical."
51. Erdely, "Doctors' Beliefs."
52. Yurcaba, "More Than 1 in 8 LGBTQ."
53. Thornton and Thornton, "Listen with Mother."
54. Zappa, Liner Notes for *Thing-Fish*.
55. Shay, "Frank Zappa: An Uninhibited Interview," 5.
56. Gray, *Mother!* 198.
57. Fisher, "Thing-Fish."
58. Zappa, "Thing-Fish Photo Fantasy," 107–28.
59. Templeton, "The Music Interview," 7.
60. Courrier, *Dangerous Kitchen*, 394.
61. Kershaw, "Frank: Fearless and Still Fighting," 8.
62. Lowe, *Words and Music*, 193.
63. Wilder, "Frank Zappa: Somebody Up There," 75.
64. Watson, *Complete Guide*, 80.
65. Watson, *Negative Dialectics*, 435.
66. Lowe, *Words and Music*, 189; Watson, *Negative Dialectics*, 435.

67. Lowe, *Words and Music*, 190.
68. Watson, *Complete Guide*, 80.
69. Prince, "Thing-Fish Rap."
70. Obama and Springsteen, *Renegades*, 132.
71. Lowe, *Words and Music*, 190.

5. PORN WARS

1. Kaduk, "The 10 Biggest Landslides."
2. "Music Censorship in America."
3. "Music Censorship in America."
4. "Record Labeling."
5. Zappa, "Opening Statement."
6. Chilton, "The Filthy Fifteen."
7. Grow, "PMRC's 'Filthy 15.'"
8. Tipper Gore, *Raising PG Kids*, 17.
9. Zappa and Occhiogrosso, *Real Frank Zappa*, 261.
10. Waxman, "The Story of Prince."
11. Zappa, "Opening Statement."
12. Quinn, "Censorship and Zappa," 7.
13. Sodaro and Wilcox, "Frank Zappa Meets the PMRC," 22.
14. Schonfeld, "Parental Advisory Forever."
15. Chepesiuk, "Sharp Words," 78.
16. Garcia, "Highway to Hell," 349.
17. Schonfeld, "Parental Advisory Forever."
18. Schonfeld, "Parental Advisory Forever."
19. Avery Anderson, "Parental Advisory," 32.
20. Pond, "Industry Said Fearful of PMRC's Sway."
21. Pond, "Industry Said Fearful of PMRC's Sway."
22. Pond, "Industry Said Fearful of PMRC's Sway."
23. Schonfeld, "Parental Advisory Forever."
24. Schonfeld, "Parental Advisory Forever."
25. Gore and Snider, "Dee Snider and Senator Al Gore Discuss Rock Lyrics."
26. Schonfeld, "Parental Advisory Forever."
27. Sodaro and Wilcox, "Frank Zappa Meets the PMRC," 22.
28. Schonfeld, "Parental Advisory Forever."
29. "Frank Zappa vs. Kandy Stroud," 3.
30. Denver, "Senate Statement"; Schonfeld, "Parental Advisory Forever."
31. McDougal and Parachini, "Art in the Eighties."
32. Honan, "Book Discloses That Reagan."
33. Johnson, "Frank Zappa Warned Us."
34. De Muir, "Artist, Businessman, Politician," 19.
35. Batten-Foster, "Marc Riley's Musical Time Machine."
36. "Music Censorship in America."

37. Graves, "The 165 Songs Banned."
38. "Music Censorship in America."
39. Less, "The White House vs. Frank Zappa," 5.
40. "Frank Zappa vs. Kandy Stroud," 9.
41. Josephs, "This 1996 Law Was Meant to Save Radio."
42. Goldstein, "The PMRC Is Back."
43. "Frank Zappa in California," 4.
44. "Frank Zappa in California," 4.
45. Avery Anderson, "Parental Advisory," 33.
46. Avery Anderson, "Parental Advisory," 34.
47. Avery Anderson, "Parental Advisory," 38.
48. Avery Anderson, "Parental Advisory," 38.
49. Trakin, "Zapping Back," 17.
50. Baêta et al., "Banned in the USA."
51. Baêta et al., "Banned in the USA."
52. Alter, "Book Bans Rising Rapidly."
53. Alter, "Book Bans Rising Rapidly."
54. Pondiscio, "Who's Afraid of Moms for Liberty?"
55. Baêta et al., "Banned in the USA."
56. Alter, "Book Bans Rising Rapidly."
57. "Governor DeSantis Announces Legislative Proposal."
58. Contorno, "Florida Bills."
59. Hemmer, "The Right-Wing Children's Entertainment Complex."
60. Gail Zappa, "25th Anniversary of Frank Zappa's Testimony."
61. Zappa, "FZ Delivered a Memorable Testimony."
62. Watson, *Complete Guide*, 101.
63. Watson, *Complete Guide*, 99.
64. Watson, *Complete Guide*, 81.
65. Watson, *Complete Guide*, 82.
66. Rense, "Frank Zappa Takes on the U.S. Senate."
67. Templeton, "Zappa on Rating Records," 7.
68. Schonfeld, "Parental Advisory Forever."
69. "A Partial List of Mass Shootings."

6. JESUS THINKS YOU'RE A JERK

1. Morrison, "Presidential Election of 1988."
2. John Swenson, "Frank Zappa—A Misunderstood Man," 20.
3. Morgenstern, "Democracy's Pitchman."
4. Robinson, "A Mind for the Body Politic," 9.
5. Morgenstern, "Democracy's Pitchman."
6. Zappa, *Zappa '88*.
7. Morgenstern, "Democracy's Pitchman."
8. "My Epitaph."

9. Watson, *Complete Guide*, 86.
10. Watson, *Negative Dialectics*, 512.
11. Watson, *Complete Guide*, 86.
12. Watson, *Complete Guide*, 56.
13. Lowe, *Words and Music*, 199.
14. Watson, *Negative Dialectics*, 512.
15. Rogers, "When Prison Food Is a Punishment."
16. Watson, *Negative Dialectics*, 515.
17. Lowe, *Words and Music*, 200.
18. "Let Me Be (Imperfectly?) Clear."
19. Slaven, "Frank's Wild Years," 7.
20. Berke, "Jackson's Rhymes."
21. Sheff, "*Playboy* Interview," 59.
22. Purnick, "Koch Says Jackson Lied."
23. Merida, "The Ebb and Flow of Jackson-Farrakhan."
24. Turner and Weisberg, "A Pre-Tour Interview."
25. Gill, "Frank's Wild Years," 94.
26. Lowe, *Words and Music*, 203.
27. Morgenstern, "Frank Zappa's Getting Out the Vote," 12E; Lisa White, "Frank Zappa," 2.
28. Zappa and Occhiogrosso, *Real Frank Zappa*, 315.
29. Zappa and Occhiogrosso, *Real Frank Zappa*, 324.
30. Zappa and Occhiogrosso, *Real Frank Zappa*, 316–17.
31. "Yes, I Am a Rich Man."
32. Guccione, "Signs of the Times," 92.
33. Winokur, "FZ: Drowning in the News Bath."
34. Watson, *Negative Dialectics*, 513.
35. "Jesse Jackson Meets Sadat."
36. Watson, *Negative Dialectics*, 514.
37. "Yes, I Am a Rich Man."
38. Watson, *Negative Dialectics*, 515.
39. "Iran-Contra."
40. Lisa White, "Frank Zappa," 16.
41. Reagan, "State of the Union."
42. Zappa and Occhiogrosso, *Real Frank Zappa*, 321.
43. Marshall, "Frank Zappa Interview."
44. *Wilk v. American Medical Ass'n.*
45. Liza Williams, "Zappa Zaps the Big Lie," 5.
46. Nolan, "Lennon Was Right," 16.
47. Franz, "Mother-Images," 7.
48. "Zappa Interview," 12.
49. Gardner, "Zappa in Concert."
50. Sheff, "*Playboy* Interview," 68.
51. Sheff, "*Playboy* Interview," 68.
52. Raup, "Allan Zavod Interview."

53. Andriote, "Doctor, Not Chaplain."
54. Andriote, "Doctor, Not Chaplain."
55. "Surgeon General's Report."
56. Andriote, "Doctor, Not Chaplain."
57. Haynes, "Donald Trump, the Christian Right and COVID-19," 2.
58. Haynes, "Donald Trump, the Christian Right and COVID-19," 6.
59. "Coronavirus: Armed Protestors Enter Michigan Statehouse."
60. Ogles, "17 Gay Sex Scandals."
61. Harris, "Jimmy Swaggart and the Snare of Sin."
62. Dart, "Swaggart Steps Down."
63. Pike, "Jimmy Swaggart."
64. Slaven, "Frank's Wild Years," 6.
65. Macnie, "Citizen Zappa," 18.
66. Rose, "Sex Workers Face Unique Challenges."
67. Altham, "Say A Good Word," 3.
68. Robinson, "A Mind for the Body Politic," 9.
69. Petrosky, "How Pat Robertson Changed Television."
70. Chepesiuk, "Sharp Words," 38.
71. Cooper and Schwartz, "Equal Rights Initiative."
72. Kramer, "Are You Running with Me, Jesus?," 24.
73. Michaelson, "Pat Robertson Is Dead."
74. Goddard, "Big Lie."
75. De Muir, "Artist, Businessman, Politician," 19.
76. John Swenson, "Frank Zappa—A Misunderstood Man," 20.
77. Petrosky, "How Pat Robertson Changed Television."
78. Posner, *Unholy*, 10–11.
79. Heyward, *Seven Deadly Sins*, 130.
80. Heyward, *Seven Deadly Sins*, 131.
81. Heyward, *Seven Deadly Sins*, 127.
82. Rechler, "Only the Weather Was Cold," 20.
83. McLeese, "Frank Zappa Waves Flag for Freedom," A5.
84. Ulrich, *The Big Note*, 56.
85. Effron, Paparella, and Taudte, "The Scandals That Brought Down the Bakkers."
86. Heyward, *Seven Deadly Sins*, 128.
87. Buxton, Samler, and Simms, "Interview of the Century—Part 1."
88. Lopez, "More Than Half of Republicans Support Christian Nationalism."

7. AMNERIKA

1. Dionne, "The 1988 Elections."
2. Menendez, "Protestant Support."
3. Gavin, "The Zappa Interview," 7.
4. Marshall, "Frank Zappa Interview."
5. Babcock, "Fund-Raisers Gear Up for Fall Race."

6. Marshall, "Frank Zappa Interview."
7. Marshall, "Frank Zappa Interview."
8. Chepesiuk, "Sharp Words," 37.
9. Zappa, "Your Vote."
10. Hoogesteger and Wünsch, "Frankfurt Press Conference."
11. Ouellette, "Frank Zappa," 50.
12. Chepesiuk, "Frank Zappa Interview," 24.
13. Varga, "That Time Frank Zappa Considered Running for President."
14. Sheff, "*Playboy* Interview," 68.
15. Sutherland, "Make a Zappa Noise Here," 69.
16. Whitaker, "The Day Frank Zappa Died."
17. Sheff, "*Playboy* Interview," 68.
18. Bruck, "Life of the Party," 31.
19. Havens, "Two Unreleased Frank Zappa Albums."
20. Courrier, *Dangerous Kitchen*, 117.
21. Havens, "Two Unreleased Frank Zappa Albums."
22. Skilling, *Charter 77*, 3, 14.
23. Stoppard, "Did Plastic People of the Universe Topple Communism?"
24. Atkins, "Frank Zappa and Eastern Europe."
25. Yanosik, "The Plastic People of the Universe."
26. Havel, "The Power of the Powerless."
27. Atkins, "Zappa and Eastern Europe."
28. Sheff, "*Playboy* Interview," 66.
29. Wheeler, "Frank Zappa's Crusade," 10.
30. Courrier, *Dangerous Kitchen*, 463.
31. Wilding, "Just When You Thought," 19.
32. Corn, "Frank Zappa: Trading Partner," 376, 378.
33. Courrier, *Dangerous Kitchen*, 465–66.
34. Corn, "Frank Zappa: Trading Partner," 378.
35. "My Epitaph."
36. Muso, "Frank Zappa 1940–1993," 22.
37. Atkins, "Zappa and Eastern Europe."
38. Watson, *Negative Dialectics*, 134.
39. Havel, "Revolutionary," 86.
40. Watson, "The Final Conflict," 37.
41. Ouellette, "Frank Zappa," 56.
42. Courrier, *Dangerous Kitchen*, 490.
43. "Mother of All Musicians," 25.
44. Courrier, *Dangerous Kitchen*, 486.
45. Courrier, *Dangerous Kitchen*, 487.
46. Courrier, *Dangerous Kitchen*, 487.
47. Little, "A Town, a Flood, and Superfund."
48. Courrier, *Dangerous Kitchen*, 489.
49. Harvey, "Scientists Deliver 'Final Warning.'"

50. Willems, "Frank Zappa Is a Man for All Seasons."
51. Zappa, "About the Abortion Issue in the United States."
52. Courrier, *Dangerous Kitchen*, 489.
53. Watson, *Negative Dialectics*, 549.
54. "1993: Shock as Racist Wins Council Seat."
55. "Jean-Marie Le Pen."
56. Zeller, "Tense Germany."
57. Langer, "This Study of American Fascism."
58. Graham, "Antisemitic Incidents Reach New High."
59. Biden, "The U.S. National Strategy to Counter Antisemitism."
60. Jeremy White, "There Are 'Nazis' in Congress."
61. Palmer, "House Republicans All Vote Against Neo-Nazi Probe."
62. Bonner, "Frank Zappa's Final Album."
63. Zappa, Liner Notes for *Civilization Phaze III*.
64. Rense, "A Different Zappa Emerges."
65. Jackson, "A Mother of Invention," 17.
66. Watson, *Complete Guide*, 100–101.
67. Rense, "A Different Zappa Emerges."
68. Menn, "The Mother of All Interviews, Part II: Waffles in Plastic," 78.
69. Menn, "The Mother of All Interviews, Part II: Waffles in Plastic," 81.
70. Rense, "A Different Zappa Emerges."
71. Rense, "Posthumous Album."
72. Hoogesteger and Wünsch, "Frankfurt Press Conference."
73. TheNilesLeshProject, "Frank Zappa—Lost Interview."
74. Frame, "Frank Zappa," 37, 41.

EPILOGUE

1. Wolf-Astrauskas, "2023 Results."
2. "George Carlin's Daughter."
3. Yazdiha, "Distortion of Martin Luther King Jr.'s Words."
4. McMullan, "What Does the Panopticon Mean."
5. Chiu, "Letter Signed."
6. "A Letter on Justice and Open Debate."
7. Chiu, "Letter Signed."
8. Chomsky and Herman, *Manufacturing Consent*, 370.
9. "A Letter on Justice and Open Debate."
10. Kershaw, "Frank: Fearless and Still Fighting," 8.
11. Watson, "Frank Zappa: Spanner in the Works."
12. "Zappa!" 29.
13. Darcy, "Trump Says Right-Wing Voices Are Being Censored."
14. Sweeting, "Rock Irony," 30.
15. Camarata, "A Talk with Frank Zappa," 9.
16. Buxton, Samler, and Simms, "Interview of the Century—Part 3."

17. Kershaw, "Frank: Fearless and Still Fighting," 8.
18. "Zappa!" 30.
19. Murray, "Frankly a Freak," 4.
20. Yanagihara, "What Should We Expect of Art?"
21. Preziosi, "Why Art Is Dangerous."
22. Abou-Ghazala et al., "A Baltimore Musician Was Hired to Organize a Protest."
23. Manilla, "Frank Zappa," 53.
24. Sheff, "*Playboy* Interview," 59.

REFERENCES

Abou-Ghazala, Yahya, Isabelle Chapman, Allison Gordon, and Donie O'Sullivan. "Exclusive: A Baltimore Musician Was Hired to Organize a Protest." *CNN*, July 26, 2023. www.cnn.com/2023/07/26/us/pro-china-information-campaign-invs/index.html.

"About HIV." *Centers for Disease Control and Prevention*, June 30, 2022. www.cdc.gov/hiv/basics/whatishiv.html.

"About the USPHS Syphilis Study." *Tuskegee University*. www.tuskegee.edu/about-us/centers-of-excellence/bioethics-center/about-the-usphs-syphilis-study.

Afary, Janet. "Iranian Revolution (1978–1979)." *Encyclopedia Britannica*, August 7, 2023. www.britannica.com/event/Iranian-Revolution.

"AIDS Crisis Timeline." *History*, June 14, 2021. www.history.com/topics/1980s/hiv-aids-crisis-timeline.

"AIDS, the Surgeon General, and the Politics of Public Health." *National Library of Medicine Profiles in Science*. profiles.nlm.nih.gov/spotlight/qq/feature/aids.

Alter, Alexandra. "Book Bans Rising Rapidly in the U.S., Free Speech Groups Find." *New York Times*, April 20, 2023. www.nytimes.com/2023/04/20/books/book-bans-united-states-free-speech.html.

Alterman, Loraine. "If You Get Headache. . . ." *Detroit Free Press*, July 15, 1966, 26. www.afka.net/Mags/Detroit_Free_Press.htm#1966Jul15.

Altham, Keith. "Say a Good Word for the Groupies, Frank." *Record Mirror*, April 10, 1971, 3. www.afka.net/Mags/Record_Mirror.htm#1971Apr.

Anderson, Avery. "Parental Advisory: Tipper Gore and the PMRC." *Women Leading Change: Case Studies on Women, Gender, and Feminism* 5: no. 10 (2020): 31–47. journals.tulane.edu/ncs/article/view/2938.

Anderson, Bryan. "Critical Race Theory Is a Flashpoint for Conservatives, but What Does It Mean?" *PBS News Hour*, November 4, 2021. www.pbs.org/newshour/education/so-much-buzz-but-what-is-critical-race-theory.

Andriote, John-Manuel. "Doctor, Not Chaplain: How a Deeply Religious Surgeon General Taught a Nation about HIV." *The Atlantic*, March 4, 2013. www.theatlantic.com/health

/archive/2013/03/doctor-not-chaplain-how-a-deeply-religious-surgeon-general-taught-a-nation-about-hiv/273665/.

Armaly, Miles T., David T. Buckley, and Adam M. Enders. "Christian Nationalism and Political Violence: Victimhood, Racial Identity, Conspiracy, and Support for the Capitol Attacks." *Political Behavior* 44 (2022): 937–60. www.ncbi.nlm.nih.gov/pmc/articles/PMC8724742/.

Askew, Joshua. "What Happened When Iran Criminalised Music after the 1979 Islamic Revolution?" *Euro News*, September 26, 2022. www.euronews.com/culture/2022/05/26/what-happens-when-a-country-criminalises-music.

Atkins, Jamie. "Frank Zappa and Eastern Europe: A Love Affair." *uDiscoverMusic*, June 24, 2023. www.udiscovermusic.com/stories/frank-zappa-eastern-europe-vaclav-havel/.

"Aung San Suu Kyi: Myanmar Democracy Icon Who fell from Grace." *BBC*, December 6, 2021. www.bbc.com/news/world-asia-pacific-11685977.

Babcock, Charles R. "Fund-Raisers Gear Up for Fall Race." *Washington Post*, June 26, 1988. www.washingtonpost.com/archive/politics/1988/06/27/fund-raisers-gear-up-for-fall-race/8c306e2f-3125-4d92-a2cd-f67cac6ab8ef/.

Baêta, Sabrina, Jonathan Friedman, Tasslyn Magnusson, and Kasey Meehan. "Banned in the USA: State Laws Supercharge Book Suppression in Schools." *PEN America*, April 20, 2023. pen.org/report/banned-in-the-usa-state-laws-supercharge-book-suppression-in-schools/.

Baker, Ed. "The Grand Wazoo Speaks." *Hot Flash*, May 1974, 1, 6–8, 13. www.afka.net/Mags/Hot_Flash.htm.

Baldwin, James. *The Fire Next Time*. New York: Modern Library, 1995.

Barlow, Rich. "How the AIDS Crisis Became a Moral Debate." *Boston University Today*, December 3, 2015. www.bu.edu/articles/2015/anthony-petro-after-the-wrath-of-god/.

Batten-Foster, Andy. "Marc Riley's Musical Time Machine: Frank Zappa and Lou Reed." *BBC Radio 4*, September 1984. www.bbc.co.uk/programmes/b05107zk.

Bender, Jeremy, and Melia Robinson. "25 Photos Show What Iran Looked Like before the 1979 Revolution Turned the Nation into an Islamic Republic." *Business Insider*, September 9, 2022. www.businessinsider.com/iran-before-the-revolution-in-photos-2015-4.

Berke, Richard L. "Jackson's Rhymes: Lilting to a Different Cadence." *New York Times*, April 16, 1988. www.nytimes.com/1988/04/16/us/jackson-s-rhymes-lilting-to-a-different-cadence.html.

Biden, Joe, and the White House. "The U.S. National Strategy to Counter Antisemitism." *The White House*, May 2023. www.whitehouse.gov/wp-content/uploads/2023/05/U.S.-National-Strategy-to-Counter-Antisemitism.pdf.

Blake, Aaron. "Trump Promised His Supporters 'Everything.' He Didn't Deliver on Much of It." *Washington Post*, January 20, 2021. www.washingtonpost.com/politics/2021/01/20/trump-promised-his-supporters-everything-he-didnt-deliver-most-it/.

Blumenfeld, Laura. "Black Like Who? Why White Teens Find Hip-Hop Cool." *Washington Post*, July 20, 1992. www.washingtonpost.com/archive/lifestyle/1992/07/20/black-like-who-why-white-teens-find-hip-hop-cool/85f66bb6-07db-475e-b266-002f5443f95b/.

Boghani, Priyanka, and James O'Donnell. "How McConnell's Bid to Reshape the Federal Judiciary Extends beyond the Supreme Court." *PBS frontline*, October 16, 2020. www.pbs.org/wgbh/frontline/article/how-mcconnell-and-the-senate-helped-trump-set-records-in-appointing-judges/.

Bonner, Michael. "Frank Zappa's Final Album Gets Release Date." *Uncut*, April 7, 2015. www.uncut.co.uk/news/frank-zappas-final-album-gets-release-date-67615/.

Bostock, Bill. "America's Richest Pastor Avoids $150,000 in Annual Taxes on a $7 Million Texas Mansion That He Said God Told Him to Build, Report Says." *Business Insider*, December 17, 2021. www.yahoo.com/news/americas-richest-pastor-avoids-150-124716761.html.

Bourne, Mike. "The Aesthetics of Freakery." *Down Beat Yearbook*, 1971. 35–38. www.afka.net/Mags/DownBeat.htm#1971%C2%A0Yearbook.

Brady, Amy. "The History (and Present) of Banning Books in America." *Literary Hub*, September 22, 2016. lithub.com/the-history-and-present-of-banning-books-in-america/.

Brichacek, Andra. "Six Ways the Media Influence Elections." *University of Oregon School of Journalism and Communication*, November 8, 2016. journalism.uoregon.edu/news/six-ways-media-influences-elections.

Brown, Jenny, Ian Meldrum, and David N. Pepperell. "The Zappa Interview." *Go-Set*, July 14, 1973, 12–13. www.afka.net/Mags/Go-Set.htm#1973Jul.

Bruck, Connie. "Life of the Party." *The New Yorker*, January 25, 1999, 30–33. www.afka.net/Mags/New_Yorker.htm#1999Jan.

Buettner, Russ, Susanne Craig, and Mike McIntire. "Long-Concealed Records Show Trump's Chronic Losses and Years of Tax Avoidance." *New York Times*, September 27, 2020. www.nytimes.com/interactive/2020/09/27/us/donald-trump-taxes.html.

Bull, Chris, and John Gallagher. *Perfect Enemies: The Religious Right, the Gay Movement, and the Politics of the 1990s*. New York: Crown Publishers, 1996.

Butler, Anthea. *White Evangelical Racism: The Politics of Morality in America*. Chapel Hill: University of North Carolina Press, 2021.

Buxton, Eric, Rob Samler, and Den Simms. "They're Doing the Interview of the Century—Part 1." *Society Pages*, April 1990. www.afka.net/Articles/1990-04_Society_Pages.htm.

———. "They're Doing the Interview of the Century—Part 3." *Society Pages*, September 1990. www.afka.net/Articles/1990–09_Society_Pages.htm.

Cagé, Julia, and Valeria Rueda. "Sex and the Mission: The Conflicting Effects of Early Christian Missions on HIV in Sub-Saharan Africa." *Journal of Demographic Economics* 86, no. 3 (2020): 213–57. www.cambridge.org/core/journals/journal-of-demographic-economics/article/abs/sex-and-the-mission-the-conflicting-effects-of-early-christian-missions-on-hiv-in-subsaharan-africa/92D19923A52263903535C96F04984DEB.

Camarata, Bill. "A Talk with Frank Zappa." *Scene*, March 3–9, 1988, 9. www.afka.net/Mags/Scene.htm#1988Mar.

Cardoza, Kerry. "28 Years of Freedom on the Wall." *Chicago Reader*, July 13, 2022. chicagoreader.com/arts-culture/28-years-of-freedom-on-the-wall/.

Carroll, Anne Berrill. "Religion, Politics, and the IRS: Defining the Limits of Tax Law Controls on Political Expression by Churches." *Marquette Law Review* 76, no. 217 (1992): 217–63. scholarship.law.marquette.edu/cgi/viewcontent.cgi?article=1644&context=mulr.

Carter, Jimmy. "Crisis of Confidence." Transcript of televised speech delivered at White House Oval Office, July 15, 1979. www.pbs.org/wgbh/americanexperience/features/carter-crisis/.

Chandler, Russell. "God's Wrath? AIDS: Rigid Church View Is Fading." *Los Angeles Times*, June 12, 1986. www.latimes.com/archives/la-xpm-1986-06-12-mn-10171-story.html.

Chepesiuk, Rob. "Frank Zappa Interview." *Overseas!* February 1990, 24–25. www.afka.net/Mags/Overseas.htm#1990Feb.

———. "Sharp Words from Music's Cutting Edge." *Gallery*, June 1989, 36–39, 78, 97. www.afka.net/Mags/Gallery.htm#1989Jun.

Chilton, Martin. "The Filthy Fifteen: Censorship, Gore and the Parental Advisory Sticker." *uDiscoverMusic*, September 19, 2023. www.udiscovermusic.com/stories/filthy-fifteen-pmrc-censorship/.

Chiu, Allyson. "Letter Signed by J. K. Rowling, Noam Chomsky Warning of Stifled Free Speech Draws Mixed Reviews." *Washington Post*, July 8, 2020. www.washingtonpost.com/nation/2020/07/08/letter-harpers-free-speech/.

Chomsky, Noam, and Edward S. Herman. *Manufacturing Consent: The Political Economy of the Mass Media*. London: Bodley Head, 2008.

Cisneros, Lisa. "40 Years of AIDS: A Timeline of the Epidemic." *University of California San Francisco*, June 4, 2021. www.ucsf.edu/news/2021/06/420686/40-years-aids-timeline-epidemic.

Contorno, Steve. "Florida Bills That Will Alter the Lives of Transgender People Await DeSantis' Signature." *CNN*, May 4, 2023. www.cnn.com/2023/05/04/politics/ron-desantis-transgender-bills-florida/index.html.

Conwright, Anthony. "American Myths Are Made of White Grievance—and the Jan. 6 Big Lie Is Just the Latest." *Mother Jones*, January and February 2023. www.motherjones.com/politics/2023/01/trump-jan-january-6-insurrection-big-lie-white-supremacy-confederate/.

Cooper, Kenneth J., and Maralee Schwartz. "Equal Rights Initiative in Iowa Attacked." *Washington Post*, August 23, 1992. www.washingtonpost.com/archive/politics/1992/08/23/equal-rights-initiative-in-iowa-attacked/f3e553a1-b768-449f-8d65-d096f9e318ee/.

Corn, David. "Frank Zappa: Trading Partner." *The Nation*, March 19, 1990, 376, 378–79. www.afka.net/Mags/The_Nation.htm#1990Mar19.

"Coronavirus: Armed Protestors Enter Michigan Statehouse." *BBC*, April 30, 2020. www.bbc.com/news/world-us-canada-52496514.

Courrier, Kevin. *Dangerous Kitchen: The Subversive World of Zappa*. Toronto: ECW Press, 2002.

Darcy, Oliver. "Trump Says Right-Wing Voices Are Being Censored. The Data Says Something Else." *CNN*, May 28, 2020. www.cnn.com/2020/05/28/media/trump-social-media-conservative-censorship/index.html.

Dart, John. "Swaggart Steps Down after Public Confession: Evangelist Admits Moral 'Sin,' Leaves for Indefinite Period." *Los Angeles Times*, February 22, 1988. www.latimes.com/archives/la-xpm-1988-02-22-mn-29975-story.html.

Davis, Michael. "Zappa Busy as Ever While Coming Out of Joe's Garage." *Record Review*, February 1980, 6–8. www.afka.net/Mags/Record_Review.htm.

De Muir, Harold. "Artist, Businessman, Politician." *East Coast Rocker*, March 30, 1988, 18–20. www.afka.net/Mags/East_Coast_Rocker.htm#1988Mar.

Demarest, Michael, and Alessandra Stanley. "Living: How To-dully Max Is Their Valley." *Time*, September 27, 1982.

Denver, John. "Senate Statement on Rock Lyrics & Record Labeling." Transcript of speech at U.S. Capitol, September 19, 1987. www.americanrhetoric.com/speeches/johndenver rockmusiclyrics.htm.

Dimery, Robert, ed. *1001 Albums You Must Hear Before You Die*. London: Cassell Illustrated, 2016.

Dionne, E. J., Jr. "The 1988 Elections; Bush Is Elected by a 6–5 Margin with Solid G.O.P. Base in South; Democrats Hold Both Houses." *New York Times*, November 9, 1988. www.nytimes.com/1988/11/09/us/1988-elections-bush-elected-6-5-margin-with-solid-gop-base-south-democrats-hold.html.

Effron, Lauren, Andrew Paparella, and Jeca Taudte. "The Scandals That Brought Down the Bakkers, Once among US's Most Famous Televangelists." *ABC News*, December 20, 2019. abcnews.go.com/US/scandals-brought-bakkers-uss-famous-televangelists/story?id=60389342/.

Elliott, Debbie. "In Tuskegee, Painful History Shadows Efforts to Vaccinate African Americans." *National Public Radio*, February 16, 2021. www.npr.org/2021/02/16/967011614/in-tuskegee-painful-history-shadows-efforts-to-vaccinate-african-americans.

Engel, Pamela. "Here's How Liberal or Conservative Major News Sources Really Are." *Business Insider*, October 21, 2014. www.businessinsider.com/what-your-preferred-news-outlet-says-about-your-political-ideology-2014-10.

Erdely, Sabrina Rubin. "Doctors' Beliefs Can Hinder Patient Care." *NBC News*, June 22, 2007. www.nbcnews.com/id/wbna19190916.

"Examining Carter's 'Malaise Speech,' 30 Years Later." *National Public Radio*, July 12, 2009. www.npr.org/2009/07/12/106508243/examining-carters-malaise-speech-30-years-later.

Falwell, Jerry. "Listen America." 1980. In *Voices of Freedom: A Documentary History*, 7th ed., ed. Kathleen DuVal, Eric Foner, and Lisa McGirr, vol. 2: 320–23. New York: W. W. Norton & Co., 2022.

———. "Sermon in Lynchburg, Virginia." July 4, 1976. Quoted in William R. Goodman Jr. and James J. H. Price, *Jerry Falwell: An Unauthorized Profile* (Cambridge, MA: Paris & Associates, 1981, 91).

Fea, John, Laura Gifford, R. Marie Griffith, and Lerone A. Martin. "Evangelicalism and Politics." *Organization of American Historians*. www.oah.org/tah/november-5/evangelicalism-and-politics/.

Fisher, Philip. "Thing-Fish—The Return of Frank Zappa." *British Theatre Guide*. web.archive.org/web/20080115113542/http:/www.britishtheatreguide.info/otherresources/interviews/Thing-Fish.htm (accessed August 9, 2023).

"500 Songs That Shaped Rock and Roll by Song (A–C)." *Rock and Roll Hall of Fame & Museum.*

web.archive.org/web/20080120174104/http:/www.rockhall.com/exhibithighlights/500-songs-by-name-ac/ (accessed August 9, 2023).

Fox, Margalit. "Owsley Stanley, Artisan of Acid, Is Dead at 76." *New York Times*, March 14, 2011. www.nytimes.com/2011/03/15/us/15stanley.html.

Frame, Pete. "Frank Zappa." *Mojo*, November 2018, 36–41. www.afka.net/Mags/Mojo.htm#2018Nov.

"Frank Zappa." *Biography*, July 30, 2019. www.biography.com/musicians/frank-zappa.

"Frank Zappa in California." *Metro Times*, September 11, 1985, 4–5. www.afka.net/Mags/Metro_Times.htm#1985Sep.

"Frank Zappa vs. Kandy Stroud: Is Labeling of Record Albums a Censorship Issue?" *Georgetowner*, September 27–October 10, 1985, 1, 3, 9. www.afka.net/Mags/Georgetowner.htm#1985Sep.

Franz, Chris. "'Mother-Images' Freak Out, Creamcheese, Psychedelics." *Wellesley News*, April 27, 1967, 7. www.afka.net/Mags/Wellesley_News.htm#1967Apr27.

"Freak Out!" *Zappa.com*. www.zappa.com/releases/freak-out/#/ (accessed August 9, 2023).

Fricke, David. "Lumpy Money." Liner notes for Frank Zappa, *The Lumpy Money Project/Object*. Zappa Records ZR20008, 2009, 3 CDs.

Fuller, George. "Zappa Shows Flair for Weirdness." *Spartan Daily*, February 20, 1974, 5. www.afka.net/Mags/Spartan_Daily.htm#1973Apr04.

Garcia, Justin D. "'Highway to Hell': Laws, Lawsuits, and Moral Panic over Heavy Metal Music." In *A History of Evil in Popular Culture: What Hannibal Lecter, Stephen King, and Vampires Reveal About America*, ed. Sharon Packer and Jody Pennington, 345–458. Santa Barbara, CA: Praeger, 2014.

Gardner, Bill. "Zappa in Concert—Unfulfilled Potential." *Chronicle*, October 20, 1976. www.afka.net/Mags/The_Chronicle.htm#1975Oct20.

Gavin, Sheila. "The Zappa Interview." *Monroe Doctrine*, March 21, 1988, 3, 7. www.afka.net/Mags/Monroe_Doctrine.htm#1988Mar.

Georgacopoulos, Christina, and Trey Poche. "Fake News, Disinformation and the George Floyd Protests." *Louisiana State University*, August 2020. faculty.lsu.edu/fakenews/about/protestfakenews.php.

"George Carlin's Daughter Says He'd 'Roll Eyes' at Far Right." *Daily Beast*, May 29, 2022. www.thedailybeast.com/george-carlins-daughter-says-hed-roll-eyes-at-far-right.

Gill, Andy. "Frank's Wild Years." *Q*, December 1989, 88–91, 93–94. www.afka.net/Mags/Q.htm#1989Dec.

Goddard, Taegan. "Big Lie." *Political Dictionary*. politicaldictionary.com/words/big-lie/.

Goldberg, Michelle. *Kingdom Coming: The Rise of Christian Nationalism*. New York: W. W. Norton & Co., 2006.

Goldstein, Patrick. "The PMRC Is Back on the Attack." *Los Angeles Times*, December 7, 1986. www.latimes.com/archives/la-xpm-1986-12-07-ca-1027-story.html.

Goodstein, Laurie. "Falwell: Blame Abortionists, Feminists, and Gays." *Guardian*, September 19, 2001. www.theguardian.com/world/2001/sep/19/september11.usa9.

Gore, Al, and Dee Snider. "Dee Snider and Senator Al Gore Discuss Rock Lyrics at the Senate Commerce, Science and Transportation Committee on Rock Lyrics and Record Labeling." Transcript of hearing delivered at U.S. Capitol, September 19, 1985. www.c-span.org/video/?c4534531/dee-snider-al-gore.

Gore, Tipper. *Raising PG Kids in an X-Rated Society*. Nashville, TN: Abingdon Press, 1987.

Goudsouzian, Aram. "'Moral Combat': Debates over Sex and Morality Caused American Political Divisions." *Knox News*, December 16, 2017. www.knoxnews.com/story/life/2017/12/16/moral-combat-marie-griffith-sex-morality-politics-religion/948875001/.

"Governor DeSantis Announces Legislative Proposal to Stop W.O.K.E. Activism and Critical Race Theory in Schools and Corporations." *Ron DeSantis, 46th Governor of Florida*, December 15, 2021. www.flgov.com/2021/12/15/governor-desantis-announces-legislative-proposal-to-stop-w-o-k-e-activism-and-critical-race-theory-in-schools-and-corporations/.

Graham, Ruth. "Antisemitic Incidents Reach New High in U.S., Anti-Defamation League Says." *New York Times*, March 23, 2023. www.nytimes.com/2023/03/23/us/antisemitism-anti-defamation-league-report.html.

Graves, Wren. "The 165 Songs Banned from American Radio Following 9/11 Terrorist Attacks." *Consequence*, September 11, 2021. consequence.net/2021/09/911-songs-banned-radio/.

Gray, Michael. *Mother! The Frank Zappa Story*. London: Plexus Publishing, 1994.

Green, John. "Bush and Evangelicals." *PBS Frontline*, April 29, 2004. www.pbs.org/wgbh/pages/frontline/shows/jesus/evangelicals/bushand.html.

Green, Joshua. "The Heroic Story of How Congress First Confronted AIDs." *The Atlantic*, June 8, 2021. www.theatlantic.com/politics/archive/2011/06/the-heroic-story-of-how-congress-first-confronted-aids/240131/.

Grieco, Elizabeth. "Americans' Main Sources for Political News Vary by Party and Age." *Pew Research Center*, April 1, 2020. www.pewresearch.org/short-reads/2020/04/01/americans-main-sources-for-political-news-vary-by-party-and-age/.

Gritter, Headley. "The Sanest Man in the World Today?" *Rock Australia Magazine*, April 4, 1980, 26–27, 29. www.afka.net/Mags/RAM.htm#1980Apr.

Grow, Kory. "PMRC's 'Filthy 15': Where Are They Now?" *Rolling Stone*, September 17, 2015. www.rollingstone.com/music/music-lists/pmrcs-filthy-15-where-are-they-now-60601/.

Guccione, Bob, Jr. "Signs of the Times." *Spin*, July 1991, 58–60, 62, 91–92. www.afka.net/Mags/Spin.htm#1991Jul.

Haberman, Clyde. "Religion and Right-Wing Politics: How Evangelicals Reshaped Elections." *New York Times*, October 28, 2018. www.nytimes.com/2018/10/28/us/religion-politics-evangelicals.html.

Hall, Madison, and Yoonji Han. "As the Supreme Court Overturns Roe v. Wade, Some Experts Fear Interracial Marriage May Be the Next Target." *Business Insider*, June 24, 2022. www.insider.com/roe-wade-loving-virginia-interracial-marriage-scotus-overturns-2022-6.

Haltiwanger, John. "5 of the Most Controversial Choices for Time Magazine's Person of the Year." *Business Insider*, December 11, 2019. www.businessinsider.com/time-person-of-the-year-most-controversial-picks-2018-12.

Hannah-Jones, Nikole. "The 1619 Project." *New York Times Magazine*, August 2019. www.nytimes.com/interactive/2019/08/14/magazine/1619-america-slavery.html.

Harris, Art. "Jimmy Swaggart and the Snare of Sin." *Washington Post*, February 25, 1988. www.washingtonpost.com/archive/lifestyle/1988/02/25/jimmy-swaggart-and-the-snare-of-sin/d07127d2-c412-4738-98d9-3b186d1b92f9/.

———, and Michael Isikoff. "PTL's Missing Millions." *Washington Post*, June 21, 1987. www.washingtonpost.com/archive/opinions/1987/06/21/ptls-missing-millions/553aa246-42b9-49bd-954e-0c3b85349514/?noredirect=on.

Harvey, Fiona. "Scientists Deliver 'Final Warning' on Climate Crisis: Act Now or It's Too Late." *Guardian*, March 20, 2023. www.theguardian.com/environment/2023/mar/20/ipcc-climate-crisis-report-delivers-final-warning-on-15c.

Havel, Václav. "The Power of the Powerless." Trans. Paul Wilson. *Hannah Arendt Center for Politics and Humanities Bard*, December 23, 2011. hac.bard.edu/amor-mundi/the-power-of-the-powerless-vaclav-havel-2011-12-23.

———. "Revolutionary." *The New Yorker*, December 20, 1993, 86–87. www.afka.net/Mags/New_Yorker.htm#1993Dec.

Havens, Lyndsey. "Two Unreleased Frank Zappa Albums Will Emerge from the Vaults This July." *Consequence*, June 13, 2016. consequence.net/2016/06/two-unreleased-frank-zappa-albums-will-emerge-from-the-vaults-this-july/.

Haynes, Jeffrey. "Donald Trump, the Christian Right and COVID-19: The Politics of Religious Freedom." *Laws* 10, no. 1 (2021): 6. doi.org/10.3390/laws10010006.

Hemmer, Nicole. "The Right-Wing Children's Entertainment Complex Is upon Us." *CNN*, April 7, 2022. www.cnn.com/2022/04/07/opinions/children-literature-disney-desantis-tuttle-twins-hemmer/index.html.

Heyward, Carter. *The Seven Deadly Sins of White Christian Nationalism*. Lanham, MD: Rowman & Littlefield, 2022.

Hilbring, Veronica. "The Pioneer: 7 Things You Need to Know about Sister Rosetta Tharpe." *Essence*, October 24, 2020. www.essence.com/holidays/black-history-month/sister-rosetta-tharpe-things-to-know/.

"Hollywood Is Losing the Battle for China." *Economist*, April 26, 2023. www.economist.com/interactive/2023/04/29/hollywood-is-losing-the-battle-for-china.

Honan, William H. "Book Discloses That Reagan Planned To Kill National Endowment for Arts." *New York Times*, May 15, 1988. www.nytimes.com/1988/05/15/arts/book-discloses-that-reagan-planned-to-kill-national-endowment-for-arts.html.

Hoogesteger, Aad, and Axel Wünsch. "Frankfurt Press Conference 21.7.92." *T'Mershi Duween* 26 (September 1992). www.afka.net/Articles/1992-09_Tmershi_Duween.htm.

Hopkins, Jerry. "Frank Zappa." *Rolling Stone*, July 20, 1968, 11–14. www.afka.net/Mags/Rolling_Stone.htm.

"Iran-Contra Affair." *History*, January 17, 2020. www.history.com/topics/1980s/iran-contra-affair.

"Iran Hostage Crisis." *Encyclopedia Britannica*, August 8, 2023. www.britannica.com/event/Iran-hostage-crisis.

Jackson, Joe. "A Mother of Invention." *Hot Press*, April 7, 1993, 16–17. www.afka.net/Mags/Hot_Press.htm#1993Apr.

"Jean-Marie Le Pen." *Encyclopedia Britannica*, August 8, 2023. www.britannica.com/facts/Jean-Marie-Le-Pen.

Jefferson, Margo. "Ripping Off Black Music." *Harper's Magazine*, January 1973.

"Jesse Jackson Meets Sadat Again and Flies to See Assad and Arafat." *New York Times*, October 3, 1979. www.nytimes.com/1979/10/03/archives/jesse-jackson-meets-sadat-again-and-flies-to-see-assad-and-arafat.html.

"Jewish American Princess." *Merriam-Webster*. www.merriam-webster.com/dictionary/Jewish%20American%20Princess (accessed August 8, 2023).

"JFK: The Legacy." *PBS*. www.pbs.org/wgbh/americanexperience/features/jfk-legacy/.

Johnson, Kimberley. "Frank Zappa Warned Us of a Fascist Theocracy in 1986." *Church and State*, April 6, 2015. churchandstate.org.uk/2015/04/frank-zappa-warned-us-of-a-fascist-theocracy-in-1986-video/.

Jonsen, Albert R., and Jeff Stryker, eds. "Religion and Religious Groups." *The Social Impact of AIDS in the United States*. Washington, DC: *National Academies Press*, 1993. 117–57.

Josephs, Brian. "This 1996 Law Was Meant to Save Radio. Instead, It Decimated Popular Black Music." *Vice*, October 21, 2020. www.vice.com/en/article/n7vjqm/this-1996-law-was-meant-to-save-radio-instead-it-decimated-popular-black-music.

Joyella, Mark. "Fox News Hits 23rd Consecutive Month as Most-Watched in Cable News as CNN Sees Gains in January." *Forbes*, February 1, 2023. www.forbes.com/sites/markjoyella/2023/02/01/fox-news-hits-23rd-consecutive-month-as-most-watched-in-cable-news-as-cnn-sees-gains-in-january/?sh=7046d7a75f59.

Kaduk, Kevin. "The 10 Biggest Landslides in Presidential Election History." *List Wire*, August 17, 2021. thelistwire.usatoday.com/lists/the-10-biggest-landslides-in-presidential-election-history/.

Kalbacher, Gene. "When Confronting Frank Zappa There Is No Middle Ground." *Aquarian Night Owl*, November 22–29, 1978, 1, 48–49. www.afka.net/Mags/Aquarian_Weekly.htm#1978Nov.

Kasthuri, A. S., and N. R. Krishnan. "Iatrogenic Disorders." *Medical Journal Armed Forces India* 61, no. 1 (2005): 2–6. www.ncbi.nlm.nih.gov/pmc/articles/PMC4923397/.

Kershaw, Alex. "Frank: Fearless and Still Fighting." *Guardian Weekend*, May 15, 1993, 6–10. www.afka.net/Mags/The_Guardian.htm#1993May.

Khatchadourian, Raffi. "High Anxiety: LSD in the Cold War." *The New Yorker*, December 15, 2012. www.newyorker.com/news/news-desk/high-anxiety-lsd-in-the-cold-war.

Kifner, John. "Khomeini Bans Broadcast Music, Saying It Corrupts Iranian Youth." *New York Times*, July 24, 1979. www.nytimes.com/1979/07/24/archives/khomeini-bans-broadcast-music-saying-it-corrupts-iranian-youth.html.

Klaess, John. *Breaks in the Air: The Birth of Rap Radio in New York City*. Durham, NC: Duke University Press, 2022.

Kofsky, Frank. "Frank Zappa (Part I)." *Jazz & Pop*, September 1967, 15–19. www.afka.net/Mags/Jazz_and_Pop.htm#1967Sep.

———. "Frank Zappa (Part II)." *Jazz & Pop*, October 1967, 28–32. www.afka.net/Mags/Jazz_and_Pop.htm#1967Sep.

Kramer, Michael. "Are You Running with Me, Jesus?: Televangelist Pat Robertson Goes for the White House." *New York Magazine*, August 18, 1986, 22–29.

Kruesi, Kimberlee. "Three More GOP-Led States Enact Abortion 'Trigger Laws.'" *Associated Press*, August 25, 2022. apnews.com/article/abortion-us-supreme-court-health-nashville-idaho-3c1fa60987ad945b4935d2ac8c1f318f.

Kurtzleben, Danielle. "Study Looks at What Motivates Trump Supporters." *National Public Radio*, July 11, 2021. www.npr.org/2021/07/11/1015120444/study-looks-at-what-motivates-trump-supporters.

Langer, Elinor. "This Study of American Fascism, Published in 1990, Is Appallingly Relevant Today." *The Nation*, June 23, 2016. www.thenation.com/article/archive/this-study-of-american-fascism-published-in-1990-is-appallingly-relevant-today/.

"The Legacy of JFK." *John F. Kennedy Library Foundation*. jfklegacy.org/legacy.

Less, Rosanne. "The White House vs. Frank Zappa on Sex." *Metro Times*, September 11, 1985, 4–5. www.afka.net/Mags/Metro_Times.htm#1985Sep.

"Let Me Be (Imperfectly?) Clear." *Richard Nixon Foundation*, October 20, 2009. www.nixonfoundation.org/2009/10/let-me-be-imperfectly-clear/.

"A Letter on Justice and Open Debate." *Harper's*, July 7, 2020. harpers.org/a-letter-on-justice-and-open-debate/.

Lewis, Trevor. "The Life & Times of Frank Zappa and the Mothers." *Woroni*, August 2, 1973, 1. www.afka.net/Mags/Woroni.htm#1973Aug02.

Liptak, Adam, and Eli Murray. "The Major Supreme Court Decisions in 2023." *New York Times*, June 29, 2023. www.nytimes.com/interactive/2023/06/07/us/major-supreme-court-cases-2023.html.

Little, Jenn. "A Town, a Flood, and Superfund: Looking Back at the Times Beach Disaster Nearly 40 Years Later." *U.S. Environmental Protection Agency*, December 15, 2022. www.epa.gov/mo/town-flood-and-superfund-looking-back-times-beach-disaster-nearly-40-years-later.

Loerzel, Robert. "A Fresh Look at *Freedom Wall*." *WBEZ Chicago*, February 25, 2014. www.wbez.org/stories/a-fresh-look-at-freedom-wall/5ba35a36-7792-4c04-9b61-edf9276904f4.

Lopez, Ashley. "More than Half of Republicans Support Christian Nationalism, According to a new Survey." *National Public Radio*, February 14, 2023. www.npr.org/2023/02/14/1156642544/more-than-half-of-republicans-support-christian-nationalism-according-to-a-new-s.

Lowe, Kelly Fisher. *The Words and Music of Frank Zappa*. Lincoln: University of Nebraska Press, 2007.

Macnie, Jim. "Citizen Zappa." *The New Paper*, March 16–23, 1988, 1, 18. www.afka.net/Mags/New_Paper.htm#1988Mar.

Mahon, Bob. "Frank Zappa Unveils Secrets of the Universe." *Sweet Potato*, November 1979, 10–11, 16. www.afka.net/Mags/Sweet_Potato.htm#1979Nov.

Manilla, Ben. "Frank Zappa." *WLIR Free Flight*, Summer 1981, 50–51, 52–55, 57, 59. www.afka.net/Mags/WLIR_Free_Flight.htm.

Marshall, Bob. "Frank Zappa Interview." October 22, 1988. www.afka.net/Articles/1988-10_Bob_Marshall_Interview.htm.

Martin, Kim. "Wielding Words 'Like Chemicals.'" *Dallas Times Herald*, October 19, 1975, 1, 7. www.afka.net/Mags/The_Dallas_Times_Herald.htm#1975oct19.

Mason, Lilliana, Julie Wronski, and John V. Kane. "Activating Animus: The Uniquely Social Roots of Trump Support." *American Political Science Review* 115 , no. 4 (November 2021): 1508–16. doi.org/10.1017/S0003055421000563.

Mattson, Kevin. *"What the Heck Are You Up To, Mr. President?": Jimmy Carter, America's "Malaise," and the Speech That Should Have Changed the Country.* New York: Bloomsbury USA: 2009.

McCammon, Sarah, and Nina Totenberg. "Supreme Court Overturns Roe v. Wade, Ending Right to Abortion Upheld for Decades." *National Public Radio*, June 24, 2022. www.npr.org/2022/06/24/1102305878/supreme-court-abortion-roe-v-wade-decision-overturn.

McDougal, Dennis, and Allan Parachini. "Art in the Eighties: Censorship: A Decade of Tighter Control of the Arts." *Los Angeles Times*, December 25, 1989. www.latimes.com/archives/la-xpm-1989-12-25-ca-781-story.html.

McKenzie, Richard B. "Was It a Decade of Greed?" *National Affairs*, Winter 1992. www.nationalaffairs.com/public_interest/detail/was-it-a-decade-of-greed.

McLeese, Don. "Frank Zappa Waves Flag for Freedom." *Chicago Sun-Times*, February 21, 1988, A1, A5. www.afka.net/Mags/Chicago_Sun-Times.htm#1988Feb.

McMullan, Thomas. "What Does the Panopticon Mean in the Age of Digital Surveillance?" *Guardian*, July 23, 2015. www.theguardian.com/technology/2015/jul/23/panopticon-digital-surveillance-jeremy-bentham.

Menendez, Albert J. "Protestant Support a Factor in Bush Win." *Washington Post*, November 26, 1988. www.washingtonpost.com/archive/local/1988/11/26/protestant-support-a-factor-in-bush-win/d831e8b3-c7ad-470a-8985-492db6c8e314/.

Menn, Don. "The Mother of All Interviews, Part II: Waffles in Plastic." *Best of Guitar Player*, 1992, 74–87. wiki.killuglyradio.com/wiki/The_Mother_Of_All_Interviews_(Part_2).

Merida, Kevin. "The Ebb and Flow of Jackson-Farrakhan." *Washington Post*, February 24, 1996. washingtonpost.com/archive/politics/1996/02/25/the-ebb-and-flow-of-jackson-farrakhan/f34d6666-a9f0-4c83-9701-430353c2591e/.

Michaelson, Jay. "Pat Robertson Is Dead. His Dystopian Legacy Lives On." *Rolling Stone*, June 8, 2023. www.rollingstone.com/culture/culture-features/pat-robertson-dead-dystopian-legacy-1234766810/.

Milkowski, Bill. "Zappa: He Are What He Is." *Good Times*, December 1–14, 1981. www.afka.net/Mags/Good_Times.htm#1981Dec.

Milton, Michael A. "How Is It That the Meek Shall Inherit the Earth?" *Christianity.com*, June 15, 2021. www.christianity.com/wiki/bible/how-is-it-that-the-meek-shall-inherit-the-earth.html.

Mitgang, Herbert. "Groups Aim to Counter Book Bans." *New York Times*, September 7, 1982. www.nytimes.com/1982/09/07/books/groups-aim-to-counter-book-bans.html.

"Moral Majority." *Encyclopedia Britannica*, February 12, 2018. www.britannica.com/topic/Moral-Majority.

Morgan, Bradley. "It's Time We Hung Out at Joe's Garage with Frank Zappa Again." *PopMatters*, September 13, 2022. www.popmatters.com/frank-zappa-joes-garage-atr.

Morgenstern, Joe. "Democracy's Pitchman." *Los Angeles Times Magazine*, October 30, 1988. www.afka.net/Mags/Los_Angeles_Times_Magazine.htm#1988oct30.

———. "Frank Zappa's Getting Out the Vote(!)" *Milwaukee Journal*, November 8, 1988, 1E, 12E. www.afka.net/Mags/Milwaukee_Journal.htm#1988Nov.

Morris, Wesley. "Why Is Everyone Always Stealing Black Music?" *New York Times Magazine*, August 14, 2019. www.nytimes.com/interactive/2019/08/14/magazine/music-black-culture-appropriation.html.

Morrison, Donald. "United States Presidential Election of 1988." *Encyclopedia Britannica*, August 4, 2023. www.britannica.com/event/United-States-presidential-election-of-1988.

"Mother of All Musicians." *Top 40*, December 1995, 24–25. www.afka.net/Mags/Top_40.htm#1995Dec.

"Mother of Two Runs Off with Uncle Meat." *Song Hits Magazine*, September 1967. www.afka.net/Mags/SHM.htm.

Mothers of Invention, The. *Absolutely Free*. Verve Records V/V6-5013X, 1967, LP.

———. *Freak Out!* Rykodisc RCD 10501, 1995, CD.

———. *We're Only in It for the Money*. Rykodisc RCD 10503, 1995, CD.

"MTV Launches." *History*, November 13, 2009. www.history.com/this-day-in-history/mtv-launches.

Murray, Charles Shaar. "Frank Zappa." *Encyclopedia Britannica*, December 17, 2022. www britannica.com/biography/Frank-Zappa.

———. "Frankly a Freak." *The Observer*, September 3, 1989, 4–5. www.afka.net/Mags/The_Observer.htm#1989Sep.

———. "How to Write, Sub, and Lay Out a Frank Zappa Lookin' Back." *New Musical Express*, November 16, 1974, 41–43. www.afka.net/Mags/NME.htm#1974Nov16.

"Music Censorship in America." *National Coalition Against Censorship*. ncac.org/resource/music-censorship-in-america-an-interactive-timeline.

Muso, Mike. "Frank Zappa 1940–1993." *Sun Zoom Spark*, January 1994, 20–22. www.afka.net/Mags/Sun_Zoom_Spark.htm#1994Jan.

"My Epitaph: Anything, Anytime, Any Place, for No Reason at All." *Humo*, December 1993. www.afka.net/Articles/1993-12_Humo.htm.

Nelkin, Dorothy. "AIDS and the News Media." *Milbank Quarterly* 69, no. 2 (1991): 293–307. doi.org/10.2307/3350206.

"1977–1981: The Presidency of Jimmy Carter." *U.S. Department of State Office of the Historian*. history.state.gov/milestones/1977–1980/foreword.

"1993: Shock as Racist Wins Council Seat." *BBC on This Day*. news.bbc.co.uk/onthisday/hi/dates/stories/september/17/newsid_2520000/2520085.stm.

Nolan, Hugh. "Lennon Was Right Says 'Mother' Frank Zappa." *Disc and Music Echo,* September 30, 1967, 16. www.afka.net/Mags/Disc.htm#1967Sep30.

Obama, Barack, and Bruce Springsteen. *Renegades: Born in the USA.* New York: Crown, 2020.

Ogles, Jacob. "17 Gay Sex Scandals That Rocked American Politics." *Advocate,* May 26, 2023. www.advocate.com/people/2018/2/02/17-gay-sex-scandals-rocked-american-politics.

Ouellette, Dan. "Frank Zappa." *Pulse!* August 1993, 48–56. www.afka.net/Mags/Pulse.htm #1993Aug.

Palmer, Ewan. "House Republicans All Vote against Neo-Nazi Probe of Military, Police." *Newsweek,* July 14, 2022. www.newsweek.com/gop-vote-nazi-white-supremacists-military-police-1724545.

Parachini, Allan. "AMA Says It Is Unethical Not to Treat AIDS Patients." *Los Angeles Times,* November 13, 1987. www.latimes.com/archives/la-xpm-1987-11-13-mn-13738-story.html.

"A Partial List of Mass Shootings in the United States in 2022." *New York Times,* January 24, 2023. www.nytimes.com/article/mass-shootings-2022.html.

"Pat Buchanan's Greatest Hits." *Washington Post.* February 3, 1987. www.washingtonpost .com/archive/politics/1987/02/04/pat-buchanans-greatest-hits/416e2224-f7cd-4271-8c9d-0712712df6f3/.

Paulsen, Don. "Frank Zappa the Incredible Boss Mother." *Hit Parader,* June 1967, 44–45. www.afka.net/Mags/Hit_Parader.htm.

Penney, Stuart. "Frank Zappa: The Early Albums." *Record Collector,* May 1987, 38–44. www .afka.net/Mags/Record_Collector.htm#1987May.

Pepin, Jacques. *The Origins of AIDS.* Cambridge, UK: Cambridge University Press, 2011.

Peters, Jeremy W., Michael S. Schmidt, and Jim Rutenberg. "Carlson's Text That Alarmed Fox Leaders: 'It's Not How White Men Fight.'" *New York Times,* May 2, 2023. www.nytimes.com/2023/05/02/business/media/tucker-carlson-text-message-white-men.html.

Petrosky, Miguel. "How Pat Robertson Changed Television and American Politics." *Religion & Politics,* December 14, 2021. religionandpolitics.org/2021/12/14/how-pat-robertson -changed-television-and-american-politics/.

Pickard, Victor. "Media Failures in the Age of Trump." *Political Economy of Communication* 4, no. 2. (2016): 118–22. repository.upenn.edu/server/api/core/bitstreams/2fc4e079 -25b1-43aa-ab1e-d9d9ec4245e3/content.

Pike, William. "Jimmy Swaggart." *Encyclopedia Britannica,* March 11, 2024. www.britannica .com/biography/Jimmy-Swaggart.

Pond, Steve. "Industry Said Fearful of PMRC's Sway." *Washington Post,* October 30, 1985. www.washingtonpost.com/archive/business/1985/10/30/industry-said-fearful-of-pmrcs -sway/1194b3f8-8255-4f25-a7d3-235161ae14fa/.

Pondiscio, Robert. "Who's Afraid of Moms for Liberty?" *Free Press,* July 13, 2023. www.thefp .com/p/whos-afraid-of-moms-for-liberty.

Posner, Sarah. *Unholy: Why White Evangelicals Worship at the Altar of Donald Trump.* New York: Random House, 2020.

Preziosi, Donald. "Why Art Is Dangerous: Making Art Is Making Trouble." *HuffPost,* April 23, 2014. www.huffpost.com/entry/why-art-is-dangerous_b_4832266.

Prince, Evil. "Thing-Fish Rap: Ike Willis Chats." *T'Mershi Duween* 54 (October 1996). www.afka.net/Articles/1996-10_Tmershi_Duween.htm.

Pryor, Lex. "Golf's Historic Problems with Race Aren't Getting Better." *Ringer*, April 7, 2021. www.theringer.com/2021/4/7/22370057/golf-diversity-issues-history-pga-lpga-the-masters.

Purnick, Joyce. "Koch Says Jackson Lied about Actions after Dr. King Was Slain." *New York Times*, April 18, 1988. www.nytimes.com/1988/04/18/us/koch-says-jackson-lied-about-actions-after-dr-king-was-slain.html.

Quinn, Patrick. "Censorship and Zappa." *The Note*, March 1989, 1, 7, 12, 22. www.afka.net/Mags/The_Note.htm#1989Mar.

Rand, Ayn. "Objectivism: A Philosophy for Living on Earth." *Ayn Rand Institute*. aynrand.org/.

Raup, Avo. "Allan Zavod Interview." July 16, 2003. www.afka.net/Articles/2003-05_Allan_Zavod_interview.htm.

Reagan, Ronald. "Address before a Joint Session of the Congress on the State of the Union." Transcript of speech delivered in House Chamber, Washington, DC, February 6, 1985. www.reaganlibrary.gov/archives/speech/address-joint-session-congress-state-union-february-1985.

"Reagan's Response." *George State University Library*. exhibits.library.gsu.edu/out-in-the-archives/hiv-aids/reagans-response/.

Rechler, Glenn. "Only the Weather Was Cold." *East Coast Rocker*, March 30, 1988, 20, 33. www.afka.net/Mags/East_Coast_Rocker.htm#1988Mar.

"Record Labeling: Hearing before the Committee on Commerce, Science, and Transportation—First Session on Contents of Music and the Lyrics of Records. *U.S. Senate, 99th Congress*, September 19, 1985.

"Registry Titles with Descriptions and Expanded Essays: 'We're Only In It For the Money' (album). Frank Zappa and the Mothers of Invention (1968)." *Library of Congress National Recording Preservation Board*. www.loc.gov/programs/national-recording-preservation-board/recording-registry/descriptions-and-essays (accessed August 9, 2023).

Rense, Rip. "A Different Zappa Emerges in Epic 'Operapantomime.'" *Milwaukee Journal*, December 18, 1994. www.afka.net/Articles/1994-12_TMJ.htm.

———. "Frank Zappa—A Would-be Chemist Who Turned to Music." *Valley News*, December 30, 1977. www.afka.net/Articles/1977-12_The_Valley_News.htm.

———. "Frank Zappa Takes on the U.S. Senate in 'Porn Wars.'" *Los Angeles Times*, October 24, 1985. www.afka.net/Articles/1985-12_The_LA_Times.htm.

———. "Posthumous Album Shows Frank Zappa in His Final Phaze." *San Francisco Examiner*, December 21, 1994.

"Republican Party Platform of 1980." Platform document adopted by Republican National Convention at Joe Louis Arena, Detroit, July 14–17, 1980. www.presidency.ucsb.edu/documents/republican-party-platform-1980.

Robinson, Julius. "A Mind for the Body Politic." *Cash Box*, November 26, 1988, 8–10. www.afka.net/Mags/Cash_Box.htm#1988Nov.

Rogers, Kaleigh. "When Prison Food Is a Punishment." *Vice*, September 23, 2015. www.vice.com/en/article/539n3d/when-prison-food-is-a-punishment.

"Ronald Reagan Becomes President." *History*, January 17, 2020. www.history.com/this-day-in-history/ronald-reagan-becomes-president.

Rose, Adrie. "Sex Workers Face Unique Challenges When Trying to Unionize." *Prism*, October 18, 2022. prismreports.org/2022/10/18/sex-workers-face-challenges-unionize/.

Rothman, Dave. "A Conversation with Frank Zappa." *Oui*, April 1979, 70–74, 123–28. www.afka.net/Mags/Oui.htm#1979Apr.

"Ruhollah Khomeini." *Encyclopedia Britannica*, August 8, 2023. www.britannica.com/biography/Ruhollah-Khomeini.

Salvo, Barbara, and Patrick Salvo. "Mother in Lore." *Melody Maker*, January 5, 1974, 23, 40. www.afka.net/Mags/Melody_Maker.htm#1974Jan.

Salvo, Patrick William. "Dialogue: Frank Zappa." *Coq*, February 1974, 56–58, 94–95. afka.net/Mags/Coq.htm#1974Feb.

Schonfeld, Zach. "Parental Advisory Forever: An Oral History of the PMRC's War on Dirty Lyrics." *Newsweek*, September 19, 2015. www.newsweek.com/2015/10/09/oral-history-tipper-gores-war-explicit-rock-lyrics-dee-snider-373103.html.

Seidel, Andrew L. *The Founding Myth: Why Christian Nationalism Is Un-American*. New York: Sterling, 2019.

Senoff, Pete. "A Bizarre Night at the Shrine." *Open City*, December 13–19, 1968, 11. www.afka.net/Mags/Open_City.htm#1968Dec13.

Sewald, Jeffrey. "I Stand Accused: Zappa Lays Down the Law." *Pitt News*, November 30, 1984, 12. www.afka.net/Mags/The_Pitt_News.htm.

Shay, Gary A. "Frank Zappa: An Uninhibited Interview with the Gloveless Rock Genius." *Songwriter Connection*, November 1984. www.afka.net/Mags/Songwriter_Connection.htm#1984Nov.

Sheff, David. "*Playboy* Interview: Frank Zappa." *Playboy*, April 1993, 55–56, 59–60, 62, 64–66, 68, 71–72. www.afka.net/Mags/Playboy.htm#1993Apr.

Sidey, Hugh. "The Presidency: The Meaning of the Cordovans." *Time*, June 30, 1980. content.time.com/time/subscriber/article/0,33009,924245,00.html.

Skilling, H. Gordon. *Charter 77 and Human Rights in Czechoslovakia*. London: Allen & Unwin, 1981.

Slaven, Neil. *Electric Don Quixote: The Definitive Story of Frank Zappa*. London: Omnibus Press, 1997.

———. "Frank's Wild Years." *Record Hunter*, July 1992, 2–7. www.afka.net/Mags/Record_Hunter.htm#1992Jul.

Sodaro, Robert J., and John Anthony Wilcox. "Frank Zappa Meets the PMRC." *Relix*, October 1986, 20–22. www.afka.net/Mags/Relix.htm#1986oct.

Starkey, Arun. "Exploring the Unusual Childhood of Frank Zappa." *Far Out*, September 29, 2022. faroutmagazine.co.uk/the-unusual-childhood-of-frank-zappa/.

Steinfels, Peter. "Moral Majority to Dissolve; Says Mission Accomplished." *New York Times*,

June 12, 1989. www.nytimes.com/1989/06/12/us/moral-majority-to-dissolve-says-mission-accomplished.html.

Stoppard, Tom. "Did Plastic People of the Universe Topple Communism?" *Times*, December 19, 2009. www.thetimes.co.uk/article/tom-stoppard-did-plastic-people-of-the-universe-topple-communism-jbq2kwf7bfq.

Strong, Robert A. "Jimmy Carter: Campaigns and Elections." *University of Virginia Miller Center.* millercenter.org/president/carter/campaigns-and-elections.

"Summary of Uncle Remus, His Songs and His Sayings: The Folk-Lore of the Old Plantation. By Joel Chandler Harris. With Illustrations by Frederick S. Church and James H. Moser." *University of North Carolina, Documenting the American South.* docsouth.unc.edu/southlit/harris/summary.html.

"Surgeon General's Report on Acquired Immune Deficiency Syndrome." Office of NIH History & Stetten Museum. history.nih.gov/download/attachments/8880323/surgeongeneralsreportonaids.pdf?api=v2 (accessed August 4, 2023).

Sutherland, Alastair. "Make a Zappa Noise Here." *Music Express*, January 1992, 68–69. www.afka.net/Mags/Music_Express.htm#1992Jan.

Sweeting, Adam. "Rock Irony from a Master Prankster." *Guardian*, December 7, 1993, 30. www.afka.net/Mags/The_Guardian.htm#1993Dec07.

Swenson, Ali. "A conservative leading the pro-Trump Project 2025 suggests there will be a new American Revolution." *Associated Press*, July 3, 2024. apnews.com/article/project-2025-trump-american-revolution-6e02a297fb91b55de01ba7e86615bb08.

Swenson, John. "Frank Zappa: America's Weirdest Rock Star Comes Clean." *High Times*, March 1980, 36–43, 96. www.afka.net/Mags/High_Times.htm#1980Mar.

———. "Frank Zappa—A Misunderstood Man." *Register-Pajaronian*, April 28, 1988, 4, 5, 20. www.afka.net/Mags/Register-Pajaronian.htm#1988Apr.

———. "Frank Zappa: The Myth of 'Joe's Garage.'" *Rolling Stone*, December 13, 1979, 21–22. www.afka.net/Mags/Rolling_Stone.htm#1979Dec.

Templeton, Bill. "Frank Zappa's Revenge." *Music*, July 2–15, 1987, 16–19. www.afka.net/Mags/Music.htm#1987Jul.

———. "The Music Interview with Frank Zappa." *Music*, January 24–February 6, 1985, 6–7, 9, 11. www.afka.net/Mags/Music.htm#1985Jan.

———. "Zappa on Rating Records." *Music*, January 9–22, 1986, 6–7. www.afka.net/Mags/Music.htm#1986Jan.

"Televangelist Jim Bakker is Indicted on Federal Charges." *History*, September 30, 2021. www.history.com/this-day-in-history/jim-bakker-is-indicted-on-federal-charges.

TheNilesLeshProject. "Frank Zappa—Lost Interview: Message to the Future." YouTube video, 00:53. January 24, 2009. youtu.be/DczLuyOvrOg.

Thornton, David, and Johnathan Thornton. "Listen with Mother: How Zappa Swapped Freaking Out for Speaking Out." *Today*, January 9, 1987.

"A Timeline of HIV and AIDS." *HIV.gov.* www.hiv.gov/hiv-basics/overview/history/hiv-and-aids-timeline/.

Trakin, Roy. "Zapping Back at Big Brother & Other Mothers." *Music Connection*, December 9, 1985, 17–19, 20. www.afka.net/Mags/Music_Connection.htm#1985Dec.

Turner, David, and Lisa Weisberg. "A Pre-Tour Interview with FZ at His House." *Mother People* 38–39, January 12, 1988. www.afka.net/Articles/1988_Mother_People.htm.

Ulrich, Charles. *The Big Note: A Guide to the Recordings of Frank Zappa*. Vancouver: New Star Books, 2018.

Usborne, David. "Wiggers Just Wannabe Black: White Middle-Class Kids Are Adopting Black Street Style and Chilling Out to Rap Music." *The Independent*, August 21, 1993. www.independent.co.uk/news/world/wiggers-just-wannabe-black-white-middleclass-kids-are-adopting-black-street-style-and-chilling-out-to-rap-music-david-usborne-reports-from-washington-1462591.html.

Valdiserri, Ronald. "In Memoriam: C. Everett Koop." *HIV.gov*, February 27, 2013. www.hiv.gov/blog/in-memoriam-c-everett-koop/.

Varga, George. "That Time Frank Zappa Considered Running for President with H. Ross Perot as His Veep." *San Diego Union-Tribune*, July 9, 2019. www.sandiegouniontribune.com/2019/07/09/that-time-frank-zappa-considered-running-for-president-with-h-ross-perot-as-his-veep-2/.

Volpacchio, Florindo. "The Mother of All Interviews: Zappa on Music and Society." *Telos* 87 (Spring 1991): 124–46. www.afka.net/Mags/Telos.htm#1991Spr.

Warburton, Moira. "Jimmy Carter's Biggest Challenges While President." *Reuters*, February 20, 2023. www.reuters.com/world/us/jimmy-carters-biggest-challenges-while-president-2023-02-20/.

Ward, Ian. "There Is a Real Sense That the Apocalypse Is Coming." *Politico*, January 27, 2023. www.politico.com/news/magazine/2023/01/27/apocalypse-coming-christian-nationalism-00079317.

"Warning! The Real Zappa." *Gold Coast Free Press*, September 29, 1979, 3–5. www.afka.net/Mags/Gold_Coast_Free_Press.htm#1979Sep.

Watson, Ben. "The Final Conflict." *The Wire*, February 1996, 36–39. www.afka.net/Mags/Wire.htm#1996Feb.

———. *Frank Zappa: The Complete Guide to His Music*. London: Omnibus Press, 2005.

———. *Frank Zappa: The Negative Dialectics of Poodle Play*. New York: St. Martin's Press, 1993.

———. "Frank Zappa: Spanner in the Works." *Socialist Review*, January 1994. www.afka.net/Mags/Socialist_Review.htm#1994Jan.

"Watts Rebellion (Los Angeles)." *Stanford University Martin Luther King, Jr. Research and Education Institute*. kinginstitute.stanford.edu/encyclopedia/watts-rebellion-los-angeles.

Waxman, Olivia B. "The Story of Prince and Those 'Parental Advisory' Stickers." *Time*, April 21, 2016. time.com/4303801/prince-dead-darling-nikki-parental-advisory/.

Wheeler, Drew. "Frank Zappa's Crusade—25 Years and Counting." *Billboard*, May 19, 1990, 3, 10, 13. www.afka.net/Mags/Billboard.htm#1990May.

Whitaker, Sterling. "The Day Frank Zappa Died." *Ultimate Classic Rock*, December 4, 2015. ultimateclassicrock.com/frank-zappa-death/.

White, Jeremy B. "There Are 'Nazis' in Congress, Says Former Republican Leader John Boehner." *Independent*, October 31, 2017. www.independent.co.uk/news/world/americas/us-politics/john-boehner-nazis-congress-republicans-trump-congress-interview-a8030026.html.

White, Lisa. "Frank Zappa." *Duckberg Times*, November 25, 1986, 2, 16. www.afka.net/Mags/Duckberg_Times.htm#1986Nov.

"White Revolution." *Encyclopedia Britannica*, August 8, 2023. www.britannica.com/topic/White-Revolution.

Wiinikka-Lydon, Joseph. "Dangerous Devotion: Congressional Hearing Examines Threat of White Christian Nationalism." *Southern Poverty Law Center*, December 28, 2022. www.splcenter.org/news/2022/12/28/dangerous-devotion-congressional-hearing-examines-threat-white-christian-nationalism.

Wilder, Elin. "Frank Zappa: Somebody Up There Doesn't Like Me." *High Times*, December 1989, 36–37, 75, 87. www.afka.net/Mags/High_Times.htm.

Wilding, Phil. "Just When You Thought It Was Safe." *Cutting Edge*, August 1993, 18–20. www.afka.net/Mags/Cutting_Edge.htm#1993Aug.

Wilk v. American Medical Ass'n. 671 F. Supp. 1465 (N.D. Ill. 1987).

Willems, Zjakki. "Frank Zappa Is a Man for All Seasons." *Oor*, September 5, 1992. www.afka.net/Articles/1992-09_Oor.htm.

Williams, Daniel K. *God's Own Party: The Making of the Christian Right*. Oxford, UK: Oxford University Press, 2010.

Williams, Liza. "Zappa Zaps the Big Lie." *Los Angeles Free Press*, December 30, 1966, 5. www.afka.net/Mags/Los_Angeles_Free_Press.htm#1966Dec.

Winokur, John. "FZ: Drowning in the News Bath." *Portable Curmudgeon Redux*, 1992. www.afka.net/Articles/1992-00_Big_Curmudgeon.htm.

Wolf, Zachary B. "'Replacement' Conspiracies Driving Gunmen Creep into Mainstream Politics." *CNN*, May 16, 2022. www.cnn.com/2022/05/16/politics/replacement-theory-buffalo-what-matters/index.html.

Wolf-Astrauskas, Marianne. "2023 Results in the Illinois Woman's Press Association Mate E. Palmer Communications Contest." *Illinois Woman's Press Association*, March 18, 2023. www.iwpa.org/2023-results-in-the-illinois-womans-press-association-mate-e-palmer-communications-contest/.

Wootson, Cleve R., Jr. "Trump and Allies Try to Redefine Racism by Casting White Men as Victims." *Washington Post*, February 5, 2022. www.washingtonpost.com/politics/2022/02/05/trump-redefine-racism/.

Yanagihara, Hanya. "What Should We Expect of Art?" *New York Times Style Magazine*, August 18, 2022. www.nytimes.com/2022/08/18/t-magazine/art-activism-social-justice.html.

Yanosik, Joseph. "The Plastic People of the Universe." *Perfect Sound Forever*, March 1996. www.furious.com/perfect/pulnoc.html.

Yazdiha, Hajar. "How the Distortion of Martin Luther King Jr.'s Words Enables More, Not Less, Racial Division within American." *The Conversation*, January 14, 2023. theconver sation.com/how-the-distortion-of-martin-luther-king-jr-s-words-enables-more-not-less-racial-division-within-american-society-195177.

"Yes, I Am a Rich Man: The Sheraton Hotel Press Conference, Oslo." *Society Pages*, August 1988. www.afka.net/Articles/1988-08_Society_Pages.htm.

Yurcaba, Jo. "More than 1 in 8 LGBTQ People Live in States Where Doctors Can Refuse to Treat Them." *NBC News*, July 28, 2022. www.nbcnews.com/nbc-out/out-health-and-wellness/1-8-lgbtq-people-live-states-doctors-can-refuse-treat-rcna39161.

"Zappa!" *Rockhead*, Summer 1990, 1, 28–30. www.afka.net/Mags/RockHEAD.htm#1990Summer.

Zappa, Frank. "About the Abortion Issue in the United States." *Tuttifrutti*, September 1989. www.afka.net/Articles/1989-09_TuttiFrutti.htm.

———. "Absolutely Free: The Complete Libretto." Liner notes for Mothers of Invention, *Absolutely Free*. Verve Records V/V6-5013X, 1967, LP.

———. *Broadway the Hard Way*. Rykodisc RCD 40096, 1989, CD.

———. *Civilization Phaze III*. Zappa Records CDDZAP 56, 1994, 2 CDs.

———. *"Congress Shall Make No Law. . . ."* Zappa Records ZR 20011, 2010, CD.

———. *Frank Zappa for President*. Zappa Records ZR20021, 2016, CD.

———. *Frank Zappa Meets the Mothers of Prevention*. Rykodisc 10547, 1995, CD.

———. "FZ Delivered a Memorable Testimony before the Maryland State Legislature." *Facebook*, March 18, 2020. www.facebook.com/Zappa/photos/a.225007574226435/2834864766574023/?type=3.

———. *Joe's Garage: Acts I, II & III*. Rykodisc RCD 10530/31, 1995, 2 CDs.

———. Liner notes for *Civilization Phaze III*. Zappa Records CDDZAP 56, 1994, 2 CDs.

———. Liner notes for *Joe's Garage Acts I, II & III*. Rykodisc RCD 10530/31, 1995, 2 CDs.

———. Liner notes for *Thing-Fish*. Rykodisc RCD 10020/21, 1986, 2 CDs.

———. Liner notes for *You Are What You Is*. Rykodisc RCD 40165, 1990, CD.

———. "Opening Statement to and Q&A with the Senate Commerce, Science and Transportation Committee on Rock Lyrics and Record Labeling." Transcript of speech at U.S. Capitol, September 19, 1985. www.americanrhetoric.com/speeches/frankzapparockmusiclyrics.htm.

———. *Thing-Fish*. Rykodisc RCD 10020/21, 1986, 2 CDs.

———. "Thing-Fish Photo Fantasy." *Hustler*, April 1984, 107–28. www.afka.net/Mags/Hustler.htm.

———. *You Are What You Is*. Rykodisc RCD 40165, 1990, CD.

———. "Your Vote." *The Learning Channel*, October 24, 1991. www.youtube.com/watch?v=gcxzpbkV2Tg.

———. *Zappa '88: The Last U.S. Show*. Zappa Records ZR20036-2, 2021, 2 CDs.

———, and Ensemble Modern. *The Yellow Shark*. Zappa Records CDZAP 57, 1993, CD.

———, with Peter Occhiogrosso. *The Real Frank Zappa Book*. New York: Poseidon Press, 1989.

Zappa, Gail. "Zappa Records Commemorates 25th Anniversary of Frank Zappa's Testimony

Against Censorship on Capitol Hill with New CD 'Congress Shall Make No Law.'" *Press release*, September 27, 2010.

"Zappa Interview." *Ann Arbor Argus*, June 19—July 3, 1969, 12–13, 23. www.afka.net/Mags/Ann_Arbor_Argus.htm#1969Jun19.

Zeller, Frank. "Tense Germany, Turkey Mark Deadly 1993 Neo-Nazi Attack." *Times of Israel*, May 29, 2018. www.timesofisrael.com/tense-germany-turkey-mark-deadly-1993-neo-nazi-attack/.

INDEX

2 Live Crew: arrest and obscenity charges, 153–54
200 *Motels* (soundtrack album), 34
"200 Years Old" (song), 35
700 Club, The, 62, 193
1619 Project, The (Hannah-Jones): analysis of systemic American racism in, 85; banning of in schools, 161
1934 Radio Act, 89
1960 Constitution of Czechoslovakia, 210
1975 Conference on Security and Cooperation in Europe, 210
1976 presidential election: Jimmy Carter's victory, 39
1980 presidential election: impact of Christian evangelicals on, 95, 106; Jimmy Carter's primary victory, 44; Ronald Reagan's victory, 59, 69, 106
1984 (Orwell), 225
1984 presidential election, 106; Jesse Jackson's campaign during, 177–78; Ronald Reagan's victory, 138
1985 State of the Union address, 182
1988 presidential election, 172; commentary in *Broadway the Hard Way* on, 174, 193; Jesse Jackson's campaign during, 177–78; Pat Robertson's campaign during, 193; Zappa as potential vice-presidential candidate during, 208; Zappa's support of Michael Dukakis in, 180
1992 presidential election: Bill Clinton's campaign during, 207; George H. W. Bush's campaign during, 207; Zappa's ambitions to campaign during, 207. See also *Freedom Wall* (1994)
2016 presidential election: evangelical support of Donal Trump during, 99, 227; impact of media on, 79, 241. See also *Frank Zappa for President* (album)
2020 presidential election: January 6 insurrection, 86; state-level book bans following, 159
2024 presidential election, 101
2025 Presidential Transition Project (Project 2025): goals and vision for, 101

abortion: C. Everett Koop's book opposing, 186; evangelical agenda to overturn during Donald Trump's first presidency, 196; evangelical efforts to restrict access to, 44, 59, 62–63, 70, 96, 98, 103, 123, 206, 217; evangelical stance on "Jesus Thinks You're a Jerk," 200; Jerry Falwell's comments on, 62; theme in "Food Gathering in Post-Industrial America, 1992," 217; Zappa's support of, 186, 217, 235
Absolutely Free (album) 19, 21, 22; censorship of, 17; division into "Underground Oratorios," 17; libretto, 17; release of, 16–17; Suzy Creamcheese appearance in, 21–22; symbolic use of vegetable imagery in, 19–20; theme of advocating for marginalized groups, 20; theme of hippie culture, 23; theme of social change, 18–20; themes of, 17, 19, 34

"Absolutely Free" (song): critique of drug culture, 25–26
"Absolutely Free" ("underground oratorio"), 17
Absolutely Free: The Complete Libretto, 17; idealistic views in, 28
AC/DC: "Filthy Fifteen" list, 141–42
Acquired Immunodeficiency Syndrome (AIDS): C. Everett Koop's response to, 110–11, 187; critique of Reagan administration's policies toward, 186; doctors refusing treatment of, 125; evangelical response to, 109, 111, 116, 121–26; history of crisis, 107–9, 119–20; legacy of, 120; media's role during crisis, 124, 125; missionary impact on HIV transmission, 118–20; origins of disease, 120; parallels to COVID-19 pandemic, 121, 189; public misinformation, 108–9, 124; Reagan administration's response to, 107–10; as theme on *Broadway the Hard Way*, 174; Zappa's criticisms of C. Everett Koop, 182–84, 186–87; Zappa's thoughts on, 114, 116–21, 125–26, 132, 189, 208. See also *Thing-Fish* (album)
"Adventures Of Greggery Peccary, The" (song), 127
Afghanistan, 69; Reagan policy concerning, 183
Alaska: Outrage at Valdez (Cousteau documentary), 215
Ali, Muhammad, 1
Alte Oper (concert hall), 216
"America Drinks & Goes Home" (song), 20
"America Drinks" (song), 20
America Online, 1
American Booksellers for Free Expression, 61
American craftsmanship: as theme in Zappa's music, 33, 52
American Dream, 3
American Library Association: on issues of censorship, 60, 151, 159
American Medical Association, 161, 183
American myths: generational passing down of, 26; racial myths, 84–87, 90; in relation to consumerism, 76; in relation to hippie culture, 11; in relation to legacy of JFK assassination, 8; in relation to racial separateness, 74–77; in relation to the American Bicentennial, 35; in relation to the American Dream, 3; role of artificial intelligence in perpetuating, 241; role of art in perpetuating, 237; Ronald Reagan's perpetuating of, 44
American Revolution, 157
Amnerika (setting), 222
"Amnerika" (song), 221–222
"Amnerika (Vocal Version)" (song), 221
"Amnerika Goes Home" (song), 221
"Amnesia America" (cultural concept): conceptual definition, 221; theme in "The Duke Regains His Chops," 19; Zappa's outlook on, 226. *See also* "Amnerika" (song)
"Amnesia Vivace" (song), 19
Amos 'n' Andy Show, 72, 133
Anderson, Avery, 146, 156–57
Andriote, John-Manuel, 186.
"Animal (Fuck Like a Beast)" (WASP song): "Filthy Fifteen" list, 141
Anti-Defamation League, 220, 221
Anti-Defamation League of the B'nai B'rith: protest over "Jewish Princess," 54
anti-Semitism: accusations of Zappa displaying, 55; allegations in "Packard Goose," 54, 56; comments by Jesse Jackson, 178; rise in violence, 221
"Any Downers?" (song), 71
"Any Kind of Pain" (song), 175
"Any Way the Wind Blows" (song), 12
Apostrophe (') (album), 30, 67
Aquarian Night Owl (newspaper), 54
Arafat, Yasser, 181
Armaly, Miles T., 102
art: role in society, 230, 237–38, 240–42
"Artificial Rhonda" (song), 128
Artificial Rhonda (*Thing-Fish* character), 128–30
As Nasty as They Wanna Be (2 Live Crew album), 153
Assemblies of God, 190
Associated Press, 115
Atlantic, The, 186
Aung San Suu Kyi, 2
"Aunt Jemima," 36, 133
Ayatollah. *See* Khomeini, Ruhollah

backward masking: Zappa's satire of, 153
"Bacon Fat" (song), 177
Baker, James, III, 143; response to Zappa's emissary designation, 213–14; Zappa's criticism of, 95–96
Baker, Susan, 213; role in PMRC, 143–44, 154; Zappa's criticism of, 141, 144–45
Bakker, Jim: financial scandal of, 96–97; media empire of, 96; thematization in "Jesus Thinks You're a Jerk," 198–99; Zappa's criticism of, 94, 96, 153; Zappa's satire of scandals, 117, 198–99
Bakker, Tammy Faye. *See* Bakker, Jim
Bald-Headed John, King of the Plookers (*Joe's Garage* character), 51
Baldwin, James, 88
Balmer, Randall, 44
Baltimore, MD: Zappa's birthplace, 9. *See also* Wright, Imani Wj
Bamboozled (film), 136
Barking Pumpkin Records, 223
"Bastard" (Mötley Crüe song): "Filthy Fifteen" List, 141
Bauman, Robert: sex scandal, 190
BBC Radio, 153, 224
Beatles (band): *Sgt. Pepper's* album cover, 23; Zappa's criticism of, 23–24. *See also* "Beatles Medley, The" (medley)
"Beatles Medley, The" (medley) 191
"Be-Bop Tango" (song), 215
"Be in My Video" (song), 36, 132
Belew, Adrian, 33
Beltway: Zappa's beliefs on, 208. *See also* "Beltway Bandits, The" (song)
"Beltway Bandits, The" (song), 170
Bentham, Jeremy, 11
Berry, Richard, 18
Biddle, Livingston, 152
Biden, Joe, 86; 1988 presidential candidate, 172; administration response to rise in anti-Semitic violence, 221
"Big Lie": theme in "When the Lie's So Big," 194–96. *See also* Hitler, Adolf
Billboard (magazine), 36, 200, 212
"Billy the Mountain" (song): plot of, 35–36
Black cultural erasure: in music industry, 74–75. *See also* "Ripping Off Black Music" (Jefferson)
Blackouts (band), 46
Black Sabbath, 142
Blake, William, 2
Bolognese, Greg, 173
Bongo Fury (album), 34–35
book bans: conservative influence on, 159–60; Falwell's influence on, 60; increase in number of, 160; targeting of books on race and gender, 159
Boone, Pat, 177
Bowie, David, 36
"Bow Tie Daddy" (song), 26–27
Bozzio, Dale, 46, 113
Bozzio, Terry, 34, 51, 113
Braden, Tom, 152
Brandt, Edward, 110
"Briefcase Boogie" (song), 129
British National Party, 219
British Socialist Workers Party, 233
Broadway. See *Thing-Fish* (album)
Broadway the Hard Way (album): as satire of America during 1988 presidential election, 174, 179, 202; "confinement loaf" imagery in, 176–77, 196; effectiveness of Zappa's satire, 201; homosexual imagery in, 198–99; legacy of, 202–3; parallels connecting Nixon and Reagan, 176–77; parallel to *We're Only in It for the Money*, 179; sexist imagery in, 175, 192; theme and lyric analysis, 174–82, 186, 188, 195–202; theme of American consumerism, 175, 179; theme of American culture, 175; theme of America's future, 201; theme of authoritarianism, 175–76; theme of C. Everett Koop, 182–84, 186–88; theme of celebrity culture, 175; theme of Christian fundamentalists, 188–89, 193–95, 197–202; theme of conservative sex scandals, 190; theme of evangelicals, 174, 175, 176, 182, 189, 190; theme of freedoms and civil liberties, 201, 202; theme of generational conflict, 26–27; theme of Jesse Jackson, 177–79; theme of Jim

Broadway the Hard Way (album) (*continued*) Bakker, 198–99; theme of Jimmy Swaggart's sex scandal, 190–92; theme of Pat Robertson, 193–95, 199–201; theme of racial violence, 199, 200; theme of religious violence, 197, 199–200; theme of televangelists, 198–201; theme of wealth disparity, 174, 193, 203; theme of white supremacy, 199, 200; theme of yuppie culture, 175; theme of Zappa leaving rock music, 175; voting advocacy in, 202
Brock, Napoleon Murphy, 112, 133
Brooks, Adam. See *Freedom Wall* (1994)
Brown, Dorothy, 166
Brownell, Herbet, 207
"Brown Moses" (song), 129
Brown Moses (*Thing-Fish* character), 127–30
"Brown Shoes Don't Make It" (song), 22–23, 34, 209
Bruce, Lenny, 2, 24
Bruister, La Marr (Frank Zappa pseudonym), 47
Buchanan, Pat: homophobic comments of, 109; Zappa's criticism of, 126
Buckley, David T., 102
Buckley, William, 125
Burton, Dan, 108
Burton, Philip, 108
Bush, George H. W., 185; 1988 presidential election, 172, 204; 1992 presidential election, 207; administration response to Zappa's emissary appointment, 213; Zappa's criticism of, 177, 186, 205–7, 224
Bush, George W.: evangelical support of presidency, 97–98. *See also* Chicks (band)
Butler, Anthea, 99, 103–4
Buxton, Eric, 200

Cage, John, 214
Cagé, Julia, 118–19
"Call Any Vegetable" (song): vegetable imagery as social commentary, 19–20
Camelot Records, 149
Camp David: Nixon's secret recordings from, 176
Camp David Accords, 40
Campbell, Bobbi, 108
"cancel culture": public discourse on, 229–30
Captain Beefheart, 35
Carlin, George: appropriation of legacy by conservatives, 229; "seven dirty words" routine, 139
Carlson, Tucker: abuse of media platform, 84, 236
Carroll, Anne Berrill, 95
Cash Box (magazine), 193
Carter, Jimmy: 1976 presidential election, 39; 1980 presidential election, 44, 69; "Crisis of Confidence" speech, 43, 44; energy and economic crises, 42–44, 69; evangelical response to, 39, 44, 59; Iranian hostage crisis, 42, 69; legacy of, 39, 40, 44; reverence for in Czechoslovakia, 212
"Catholic Girls" (song), 46–48; homophobic and sexist language in, 65; Zappa's reaction to anti-Semitism, 55
censorship: impact on *Absolutely Free*, 18; mass media influence of, 230; religious influence on, 60, 157; Václav Havel's fight against, 210; Zappa's criticism of, 59–60, 88, 90, 152, 170–71, 213, 224; Zappa's response to, 24, 54. *See also* book bans; Parents Music Resource Center (PMRC)
Central Scrutinizer, The (*Joe's Garage* character), 46–50, 53, 228
"Central Scrutinizer, The" (song), 46
"Charlie's Enormous Mouth" (song) 71
Charter 77, 210
Chef, Alice, 173
cheese: as allegory for mass consumerism, 76–78, 80, 91. See also *You Are What You Is* (album)
Chepesiuk, Ron, 206
Chicago Sun-Times (newspaper), 198
Chicks (band), 154
China: influence on American entertainment, 32; relationship with the United States, 40
Chomsky, Noam, 2, 230
Christian Broadcasting Network, 193
Christian evangelicals/fundamentalists: agenda/goals of, 63; complicit attitude toward church financial exploitation of, 93; impact

on abortion rights, 217–18; impact on AIDS crisis, 123–26, 186, 189; impact on book bans, 151; impact on government and culture, 5–6, 37, 70, 91, 93, 170, 184, 201, 203–4, 233, 235; impact on marginalized groups, 37–38; Jerry Falwell's mobilization of, 59; opposition to LGBTQ community, 96, 108–9, 121–23, 125, 194; opposition to secularism, 61–62, 70, 123, 188, 196; racial violence by, 200; yearning for pre-1960s nostalgia, 37–38; Zappa on, 5–6, 92–93, 100–101, 104–5, 111–12, 126, 153, 168–69, 176, 180, 189, 193–95, 200–201, 206, 213, 217
Christian nationalism/fascism: part of Republican Party platform, 5; pre–Moral Majority movements, 59; rise during the Trump administration, 227; as theme in *Joe's Garage*, 48, 59, 63–66, 68
Christian Right: agenda and goals for Reagan's presidency, 44; bringing religion into politics, 44; counterrevolution during 1960s, 9, 38; counterrevolution during 1970s, 38; emergence as a political force, 95–96; George W. Bush's support for, 97; impact on AIDS crisis, 123; impact on civil liberties and freedoms, 38; impact on COVID-19, 188; impact on marginalized groups, 38; opposition to liberalism, 38, 44; Reagan's support for, 44; support of Trump, 196–97; support of Reagan, 44; support of Republican Party, 44
Christians Against Christian Nationalism, 101
"Chrome Plated Megaphone of Destiny, The" (song), 24
Chronicle, The (newspaper), 184
Chunga's Revenge (album), 33, 175
Civic Forum Party (Czechoslovakia), 211
Civil Rights Act of 1964, 8, 85
civil rights movement: as theme in "Uncle Remus," 30–31
Civilization Phaze III (album), 20, 165; analysis of themes, 222–24; release of, 223; as Zappa's final work, 223–24
CKLN (Canadian radio station), 205
Clear Channel (radio network): banned songs after September 11 attacks, 154
Clemons, Clarence, 135
Clinton, Bill: Gail Zappa's support of, 209; Zappa's criticism of, 207
Clinton, Hillary, 209
"Clowns on Velvet" (song), 127
CNN, 80, 132, 152; Zappa's criticism of, 81, 185, 208
Columbia College, 1
Colwell, Cerphe, 147
communism: 1980 Republican Party Platform on, 69; JFK's fight against, 8; Reagan's fight against, 59; Zappa's comment on fascism being a bigger threat than, 152
"Concentration Moon" (song): theme of government imprisoning hippies, 29
"Conehead" (song), 71
"confinement loaf." See under *Broadway the Hard Way* (album)
Congress Shall Make No Law . . . (album), 163–65
"Congress Shall Make No Law" (spoken-word track), 164
Congressional Record: comments about AIDS in, 108, 115; regarding satire in "Porn Wars," 168
Connecticut: Zappa radio airplay in, 88
conservative politicians: using violent imagery in campaign ads, 16
"conspicuous opulence" phenomenon, 76
Conwright, Anthony, 87
Copeland, Kenneth, 97
Corn, David, 212
Courrier, Kevin: on Christian fundamentalism, 213; on messianic figures in hippie culture, 93; on myths of the hippie generation, 37; on Reagan administration's efforts to erase reform, 37; on satire in "Who are the Brain Police?," 11
Cousteau, Jacques, 215
COVID-19: conspiracy theories regarding, 121, 188; Donald Trump's handling of, 188, 189; impact on and response by religious conservatives, 188–89; impact on school restrictions, 159; media response and coverage of, 188–89; politicization of, 188–89; racial disparity regarding treatment of, 116

"Crab-Grass Baby, The" (song), 128
Crab-Grass Baby, The (*Thing-Fish* character), 128–30
Craig, Larry, 190
Creamcheese, Suzy (*Freak Out!* and *Absolutely Free* character), 21–22
"Crew Slut" (song), 34, 47; sexist language in, 65
"criminalization of America": as theme in *Joe's Garage*, 51
"Crisis of Confidence" (Carter speech), 43–44; theme of preserving American values, 43–44; theme of threats to democracy, 43. *See also* Carter, Jimmy
"critical race theory": conservative response to, 85–86; Ron DeSantis's legislation to ban, 161
Cronos (Venom singer), 147
Crossfire (CNN program), 152
Cruise, Tom, 50
Cruising with Ruben & the Jets (album), 30
C-SPAN, 182
Cuccurullo, Warren, 50
cultural appropriation: white appropriation of rap culture, 73–74. *See also* "You Are What You Is" (song)
Culture Club, 132
Cuomo, Mario, 173
Czechoslovakia: government abuse in, 210–11; government view on Zappa, 212; Havel as president of, 211; musical underground in, 211; Zappa's efforts toward promoting economic independence, 212; Zappa's impact on, 214; Zappa's visit to, 211
Czech Republic, 211

"Daddy, Daddy, Daddy" (song), 34
Dalai Lama, 2
Dallas Times Herald (newspaper), 35
"Dancin' Fool" (song), 36
Danforth, John: audio in "Porn Wars," 166; Center at Washington University, 98, 122; in PMRC hearings, 163
Dannemeyer, Bill, 108
"Darling Nikki" (Prince song): "Filthy Fifteen" list, 141; as inspiration for formation of the PMRC, 142–43
Dartmouth College, 44
Def Leppard: "Filthy Fifteen" list, 141–42
Democratic National Convention: Jesse Jackson speaking at the, 178
Democratic Party: Jesse Jackson's campaign for, 177, 181; Jimmy Carter's nomination for 1976 presidential election, 39; Richard Nixon's "silent majority" impact on, 58; Zappa on, 181
DeMoss, Bob, 158
DeNameland, Quentin Robert (*Thing-Fish* character), 127–30
Denver, John, 231; PMRC testimony, 150–51, 167
deregulation: of the telecommunications industry, 70, 97, 106–7, 155, 232; Reagan administration's impact on, 162, 184; Republican Party platform on, 69
DeSantis, Ron, 160–61
Detroit Free Press (newspaper), 19
"Dickie's Such an Asshole" (song): parallels between Nixon and Reagan, 176–77; theme and lyric analysis of, 176–77
"Dirty Love" (song), 34
"Disco Boy" (song), 36
"discorporate": drug use satire in "Absolutely Free" (song), 26
"Does Rock Music Cause AIDS?" (*Crossfire* topic): Zappa's response to, 132
"Dog Breath Variations" (song), 215
Domestic Policy Council, 111
"Dong Work for Yuda" (song), 51; homophobic language in, 65
"Don't Eat the Yellow Snow" (song), 36
doo-wop: Zappa's musical use of, 4, 12, 26, 30
"Doreen" (song), 71
Douglass, Frederick, 1
Down Beat (magazine), 24
"Do You Really Want to Hurt Me?" (Culture Club song), 132
"Dr. God" (C. Everett Koop nickname), 182
"Drafted Again," 72
"Dress You Up" (Madonna song): "Filty Fifteen" list, 141
Drinan, Robert, 94–95
"Drop Dead" (song), 130
Duckberg Times (newspaper), 182

Dukakis, Michael: 1988 presidential campaign of, 172, 204, 205; Zappa's support of, 180
"Duke of Prunes, The" (song), 19
"Duke Regains His Chops, The" (song), 19
Duke University, 184
Duke, George, 30
"Dumb All Over" (song), 91; theme and lyric analysis of, 99–102; theme of religious hypocrisy, 99–100; theme of religious violence, 100; theme of religious xenophobia, 101, 103; theme of the apocalypse, 102
Dunbar, Paul Laurence, 134
Dylan, Bob, 33

East Coast Rocker (magazine), 153
Easton, Sheena: "Filthy Fifteen" list, 141, 159
"Eat Me Alive" (Judas Priest song): "Filthy Fifteen" list, 141
EIHN (Everything Is Healing Nicely) (album), 221
Einstein, Albert, 1
Eisenhower, Dwight, 207
"Elvis Has Just Left the Building" (song), 175
Enders, Adam M., 102
Ensemble Modern, 214–16, 218, 221–22
E Street Band, 135
Evil Prince, The (*Thing-Fish* character), 112, 114, 126, 129–30; on *Frank Zappa for President,* 222
Exon, Jim, 163

Falwell, Jerry: as pioneer of televangelism, 94; Christian fundamentalist views of, 59–62, 64, 94, 125; dissolving the Moral Majority and achieving its mission, 64; formation of the Moral Majority, 58; impact on book bans, 60; influence on Reagan administration, 62, 111; involvement with Swaggart sex scandal, 198; on AIDS, 125–26; on September 11 attacks, 62; similarity of rhetoric to that of Ruhollah Khomeini, 59; Zappa on, 126
Farrakhan, Louis, 178
Father Riley (*Joe's Garage* character), 46–47, 51, 65. *See also* Jones, Buddy (*Joe's Garage* character)
Fauci, Anthony, 187
Federal Bureau of Investigation (FBI), 176
Federal Communications Commission (FCC): Reagan's deregulation of, 97; regulatory function of, 89; Telecommunications Act of 1934, 89
"Fembot In a Wet T-Shirt" (song), 47; sexist language in, 65
Feminine Mystique, The (Friedan), 24
Fight Club (Palahniuk), 175
Fillmore East, 25
Fillmore East, June 1971 (album), 34, 190
"Filthy Fifteen" song list, 141–42, 147–48. *See also specific songs*
Finan, Chris, 61
Financial News Network, 212
First Amendment, 61, 64, 140–41, 145, 150, 164, 168
"Flakes" (song), 32–33; Bob Dylan monologue in, 33; theme of American consumerism in, 33; theme of union laborers, 33, 65
"Flower Punk" (song): satire of hippie movement in, 65
Floyd, George, 16
Focus on the Family (religious organization), 158
Foley, Mark, 190
"Food Gathering in Post-Industrial America, 1992" (song), 218; theme and lyric analysis of, 216–17; theme of abortion ban, 217; theme of Republican influence, 216–17
Foucault, Michel, 11
Fourteenth Amendment, 62
Fox News, 80, 84
Frank Zappa for President (album), 209, 221
Frank Zappa Meets the Mothers of Prevention (album), 37, 165; title and music criticizing PMRC, 165; warning label on cover of, 168, 169; Zappa testimony audio (*see* "Porn Wars" [song])
Frank, Anne, 2
Frankfurt Festival, 214
Freak Out! (album), 16, 18, 21, 30, 67; liner notes encouraging self-education, 10; subversion of pop music stylings in, 12–13; theme and lyric analysis of, 9–13; theme of American culture, 9–13; theme of "freaking out," 12–13; theme of inclusivity, 10; theme of youth culture, 12

Freedom from Religion Foundation, 94
Freedom Wall (1994), 1, 3–4, 231, 237; names on, 1–2; theme of representing diverse voices, 2–3, 7
Friedan, Betty, 24
Friedman, Jonathan, 159
Fruit of Islam, 178
Frye, Marquette, 13
Frye, Ronald, 13

Gallery (magazine), 144, 193, 206
Galoot Cologne (*Thing-Fish* reference), 112–14, 129–30
"Galoot Up-Date" (song), 113–14
Gardner, Bill, 184
Gay Men's Health Crisis (AIDS service organization), 107
Germany: resurgence of neo-Nazism in, 220
Gifford, Laura, 98
"Goblin Girl" (song), 71
"Go Cry on Somebody Else's Shoulder" (song), 12
Goldberg, Danny, 146
Gold Coast Free Press (newspaper), 51
Good Times (magazine), 88, 100
Goodman, Robert O., Jr., 178
Gore, Al, 144; 1988 presidential campaign, 172; Gail Zappa's support of, 209; in PMRC hearing, 163; sample audio in "Porn Wars," 166–67
Gore, Tipper: Dee Snider's response to, 148; parenting philosophy of, 157; relationship with Al Gore, 144; role in PMRC, 142–43, 145; Zappa's criticism of, 141
Gorman, Marvin, 190
Gortikov, Stan, 145–47
Gorton, Slade, 166–67
gospel: musical influence in "You Are What You Is" (song), 87; white appropriation of, 74
Graham, Billy, 92
Grammy award, 169
Grateful Dead, 25, 71
"Great Satan": Ruhollah Khomeini's name for U.S., 42
"Great Society" (domestic programs), 8; reference in "Hungry Freaks, Daddy," 10; reference in "Trouble Every Day," 15
Greely, Andrew, 123
Greenblatt, Jonathan, 221
Griffith, R. Marie, 122
Groening, Matt, 223
groupies: imagery in Zappa's music, 34, 190; reference in "Motherly Love," 12; reference in *Joe's Garage*, 47; Zappa's attitude toward, 192. *See also* Creamcheese, Suzy (*Freak Out!* and *Absolutely Free* character)
Guardian Weekend (magazine), 235
Guitar Player (magazine), 223
Gun Violence Archive, 170

Hannah-Jones, Nikole, 85. See also *1619 Project, The* (Hannah-Jones)
Harper's (magazine): 2020 open letter in, 230–232; Margo Jefferson essay, 74–75
Harris, Art, 96
Harris, Bob, 127
Harris, Joel Chandler, 31
"Harry & Rhonda" (song), 113
Harry (*Thing-Fish* character), 113–14, 126–31, 133
"Harry, You're a Beast" (song), 24
Harry-As-A-Boy (*Thing-Fish* character), 127–30
"Harry-As-A-Boy" (*Thing-Fish* song), 127
Havel, Václav: advocacy for the release of the Plastic People of the Universe, 210–11; becoming president of Czechoslovakia, 211; meeting Zappa, 210, 212–14; tribute to Zappa, 214
Havlová, Olga, 212
Hawkins, Paula, 164
Haynes, Jeffrey, 188
"He Used to Cut the Grass" (song), 52
"Health Nazis": Zappa's comments on, 207–8
"Heavenly Bank Account" (song), 91, 94, 100; theme and lyric analysis of, 93–94, 96–97; theme of religious followers, 93; theme of religious influence on government, 93–94; theme of tax-attempt status for religious organizations, 96–97; theme of televangelists, 93–94
"He's So Gay" (song), 127–28; homophobic lyrics in, 132

Heller, Jean, 115
"Help, I'm a Rock" (song), 13
Hemmer, Nicole, 161
Heritage Foundation, 101
Heritage USA (Christian amusement park), 96
Herman, Edward S., 230
"Hey Joe" (Jimi Hendrix Experience song), 25
Heyward, Carter, 197, 199
"High 'n' Dry" (Def Leppard song): "Filthy Fifteen" list, 141
High Times (magazine), 59, 81, 117, 132
Hilliard, Bobby, 108
Hinson, Jon, 190
hippie culture: as theme in Zappa's music, 12, 22–23, 25–26, 29, 37, 179; in relation to Christian fundamentalism, 93; Zappa's comments on, 27–28
Hitler, Adolf, 42, 220; Louis Farrakhan's comments on, 178; "the Big Lie," 194–96
Hit Parader (magazine), 22
Hoch, Studebaker ("Bill the Mountain" character), 36
Holiday, Billie, 200
Hollings, Ernest F.: PMRC hearing, 164; reference in "Jezebel Boy," 190; sampled audio in "Porn Wars," 166
Holocaust, 219
Home Audio Recording Act ("blank tape tax"). *See* H.R. 2911 (legislation)
homophobia: accusations of against Zappa, 236; Zappa's attitudes toward, 235; Zappa's use of language in music 46, 50, 65–66, 132
hooks, bell, 2
Hoover, L. Ron (*Joe's Garage* character), 50
Hot Flash (magazine), 31, 82
"Hot Plate Heaven at the Green Hotel" (song): theme and lyric analysis of, 179–81; theme of Republicans and Democrats, 179–80; theme of wealth disparity, 179–80
"Hot Poop" (song), 24
Hot Press (magazine), 222
House Oversight Subcommittee on Civil Rights and Civil Liberties, 101
"How Could I Be Such a Fool" (song), 12
Howar, Pam, 144
Howard, John Tasker, 17
H.R. 2911 (legislation), 143
"H.R. 2911" (song), 165
Hradčany Castle, 212
Human Immunodeficiency Virus (HIV). *See* Acquired Immunodeficiency Syndrome (AIDS)
Humo (magazine), 174
"Hungry Freaks, Daddy" (song): theme and lyric analysis of, 10–11; theme of American government and education, 10; theme of free speech advocacy, 10; theme of small-town American values, 10
Hustler (magazine), 131
"Hymietown" remark. *See* "Rhymin' Man" (song)

"I Ain't Got No Heart" (song), 12
"I'm a Beautiful Guy" (song), 71
"I'm Not Satisfied" (song), 12
iatrogenic diffusion, 119
"Idiot Bastard Son, The" (song), 29; theme and lyric analysis of, 27; theme of generational conflict, 27
"'If I Was President . . .'" (song), 209
"If Only She Woulda" (song): theme of gender violence, 71–72
"I'm the Slime" (song): modern analysis related to social media influence, 32; theme of television propaganda, 31–32, 184
"Imagine" (John Lennon song): banning from radio after September 11 attacks, 154
immigration: conservative restrictions on, 83. *See also* "Welcome to the United States" (song)
"In France" (song) 132
"In My House" (Mary Jane Girls song): "Filthy Fifteen" list, 142
Industry of the Ordinary (conceptual art collaborative), 1. See also *Freedom Wall* (1994)
Intergovernmental Panel on Climate Change, 217
Internal Revenue Service (IRS), 94, 200
"Into the Coven" (Mercyful Fate song): "Filthy Fifteen" list, 141

"Invocation & Ritual Dance of the Young Pumpkin" (song), 20

Iran: Iranian hostage crisis, 42; Iranian Revolution, 42–43; opposition to the Shah in, 40–41; pro-Western secularization of, 40; rise of the Shah's authoritarianism in, 40–41; role in oil crisis, 42; the Shah's modernization programs in, 40–41

Iran-Contra affair, 182

Isikoff, Michael, 96

Islam: impact of Trump administration on, 83, 99; Pat Robertson's comments on, 194. *See also* Khomeini, Ruhollah

Israel, 40, 181

It Can't Happen Here (Lewis), 13, 220

"It Can't Happen Here" (song): theme and lyric analysis of, 13; theme of American totalitarianism, 13

Jack-in-the Box (restaurant), 47

Jackson, Jesse: foreign and domestic policies, 181; voter registration advocacy, 173. *See also* "Rhymin' Man" (song)

Jackson, Joe, 222

Jackson, Michael, 175

Jakes, T. D., 96

January 6th insurrection, 83–87, 240

Jazz & Pop (magazine), 12, 17, 20

Jazz from Hell (album), 169, 215, 222

Jefferson, Margo, 74–75

Jefferson, Thomas, 1

"Jesus Thinks You're a Jerk" (song): effectiveness of satire in, 201–2; homosexual imagery in, 198–99; theme and lyric analysis of, 198–202; theme of Pat Robertson controversies and campaign, 198, 200; theme of televangelist scandals, 198–99; theme of white Christian nationalism, 198–201

"Jewish American Princess" (slur), 54, 55. *See also* "Jewish Princess" (song)

"Jewish Princess" (song): accusations of anti-Semitism in, 54–55; use of satire in relation to "Catholic Girls," 55–56

"Jezebel Boy" (song), 190

Jimi Hendrix Experience, The, 25

Joe (*Joe's Garage* character), 45–47, 49–53, 56–57

Joe's Garage (album), 30, 34, 36; accusations of anti-Semitism in, 54–56; act 1 summary and analysis, 46–48; act 2 summary and analysis, 50–51; act 3 summary and analysis, 52–54; album cover controversy, 65; as allegory of the United States, 48–52, 58–59, 62, 64–65; biographical connections to Zappa, 52; criticism of environmental laws in liner notes of, 47; effectiveness of satire in, 64–68; recording of, 48–49; release of, 45; as response to Iranian Revolution, 45, 47–48, 58, 64–65; sexism in, 47, 65; sexual themes in, 46–47, 50–51, 65; significance of garage as setting in, 49–50; theme and lyric analysis of, 45–49; theme of authoritarianism, 46, 51–54, 57, 65; theme of business influence on government, 48, 53–54; theme of Christian evangelicalism, 62–64, 66, 68; theme of consumerism, 46, 52–53; theme of criminalizing music, 45–46, 52–53, 56–58, 62; theme of free expression, 47, 49, 52, 56–58; theme of freedoms, 47–48, 51–53, 57–58, 62, 64–65; theme of government control, 47–49; theme of government influence on media, 48, 52; theme of individualization, 49, 53; theme of institutional power, 47, 65; theme of music corrupting youth, 45, 49; theme of music journalism, 52, 54, 56–57; theme of nostalgia, 50; theme of prisons, 51–52, 65; theme of religion, 46–47, 50, 53, 65; theme of the music industry, 51–52; theme of "Total Criminalization," 51, 53, 57–58; theme of uniformity, 53, 57; use of sexist, homophobic, and racist imagery in, 65–66; as vision of future of America, 53–54, 58, 64. *See also* "Catholic Girls" (song); "Packard Goose" (song)

"Joe's Garage," (song) 46, 48

John Birch Society, 59

Johnson, Lyndon, 10, 15, 18, 22; Presidential legacy of, 8

Jolson, Al, 56

Jones, Buddy (*Joe's Garage* character), 47, 51. *See also* Father Riley (*Joe's Garage* character)

Judas Priest: "Filthy Fifteen" list, 141
"Jumbo Go Away" (song): theme of gender violence in, 71–72
Just Another Band from L.A. (album), 34, 35

Kane, John V., 82
"Keep It Greasy" (song), 51; theme of prison rape in, 65
Keneally, Mike, 177–78, 191
Kennedy, John F., 2, 38, 138; legacy and impact as president, 8–9
Kennedy, Ted, 44
Kent State shootings, 26
Kershaw, Alex, 235
Kevorkian, Jack, 1
Khomeini, Ruhollah: adversary of Western nations, 41; banning music in Iran, 45, 61, 64; control of media in Iran, 45l; development of fundamentalist beliefs, 41; exile from Iran, 41–42; as leader of Iran, 42, 44–45, 64; opposition to the Shah, 41; overthrow of the Shah, 41; role in Iranian hostage crisis, 42; similar rhetoric to Jerry Falwell, 59, 61; *Time's* "Person of the Year," 42
"Kill Ugly Radio" (song), 17
King, Martin Luther, Jr., 1, 177, 229
Kingfish (*Amos 'n' Andy Show* character): allusion to in *Thing-Fish*, 132–34; allusion to in "You Are What You Is," 72
Kingsmen (band), 18, 219
Knaifel, Alexander, 214
Kocáb, Michael, 211
Koch, Ed, 178
Komárek, Valtr, 213
Koop, C. Everett: efforts to manage AIDS crisis, 110–11, 187; legacy of, 186–87; Zappa's criticism of, 116, 189, 208. *See also* "Promiscuous" (song)
Koppel, Ted, 150
Kramer, Larry, 107
Kremlin, 241
Kretschmar, Hermann, 218–19
KROQ (radio station), 54
Krug, Judith: on conservative efforts to ban books, 60, 151
Ku Klux Klan: imagery in "Jesus Thinks You're a Jerk," 200

Langer, Elinor, 220
Lauper, Cyndi, 142
Law, Bernard, 109
Lawrence, Regina, 80–81
League of Women Voters: partnering with Zappa for voter registration, 173, 235
Learning Channel, The, 207
Lee, Spike, 136
Lennon, John, 2; "Imagine" banned on radio, 154
Le Pen, Jean-Marie, 219–20
Lesh, Niles, 224
Let's Dance (David Bowie album), 36
"Let's Make America Great Again": Donald Trump's adoption of Ronald Reagan campaign slogan, 98
"Let's Make the Water Turn Black" (song) 24
"Let Me Put My Love into You" (AC/DC song): "Filthy Fifteen" list, 141
Levin, Sis, 145
Lewis, John, 207
Lewis, Sinclair, 13, 220
LGBTQ community: evangelical Christian opposition to 101, 198; healthcare restrictions for, 125; as target in book bans, 159–162
liberalism: evangelical Christian opposition to, 49, 138, 194, 196–97, 199, 202
Libertarian Party, 208
Library of Congress, 23
"Like a Virgin" (Madonna song): inspiration for formation of the PMRC, 143
Limbaugh, Rush, 2
Lincoln, Abraham, 2, 193
Ling, Jeff, 132, 157
"Listen America" (Falwell statement), 60–61. *See also* Falwell, Jerry
"Little Green Rosetta, A" (song), 53
Lofton, John, 152–53
London Metropolitan University, 188
"Lonely Little Girl" (song), 26
Loop (Chicago neighborhood), 1
Lorraine Motel, 177

Los Angeles, CA: hippie subculture scene in, 22; Pandora's Box riot, 18; Zappa's pro-choice rally speech in, 235. *See also* "Trouble Every Day" (song)

Los Angeles Police Department. *See* "Trouble Every Day" (song)

Los Angeles Times Magazine, 56

Los Angeles Times (newspaper), 155, 168

"Lost Interview, The" (interview), 224

"Louie Louie" (Kingsmen song), 18, 219

"Louisiana Hooker with Herpes" (song), 191

Lowe, Kelly Fisher: on "Dub All Over," 100; on "Hot Plate Heaven at the Green Hotel," 180; on "Jewish Princess," 55; on Republican presidential administrations, 177; on *Thing-Fish*, 136

LSD, 25, 118

Lucille (*Joe's Garage* character), 47

"Lucille Has Messed My Mind Up" (song) 47

"Lucy in the Sky With Diamonds" (Beatles song), 191

Lukeš, Milan, 212

Lumpy Gravy (album), 30, 222

Madonna: "Filthy Fifteen" list, 141–42; role in inspiring PMRC, 143

"Magdelena" (song), 34–35; sexual imagery in, 34–35

Maines, Natalie, 154

Make a Jazz Noise Here (album), 191

"malaise speech" (Carter). *See* "Crisis of Confidence" (Carter speech); Carter, Jimmy

Mammy Nuns (*Thing-Fish* characters), 112–13, 126–30, 132–33

"Mammy Nuns, The" (song), 113

Mandela, Nelson, 1

Man from Utopia, The (album), 33

Mankiller, Wilma, 1

Mann, Ed, 50

"manufacturing consent" (concept), 230–31

Mapplethorpe, Robert, 2

Marsh, Dave, 146

Marshall, Bob, 51, 57, 205

Martin, Lerone A., 98–99

Mary (*Joe's Garage* character), 46–47; *Joe's Garage* monologue, 57

Mary Jane Girls (band): "Filthy Fifteen" list, 142

Mason, Lilliana, 82

mass shootings, 84, 170, 194

"Massive Improve'lence, The" (song), 128

Mattson, Kevin, 44

MCA (record company), 131, 169

McConnell, Mitch, 63

McDuffie, Joanne, 148

McGovern, Goerge, 207

McHenry, Barnabas, 152

media: perpetuating racism and prejudice, 86–87; prejudices and biases of, 80; propaganda in, 230–31; role in Donald Trump's election, 79–80; role in political polarization, 80, 81

Medicaid: Reagan administration's funding cuts to, 106

"Medieval Ensemble" (song), 209

"Meek Shall Inherit Nothing, The" (*Thing-Fish* version), 127

"Meek Shall Inherit Nothing, The" (*You Are What You Is* version), 100; lyrical connection to biblical passage, 91–92; theme and lyric analysis of, 91–92; theme of complicity of religious exploitation, 91–92, 96; theme of counterculture captivation with messianic figures, 93; theme of hippie culture becoming yuppie culture, 93

Meese, Ed, 182–83

Menn, Donn, 223

Mercyful Fate: "Filthy Fifteen" list, 141

Meta (Facebook); impact on 2016 election, 79

Metro Times (newspaper), 154, 156

MGM, 17

Michaelson, Jay, 194

Miller, Dennis, 207

Missouri: 2020 election impact on book bans in, 159. *See also* Times Beach, Missouri flood disaster

"M.O.I. American Pageant, The" ("underground oratorio"), 17

Mölich-Zebhauser, Andreas, 214

"Mom & Dad" (song): theme of generational conflict in, 26–27
Moms for Liberty: efforts to ban books, 159–61
Mondale, Walter, 138
Monroe Community College, 205
Monroe Doctrine (student newspaper), 205
Moore, Nancy Janice, 144
Moral Majority, The: formation of, 58; influence on book bans, 60; influence on culture, 62, 64, 94; influence on Reagan administration, 59, 61, 125, 152; Zappa's criticism of, 58–60, 84, 152
Morris, Wesley: ideas on myth of racial separateness, 74–76
Mosaddegh, Mohammad, 40
Moscow Ministry of Culture, 211–12
Mother Jones (magazine), 87
"Motherly Love" (song), 12
Mother People (fanzine), 179
"Mother People" (song): theme of social acceptance in, 28–29
Mothers of Invention, 4, 9–10, 16–18, 21, 23–25, 28–30, 33, 35, 37, 67, 176, 215. See *Absolutely Free* (album); *Frank Zappa Meets the Mothers of Prevention* (album); *Freak Out!* (album); *We're Only in It for the Money* (album)
Mother Teresa, 2
Motion Picture Association of America, 142
Mozart, Wolfgang Amadeus, 2
"Ms. Pinky" (song): sexual imagery in, 34; *Thing-Fish* version, 128
MTV: and banned Zappa video, 90; influence on entertainment media, 70–71, 156; Zappa's criticism of, 36, 89–90, 132
"Mudd Club" (*Thing-Fish* version), 127
"Mudd Club" (*You Are What You Is* version), 71, 92
"Murder by Numbers" (Police song), 175
Murphree, Debra, 190
Music (magazine), 131, 168
Music Connection (magazine), 158
Music Express (magazine), 208
musique concrète: Zappa's use of, 9, 21–24, 30, 165, 222
Musical Majority, 146
Myanmar. *See* Aung San Suu Kyi, 2

"Nasal Retentive Calliope Music" (song), 24
Nassau Coliseum, 173
Nation of Islam, 178
Nation, The (magazine), 212, 220
National Academy of Sciences, 120
National AIDs Hotline, 108
National Association for the Advancement of Colored People, 133
National Association of Record Merchandisers, 146
National Coalition of Black Lesbians and Gays, 110
National Endowment for the Arts, 152
National Front (France), 220
National Front (Iran), 41
National Guard, 14
National Hemophilia Foundation, 110
National Opinion Research Center, 123
National Parent Teacher Association (PTA), 138, 146
National Recording Preservation Board, 23
National Religious Broadcasters, 95
National Rifle Association, 199
National Security Council, 185
Nazi Germany, 151, 219
Nazis: book burnings by, 151; members of Congress accused of being, 221; reference in "Plastic People," 18; reference in "Welcome to the United States," 219; rise of neo-Nazis, 219–20, 240–41; sympathizer groups, 59, 219; Zappa's attitudes toward medical establishment, 207
Nelkin, Dorothy, 124–25
neo-Nazism: European history of, 219–20; in America, 220–21
Ness, Eliot, 181
Nevius, John, 144
Nevius, Sally, 144
New America: Zappa's outlook on postindustrial America, 216
New Deal, 8

New Musical Express (magazine), 11
New Paper (magazine), 191
Newsweek (magazine), 76, 108, 147; PMRC oral history, 150, 151, 169
New York: Zappa radio support in, 88
New Yorker (magazine), 209, 214
New York Times (newspaper), 85, 108, 161
New York Times Magazine, 74
Nightline (ABC program), 150, 154
Nixon, Richard: "The Idiot Bastard Son" dedication, 27; "silent majority," 58; Zappa's criticism of, 177. *See also* "Dickie's Such an Asshole" (song)
No Commercial Potential (project), 30
"No Not Now" (song), 129
Nobel Peace Prize, 2
North, Oliver, 185
"Norwegian Jim" (song), 191
"Norwegian Wood" (Beatles song), 191

Obama, Barack: evangelical response to, 103; podcast with Bruce Springsteen, 135
Obergefell v. Hodges, 103
objectivism (Ayn Rand concept), 2
Observer, The (newspaper), 235
Office of Faith-Based Initiatives, 97
Office of Intellectual Freedom, 60
Old Executive Office Building, 176
"Old South," 31
"On the Bus" (song), 47
"One Man, One Vote" (song), 165
Onishi, Bradley, 102–3
Oor (Dutch music magazine), 217
Organization of American Historians, 98
Organization of the Petroleum Exporting Countries (OPEC), 42
Orwell, George, 225; "Orwellian," 19
Osteen, Joel, 97
Ouellette, Dan, 214
Oui (magazine), 56–57
"Outrage at Valdez" (song), 215
"Outside Now" (song), 51
Over-Nite Sensation (album), 31, 34, 67
"Overture to 'Uncle Sam'" (song), 209

"Packard Goose" (song), 52; anti-Semitic language in, 54–56; criticism of journalists in, 54, 56–57; "music is the best" monologue, 57–58; theme of social uniformity, 56
Pahlavi, Mohammad Reza, 50; efforts to modernize Iran, 40–41; Khomeini's overthrow of, 41–42; rule as the Shah, 40
Palahniuk, Chuck, 175
Palestine Liberation Organization, 181
Pandora's Box (Los Angeles restaurant), 18
panopticon: in relation to current culture, 230; in relation to Zappa's comments on self-policing, 11
Pape, Robert, 86–87
Parents Music Resource Center (PMRC): absence of country music in proposal, 155; accusations of being a lobbying group, 140, 145–46, 154, 156, 162, 163, 165; and accusations of obscenity in rock music, 139–42, 145, 147–49, 152–56, 158, 162–63; advocacy for music warning labels, 139, 142, 145–46, 148–50, 155, 162–63, 165, 168–69; agenda of and proposals by, 138, 140–41, 143–50, 154, 155–58, 160, 162–65, 168–69; beliefs on music's damage to children, 138, 142, 145, 147, 155, 157; connections with Christian right, 140, 144, 149, 153, 155, 157–58, 170; cultural attitudes toward women, 156–57; Dee Snider testimony, 148; effect on musicians, 140–41, 146, 148–49, 163, 169; "Filthy Fifteen" list, 141–42, 147–48; formation and organization of, 142, 144–45; H.R. 2911 act, 143; historical background of parents' rights groups, 139; historical context of parenting philosophy of, 157; impact on consumer education, 138, 141–43, 148, 154, 157, 162–63; impact on free speech, 141–42, 144–51, 153–54, 156, 162, 165, 168, 170–71; influence and legacy of, 153–55, 158–62, 170; issue of music education, 147; John Denver testimony, 150–51; media coverage and strategy of, 139, 144–46, 149, 154, 157–58, 163; music industry cooperation with, 139, 143, 145–47; music retailer response to, 149; opposition from music industry, 139,

146–48, 155–56; "porn rock," 139, 146, 156, 158, 166; relationship with senators at hearing, 139, 144–45, 162; Senate hearing, 139–41, 143–45, 147–49, 163–64, 166–68; sexism of "Washington Wives" label, 139; tax legislation impact, 140, 143–47, 162–63; theme on *Congress Shall Make No Law . . .* album, 163; Zappa's comments on danger of words, 60; Zappa's criticism of music industry, 143; Zappa's testimony, 140–41, 143–45, 147, 149, 162–65, 170
Parks, Rosa, 1
Payne, Leah, 196
Peace Corps. *See* "Who Needs the Peace Corps?" (song)
PEN America: report on censorship, 158–60
"Penguin in Bondage" (song), 34
"Pentagon Afternoon" (song), 216
Penthouse (magazine), 190
"Perhaps in Maryland," (spoken-word track) 164
Perot, Ross, 208
Perry, Scott, 84
Petro, Anthony, 122
Pew Research Center, 80
Philharmonie Berlin (concert hall), 216
Phillips, Kevin, 76
"Pick Me, I'm Clean" (song), 34
Pickard, Victor, 79
Pitt News (student newspaper), 88
"Planet of the Baritone Women" (song), 175
"Plastic People" (song): inspiration for Plastic People of the Universe, 210; plastic as allegory for conformity in, 18–19; theme and lyric analysis of, 18–19; vegetables as allegory for misinformation, 19
Plastic People of the Universe: trial of, 210–11
Playboy (magazine), 178, 184–85, 209, 211–12
"plooking" (Zappa term), 51
PMRC. *See* Parents Music Resource Center (PMRC)
Pneumocystis carinii pneumonia, 107
"pollstergeists" (Zappa term), 205
"Poofter's Froth Wyoming Plans Ahead" (song), 35
PopMatters (magazine), 227
"porn rock." *See under* Parents Music Resource Center (PMRC)
"Porn Wars" (song): accusations of Zappa profiting off of publicity, 168; accusations of Zappa's bias, 168; sampled Senate hearing audio in, 166–68; theme and lyric analysis of, 165–68; theme of PMRC, 165–66; Thing-Fish segment in, 167
Posner, Sarah, 196
"Possessed" (Venom song): "Filthy Fifteen" List, 142
"Pound for a Brown" (song), 215
"Power of the Powerless, The" (Havel), 210
Pražský Výběr, 211
Preziosi, Donald, 238
Prince: "Filthy Fifteen" list, 141; Role in inspiring PMRC, 142, 159
Prince William Sound oil disaster, 215
"Prologue" (song), 112
"Promiscuous" (song): conspiracy theory lyrics in, 186; criticism of American Medical Association, 183; in relation to Zappa's view on AIDS crisis, 187–188; theme and lyric analysis of, 182–84, 186; theme of C. Everett Koop, 182–84; theme of religious influence on medical establishment, 184
PTL Club ("Praise the Lord" Club), 96
Public Enemy (hip-hop group), 182
Pulse nightclub shooting, 194
Pulse! (magazine), 16, 207, 214
Purple Rain (film), 142

Q (magazine), 179
Quayle, Dan, 213

racial violence: committed by Christian fundamentalists, 103, 194–95, 197–200; committed by neo-Nazis, 220; committed by white men, 72, 82; motivation for January 6th insurrection, 87. *See also* "Trouble Every Day" (song)
racism: as theme in Zappa's music, 15, 35; Broadway tradition of, 133; criticism in relation to Zappa's music, 66, 112, 121, 131–36;

racism (*continued*)
Donald Trump's influence on, 83; impact on book bans, 159; media's role in perpetuating, 86–87; white evangelicalism, 99, 101, 103–4; Zappa on religious racism, 104; Zappa's comments on racism in America, 78, 81–82, 135. See also *1619 Project, The* (Hannah-Jones); "critical race theory"; *Thing-Fish* (album); "Trouble Every Day" (song); "You Are What You Is" (song)
Radio Darya, 45
Rage Against the Machine: music banned on radio after September 11 attacks, 154
Raising PG Kids in an X-Rated Society (Gore), 142
Rancho Park (Los Angeles neighborhood), 235
Rand, Ayn, 2
Raup, Avo, 186
Ray, James Earl, 177
Reagan, Ronald: 1980 presidential victory of, 69; 1984 presidential victory of, 138; 1985 State of the Union address, 182–83; administration's enforcement of tax code, 96; administration's impact on the arts, 147, 152; administration's response to AIDS crisis, 107–112, 116–17, 120, 182, 186–87; administration's cuts to Medicaid, 106; continuation of agenda during 1988 presidential election, 172; deregulation of telecommunications industry by, 70, 89, 97, 155; economic policy of, 69, 106; emboldening of Christian evangelicals by, 180–81; influence on 1988 presidential election, 204–5; Iran-Contra affair, 182; "Let's Make America Great Again" campaign slogan of, 98; meaning of "conservatism" during presidency, 180; on communism, 183; refusal to visit concentration camp, 165; support from evangelical Christians, 44, 59, 70–71, 95, 106, 140, 152, 187, 228; Zappa on, 81, 147, 174, 180–83, 185, 193, 205–6, 208; Zappa's criticism of in music, 71–72, 76, 176–77, 179–82. *See also* Bakker, Jim; "Concentration Moon" (song); "Dickie's Such an Asshole" (song); Falwell, Jerry; "Idiot Bastard Son, The" (song)
"Reagan at Bitburg" (song) 165
"Reagan at Bitburg Some More" (song) 165
Real Frank Zappa Book, The (Zappa and Occhiogrosso): criticism of C. Everett Koop in, 116; criticism of evangelical influence on AIDS, 117, 119; criticism of media in, 81; criticism of Reagan national security policy, 183; criticism of tax-exempt status for churches in, 94–95, 96; criticism of Tipper Gore, 142–43; criticism of drug use, 25–26; thoughts on federal programs, 180
Rebozo, Bebe, 177
Record Hunter (magazine), 177
Record Review (magazine), 49
Recording Industry Association of America (RIAA): "blank tape tax" proposal, 143; criticism of by anti-censorship groups, 146; Dee Snider's criticism of, 148; warning label efforts, 145–46, 149; Zappa's criticism of, 149
Register-Pajaronian, (newspaper), 173, 195
religious violence 102–3, 195, 197–200, 221
Relix (magazine), 149
Renegades: Born in the USA (Obama and Springsteen podcast), 135
"replacement theory," 84
Republican Party: 1980 platform of, 69; accusations of Nazis in, 221; Donald Trump's impact on, 83; emboldening of Christian fundamentalism, 84; evangelical support of, 44, 70, 95–96, 193–94; impact on religious tax exemption, 94–96; news-consumption habits of people in, 80–81; stance on racial progress in America, 85–86; white Christian nationalism in, 202; Zappa on, 180–81, 208. *See also* "Hot Plate Heaven at the Green Hotel" (song); "Jesus Thinks You're a Jerk" (song); "What Kind of Girl?" (song); "When the Lie's So Big" (song)
"Return of the Son of Monster Magnet, The" (song), 21
Rexroth, Dieter, 214
Rhonda (*Thing-Fish* character), 113–14, 126, 128–31, 133
"Rhymin' Man" (song): theme and lyrics analysis of, 177; theme of Jesse Jackson presidential campaign, 177–79; theme of Jesse Jackson's relationship with Louis Farrakhan, 178; theme

of Jesse Jackson's use of anti-Semitic language, 178; Zappa's criticism of Jackson in relation to Martin Luther King Jr. death in, 177–78
"Ripping Off Black Music" (Jefferson), 74–75
River North (Chicago neighborhood), 1
Robertson, Pat: 1988 presidential campaign of, 193–94, 198, 200–201; evangelical influence on politics, 193, 194, 196; impact on Donal Trump, 196; influence on American culture, 195–96; legacy of, 194, 196, 200; references in "Jesus Thinks You're a Jerk," 198–200; Zappa's criticism of, 94, 193–95, 198–201
Rock & Roll Hall of Fame, 23
Rock Australia Magazine, 57
Rockhead (magazine), 234
"Rocky Mountain High" (John Denver song): accusations of drug use imagery in, 150; banned on radio, 151
Rodney King riots: Zappa's comments connecting Watts Rebellion with, 16
Roe v. Wade: evangelical goal to dismantle, 62; Supreme Court reversal on, 62, 227
Rolling Stone (magazine), 21, 48, 49, 50, 52, 194
Roman Catholic Archdiocese of Boston, 109
Roman Catholic Diocese of San Jose, California, 122
Römer, Rainer, 218
Roosevelt, Franklin D., 138
Rowling, J. K., 230
Roxy & Elsewhere (album), 34
"Rudy Wants to Buy Yez a Drink" (song), 33
Reuben, Josh, 173
Rueda, Valeria, 118–19
Rundel, Peter, 218
Rushdie, Salman, 230
Ruzyne Airport (Prague), 211

Sadat, Anwar, 181
San Fernando Valley (Los Angeles County, CA): sampled audio in "Waffenspiel," 223; satire in "Valley Girl," 37
San Francisco, CA: satire of hippie subculture in, 25
San Francisco General Hospital, 108
San Quentin (prison), 112, 127
Sandinistas, 182
Satanic Panic, 153
Schrock, Ed, 190
secularism: evangelical Christian opposition to, 61–62, 70, 123, 188, 196; Iran's adoption of, 40–41
Seidel, Andrew L., 94
Senate Commerce, Science and Transportation Committee. *See* Parents Music Resource Center (PMRC)
Senate Judicial Proceedings Committee of the Maryland state legislature, 164
September 11 attacks: Clear Channel banning music after, 154; evangelical disappointment in wake of, 99; Jerry Falwell's comments on, 62; Pat Robertson's comments on, 194
sexism: imagery in Zappa's music, 33–35, 71, 90, 175, 192, 235; sexual imagery in music of, 33–35
Sgt. Pepper's Lonely Hearts Club Band (Beatles album), 23
"She Bop" (Cyndi Lauper song): "Filthy Fifteen" list, 142
Sheik Yerbouti (album), 32–33, 36, 52, 54, 67
Shi'i, 41
Ship Arriving Too Late to Save a Drowning Witch (album), 37, 129
Shopping Mall Owners Associations, 149
Sidey, Hugh, 22
Simmons, Jeff, 47
Sister Ob'dewlla X (*Thing-Fish* character), 113, 129–30
Sister Owl-Gonwkin-Jane Cowhoon (*Thing-Fish* character), 128
Slaven, Neil, 114
Snider, Dee: PMRC testimony, 148, 150–51, 231
Social Security: Reagan administration's cuts to, 106; Zappa's beliefs on, 180
Society Pages (fanzine), 233
"Society Pages" (song), 71
"Soft-Sell Conclusion" (song), 20; vegetable imagery as commentary in, 20
"Son of Suzy Creamcheese" (song): inspiration for Suzy Creamcheese, 22; theme and lyric analysis of, 21–22; theme of hippie counterculture, 21–22

Song Hits (magazine), 17
Songwriter Connection (magazine), 131
South Carolina: role in book bans after 2020 election, 159
South Park (TV show), 50
Southern Baptist Convention: Jerry Falwell's comments on accomplishing mission, 64
Southern Poverty Law Center, 102
Soviet Union: Zappa's music distributed in, 212
Spin (magazine), 89
Springsteen, Bruce: on racial dynamics in his band, 135
Stanley, Augustus Owsley, 25
"Status Back Baby" (song): critique of education system, 21; theme and lyric analysis of, 20–21; theme of high school culture, 20–21
Steinem, Gloria, 230
"Stick It Out" (song), 50
"Stick Together" (song), 33
Sting (musician), 175
Stockhausen, Karlheinz, 214
Stop the Wrongs to Our Kids and Employees [W.O.K.E.] Act, 160–61
"Strange Fruit" (Billie Holiday song), 200
"Strap On 'Robbie Baby'" (Vanity song): "Filthy Fifteen" list, 141
Stravinsky, Igor, 9
"Strawberry Fields Forever" (Beatles song), 191
Stroud, Kandie, 145, 154–55
Studio Tan (album), 127
Sturt, Hilary, 216–17
"Sugar Walls" (Sheena Easton song): "Filthy Fifteen" list, 141
"Suicide Chump" (song): suicidal imagery in, 71–72
Sunset Boulevard: reference in "Plastic People," 18
Sununu, John, 185
Supreme Court: obscenity ruling pertaining to 2 Live Crew, 153; obscenity ruling pertaining to George Carlin, 139; overturning of *Roe v. Wade*, 62–63, 217, 227; Republican goal to make conservative majority in, 63, 98; ruling prioritizing religious freedom and effect on LGBTQ community, 125; Zappa on evangelical influence of, 218
Surgeon General's Report on Acquired Immune Deficiency Syndrome (Koop) 110, 187
Swaggart, Jimmy: reference to in "Murder by Numbers," 175; satire of in Zappa's music, 191–192, 198; sex scandal of, 190–191; Zappa's criticism of, 94, 153, 192–93
Sweet Potato (magazine), 58
Sy Borg (*Joe's Garage* character), 50
"Sy Borg" (song), 50
Synclavier (musical instrument), 169, 209, 215, 222
Syria: Jesse Jackson's trip to, 178

"Take Your Clothes Off When You Dance" (song): theme and lyric analysis of, 28–29; theme of idealism, 28–29; theme of social utopia, 28–29
tax exemption: Zappa's criticism of religious tax exemption, 94–97, 180–81
Teach for America, 160
"Teenage Wind" (song) 71
Tehrān, Iran: U.S. embassy hostage crisis, 42
Telecommunications Act of 1934, 89
"Telephone Conversation" (song) 24
televangelism: impact on AIDS crisis, 125; impact on Christian nationalism by, 94; Zappa on, 93–97, 100–101. See also *Broadway the Hard Way* (album); "Heavenly Bank Account" (song); Falwell, Jerry; "Jesus Thinks You're a Jerk"; Robertson, Pat; Swaggart, Jimmy; *You Are What You Is* (album)
"Tell Me You Love Me" (song), 175
Telos (journal), 78
Templeton, Bill, 131, 168
Tennessee: criticism of PMRC excluding country records from proposals, 156; role in book bans after 2020 election, 160
Texas Motel (Louisiana motel), 191
"Texas Motel" (song), 191
"That Evil Prince" (song), 114
Them or Us (album), 36, 153
Thing-Fish (album), 183, 222; as commentary on

AIDS, 121, 131, 134–35; Broadway aspirations for, 36, 131; criticism of racism in, 112, 121, 131, 132–36; homophobic language in, 132; homosexual themes in, 127–28; Ike Willis's comments on, 133–35; legacy, 135–36; parallels with Tuskegee syphilis study, 112, 114–16, 135–36; plot overview, 112–14, 126–30; sexist language in, 127–30, 132; sexual themes in, 127–32; subversion of Broadway tradition as commentary on racism, 133; theme and lyric analysis of, 112, 126, 130–31; theme of women's liberation, 128–30; warning label on album, 131; Zappa on origin and messaging of, 114–15, 131
Thing-Fish (*Thing-Fish* character): Ike Willis's inspiration for, 134; in *Thing-Fish*, 112–14, 126–28, 130; segment in "Porn Wars," 167
Third Reich, 149
This Is Spinal Tap (film), 36
Thomas, Clarence: on outcome of overturning *Roe v. Wade*, 62
"Thou Shalt Have No Other Gods Before Me" (spoken-word track), 164
"Thou Shalt Not Commit Adultery" (spoken-word track), 164
"Though Shalt Not Steal" (spoken-word track), 164
Thurmond, Strom, 144
Time, 22; Ruhollah Khomeini as "Person of the Year," 42
Times Beach, Missouri flood disaster, 216
"Times Beach II" (song), 216
Tin Pan Alley, 26, 29
Tinsel Town Rebellion (album), 34
"Tinsel Town Rebellion" (song), 37
"Titties & Beer" (song), 34
T'Mershi Duween (fanzine), 134
"To Is a Preposition, Come Is a Verb" (Lenny Bruce joke routine), 24
Today, 126
"Token of My Extreme, A" (song), 50
"'Torchum' Never Stops, The" (song), 114
"Torture Never Stops, The" (song), 114
transgender people: conservative and evangelical impact on safety of, 125, 161, 199; J. K. Rowling comments on, 230
"Trashed" (Black Sabbath song): "Filthy Fifteen" list, 142
"Tricky Dick." *See* Nixon, Richard
"Trouble Every Day" (song): modern parallels of, 16; theme and lyric analysis of, 13; theme of media exploitation of racial violence, 14–16, 30, 105; theme of Watts Rebellion, 13–14; Zappa as social commentator, 14–16; Zappa's commentary on class, 15–16; Zappa's commentary on race, 14–15; Zappa's commentary on racial violence in America, 16
True Glove (maxi-single), 132
Trump, Donald: bias against marginalized communities by supporters of, 82–83, 86–87, 99; effect on book bans, 159; emboldening of aggrieved white men, 79; evangelical support of, 98–99, 101, 188, 196; financial records of, 97–98; handling of COVID-19, 188; impact of first presidential term, 227, 228; impact on conservative judge vacancies, 63; influence of Pat Robertson on, 196; influence on January 6th insurrection, 83, 86–87; influence on public discourse, 83, 97–98, 234, 236; media coverage of, 79; supporter appropriation of George Carlin, 229; theme of *Frank Zappa for President*, 209
Tubman, Harriet, 1
Tūdeh, 41
Turner, Tina, 34
Tuskegee syphilis study: and AIDS crisis within *Thing-Fish*, 121, 135–36; history, investigation into, and legacy of, 115–16
Tuttifrutti (Italian magazine), 217
Twilight Zone, The (TV show), 200
Twisted Sister: "Filthy Fifteen" list, 141. *See also* Snider, Dee
Tyler, Amanda, 101

"Uncle Bernie's Farm" (song): theme and lyric analysis of, 18–19; theme of government indoctrinating children, 19
Uncle Meat (album), 30

"Uncle Meat" (*The Yellow Shark* version), 215
Uncle Remus (fictional character), 31
"Uncle Remus" (song); theme and lyric analysis of, 30–31; theme of racial progress in America, 30–31
"Under the Blade" (Twisted Sister song): accusation of promoting violence by the PMRC, 148
United Kingdom: 1993 victory of far-right fascist party, 219; alliance with Iran, 40
United Kingdon Secret Intelligence, 40
United Nations, 210
United States Capitol: 2016 insurrection on, 83, 86, 98, 102, 240
United States Centers for Disease Control (CDC), 107–8, 120
United States Central Intelligence Agency (CIA), 40, 184
United States Department of Health and Human Services: Reagan administration's cuts to, 106
United States Department of Justice: Immigration form used in "Welcome to the United States," 218
United States embassy hostage crisis in Iran. *See* Carter, Jimmy
United States House of Representatives, 138
United States National Strategy to Counter Antisemitism, 221
United States Public Health Service, 115
"Untouchables, The" (song), 181–82
Utah: role in book bans after 2020 election, 159
Utah Parents United, 159

"Valley Girl" (song): cultural impact of, 37; theme of youth culture in, 36–37
Vanity (band): "Filthy Fifteen" list, 141
Varèse, Edgard, 9
Velvet Revolution, 211
Venom (band): "Filthy Fifteen" list, 142, 147
Verve Records, 16
Vietnam War, 38
Village Voice, (newspaper), 146
Volpacchio, Florindo, 78
Voting Rights Act, 85

"Waffenspiel" (song), 223
Wagner, Richard, 212
Ward 86, 108
warning labels. *See* Parents Music Resource Center (PMRC)
Washington, George, 1
Washington Post (newspaper), 83, 96, 147, 178, 205
Washington Times (newspaper), 152
"Washington Wives." *See* Parents Music Resource Center (PMRC)
WASP (band): "Filthy Fifteen" list, 141
Watergate scandal. *See* "Dickie's Such an Asshole" (song)
"Watermelon in Easter Hay" (song), 53
Watson, Ben: on *Civilization Phaze III*, 165, 223; on criticisms of Zappa's music, 233; on Jessie Jackson's domestic and foreign policies, 181; on "Packard Goose," 57; on "Planet of the Baritone Women," 175; on "Uncle Bernie's Farm," 18–19; on "Uncle Remus," 30; on "You Are What You Is," 90; on *The Yellow Shark*, 219; on *Thing-Fish*, 133; on Zappa's emissary status being revoked, 214
Watson, Johnny "Guitar," 128
Watts Rebellion. *See under* "Trouble Every Day" (song)
Waxman, Ben, 173
Waxman, Henry, 107
"We Are Doing Voter Registration Here" (song), 173
"We're Not Gonna Take It" (Twisted Sister song): "Filthy Fifteen" list, 141, 148
We're Only in It for the Money (album), 30, 67, 222; album cover, 23–24; legacy of, 23; parallels to *Broadway the Hard Way*, 179; theme and lyric analysis of, 23–29; theme of counterculture, 23, 26–29; theme of cultural conservatism, 23, 26–27; theme of generational conflict, 26–27; theme of hippie subculture, 23, 25, 27, 29; theme of individualism and institutional resistance, 29; theme of outsider acceptance, 28–29; vision for the future of America in, 29

"We're Turning Again" (song), 37
Weiss, Ted, 108
"Welcome to the United States" (song), 220, 221
"What Homosexuals Do" (Bill Dannemeyer speech), 108
"What Kind of Girl?" (song): Jimy Swaggart sex scandal inspiring, 190–92; sexist imagery in, 192; theme and lyric analysis of, 190. *See also* Swaggart, Jimmy
"What Kind of Girl Do You Think We Are?" (song): groupie imagery in, 34, 190
"What's the Ugliest Part of Your Body?" (song): theme of youth generation in, 26
"When the Lie's So Big" (song), 19, 209; allusion to Hitler's concept of the Big Lie, 194; theme and lyric analysis of, 194–95, 197; theme of Christian violence, 197; theme of religious influence on culture, 194; theme of religious influence on media, 194–96; theme of religious manipulation of American iconography, 195; theme of Republican dishonesty, 195
White, Ray, 87, 93, 101, 128, 133
"White Boy Troubles, The" (song), 129
white grievance/self-victimization: Zappa's thoughts on, 83. *See also* "You Are What You Is" (song)
White House: evangelical programs in, 97; reference in "Brown Shoes Don't Make It," 22; Nixon's secret audio recordings in, 176; Zappa's criticism of smoking ban in, 207
white nationalism: rise of, 101–2; Zappa's music opposing, 6, 239
White Revolution (program), 41
white supremacy: American myth of, 86; as foundation of Christian fundamentalism, 91, 98–100; impact on media by, 82, 84; influence on January 6th insurrection, 87; rise of, 220–21. *See also* "Jesus Thinks You're a Jerk" (song); "You Are What You Is" (song)
Willis, Ike, 46, 65; relationship with Zappa, 134–35; on *Thing-Fish* criticism, 134–35; vocals on "Dickie's Such an Asshole," 176–77; vocals on "Dumb All Over," 101; vocals on "Jesus Thinks You're a Jerk," 200; vocals on "Promiscuous," 182–84; vocals on "The Untouchables," 181; vocals on "What Kind of Girl?," 191; vocals on "You Are What You Is," 87; vocals on *Thing-Fish*, 112–13, 134–35
"Who Are the Brain Police?" (song): imagery of plastic in, 11–12; theme and lyric analysis of, 11–12; theme of self-policing, 11
"Who Needs the Peace Corps?" (song): theme and lyric analysis of, 24–25; theme of San Francisco hippie culture, 24–25
"Why Does It Hurt When I Pee?" (song), 47
"Why Don't You Like Me?" (song), 175
Wiener Konzerthaus (concert hall), 216
Wiesel, Elie, 2
Wiinikka-Lydon, Joseph ,102
Wilder, Elin, 81
Wilk v. American Medical Association, 183
Williams, Andre, 177
"Wistful Wit a Fist-Full" (song), 129
WLIR (radio station), 50
WLIR Free Flight (publication), 92
"Won Ton On" (song), 132
World Health Organization: first meeting on AIDS crisis, 108
World Trade Center: Zappa's comments on 1993 bombing, 291
World War II: Germany's role in, 220; Japanese internment camp reference in "Concentration Moon," 29
"Wowie Zowie" (song), 12
Wright, Imani Wj, 241
Wronski, Julie, 82

"Ya Hozna" (song): backward masking in, 153
Yellow Shark, The (album): concerts for, 215–16, 219, 221, 224; origin of, 214; theme and lyric analysis of, 216–19, 221; theme of abortion, 216; theme of consumerism, 216–17; theme of immigration, 218–19; theme of postindustrial America, 216–17; theme of the environment, 216–17; themes of Nazism, 219. *See also* "Amnerika" (song); "Food Gathering in Post-Industrial America, 1992" (song); "Welcome to the United States" (song)

You Are What You Is (album), 74, 80, 99, 126; gender violence in, 71–72; poor sales of, 88; social commentary in, 71; theme and lyric analysis of, 70–77, 81, 84, 86–87, 91–93, 96, 99, 100–105; theme of Christian fundamentalism, 91–94, 96, 99–104; theme of Christian violence, 100–101; theme of connecting hippie and yuppie subcultures, 92–93; theme of racial appropriation, 72, 75, 77, 81, 84, 86–87, 90; theme of racial violence, 100–101, 103–4; theme of televangelism, 93–94; theme of white male grievance, 71–73, 75, 77, 79, 81–82; Zappa's essay in liner notes on commercialism, 76–77

"You Are What You Is" (*Thing-Fish* version), 126–27

"You Are What You Is" (*You Are What You Is* version), 103; banned on radio and MTV, 90; modern relevancy as commentary on systemic racism, 90–91; music video for, 89; theme and lyric analysis of, 72–73, 75, 77; theme of Black assimilation, 84, 86–88; theme of cultural appropriation, 72–73, 75; theme of white male grievance/victimization, 81, 84, 86; use of racial tropes and imagery, 77

"You Didn't Try to Call Me" (song) 12

Your Vote (education special), 207

"You're Probably Wondering Why I'm Here" (song): theme of counterculture and American commercialization in, 12

Yugoslavia: Zappa bootlegs in, 212

Zappa '88: The Last U.S. Show (album), 173, 191, 209

Zappa in New York (album), 34

Zappa, Dweezil, 163

Zappa: Electric Don Quixote (Slaven), 114

Zappa, Frank: and accusations of anti-idealism, 27–28; advocacy for democracy, 173, 232; anti-Semitism in music of, 54–56; appropriation of Black music, 74; as cultural emissary for Czechoslovakia, 212–14; as social commentator, 14, 91, 174–75, 190, 225–27, 231–35; cancelled talk show, 212; cancer diagnosis and health, 209, 215–16, 224–25; censorship of, 17–18, 131; controversial qualities of, 5–6, 34–35, 71, 72; criticism of, 4–6, 16, 27–28, 33, 35, 54–55, 66, 71–72, 132–33, 135–36, 175, 186, 192, 202, 225, 228, 231–36, 239, 240; cynical attitude of, 11, 16, 52, 27, 28, 169, 185–86, 201, 206, 225–26; Czechoslovakians' admiration for, 211, 214; death of, 223–26; effectiveness of own satire, 130–31, 201; fan base of, 57, 136, 233, 240; general biography of, 3–5, 9; homophobic themes in music of, 132; idealism in music of, 28; legacy of, 5–7, 9, 27, 32–33, 55, 136, 214–15, 224–26, 231–33, 235–36, 239–40, 242–43; meeting Václav Havel, 210–12; musical influences of, 9; name on *Freedom Wall*, 3; offensiveness of lyrics, 35, 55–56, 71–72, 90, 104, 131, 133, 192, 225, 227, 232–36, 238; on AIDS, 111, 114–21, 125, 126, 208; on American authoritarianism, 51–52, 235; on American corporatization, 23, 35, 37, 76–77, 175; on American culture, 20–21, 23, 30, 34, 76–78, 132; on American education system, 21, 78; on American evangelical influence, 173; on American hypocrisy, 35, 78; on American music culture, 20; on arts education, 223; on bands capitulating to the music industry, 37; on banning music, 58; on being American, 241–42; on Bill Clinton, 207; on C. Everett Koop, 189, 208; on censorship, 60, 150, 153, 155, 168; on Christian evangelicals/fundamentalists, 91, 99–105, 116, 152, 153, 176, 180–82, 184, 188, 193, 198–200; on Christian fundamentalist impact on 1988 election, 206; on Christian fundamentalist impact on abortion, 217; on Christian fundamentalist impact on freedoms, 202; on Christian fundamentalist impact on legislation, 195; on Christian fundamentalist threat to democracy, 193–95; on Christian white supremacy, 199–200; on class in America, 15–16, 37, 71; on commercialism, 12, 33, 35 37, 76–77; on complicit attitude of Americans, 33, 51–52, 91–93, 96–97, 225; on complicit attitudes toward religious exploitation, 92–94, 96–97; on consumerism, 37, 78, 216–17; on counterculture, 9–10, 12, 23, 25; on criminalization of personal freedoms, 51; on Czechoslovakian economic independence, 212; on desensitization of Americans, 51; on disco culture, 36, 54; on drug use, 25–26; on education, 77–78, 147, 184; on election polling, 205, 206; on establishment institutions, 184–86, 189, 231–34; on fascist theocracy in America, 152–53; on free speech/expression, 5, 9, 13, 18–19, 59, 131, 140, 153, 155, 162, 165, 168–70, 180, 201, 203, 213, 223 225, 232–36, 239; on generational conflict, 20, 26; on George H. W. Bush, 205–7; on government impact on culture, 47–48; on government impact on freedoms, 22, 51; on government impact on media, 32, 81, 234; on greed in America, 35; on groupies, 22; on hippie subculture, 27–28, 37; on hippies becoming yuppies, 37; on his music being banned in Soviet Union, 211–12; on influence of money in media, 32; on institutional authority, 28; on intellectual development, 37, 78, 90; on Jesse Jackson, 178–79; on Jimmy Swaggart sex scandal, 191–92; on journalists, 56–57; on liberal media bias, 81; on love, 27; on media coverage of 1988 election, 205; on media impact on American culture, 31–32, 51, 76–77, 83, 184; on media impact on expression, 31; on media impact on government, 48, 185; on media impact on race, 77–78, 81–82; on media impact public education, 15, 77–78; on media industry, 16 , 31–32, 76–78, 81, 83, 88–90; on mental health in America, 76; on MTV, 36, 89–90; on music as resistance to power, 18–20, 28; on music journalists, 54, 56, 225; on music-video culture, 36, 88–89; on neo-Nazism, 220; on news media, 81–82; on outsider, fringe, and marginalized groups, 17–18, 20, 22, 28; on Pat Robertson, 192–95, 200; on personal freedom and civil liberties, 18, 22, 60, 65, 105, 117, 140, 168, 204, 207; on popular culture, 36–37, 71, 76; on "porn rock," 156; on postindustrial America, 216–17; on racism in America, 78, 81–82, 135; on radio, 88–89; on religion's impact on government, 93–95; on religious hypocrisy, 99; on religious impact on censorship, 59–60, 152–53; on religious impact on culture, 59–60, 91, 94; on religious racism and xenophobia, 104; on religious tax exemption, 94–97, 180–81; on religious violence, 100–103, 105, 195, 197; on Richard Nixon, 177; on Ronald Reagan, 177, 180, 182–83, 193, 205–6; on self-education, 21, 184; on self-policing and self-censorship, 11; on separation of church and state, 173; on sex in American culture, 35; on sexually repressed politicians, 22; on sexual promiscuity of missionaries, 117; on social change, 18, 20, 28; on televangelists, 93–97, 100–101; on the American Medical Association, 183; on the American public, 33; on the Beatles, 23–24; on the "blank tape tax," 143–45; on the environment, 216–17; on the medical establishment, 207–8; on the Moral Majority, 58; on the music industry, 223, 233; on the PMRC, 165, 158; on the PMRC connections with religious right, 153, 157; on the PMRC excluding country music from proposal, 156; on the PMRC's impact on culture, 144, 147; on the PMRCs' impact on the music industry, 140, 143–44; on the power of music, 17, 18; on the responsibility of the American public, 33; on Tipper Gore, 142–43; on unions, 33, 77; on violence in America, 16, 31, 35; on wealth disparity, 179–80; on words in music, 60; on youth culture, 12–13, 16, 20–22, 26, 37, 71, 72; PMRC testimony, 140–41, 143–45, 147, 150, 162–64, 168, 170; personal and professional grievances, 32–33, 54, 56, 130, 181; political beliefs of, 180–81, 184–86, 189–90; political goals/agenda of, 208–10; presidential ambitions of, 208–9; racist imagery in music of, 16, 72–75, 77, 90, 112, 132–33, 135–36; relevancy of, 6, 9, 16, 72, 79, 90–91, 160, 170–71, 202, 214, 232, 235, 239; reputation of, 32–33, 35, 55–56; sexism in music of, 33–34, 35, 71, 90, 175, 192, 235; sexual imagery in music of,

Zappa, Frank (*continued*)
33–35; theme of American culture in music of, 9, 13, 16, 18, 25–26, 30; theme of American education system in music of, 21; theme of authoritarianism in music of, 38, 66, 176; theme of business influence of government in music of, 48; theme of Christian fundamentalism in music of, 5–6; theme of groupies in music of, 34; theme of institutional power/oppression in music of, 31, 33, 47; theme of media exploitation of racial violence in music of, 13–15; theme of police violence in music of, 14, 30; theme of race in music of, 72–73, 90; theme of racial progress in America in music of, 30–31, 78; theme of racism in America in music of, 15, 35; theme of the power of the individual in music of, 36; theme of white supremacy in music of, 100; theme of yuppie culture in music of, 37; use of racial slurs in music of, 73, 90; Václav Havel's tribute to, 214; vision for the future of America, 18, 19, 35, 66, 100, 101, 104–5, 173–74, 198, 201, 208, 213, 216, 221–26; voting advocacy of, 172–74, 177, 185–86, 202, 206–7, 235, 239

Zappa, Gail: on *Congress Shall Make No Law . . .*, 164; on Frank's involvement with the PMRC, 150, 169; political advocacy of, 209; release of *Civilization Phaze III*, 223–24

Zappa, Moon Unit: PMRC hearing, 163; "Valley Girl," 37

Zavod, Allan, 186

Zoot Allures (album), 34, 67, 114, 128